OUR HISPANIC ROOTS:

WHAT HISTORY FAILED TO TELL US

SECOND EDITION
Revised and Expanded

CARLOS B. VEGA, Ph.D.

JANAWAY PUBLISHING, INC.
Santa Maria, California

Our Hispanic Roots: What History Failed to Tell Us. Second Edition

Copyright © 2013 Carlos B. Vega

Originally published as First Edition:
Copyright © 2007 Carlos B. Vega
Baltimore: 2007

Published by:

Janaway Publishing, Inc.
732 Kelsey Ct.
Santa Maria, California 93454
(805) 925-1038
www.JanawayGenealogy.com

2013

Library of Congress Control Number: 2013948324

ISBN: 978-1-59641-284-2

Cover design by Nicholas Sutton Bell

Made in the United States of America

DEDICATION

To the truth, and to all those who cultivate and stand behind it.

SOME PRELIMINARY THOUGHTS

-The discovery of America was a collaborative effort of Columbus, Spain and the knowledge and technology of the time—which came mainly from Spain and Portugal—, just like the trip to the moon was a joint effort of three astronauts, the United States, and the knowledge and technology of the time.

-It is true that it could have been "discovered" by someone else at a different time, but such can't be affirmed or denied. Anyone can claim having been in America before 1492, but historical events must be recorded or they would simply become a theory or a myth. No such event was ever recorded.

-Spain led the way, but many of today's Hispanic countries also contributed greatly to the making of the United States, among them: the Dominican Republic, Cuba, Puerto Rico, Mexico and Peru. Looking at it from today's perspective, it was most certainly a Hispanic enterprise. For the first 50 years, while other Europeans were tip-toeing along the eastern seaboard and the Canadian border, Hispanics were toiling and crisscrossing the continent in all directions discovering, exploring, and settling the new lands.

-In North America, by royal decree, Hispanics sought to "poblar" (settle, civilize) the newly discovered lands, while other Europeans sought to colonize or turn the lands they discovered into colonies. Hispanics never referred to their lands as colonies but as "provinces" (of Spain.) That set the tone between one culture and the others in America.

-Who founded the United States? There were two foundings of the United States: one in the east with Anglo-Saxon roots in the 17th and 18th centuries, and one in the south, southwest, and west with Spanish/Hispanic roots in the 16th and 17th centuries. The one with Anglo-Saxon roots founded *the republic*, and the one with Spanish/Hispanic roots founded *the country*. Both fused into one during the 19th century becoming the United States as it is known today. Not only did Hispanics found the country, but they also helped found the republic. Based on this premise, there were two sets of founding fathers: for the republic, among others, Washington, Jefferson, Adams, Madison, Franklin, and for the country, among others, De León, De Soto, Coronado, De Vaca, Father Serra.

In time it is conceivable that the United States may become a Hispanic country with the Anglo-Saxons and others being the minority of the population, just the opposite of what it is today.

-The root for the lessened appreciation toward the Hispanic people.

The Spanish Black Legend contributed to the diminished role of Latinos in our national history. Spawned in the 16th-century Spain-England rivalry that ended in England winning the war of propaganda, the Black Legend perpetuated negative stereotypical notions about Spain and its people who settled in the Americas. Thus the dichotomy of England as the good empire and Spain as the evil empire emerged in American lore, history, and literature.

The negative beliefs about Spain prevailed and became embedded in U.S. history textbooks.

Joseph P. Sánchez, Ph.D / American Latino Heritage, National Parks Service

CONTENTS

PREFACE

We are not afraid to follow truth wherever it may lead,
not to tolerate any error so long as reason is left free to combat it.
—Thomas Jefferson

This is a book about the United States and how the country that
is today was formed five centuries ago. We have gathered
overwhelming hard historical data that demonstrates that for the
first two hundred years it was Spain, together with other Hispanic
countries, such as Mexico, that were the ones that laid the
foundations and paved the way for the creation of the entire
country and not only a section of it, as is commonly believed.
Spain made America known to the world, and made it possible for
all others to find their way to it, carried out their deeds, and profit
enormously from it. Other countries, mainly England, may have
contributed, although indirectly, to the establishment of a political
philosophy and institutions in the Northeast, which 300 years later
spread out and took hold throughout the land. But thirteen colonies
alone did not make what the United States is today, just like the
kingdoms of Castile or Aragon alone did not make what is today
Spain. Taking out the territories comprised in the thirteen colonies,
everything else was done principally by one nation, and that nation
was Spain which operated directly from its American possessions,
like Mexico and the Caribbean. What would the United States be
today without all of Florida, the Louisiana territory as it was

known then (comprising ten of today's states), California and the entire Southwest, and without direct access to the Pacific Ocean, the Gulf of Mexico, and the Caribbean Sea?

Even in the 18th century Spain was busy furthering its North American enterprise, discovering, exploring, and settling vast territories in the Southwest and Northwest, chartering new sea routes to and in the Pacific and elsewhere, and studying their flora and fauna as well as their people and culture. Indeed, Spain did not take a single rest for over 400 years, from the time it landed in North American shores in 1513, to the time it finally departed in 1898—385 long years. Yet, at the end, exhausted and disillusioned, Spain abandoned its North American holdings, and, if that was not in itself punishment enough, unfairly impugned for alleged mistakes made in America during that long period of time. Conventional history owes an apology to Spain, and it is hoped that this book will contribute to making that happen sooner rather than later.

This book is honest and straight-forward, setting forth the truth as it really stands. It is written in language that is basic and transparent, thus making it accessible to readers from all walks of life. It includes two substantial appendices, Appendix A and Appendix B, which contains additional data supporting the historical facts, and which are designed to stand on their own and be used, if so desired, independently from the rest of the book.

In writing this book we have consulted the most authoritative and reliable sources available today, most of which are quoted verbatim throughout the text. To the possible surprise of many of the readers, a vast number of these sources are either American or British, true scholars who investigated and wrote copiously about the historical truth which, unfortunately, had been ignored, diluted or distorted by historians and a long legion of academicians on the true beginnings of the great American republic.

By no means was Spain the only one to contribute to the creation, formation, and development of the United States. Right from the outset, Spain had many close allies within her American possessions that joined in the enterprise with equal dedication and fervor, among them Cuba, Dominican Republic, Puerto Rico, Mexico, and Peru. In this regard, it was not a Spanish enterprise but rather a Hispanic enterprise of combined ideas, skills, resources, and effort. Yes, Spain led the way, but without the others the end result would have been quite different.

INTRODUCTION

*If Spain had not existed 400 years ago
the United States would not exist today.*
—Charles F. Lummis

In writing this book we have embarked on a very arduous and ambitious mission. In essence, what we have set out to do is to challenge conventional history as it pertains to the role Spain and other Hispanic countries played in the making of the United States. The fact is that the vast majority of historians have simply squeezed out of their accounts most of the great deeds achieved by Spain in North America. Consequently, we, as a nation, know very little about the true historical facts, perhaps as little as two per cent of the whole truth. The rest, or the other ninety-eight per cent, has remained entombed until now in the catacombs of history. These words from the eminent American historian Charles F. Lummis should enlighten most readers on this historical injustice perpetrated on Spain. This is what he had to say over 100 years ago:

It is because I believe that every other young American loves fair play and admires heroism as much as I do, that this book has been written. That we have not given justice to the Spanish pioneers is simply because we have been misled. They made a record unparalleled; but our text-books have not recognized that fact, though they no longer dare dispute it. Now, thanks to the New School of American History, we are coming to the truth—a truth which every manly America will be glad to know. In this country of free and brave men, race prejudice, the most ignorant of all human ignorance, must die out. We must respect manhood more than nationality, and admire it for its own sake wherever, found—and it is found everywhere. The deeds that hold the world up are not of any one blood. We may be born anywhere—that is a mere accident; but to the heroes we must grow by means which are not accidents nor provincialisms, but the birthright and glory of humanity.

We love manhood; and the Spanish pioneering of the Americas was the largest and longest and most marvelous fact of manhood in all history. It was not possible for a Saxon boy to learn that truth in my boyhood; it is enormously difficult, if possible, now. The hopelessness of trying to get from any or all English text-books a just picture of the Spanish hero in the New World made me resolve that no other young American lover of heroism and justice shall need to grope so long in the dark as I had to...[1]

As if echoing Mr. Lummis' opinion, American historian Charles Gibson wrote:

Spain in America is a substantial subject. In space, time, and complexity, it is a more substantial subject than England in America, and it carries the additional difficulty, for English-speaking students, that it is alien and easily misconstrued. Though impressive advances have been made, Spanish America still lags behind equivalent fields of historical investigation. In certain of its topics, the overtones are such that one can hardly make any comment without sounding biased. Our ignorance of other topics is abysmal.[2]

And the much-respected American historian Samuel Eliot Morison, in comparing the Spanish enterprise in America with England and other European nations, stated:

By 1600, Spain had conquered almost the whole of coastal South America except Brazil, and much of the interior as well, down to the River Plate. Thus, foundations had been laid for every one of the twenty republics of Central and South America, excepting the Argentine. No other conquest like this has there been in the annals of the human race. In one generation the Spaniards acquired more new territory than Rome conquered in five centuries. Genghis Khan swept over a greater area but left only destruction in his wake; the Spaniards organized and administered all that they conquered, brought in the arts and letters of Europe, and converted millions to their faith. Our forebears in Virginia and New England, the pathfinders of the Great West, and the French pioneers of Canada, were indeed stout fellows, but their exploits scarcely compare with those of brown-robed Spanish friars and armored conquistadors who hacked their way through solid jungles, across endless plains, and over snowy passes of the Andes, to fulfill dreams of glory and conversion; and for whom reality proved ever greater than the dream.[3]

Have most historians been afraid of telling the truth and if so why? The United States has always trumpeted its Anglo Saxon ancestry as paramount for achieving its great political and economic success, from the time of the landing of the Mayflower through today. Those Anglo Saxon immigrants and their descendants forged the nation and made it bloom. While they were toiling in that majestic endeavor, a band of interlopers encroached upon the uncharted territory either searching for gold or trading furs with the natives. Those Anglo Saxon immigrants were the nation's builders, the true pioneers, statesmen, patriots, philosophers, cavaliers, in short, the patriarchs of the motherland. The others, well, they were merely unscrupulous adventurers lured by fame, glory and, of course, gold. Ultimately they were driven out and the "true Americans" seized control of the continent and a great new nation emerged.

This is history in reverse, a fundamentally distorted interpretation of the true historical facts as the reader will ascertain in reading this book. For many years historians, the "Herodotus" of modern times, have been exalting this fallacy which the nation has ultimately accepted as fact. Consequently, the United States has long regarded non-Anglo Saxons immigrants as extrinsic to true North Americanism.

Basically, we have set out to achieve three main objectives: one, to bring forth the major contribution that Spain and other Hispanic countries, namely Mexico, have made to the forging of the United States, not only to a portion of it but to the nation as a whole; two, to set the record straight about the Spanish enterprise in the Americas and her victimization by rival nations; three, to instill in all who may read the present book a deeper sense of pride and appreciation toward this nation's Hispanic heritage. True, the nation has Anglo Saxon roots of which we should feel very proud. True also that our nation has Hispanic roots of which we should feel equally proud. Neither one should be above the other for they are both as crucial to the nation's heritage. All of the other roots, French, German, Dutch, Swedish, Irish, Italians, although very important also, are not and cannot put at the same level of the other two. In conclusion, the heritage of the United States is predominantly Anglo and Hispanic and to a much lesser degree all the others.

We have also endeavored to uplift the spirits of Hispanics, to make them feel welcomed and at home here for this is their land also. They and others must remember that before there was a United States there was a Santo Domingo, a Cuba, a México, and a Perú, and that much before others arrived here Western civilization had made its triumphant entry into the future United States through México. It must also be remembered that before they said "Good morning!" we said "¡Buenos días!," for Spanish was spoken here one hundred years before English (or any other European language.) When the first wave of North American adventurers (here the name does fit) crossed the waters of the Mississippi toward the west in the 19th century, what they found were not barren lands but a region in full bloom, so attractive in fact that they tried to keep it for themselves, which they ultimately did. That was back then. Today, the proud descendants of those *first North American pioneers,* the Hispanic-Americans, continue to help advance the nation. And, in another fifty years, the future of the United States may very well hinge on their continued hard work and support. And who knows—one may wonder—, maybe one day, in a hundred years henceforth, "¡Buenos días!" will be just as acceptable as "Good morning!"

CHAPTER ONE

A CALL TO REASON

The United States of America is a great nation, among the greatest the world has ever known. Politically savvy, daring, visionary, with a deep sense of purpose and history. To fully comprehend the magnitude of what this nation truly represents we need only to reflect on this fact: In just 225 years (1776 to the present), the dream of a group of passionate rebels bloomed into a democratic republic widely respected, admired, revered, and emulated around the globe. A nation shaped by common people, humble, socially and economically deprived and mostly uneducated, and not by royalty or nobility or by the social elite. They were not driven by fame or glory, nor by king and country, nor were they crusaders of religious or philosophical beliefs, nor were they heroes. No traditions or heritage to fight for but rather the pursuit of a dream of a new beginning, of a totally different way of life. It is most singular that such people, under such circumstances, were able to forge what is considered today the most advanced and powerful nation on earth.

The United States is the land of "eternal dreams," constantly searching for an utopian world in which liberty, justice, civil rights, and equality are the birthright and patrimony of all the people. A Don Quixote of modern times, refusing to accept the reality of man with all of its intrinsic flaws, weaknesses, and paradoxes, eagerly confronting not one but many windmills and claiming victory in every encounter. The rightly called "American Experiment" is one of man's greatest endeavors and a powerful legacy to the world of the future.

How did all begin? What made the United States the great nation that it is today? Many people would say that it all began in 1607 with the arrival of the English and, therefore, give full credit to England for forging the nation while perhaps acknowledging the contribution of other European nations, namely Germany and Holland. This has been the consensus for over two hundred years continuing through today. However, this is not how the distinguished American historian Charles F. Lummis interpreted it when he wrote: "If Spain had not existed 400 years ago, the United States would not exist today."

Much happened in the Americas (and that includes North America) many years before the English dared to brave the rigors of the Atlantic, and much more after they settled in Jamestown. For two hundred years, while the English were tending to their meager crops in a tiny piece of land and going about the business of setting camp in their new environs, the Spanish swept across both continents advancing the cause of what they thought was man's greatest endeavor: Western civilization. They may have been partially lured by America's hidden riches, as all men are, but such a heroic undertaking could not have taken place only because of their quest for the glimmering metals, just like we would not dare say that because the United States is a capitalist nation all that matters to it is the pursuit of wealth. Some may claim so, for the United States has its share of enemies around the globe, but those who know the nation well think otherwise. In the words of American historian Bern Keating:

> After Columbus, for 400 years, came a certain breed of men—the explorers. They came for gold, God, glory, or the lure of the unknown. They were sometimes idealistic, ruthless, religious, greedy, romantic, and

often foolish. They were chased by grizzlies, tortured by Indians, shipwrecked by storms, frozen by blizzards. [4]

And Bernal Díaz del Castillo, in his *True History of the Conquest of New Spain*, reminded us that wealth was but one goal of the conquistador's quest:

> To me it appears that the names of those (the soldiers who accompanied Cortés in 1519) ought to be written in letters of gold, who died so cruel a death, for the service of God and His Majesty, to give light to those who were in darkness and to procure wealth which all men desire.

The lust of gold is inherent to all men since Creation.

The glory of the discovery, conquest, and colonization of both Americas for the first two hundred years belongs to Spain and to her people, whose heroic deeds have marveled all those who have cared to know the facts. They were the first to venture into the unknown, to cross the feared and treacherous ocean by the most rudimentary means, to confront a totally new and foreign world with unwavering resolution, stoicism, and sense of purpose. Commenting on the incredible deeds of the Spaniards, Mr. Charles F. Lummis had this to say: (translation by the author)

> There are no words with which to express the enormous preponderance of Spain over all the other (European) nations in the exploration of the New World. The Spaniards were the first ones to see and sound out the largest of the gulfs; Spaniards were the ones to discover its two largest rivers; Spaniards were the ones who for the first time saw the Pacific Ocean; Spaniards were the first ones to realize that there were two continents in America; Spaniards were the first ones to circle the globe. Spaniards were the first ones to journey into the remote confines of our own country and to all the lands to its south, and the ones who founded cities thousands of miles inland much before the first Anglo-Saxon landed on our shores.[5]

When the reader finds out that the best English textbook does not even mention the name of the first mariner who circumnavigated the globe (a Spaniard), nor of the explorer who discovered Brazil (another Spaniard), nor of the discoverer of California (also a Spaniard), nor of the Spaniards who discovered and settled colonies in what is today the United States, and that said book contains such blatant omissions and a hundred historical accounts that are as false as the omissions are inexcusable, he will then understand that the time has come for us to do more justice to a subject that should be of the utmost interest to all true Americans.[6]

This historical fact has been systematically glossed over by most historians and general academia in the United States for over two hundred years. Consequently, people in this country have long had a blurred vision of Spain's awesome contribution to United States history. In the halls of learning across the nation, in everyday classrooms where American history is taught, teaching centers around British America while disregarding the hundred plus years that proceeded to the true dawn of the nation. On the subject of Spain's aid to the Thirteen Colonies during their struggle for independence, discussed below, we will present hard historical facts unknown to most to this day. Regrettably, most historians chose to ignore those facts to the detriment of the nation. Let us bring forth some of those facts relating to the American Revolution.

CHAPTER TWO

SPAIN'S AID TO THE AMERICAN REVOLUTION

To begin, we would like to quote a respected American historian, Buchanan Parker Thomson. In her book, *Spain: Forgotten Ally of the American Revolution*, she stated:

> Ask any American, with the exception of the trained historian, "What do you know of the aid given by Spain to the United States in its struggle for independence during the Revolutionary War? " The answer will be short and instantaneous: "Nothing! I never knew that Spain gave us any assistance during our Revolutionary War." Ask the same question of many students of American history and the answer will be the same.[7]

What are we to make of this? How can historians write copiously about France's or even Holland's aid to the American Revolution and leave Spain out? Do they know or care about the facts, about the truth? Mrs. Parker Tomson's book, written in 1976, has also been consigned to obscurity. The author of this book was able to get a copy through a friend in Spain, a rarity given the circumstances. Although France (primarily through Charles Gravier, Count of Vergennes, Minister of Foreign Affairs at the court of Louis XVI, and Pedro Carón de Beaumarchais, the author of *The Barber of Seville*) played a significant role in aiding the American Revolution (as stipulated in the "Family Compacts of

1733," and in the most important one of 1761, in which both England and France sought Spanish support in the Seven Years War), it was Spain that was the nation that did the most. Based on the Family Compact accord, France was expected to supply a variety of goods for which Spain would pay and later be reimbursed. In other words, Spain put up the funds. Moreover, the person duly credited with forming the alliance between the three nations (which included Holland) and formulating the plan was King Charles III of Spain and his representatives. Further, it was in the Spanish possessions of Cuba and Santo Domingo where the American colonists went to trade for arms, just like it was in the port of Havana where their vessels often docked to conduct business. And it was in the Spanish factories of Mexico where gunpowder was produced and sent to the American colonists along with many other provisions via the city of Havana.

Among Charles III's representatives, all of whom played a key role in advancing the cause of the American Revolution, were:

*Don Pedro Pablo Abarca de Bolea, Count of Aranda, Charles III's ambassador to Paris (Court of Louis XVI.)

*Don Gerónimo Grimaldi, Prime Minister at the Spanish Court.

*José Moñino y Redondo, Count of Floridablanca, who replaced Grimaldi who had been assigned ambassador to the Vatican.

*Diego María de Gardoqui, a Basque merchant well-known and respected among the colonists as well as in England, who was later Spain's representative in the United States.

*José de Gálvez, Minister of the Indies.

*Bernardo de Gálvez, governor of Louisiana.

They were known as the "Famous Six" the ones responsible for providing Spain's, France's, and Holland's direct aid to the American colonists. The Count of Floridablanca was the one who authorized the first monetary aid to the colonists, which he personally gave to Author Lee, the United States ambassador in Madrid. José de Gálvez was the one who, following orders from Madrid, dispatched emissaries from Havana (namely Miguel Eduardo and later Juan de Miralles) to the Thirteen Colonies in a reconnaissance mission to ascertain the status of the conflict. His nephew, Bernardo de Gálvez, governor of Louisiana, according to historian Lorenzo G. LaFarelle, "...embodied and exemplified the mission and driving force of the noblest and truest Spanish tradition of his time, which is best summarized by the motto: 'Por Dios y por el Rey' (for God and King). All his endeavors were guided by this noble and exalted principle." And Mr. LaFarelle added: "...He served his king on three continents: Europe, the Americas, and Africa. In all three he shed his blood for the cause he believed in and to which he was committed. Furthermore, the drove the British from the Gulf of Mexico and helped in the birth of a new nation, the United States of America, soon to become the most powerful nation on earth. Through his invaluable assistance he helped to make this possible."[8]

And also regarding Bernardo de Gálvez, Ms. Parker Thompson stated:

January 1, 1777, when Gálvez became Acting Governor of Louisiana, was an important day in American history. His orders from his uncle, the power behind the throne as Secretary of State and President of the Council of the Indies, were precise. He was to make an immediate survey of the territory from Natchitoches, Opelousas and at Arkansas, inform himself fully at once concerning conditions along the English frontier, to map the whole Mississippi and the southern coast from Belize to Bahía del Espiritu Santo. He was to take strong measures against illicit commerce, and curtail the trading activities of foreign vessels. He was to cultivate friendly relations with the Indians. Particularly significant was the injunction to collect all possible information about affairs in the English colonies, through secret agents sent for the purpose. The coming of Bernardo de Gálvez marked at once a change of policy toward both

Americans and English. It meant more vigorous measures to get speedy aid to the former. By July 1777, in answer to the plea of General Lee, the government of Spain had deposited at New Orleans 2000 barrels of powder, a great quantity of lead and large amounts of clothing, subject to the order of Virginia. Spanish aid also meant sanctuary for refugees: Louisiana was rapidly becoming a refuge for hundreds of Americans fleeing the depredations of the English from across the Great River. They flocked into the province with their women, their children and their slaves and with whatever household possessions it was possible to carry with them: All of them were desperate for food, clothing and ammunition. At all the Spanish posts along the river and in New Orleans they found a haven and the wherewithal to establish themselves in safety.[9]

Moreover, tons of war supplies destined for the American colonies routinely left port from the Spanish cities of Barcelona, Cadiz, La Coruña, and Bilbao. And it was in a Spanish city, Burgos, in Old Castile, where Spain's representatives Diego de Gardoqui and the Count of Grimaldi met with Arthur Lee (who had been asked by Benjamin Franklin to attend the meeting in his place due to his advanced age and illness) and cemented the accord to provide aid to the American colonies. After the meeting, Arthur Lee was asked to go the city of Vitoria to meet Grimaldi who carried with him all official letter from the Count of Floridablanca. The letter said in part:

The fate of the Colonies is of the utmost importance to Spain and we shall help them in every way possible as dictated by circumstances. As can be testified by Mr. Diego Gardoqui there, we have already provided for such help not only through Louisiana but through other routes as well. That we shall faithfully and actively execute said dispositions sending from Spain and other areas all the goods we may be able to supply, and make available in Paris letters of credit for the purchase of goods in Holland... that our ambassador, Count of Aranda, will be duly notified and authorized to proceed...Finally, I am informing your Excellency that the king has authorized for now to give you 500,000 livres tournoises, half in goods from Spain and the other half in cash...[10]

18

It is interesting to note that around that same time Benjamin Franklin sent to the Spanish Court a memorandum containing a U.S. Congress resolution dated December 30 1776 proposing that:

A) The United States would aid Spain in the conquest of Panzacola, provided it would join forces with the Colonies and allow for easy access to same and be free to navigate the Mississippi;

B) The United States would agree to declare war to Portugal if Spain so wished;

C) The United States would facilitate to Spain to conquer The Bahamas.

The letter received no response from the Spanish Crown, but it evidenced the Colonists' keen interest in procuring Spanish aid.

And, in another letter dated September 1777, the colonists' representatives again turned to Spain and France petitioning further aid, primarily for the acquisition of war supplies payable in commercial goods, plus a loan for the amount of up to 2 million sterling pounds.

France, through Vergennes, immediately turned it down. On the other hand, upon learning of that decision, the Spanish Minister sent a letter to France emphasizing the importance of continuing the aid and encouraging the colonists. Moreover, he stated that because the Spanish aid consisted mainly of foreign goods which had to be purchased in other countries, it represented a bigger burden for Spain while France could provide its own goods manufactured locally. He further stated that Spain would proceed immediately to grant the aid as it had promised.

Pursuant to the pledge made to Lee, Spain granted to the American colonists the funds. To this end, the Spanish treasurer Manuel Ortiz de la Riba authorized 70,000 pesos which were given to Diego de Gardoqui (who had already given the colonists an equal amount by order of the king.) A month later (May) the Spanish government authorized another loan of 50,000 pesos plus several letters of credit totaling 50,000 pesos earmarked for the purchase of goods in Holland and other countries. Soon after, Benjamin Franklin acknowledged receipt of the funds and expressed his appreciation to the Count of Aranda. He also confirmed the arrival of a Spanish ship in Boston carrying 12,000 rifles while requesting several more ships. Ms. Parker, Thomson added:

> Thus, in June 1776, when the American Revolution had just begun, we find both Spain and France acting officially, though under seal of secrecy, as allies of the English Colonies against their mother country. Even before this date, however, supplies had been going out on a haphazard basis through the ports of Spain, France and also Holland, as ships captains picked up arms and ammunition in personal trading ventures. Moreover, much important trade of this nature had been going on through the Spanish ports in the West Indies as well as through the famous port of St. Eustatius in the Dutch West Indies. With the connivance of Spanish, French and Dutch traders in the Islands, American smuggling and privateer operations had been keeping the Colonial forces supplied with the sinews of war. From these same ports as bases, American captains had been able to prey upon British merchants vessels during the first months of the war to an appalling extent. They had captured some seven-hundred British ships carrying valuable cargoes destined for England. The goods thus captured were traded in the Islands for war materials or for any goods badly needed in the Colonies.[11]

Spain and also France were committed to aid the colonists in their struggle for independence, even if it meant going to war with England. In April of 1779, the Spanish Crown sent England an ultimatum demanding A) a cease to hostilities in America; B) a formal representation at the Spanish court of the conflicting parties; and C) treating the Colonies during this time as independent states. England ignored it. Both Spain and France prepared for war and entered into a secret accord to that effect. Spain broke diplomatic relations with England on the basis of the harm inflicted on Spanish possessions and the Spanish ambassador in London, the Marquis of Almodóvar, left the embassy. The hostilities between the three powers had thus begun. Needless to say, Franklin and his compatriots rejoiced at the news.

Spain sought to aid the colonists on two fronts: One by undermining England's power in North America and elsewhere; and two by providing funds and supplies. Very soon, a stream of Spanish gold and silver (which had been mined in Spanish America) began flowing into the Thirteen Colonies.

In June of 1778, governor Gálvez of Louisiana gave to Oliver Pollock, commissioner of the Colonial Congress, 24,023 pesos; in October of the same year an additional 15,948 pesos to refurbish the frigate Rebecca; in July of 1779 another 22,640 pesos for the same frigate; and in 1781 another 5,000 pesos. In Europe, in July 1778, pursuant to the pledge made by the Count of Floridablanca, the Spanish treasurer Miguel de Muzquiz reimbursed Gardoqui 53,000 pesos he had previously given to Lee in May. Finally, in October Gardoqui sent to the colonists goods valued at 50,000 pesos plus 30,000 pesos in blankets. All together, the loans given by Spain to the colonists amounted to 7,944,906 reales and 16 maravedís vellón which at the rate of 20 reales to one hard peso totaled 52,966 hard pesos. (Spanish historian Ramón Ezquerra sets the total amount at over 9 million reales.) At the time the loans were made, the peso was worth 40 continental dollars. Thus, in American currency, the grand total of the loans amounted to $2,118,640, an enormous sum of money at the time especially when converted into the very strong and stable Spanish peso. In addition, Spain also provided a large number of supplies, including 30,000 blankets for use during the harsh winter months. That takes care of some of the tangible aid. With regard to the intangible aid, we will let Ms. Parker Thompson describe it in her own words:

The archives of Seville and Simancas are filled with thousands of documents that provide a more heart-warming tale of the ability and the personal sacrifice of such men as Gálvez in America, Aranda in Paris, and Gardoqui both in Spain and America. Therein are the evidences of deep friendships established in the heat of the crisis. In these documents, we find the intangibles that form the warp and woof of the real story. When one remembers the blanket-weavers of Palencia and the wave of enthusiasm that swept that province when the news came to the pueblos of the need of Washington's freezing army, one can imagine these families, all too well acquainted with the cruel winters in northern Spain, murmuring as they wove, "Los pobrecitos!"

We must consider the militiamen and "habitants" of Louisiana, their courage, their endurance and fortitude as they struggled through swamps, forests and raging rivers; the friendship of the Trader Vigo and of Commandant Leyba for Clark in the battle for the Illinois; the remarkable accomplishment of the people of Havana, in raising 1,500,000 pesos for Rochanbeau by public subscription in twenty-four hours, a feat of the 20th century that actually took place in the 18th. Let us remember also the close and affectionate bond between Bernardo de Gálvez and the American Oliver Pollock, which extended even to the doors of the prison in Havana when Pollack, in deepest degradation and despair, was forgotten by his own people; the quality of loyalty that could bring about the unostentatious gift of his private fortune to the American Cause by Juan de Miralles.

Let us recall that in focusing attention on Madrid, Burgos, and Paris, Philadelphia, New York, New Orleans and Havana, we should also bear in mind that other front, the sea. One of the most difficult of all intangibles to assess, the aid given by the fleet of Spain during the years 1776 to 1779, was most significant. As a deterrent to the ability of England to send troops and supplies to America almost at will, Spanish sea power enabled the revolting Colonies to gather their strength by presenting them the priceless gift of time. While forcing England to retain a sizeable part of her naval strength in home waters, it was successfully keeping German mercenaries idle in all the principal ports, where they piled up maintenance costs and created widespread bitterness among all classes of the English people. Spain's sea power also forced the English to alert and keep a substantial fleet of powerful ships in constant readiness to protect Gibraltar, if and when Spain should declare open war.[12]

Fearing a showdown with Spain, England seemed willing to negotiate by ceding Florida, Gibraltar, and cod fishing in Terranova, provided Spain would stay out of the conflict, closed all ports to the rebels, and joined her in defeating the colonists. Spain flatly refused and the tension increased on both sides. Bernardo de Gálvez was appointed commander of all military operations, and in August 1779 pushed for a colonists' settlement in west Florida. The Spaniards captured Fort Manchack, a month later the Baton Rouge Fort was seized, and Pamure and other towns on the banks of the Mississippi were captured. In the meantime, the attack on Mobila was being planned with Spanish reinforcements to be sent from Cuba. A total of twelve military vessels sailed from Havana but they were soon hit by a storm and only four reached their destination. The English were ordered to surrender but refused and the Spanish forces attacked. In February 1780 the English finally surrendered and Mobile was captured. The American colonists were in desperate need for more aid and again turned to Spain. Now it was John Jay their representative. While in Spain, he informed the Count of Floridablanca that he was unable to pay a $300 letter of credit and asked him to pay it. Floridablanca agreed on the condition that he would refrain from getting into further debt. But Jay was not the only one in deep debt. The Thirteen Colonies were in far worse shape. They lead issued $200 million in currency through letters of credit which they could not afford to pay. Before the letters became due, and in order to pay them, they issued more letters of credit now totaling 100,000 sterling pounds which would have to be paid by Spain within six months. When Spain found out that such a deal had been struck without consulting her, she was naturally annoyed but nonetheless agreed to pay the debt plus the interest, although not in six months but within two years. In return, Spain asked for the building of several war ships for which it would provide all the necessary materials. Surprisingly Jay objected to the proposal and an agreement was never reached. Sometime later, Jay went back to Gardoqui, now the Spanish representative in the Thirteen Colonies, and reminded him that the letters of credit would soon become due and needed to be paid and that he was counting on Spain to make good for them. In addition to the 18,000 pesos previously given to Jay, he received 17,000 hard pesos in cash plus 15,000 pesos to cover the clothes already purchased on Spain's credit by Harrison, plus an additional 12,000 pesos. As if all this was not enough, Spain had agreed to pay within six months the three million reales de vellón it had pledged to the Colonists giving an additional 12,000 hard pesos in May, another 12,000 on the following month, plus 12,000 more in August.

The Spanish aid continued through the battle of Yorktown, which ended England's despotic reign in the Thirteen Colonies. This battle was won partially by Spanish aid coming not from Spain but from Havana, Cuba. Needing money to confront the enemy, the colonists, under the command of George Washington, asked France for help which in turn asked the French colonists in the Dominican Republic. The aid was denied. The American army was in despair, and it was at that critical moment that the Spaniards in Cuba volunteered to collect the funds through a national campaign. They collected over $1.5 million livres tournoises which were immediately forwarded to Washington. Neither Spain nor Cuba ever asked or expected to be repaid for those funds.

Large sums of money, made available mostly through a secret third party and payable in livres tournoises and reales de vellón: one million livres tournoises in June, 1776, just one month before the Declaration of Independence, and four million reales de vellón a month after on August 5, 1776, plus letters of credit and war supplies, including weapons, brass cannons, bayonets, gun-carriers, mortars, ammunition, shells, bullets, powder, clothing, blankets, threads, buttons, needles, uniforms, shoes, tents, and countless other supplies of every denomination. On orders from the king, carried out through his competent representatives Aranda and Gardoqui, cities and towns across Spain feverishly pulled together to manufacture the goods needed by the American colonists. Regarding this, Ms. Parker Thomson added:

> Gardoqui gave the order for the weaving, collection and baling of the blankets and other woolen articles to the weaving centers of the province of Palencia of which Vitoria is the capital. Palencia was at this time the center of the finest of the wool-weaving industries in the country. Gardoqui's orders threw this peaceful province into a fever of activity; in every pueblo men, women and children worked furiously in order to complete the work. The plazas in the small towns were piled high with the product of their hands while being baled for shipment to the city of Palencia. Excitement spread throughout the province when it became known that the blankets were destined for the army of Washington in America.
>
> The influx of Gardoqui's orders brought feverish activity to the ports of Barcelona, Bilbao and Cadiz. In the matter of arms and ammunition, absolute secrecy was required since Spanish arsenals, like the arsenals of France, were under the direct ownership of the Crown. Gardoqui made arrangements with De La Riva, a banker of Madrid, to handle the release of such material by the government and in this way effected its transferal without arousing undue suspicion. By September, 1977, Spain had given Lee directly 187,500 livres for expenditures made outside of Spain besides having contributed a priceless amount in goods not listed in value, all this without any qualification whatever as to repayment.[13]

Spain's aid to the American Revolution carne in multiple ways both in and outside of Spain. The truth is that for many years up to 1776 and beyond, the nation of Spain and her people embraced the American cause as their own and joined collectively in seeing it succeed at a time, we may add, when Spain was confronting many other problems and experiencing a dwindling national treasury, especially due to the financing of Cevallo's expedition to the Río de la Plata. Furthermore, in so doing, she risked sparking an equal sentiment for independence in her Spanish American possessions, as it ultimately happened. In spite of this, and even though she was going squarely against her own self-interest, she went ahead losing it all in the end. It is important to note that at no time Spain expected re-payment of her many loans as clearly stated by Floridablanca in one of his letters to Arthur Lee: "... That these things the king did and would do out of his own generosity, without stipulating any recompense." One more ill-investment for Spain—heart over matter—the deciding factor of her inevitable and eventual downfall. No capitalist nation, then, and much less today, would ever be so generous in a foreign cause. By the way, in 1778 Spain attempted to mediate an Anglo-French truce and de facto English recognition of American independence, which was reported in the Gazeta of Madrid in 1779, and translated into English in the Annual Register for 1779. We should mention also at this juncture that almost 5,000 Spaniards died in the American cause as prisoners of war of the English off New York harbor. Also that Francisco de Miranda (born in Caracas, Venezuela), one of the great patriots of Spanish-American independence, took active part in the seizure of Pensacola in 1781 fighting the British, for which he was elevated to the rank of lieutenant colonel.

It must be pointed out that the funds given to the colonists, amounting to millions of what we would call today hard currency—Spanish gold and silver—were derived mainly from the mines of Mexico, Peru, and Bolivia. Thus, when historians write that the Spaniards plundered the gold of the Incas and the Aztecs, guess where a considerable portion of those treasures ended up? Well, you guessed it, in the very heart of Colonial America, in the war chests of the insurgents to help finance their struggle against the tyrant, as Jefferson called archenemy King George III. *Should we, meaning the United States, be grateful to the conquistadors and to the natives of those three countries for so contributing to our independence?* Indeed we should. Many papers were signed, many meetings held, and many promises made, but they all went up mostly in smoke. The United States only partially repaid that debt and never thanked Spain, Mexico, or Peru for it which it should have done, even if belatedly. And among those to be thanked should also be Cortés and Pizarro, Moctezuma and Atahualpa, as well as the Indians and Black slaves who labored the mines.

This historical injustice perpetrated on Spain did not just surface overnight. It began soon after Spain took the lead upon discovering the New World and suddenly became the reigning power in Europe. By the time the other nations arrived, most of the Americas had been discovered, explored, and settled by the dauntless Spaniards.

FAME AND GLORY TURNS EUROPE AGAINST SPAIN

Referring to the reign of Spain's Catholic Kings, American historian Theodore Maynard wrote in his book *De Soto and the Conquistadors*:

> It is true—especially as applying to the hundred glorious years then begun, during which occurred that explosion of Spanish energy which is perhaps the most brilliant chapter in history. While that energy exploded around the world, the rest of Europe watched the succession of astonishing events in discovery and exploration with awe, perplexity, and increasing envy.[14]

The truth is that those European nations, chafed by Spain's sudden ascent to fame, have never to this day forgiven her for taking that lead. Thus, she had to be maligned, ostracized, ridiculed, criticized, undermined, punished and stopped at all cost. This widespread sentiment and none other fueled the so- called Black Legend against Spain, taking instant hold among Spain's many foes in Europe and elsewhere. Regarding the fierce jealousy and envy eating away the hearts and souls of other European nations upon Spain's absolute supremacy in America and elsewhere, the noted American historian Philip Ainsworth Means wrote:

Whatever else the Spaniards were they were soldiers and men of unsurpassed virility who built an empire in a crusading spirit compounded equally of piety and intolerance. Judged by the standards of that time—which are the only standards that may be fairly used—both the piety and intolerance of the Spaniards were laudable, and the title which they conferred upon the original conquerors of America was valid and remained so as long as the descendants of those conquerors could maintain it by force of war. European rivals were destined to come and to build lesser realms of their own in the territories claimed by Spain, but wrested from her. The efforts of the rival nations to break up the Spanish empire in America were informed by a crusading spirit no less real and vigorous than that of Spain, and compounded of precisely the same ingredients, piety and intolerance. Moreover, Spain and her foes were alike also in the fact that they sought for wealth in America greater than that which any of them had known previously. Altogether, we may say that on all sides the religious motives, the motive to crush departure from an accepted pattern of righteousness, and a hunger for riches gave to all the contenders a deep-rooted determination to hold the chief place in the colonial game.

In short, Spain the first-corner, soon became and long remained the target for furious attacks. Nevertheless, in spite of her enemies, and in the face of tremendous calamities to her cause, Spain was to hold against all comers most of what she originally took through the vigor of her subjects, and she did so for over three hundred years. In other words, of the nearly 450 years that Europeans have known about America, 325 were years during which Spain was the dominant power in the most enviable parts of the Western Hemisphere.[15]

And later, discussing the effect that the Spanish Main had on Spain's European foes, historian Ainsworth Means added:

It was, therefore, because the ports in and around the Spanish Main were so many emporiums for a majestic flow of riches from far-flung interior points on the mainland to Seville, chief port of Spain, that the Spanish Main became, by 1525, a focus of foreign envy—and remained so for 275 years. It was there, principally, that Spain had to fight with her enemies who, naturally enough, were eager to sever her trade-routes and to capture for themselves her laboriously collected wealth.

If Roger Barlow [an Englishman who had accompanied Sebastian Cabot on his expedition to South America in 1526-1530 under the service of Spain], after his return to England soon after 1530, had had his way, England would have attacked Perú by way of the Amazon with an army of 4,000 men traveling in a great fleet of river-craft. This was a scheme which he tried to foster between 1550 and 1553... . Still, had the daring scheme of Barlow and his associates gone through, the Amazon and not the Caribbean might have been the area upon which, in later chapters, we would have to concentrate our attention in studying the long and implacable struggle between Spain and her rivals.[16]

However, none of those nations dared to openly confront Spain in the plenitude of her power. Therefore, they resorted to the implementation of a more subtle yet very effective accomplice—propaganda, as well as to what we would call today guerilla warfare, the masters of which were well-known pirates and saboteurs who carried out their infamous deeds with the explicit consent and blessings of their respective monarchs.

Spain was too busy to retaliate. Her many burdens around the globe demanded constant vigilance and effort and she was determined to succeed. Although she was well aware of the prevailing ill-sentiment toward her, she pushed them aside and kept pressing forward. On the other hand, and in view of Spain's apparent passiveness, the other European nations grew in arrogance and stepped up their unrelenting guerilla maneuvers.

By 1588 King Philip II 's patience, after thirty years of intrigue and hesitation, had reached its peak and, upon learning of the execution of queen Mary Stuart, the deposed Queen of Scots, boldly launched all of his military might against England hoping to silence it forever, "because such was the mission he had received from God". But it was not to be. The king's hopes were crushed and Spain, badly wounded, had to double her efforts to hold on to her achievements. In his book, *Treasures of the Armada*, Belgian archeologist/writer Robert Sténuit put it this way:

The sun never set on Philip's empire, and never had so scattered an empire depended to such an extent on supremacy at sea. Each year more gold was mined in America than had existed in the whole of Medieval Europe. Special fleets of armed galleons, the "Platas Flotas, " the plate fleets, carried this annual haul back to Cádiz. Pirates of all nations dreamed about it, and so did the sailors of Her Most Gracious Majesty Queen Elizabeth's Royal Navy. Sometimes they did more than dream. If Philip was going to keep the world in his clutches for himself, if he was going to protect the Spanish trade monopoly with the Americas, to continue unhindered transporting from Perú and México to his own coffers the gold necessary to maintain Christ's army, there was one last rival still to be swallowed, Elizabeth, who obstinately persisted in putting England and her ships in his way.[17]

As stated in the beginning, in the annals of United States' history little recognition has been given to Spain's major contribution to the making of the United States as a whole, especially by modern historians. Once in a long while a distant cry is heard clamoring for the truth but it is quickly silenced by forces deeply-rooted in our traditional beliefs. Evidently, echoes of the Black Legend made their way across the Atlantic where they found fertile grounds, especially with the advent of America's Expansionist Movement inspired by the "Manifest Destiny."

CHAPTER FOUR

THE U.S. EXPANDS WESTWARD TO FORMER SPANISH TERRITORY

After gaining its independence, the ambitious young republic sought to expand westward but Spain stood in the way as a major impediment. By 1763, just 13 years before the Declaration of Independence, all lands west of the Mississippi, or almost two-thirds of today's United States, was under Spanish domain (the territory was ceded by France to Spain on November 3, 1762 as compensation for the loss of Florida to England.) As historian E.G. Bourne wrote in his book *Spain in America*: "More than half the present territory of the United States at one time or another has been under Spanish rule."[18]

However, this was soon to change by virtue of one of the most extraordinary and fascinating territorial expansions in history, as we will now summarize it. In 1783 the Thirteen Colonies occupied the region between the Atlantic Ocean and the Mississippi River, and from the present Canadian boundary as far south as Florida. In 1803 the United States purchased Louisiana from France, which had belonged previously to Spain, for $15 million, or for four cents an acre, according to historian Burt Hirschfeld (*Four Cents an Acre: The Story of the Louisiana Purchase*, Julian Messner, 1965), thus doubling the land mass of the United States. Most people may not realize the actual size of the "Country" of Louisiana as it was then called, but it comprised the following present-day states: Louisiana, Arkansas, Oklahoma, Kansas, Missouri, Nebraska, Iowa, the Dakotas, Montana, and parts of Minnesota, Colorado and Wyoming. (After De Soto discovered the Mississippi on May 8, 1541, 132 years passed before white men ventured near the great stream. Then, in April 1682, the Frenchman René Robert Cavelier, standing at its mouth, claimed the entire Mississippi Valley for France and named it Louisiana in honor of his king, Louis XIV, which is how the name Louisiana originated.) By the Treaty of 1819 with Spain, Florida and part of Louisiana were added. Then Texas was annexed in 1845, and title to the Oregon Territory (including Idaho and Washington) was established in 1846. After the Mexican-American War in 1848, Mexico ceded by the Treaty of Guadalupe-Hidalgo what is now California, Nevada, Utah, Arizona and New Mexico, with the exception of some disputed lands which were later bought in the Gadsden Purchase in 1853. The Rio Grande boundary was settled in 1848. Then Alaska (which had been a Russian province since the 18th century following Bering's voyages) was purchased from Russia for a little over $7 million in 1867; Hawaii was annexed in 1898; Cuba, Puerto Rico, Guam and the Philippines were ceded by Spain after the Spanish- American War in 1899; American Samoa by treaty in 1900; the Virgin Islands, formerly the Danish West Indies, were purchased from Denmark in 1917. Thus, in less than 114 years, the United States had expanded an incredible 2,850,749 square miles at the amazingly low cost of only $100 million. Approximately half of that territory was purchased while the other half was ceded by Mexico and Spain. Combining all of the purchases, acquisitions, territories ceded or transferred, and the time it took to bring them into the Union, it remains to this day the biggest and most profitable real estate business ever! The reader is urged to read Donald Barr Chidsey's *Louisiana Purchase: The Story of the Biggest Real Estate Deal in History*, New York, Crown Publishers, 1972; and also John Keats' *Eminent Domain: The Louisiana Purchase and the Making of America*, New York, Charterhouse, 1973. Basically, the Louisiana Purchase had provided to the young republic an outlet to the Gulf of Mexico, just like the Oregon country and the cession by Mexico of half her lands had provided an outlet to the Pacific. The United States now controlled the outlets to both oceans, the Gulf, the Caribbean Sea, and, with the Mississippi, the continental west. Clearly, after the Louisiana Purchase, the West ignited the young republic to expand its borders beyond the Mississippi. Lewis and Clark set out to find the Northwest Passage; the Virginian Henry Sager set out on the Oregon Trail to reach the continent's farthest shore; Sam Houston was able to carve out his own independent republic in Texas. After the Civil War, the building of the transcontinental railroad took care of the rest. Divine Providence was blowing fair winds across the nascent republic.

(Note: In the above-cited $100 million figure, we have not included the $250,000 the United States paid annually to Panama for the lease of the canal, but did include the $25 million reimbursement to Colombia for said lease. Therefore, the overall figure of $100 million could be higher.)

However, not all Americans were in favor of purchasing Louisiana. For example, D. Humphrey, in his valedictory discourse before the "Society of the Cincinnati for the State of Connecticut," Hartford, July 4, 1804, (Boston, 1804.), referring to the purchase asks rhetorically: "Who, but land jobbers and negro-owners will reap any emolument from it." Whatever the mood of the nation at the time, the fact remains that with the purchase the United States catapulted into world prominence and was very much on its way to achieving its present-day leadership. Destiny played a role too in the timing of the purchase for Mexico was in a state of total anarchy, Spain exhausted, and France was willing to unload it as Napoleon had his eyes set on expanding his European empire. He needed to make money, not spend it. As scholar John Keats wrote: "Napoleon intended to make war on Britain. He cared nothing for the United States, whose friendship or enmity was unimportant to him, but he was entirely willing to use the little republic, in any way he could, to claw at the British."[19]

In 1793, Jedediah Morse published the *American Universal Geography*, in which he wrote: "The Mississippi was never designed as the western boundary of the American Empire," echoing the general sentiment favoring the territorial expansion and North America's imperial quest embodied in one of the principal statements of the Manifest Destiny. President Thomas Jefferson had already envisioned a continental United States, but kept it a secret fearing controversy. In 1802 he instructed his ambassador to Paris, Robert Livingston, to convince Napoleon that the United States lead no intentions of expanding west of The Mississippi when in reality he was forging just the opposite plan. The astute statesman was well aware that both Florida and Louisiana commanded the only outlets to the sea and he sought to control both. In 1803, a congressional committee released a report authorizing Jefferson to start negotiations with France and Spain for the purchase of Florida (east and west) and New Orleans. The report made quite clear the United States' intention to expand westward when it stated: "…it must be seen that the possessions of both Floridas and New Orleans will not only be required for the convenience of the United States, but will be demanded by their utmost necessities." James Monroe was asked to effectuate the purchase at any cost—for as low as $2 million or as high as $10 million.

In the end, the United States paid $15 million for Louisiana and nothing for both Floridas. It is interesting to note that in the 1803 issue of "Scots Magazine," (published by Alex. Chapman & Co. for Archibald Constable, Edinburgh), there is an article with the heading, "Jefferson and Napoleon Swindle Spain," which partially states:

> Jefferson joins Napoleon in fraudulent Louisiana Purchase, covertly cutting a deal on land not theirs to dispose a land that belonged to Spain, as both knew. 1803 was the year Thomas Jefferson and Napoleon defrauded Spain by illicitly arranging the Louisiana Purchase, sidestepping Congress and evading rightful owner Spain, regarding an invaluable tract of land that had been coerced from Spain by Napoleon and supposedly held in trust, a fact well known to Jefferson, a compatriot of the French Revolution.

Such piece of news, indeed a hard historical fact, leaves one simply breathless...

The mainland territory, although immense, was merely seen as a stepping stone for what laid ahead—Mexico, Cuba, Panama, and beyond. In short, the entire Western Hemisphere. And why not? Was not the United States the country "chosen" to keep it all under God's guidance? To attain its ambitious goals, the United States (aided by England) devised a two-phase stratagem: One, the declaration of the Monroe Doctrine, whereby all European nations were henceforth forbidden to intervene in the internal affairs of the Americas; two, to provide covert-action support to the emerging South American countries seeking to gain independence from Spain. Once they were "free and independent states," the United States would not only "protect" them from foreign intervention but also lend political and economic support. The plan ultimately bore fruit and cemented the United States' absolute economic and political dominance in the Western Hemisphere. In February, 1859, Florida's senator Stephen R. Mallory, in the speech delivered in the Senate of the United States, dreamed of an American slave empire in the Caribbean, arguing that the acquisition of Cuba had been a bipartisan cornerstone of American foreign policy, and adding:

> ... its purchase (of Cuba) is the necessary consequence of the purchase of Louisiana... and that unless Cuba is acquired, the United States will sit by helplessly while the Island is Africanized by sentimental and misguided emancipation policies of Spain and England. (Baltimore, John Murphy, 1859.)

Also, in 1859, the U.S. Senate proposed the Bill S.497 "...making appropriations to effect the acquisition of the island of Cuba by negotiation." (U.S. Congress, Senate Committee on Foreign Relations, 1859.) But, despite the many attempts, it was not to be and Cuba remained "free" for a while.

In this regard, it is worth noting that in 1803, upon the purchase of Louisiana, the United States minted a silver medal inscribed as follows: "Westward The Course of Empire Makes Its Way." That the United States sought control of South America from the Río Grande all the way down to Patagonia is not a hypothesis but a hard fact. All of the presidents at the time, Jefferson, Madison, Monroe, and many of the others who followed, and very especially Buchanan and Pierce, wanted not only to dominate the continent but Cuba, Santo Domingo, and even Mexico with the attempt of Governor James Wilkinson in cahoots with Aaron Bur in 1806. In this regard, historian James W. Cortada had this observation:

> During the 1820s evidence of American interest in Cuba was consistently there. John Quincy Adams, for example, envisioned Cuba being drawn into the sphere of North American influence in years to come through the dint of geographic proximity and intimate trade relations.[20]

The same author quoted a Spaniard who at the time had this to say about the United States' intentions: "...Americans consider themselves superior to all nations of Europe; and believe that their domination is destined to extend, now to the Isthmus of Panama, and hereafter, over all the regions of the New World."[21]

The plan for the acquisition or annexation of Cuba became inoperative only because of the United States' Civil War. It was a difficult century for the declining Spain and the United States, emerging as a new world power, saw the opportunity to sweep it all, playing the game of "Red Riding Hood." Respecting this point, historian Joseph Burkholder Smith had this to say commenting on "filibustering" in Latin America as a main feature of the United States' foreign policy toward Latin America:

> The common pattern is established, from which the others were cut, consisted of a preliminary propaganda phase—working up excitement in and about the target—then the organizing of a "patriot government" opposed to the group we wished to get rid of then an armed attack by the "patriots" on the nearest legitimate authority over which the targeted group held sway, then an appeal to the United States government to assume control and restore "order," a call which the United States government usually answered. Often, in came the marines.[22]

And he even had harsher words of criticism when commenting on the Louisiana Purchase:

> When Jefferson authorized negotiations for the purchase of New Orleans from France, he, his secretary of state, James Madison, and his special envoy, James Monroe, immediately launched a devious diplomatic ploy. As soon as Napoleon indicated he would sell all of Louisiana, they quickly made sure the eastern boundaries of that territory were left unclear. Their aim was to create a claim to Florida out of a mist of vague language. Subsequent moves in their maneuvering matched the moral standard thereby established. These included, at a later date, a two-million dollar bribe attempt to get France to put pressure on Spain to cede Florida, and Madison's changing dates on documents to help the cause along. All diplomatic efforts to gain acceptance of the claim that the Louisiana Purchase included West Florida—the rich area of present-day Louisiana north of New Orleans, plus parts of the present states of Alabama and Mississippi failed. So a covert- action operation was used.

The area north of New Orleans was occupied in 1810 after the United States-sponsored rebellion of settlers there provided the excuse for our troops to move in. The remainder of West Florida was left dangling. So was East-Florida—the present state.[23]

That policy responded to a clash between two opposing civilizations, carried over from Anglo-Saxon/Protestant England to Anglo-Saxon/Protestant North America, and from Latin and Catholic Spain to Latin/Indian Catholic South America. The struggle between these two worlds rather than being an economic or political one has been and continues to be cultural above all. In other words, the conflict and rivalry that was once staged in Europe between Spain and England shifted to America where it has been raging for the past three hundred years: Anglo-Saxon vs Hispanicism. Up to now, the first has triumphed but no one knows what the future may hold. We are not bringing all this up merely to criticize the United States' conduct at that time (although some criticism is deserved) but to make evident that all nations, especially the powerful ones, seek at one time or another the same goal of world preeminence; some do it openly, like Spain did in her apogee during the reigns of Charles V and Philip II, and some others not openly at all, like England, for instance, during the time of queen Elizabeth I, while others do it resorting to subterfuge, like the United States during the time of Jefferson and others. With regard to the Monroe Doctrine it must be said that the United States did not act alone but in concert with its close ally, Great Britain. Not for a long while did such opportunity present itself by which this nation could expand its markets and at the same time establish a legitimate foothold in the Americas. And though such alliance was at first rejected by President Monroe on the advice of his Secretary of State, John Quincy Adams, England ultimately got its wish. It is interesting to note that, earlier, both Jefferson and Madison had been in favor of such alliance. In this regard,

American historian Milton Meltzer wrote:

The United States feared that European intervention in Latin America might result in new empires at our borders, and especially desired to keep declining Spanish power from transferring Cuba to any other European country. Great Britain's interest lay in the promise of rich markets in South America, with the continent freed of Spanish control.[24]

CHAPTER FIVE

SPAIN FALLS VICTIM TO OPPORTUNISTIC HISTORIANS

Over the years people in the United States have been led to believe that their history truly began in the early 17th century, claiming that all that may have transpired prior to that time had but little consequence in the forging of the nation. To them, American history centered on the Thirteen Colonies, the cradle of the great republic. Whatever else took place from the time America was discovered to the time of the founding of Jamestown in 1607, a span of 115 years, has been virtually left as a blank page in the annals of this nation's history. Further, all the glory has been bestowed on four countries: England, France, Germany, and Holland, while Spain has been grossly neglected. Indeed, the most important events (and we say the most important because there were many) in United States history up to 1776 were, besides the discovery of America in 1492, the discoveries of the Pacific Ocean, the Gulf of Mexico; the conquests of Perú, México and of the Caribbean islands; the expeditions of Ponce de León, Hernando de Soto, Francisco de Coronado and Cabeza de Vaca; and the arrival of the Franciscan and Jesuit missionaries. After 1776, among the most far-reaching events were the purchase of Louisiana and the territorial cessions by Spain and Mexico. Had these events not taken place, we would be looking today at a totally different United

States. Historians may claim otherwise, but we know, and they know, that those are the facts. When Spain discovered America, and became in fact the world's center of gravity, England was an island on the fringe of world affairs, or as American historian Richard B. Morris noted:

> ...still a nation of shepherds and farmers, just emerging from the paralyzing dynastic Wars of the Roses. England had no maritime power, and in any case its Tudor Kings were too concerned with domestic problems to think of vying with Spain in the New World. Spanish initiative did awaken feelings of envy and regret among Englishmen, but at that particular time England was not prepared to do anything about it.[25]

And not only was England at the time a country of farmers and shepherds, but also a land crawling with unruly, slothful folks. In their book, *The Bold and the Magnificent: America's Founding Years, 1492-1815*, authors Bruce Catton and William B. Catton wrote:

> England in the late fifteenth century stood in sore need of such rulers (the Tudors.) Generations of wars with France, punctuated by the Black Death and sporadic peasant revolts and followed by decades of domestic strife growing out of the War of the Roses, had created conditions of turmoil and disorder from one end of the land to the other. "There is no country in the world, " the Venetian envoy noted, "where there are so many thieves and robbers as in England, insomuch that few venture to go alone in the country excepting in the middle of the day, and fewer still in the towns at night, and least of all in London.[26]

In this book we intend to prove that United States history began with the arrival of the Spaniards who played as an important a role as England and a far superior one than all of the other European nations put together. We also intend to establish that those Spaniards were not, as they have been portrayed, a band of marauders and brigands. They were, quite to the contrary, our first true heroes and pioneers, contributing immeasurably to the making of the United States from the very beginning up to and beyond the American Revolution. De Soto, Cabeza de Vaca, Coronado, Friar Junípero Serra and hundreds of others were here first and paved the way for what was to come one hundred years later, thus becoming this nation's first true heroes and pioneers. If the United States had been confined within the boundaries of the original Thirteen Colonies, which occupied a mere third of the size of its present-day territory along the Atlantic coastal plain, the great North American republic would have never come to exist. What would the United States be today without California, Texas, Florida and two-dozen other states? Who would control the Mississippi river and the outlets to the Pacific Ocean, the Gulf of Mexico and the Caribbean Sea? Who would claim domain over such natural wonders as the Grand Canyon, Yellowstone Park, Yosemite National Park and the vast natural resources therein? What would have happened to our agriculture and industry? And what would the United States today be without such cities as Los Angeles, San Francisco, Houston, Denver, Miami? Look at map of today's United States. Color in blue all the area east of the Mississippi, north to south. Then, color in red all the area west of the Mississippi, north to south. Take a step back and look at the colored map. The red area would correspond to the territory that was once under Spanish domain, while the blue area would correspond to the original territory occupied by the Thirteen Colonies, just thirteen years before the Declaration of Independence. If history had taken a different course, who knows how the United States would have looked today?

However, history did not take that turn. Taking cyclopean leaps, as we have already seen, the young republic soon laid claim to the entire continent. However, what most people fail to recognize is that when the colonists expanded westward they did not set foot on barren lands (as the Spaniards did in the 16th century), but on a vast region where the seeds of Western civilization were already sprouting. This in itself may constitute one of Spain's and Mexico's greatest contributions to the making of today's United States. But there was another contribution also often overlooked. At the same time that the United States envisioned a westward expansion, so was Russia seeking to expand eastward which may have caused an eventual clash between both cultures. Through the Imperial Russian-American Company, established in 1799, Russia had already claimed the Pacific Northwest and was headed for more. Fearing an intrusion on her western front, and also upon learning of Russia's proposed alliance with England (whereby it would provide, besides its navy, 20,000 troops to combat the Thirteen Colonies), Spain stepped in and held the Russians back thus shattering their imperialistic quest.

On the subject of the Black Legend, from which most of this modern aberration against Spain originated, we can now say that it is no longer valid or credible. At long last, after many years of scholarly work by some of the world's most distinguished historians, it has been proven to have been nothing more than a propagandistic scheme concocted by Protestant Europe to undermine Catholic Spain's well-earned fame and glory. The conquistadors lust of gold and their inhumane treatment of the natives was a blatant exaggeration of the facts propagated around the world by Spain's eternal rivals.

The quest for gold is as ancient as civilization itself. Actually it goes back thousands of years to ancient Egypt, where it was habitually used for burial purposes; then to Rome, which used it to finance its far-flung empire; then to Spain via Mexico and Peru for the same purpose; then to California for sheer greed; then to South Africa exclusively for export; and finally to Wall Street for trade. Back then it was called gold. Today, it is called the dollar. Mexico lost more than its pride when it ceded California to the United States, as the gold mines of Sierra Nevada during the gold rush of the 19t[h] century (which caused the largest migration in history as well as despicable acts of violence against minorities—Chinese, Mexicans, and others) yielded well over $2 billion just in a decade, not counting the discovery of oil and gas in California in the 1850s with a cumulative value of well over $5 billion (the reader is urged to read *Early California Oil-A Photographic History, 1865-1940,* by Kenny A. Franks and Paul F. Lambert.) After gold was found by General George Custer in the Homestake mine of Black Hills, South Dakota, the area was flooded with frantic adventurers who crushed all obstacles on their path to mine the gold and become instant tycoons (by the way, the area had been given to the Plain Indians through a treaty but it was later rescinded and the land seized upon the discovery of gold.) Historian James Schouler described the unprecedented madness this way:

> Here within one hundred and sixty thousand square miles of our Mexican conquest, within that country alone, west of the Sierras, which was drained by the Sacramento and San Joaquín Rivers, was more gold probably than would pay the cost of our late war a hundred times over... Within four months of the first discovery over four thousand persons were about the Sacramento, working as if for dear life, dwelling in coarse canvas tents and huts, and coaxing fortune with the rudest implements ...Fleets of launches, from the sloop to the cockleshell, left San Francisco in early May for the Sacramento saw-mill region, and the town was nearly stripped of its male population in course of the Summer. Soon, the whole country, from San Francisco to Los Angeles, and from the seashore to the base of the mountains, echoed the cry of "Gold, gold, gold!" The house was left half-built, the field half-planted; women looked after the shop. Foreign vessels began to arrive; but before they could unload, their crews deserted for the "diggings. "...And quickly as sails or steam could bear the tidings to different points of the compass, adventurers hastened from China, from the Sandwich Islands, from Australia, and from the whole Pacific coast between Vancouver Island and Valparaíso... The new year witnessed the exodus of our modern Argonauts. A stream of population, swollen beyond all precedent, drained the drifting elements from Europe, to mingle in a current whose American element predominated. Never again was delirium known, for it is novelty that makes the blood leap avidly.[27]

And we wonder how these Argonauts would have behaved had they descended on Cajamarca or Tenochtitlán three hundred years past. But we will let historians, sociologists, political science analysts, and other so-called pundits of human behavior ponder the question and figure the answer.

Imperial Rome, many centuries past, plundered the rich gold mines of Asturias in northern Spain through an intricate mechanism of channels and tunnels at a high cost of human lives especially of slaves. In 35 BC, the Emperor Augustus left Rome accompanied by an army of 70,000 men bent on a mission to get his hands on the Asturias gold, estimated to have been 30 million ounces of gold (valued at $12 billion today), all of which he hauled directly back to Rome. Although a known historical fact, it has never made any historian turn blue with repudiation. Yet, in the case of Spain, they have all turned deep purple. The difference between the gold mined by the Romans in Asturias in one single scoop and the one mined by Spain over a period of 400 hundred years was $5 billion—$12 billion versus $17 billion—, with one major difference: Rome took all the gold back to Rome while only a fraction of America's gold ever reached Spain. Yet, one is exonerated and the other is vilified which is hardly logical and just.

As we have said, the lust for gold has been with us since biblical times, and no nation can claim exemption from it. With regard to America's gold, all nations, but especially England and Holland, fought furiously to get their share partially to finance their own imperialistic ventures but also for sheer greed. It must be remembered that the Virgin Queen of England quadrupled her wealth by the dividends she received from the investments she personally orchestrated with her pirate cohorts. In fact, in the late 1770s, England became a world military power not only by the defeat of the Spanish Armada, but very especially by the gold the English managed to seize from Spain, which indeed was an enormous amount, enough in fact to make them and all of Europe very rich. But, instead of sweating it out to get it, as Spain did, England and Holland quietly walked away with it fooling the world in the process. Spain was used as a scapegoat and the Black Legend ensued. On the other hand, the world saw them as heroes for having inflicted another blow to the very despised Spanish power.

England may have been seen as a hero back then but certainly is no hero today. Enter South Africa, the 20 century. For the past one hundred years, the gold mines of South Africa have yielded over $4 billion annually, including other precious metals such as emeralds and diamonds. We will let the reader do the math and figure out the total mined over that period of time—$4 billion times 100. The shocking fact is that almost the totality of that immense wealth (which accounts for half of all the gold ever produced in the world) has been sold on the world market with an infinitesimal amount staying in South Africa. It stands to reason that if only a fraction of that wealth had been invested in building and helping not only South Africa but the entire continent, the abysmal situation existing in that region today would have been totally eradicated. In sharp contrast, much of the gold that Spain mined in America stayed in America and was used in building it.

During Colonial times, under the watchful eyes of some of the world's greatest administrators—the Spanish viceroys—Mexico City and in special Lima became the envy of the world rivaling with Europe's finest cities. Mexico City was re-built by Cortés, mirroring the most majestic Spanish and European cities; Lima (named by Pizarro "Ciudad de los Reyes" and later re-named Lima—the name taken from the river the Incas used to call "Rimac"— was built by Pizarro and other Spaniards brick by brick, turning it into the jewel of Colonial America. According to historian Salvador de Madariaga, Humboldt had much to say about these and other cities. On the province of Guanajuato, México (translation by the author):

The culture in this beautiful city is owed totally to the Europeans who in the 16th century provided the first seeds of civilization.... Of course, he was especially interested in any sign of scientific progress since, above all, Humboldt was a man of science. In this regard his testimony is of inestimable value. As he saw it, cultural progress is "most notable in Mexico City, Havana, Lima, and Santa Fe, Quito, Popayán, and Caracas. Despite the efforts of the patriotic society of the Island of Cuba, which fosters the sciences with the most generous zeal. .... the study of mathematical chemistry, mineralogy, and botany are more developed in México, Santa Fe and Lima....Everywhere one can observe a great intellectual movement, young people endowed with an exceptional facility to understand the principles of science. ...There is no city in the new continent, without excluding those in the United States, that would offer scientific establishments as great and as solid as the capital of México.[28]

Regarding the working of precious metals in México, Madariaga quotes Humboldt's observations:

The smaller of cities have their silversmiths in whose shops there are artists of all ethnic groups—white, mestizos, and Indians. The Academy of Fine Arts and the School of Art in México and Xalapa have contributed greatly to propagate a liking for all classical forms. Over the past few years, México has produced silver goods amounting to 150,000-200,000 Francs which, for the elegance and care of its execution, can rival with goods of the same kind produced in the most civilized parts of Europe.[29]

And regarding the study of natural sciences, Madariaga is impressed by Humboldt's words:

Respecting botany, he finds that the Indies have even achieved greater progress: "Since the end of the reign of Charles III—writes Humboldt who was himself an excellent botanist—the study of the natural sciences has been greatly developed not only in México but in all Spanish possessions. No other European government has sacrificed larger sums of funds to foster the knowledge of plants than the government of Spain.[30]

And on the subject of public health, the cure of smallpox in particular, Madariaga is also impressed by this Humbolt observation:

> In the Indies, this disease flared up every 17 or 18 years. The Spanish government wasted no time to put into effect Jenner's discovery. By 1797, less than a year after the vaccine had been discovered, the inoculation ...was in general use in all of New Spain, especially in México and in the province of Michoacán, where considerable improvement had been observed regarding the mortality rate from the disease in that critical year. While in 1779 9,000 people had perished from the disease only in the capital, in 1797 only 170 had died of the 6,800 people who had contracted it.[31]

In general terms, as documented by Madariaga in this and in other passages, Humboldt had high praise for the work Spain had done in Americas after 300 years of Spanish intervention. No city was ever erected in North America during or after its colonial period that could be compared with Mexico City or Lima, not even with Havana, Santo Domingo or San Juan, and most definitely not with any which may have ever been erected by England in any of its multiple colonies. (The reader is urged to read *El virreinato del Perú*, by José M. Valega, Editorial Cultura Ecléctica, Lima, 1939, for a very detailed account of the history of Perú during that era. A truly engrossing and fascinating book.)

In addition to Spain, Mexico should also be recognized as a major contributor to the making of the United States. After all, one-third of its territory was "ceded" to the United States comprising today five of its largest and most prosperous states. Further, the silver mined at Zacatecas made North America's first millionaires and infused new life in the economy of Colonial North America. The Treaty of Guadalupe-Hidalgo of 1848 (ratified by the United States Senate on March 10, 1848, and by the Mexican Congress on May 25th) manifests in plain language the magnitude of the lands "ceded" by Mexico to the United States. Drafted by the United States government it reads in part:

New Mexico and Upper California have been ceded by Mexico to the United States, and now constitute a part of our country. Embracing nearly ten degrees of latitude, lying adjacent to the Oregon territory, and extending from the Pacific ocean to the Río Grande, a mean distance of nearly a thousand miles, it would be difficult to estimate the value of these possessions to the United States. They constitute of themselves a country large enough for a great empire, and their acquisition is second only in importance to that of Louisiana in 1803. Rich in mineral and agricultural resources, with a climate of great salubrity, they embrace the most important ports on the whole Pacific coast of the continent of North America. The possession of the ports of San Diego and Monterey and the bay of San Francisco, will enable the United States to command the already valuable and rapidly increasing commerce of the Pacific. The number of our whale ships alone now employed in that sea exceeds seven hundred, requiring more than twenty thousand seamen to navigate them, while the capital invested in this particular branch of commerce is estimated at not less than forty million of dollars. The excellent harbors of Upper California will, under our flag, afford security and repose to our commercial marine, and American mechanics will soon furnish ready means of ship-building and repair, which are now so much wanted in that distant sea.

By the acquisition of these possessions, we are now brought into immediate proximity with the west coast of America, from Cape Horn to the Russian possession north of Oregon, with the islands of the Pacific ocean, and by a direct voyage in steamers we will be in less than thirty days of Canton and other ports of China.

In this vast region, whose rich resources are soon to be developed by American energy and enterprise, great must be the augmentation of our commerce, and with it new and profitable demands for mechanic labor in all its branches, and new and valuable markets for our manufactures and agricultural products. ("30th Congress, 1st Session, [Senate] Executive, No. 60, Message from the President of the United States—A copy of the treaty with the Mexican republic, of February 2, 1848, and of the correspondence in relation thereto, and recommending measures for carrying the same into effect, July 6, 1848.")

Imagine for a moment what the United States would be today without the Louisiana territory and the lands ceded by Mexico and Spain.

And Cuba too, since many of North-America's famed explorations were launched from what once was the leading outpost of the Spanish empire in America. Moreover, all the Spanish gold and silver flowing into Colonial North America during the 17th and 18th centuries, which proved to be so vital to its future development, was derived, in addition to Mexico, from the mines of Peru and Bolivia. Thus, a case could be made that these two countries also played a significant role in the making of the nation. We should mention here that in the late 1700s the Spanish brigantine of war, El Cazador, which sailed from the port of Veracruz for New Orleans with a cargo of 450,000 pieces of newly minted silver coins (dated 1783), or Spanish milled dollars, disappeared off the coast of New Orleans. Had these coins reached their destination they would have stabilized the Spanish monetary system in Colonial North America and solidified Spain's holdings. After this great loss, King Charles III reluctantly commenced negotiations to sell the Louisiana territory to France, finally giving it up in 1800 for some minor European considerations. We know that part of that cargo has recently been salvaged and that some of those coins have been sold on the world market.

For the first one hundred plus years, both Americas were interconnected with one another under the flag of Spain, meaning that all major historical, political, geographical, economical, and social events taking place in one region would greatly impact the others. The conquests of Peru, Mexico, the Dominican Republic, Cuba and Puerto Rico; the discoveries of the Pacific Ocean, the Amazon River, the Gulf of Mexico, and the Potosí and Zacatecas mines; Magellan's and Humboldt's explorations plus many others had profound repercussions on North America. In addition, all of North America's great Spanish explorers—De Soto, Coronado,

Ponce de León, Narváez, Cabeza de Vaca, Cabrillo, Vizcaíno and numerous others, came to North America not from Spain but from South America, mainly from Mexico and also from Peru. What this means is that those countries, as well as others, were the proving grounds and seedbed for the future discoverers, explorers, and settlers of North America, among them, De Soto with Pizarro in Perú and in Cuba; Cortés in Cuba, Mexico and Central America; Coronado in Nueva Galicia, Mexico (where he served as governor); Narváez in Jamaica, Cuba, and Mexico; Cabeza de Vaca in Mexico; Marcos de Niza first in Nicaragua and later in Peru (where he witnessed Atahualpa's death); Ponce de León in Santo Domingo (which he helped conquered), Puerto Rico (where he was governor), and Cuba; Friar Junípero Serra in Mexico and Baja California. Menéndez de Avilés was among the very few who was trained in Spain in the wars against the French corsairs under Charles V, and later as a Commander of the Indies fleet under Philip II. The same could be said about the hundreds of Spanish missionaries who trudged North America in all directions, bringing with them the seeds of Western civilization. And similarly about the Spanish viceroys, especially Antonio de Mendoza, the first true Administrator of the New World, under whose leadership Mexico flourished and many North American expeditions were launched. The reader is urged to read Arthur Scott Aiton's book, *Antonio de Mendoza: First Viceroy of New Spain*, New York, Russell & Russell, 1967 (a reprint of the 1927 edition.) Thus, the great training ground for the conquest of the north was the conquest of the south, not only for the Spaniards but also for many English explorers, including Francis Drake and Walter Raleigh. But even today Spain continues to be ignored or disparaged in most American history books. Let us look at a few examples (we are omitting titles and authors as we do not wish to embarrass them.)

In a recently published 1000-page American history textbook, which we assume is read by thousands if not millions of students across the country, only six pages touch on the early Spanish explorations of the southwest, repeatedly interjecting trite remarks about the Spaniards' insatiable thirst for gold and their brutality toward the Indians. Gorging on their negative depiction of the Spaniards, the authors cite a supposed Nahua witness lament which in their own translation reads: "(The Spaniards) picked up the gold and fingered it like monkeys. They hungered like pigs for that gold." Referring to Cortés and his Spanish "invaders," they lashed out these words: "They sacked and burned Tenochtitlán." And of Pizarro: "Dreams of gold-filled continents stirred anew when Francisco Pizarro, with the help of guns and disease, plundered the fabulously wealthy Inca empire."

In another best-selling book, first published in London and now in a new American edition, under the heading "The Colonies and Dependencies of the States of Europe," Spain is listed as having only three colonies in America: Cuba, Puerto Rico, and what appears to be the name Pinos, (which we have never heard of.) Yet, those of England, France, and even Holland surpassed twenty! And then, in another section titled "Principal European Battles," only the Spanish battle of Lepanto against the Turks (which is misspelled as Lepanito) is mentioned. It seems that the greatest of all European battles, that of Philip II and his formidable Armada against England, never took place. In an encyclopedia of world history, compiled and edited by a distinguished history professor from one of the United States' elite universities, in the section titled "North America—Exploration and Settlement," no reference is made to Spain or the Spaniards, while mentioning the other nations under different headings: "The French in North America," "The English in North America," "Dutch and Swedish Settlements." This omission of Spain is appalling. Mentioning the Dutch and the Swedish and leaving Spain out defies reason. Besides the purchase of Manhattan Island from the Indians, a few spotted settlements along the eastern seaboard in Connecticut, New Jersey, Delaware and Pennsylvania, the exploration of the Hudson river by Henry Hudson (who was English, not Dutch) and the trading of furs with the Indians through a monopoly given to the New Netherland Company and a few others, the Dutch contribution to North American was virtually nil. In South America they became the consummate pirates and profiteers of black slaves rivaling with the English. With regard to the Swedish, their claim to fame in North America consisted of the establishment of two or three fur trading companies, such as the South Company (which ultimately failed) and the New Sweden Company in the Delaware region. Nothing else.

Also, in a large chronological guide of American history, published by a respected publisher, the name of Spain is mentioned (slightly) about twenty times from 1492 through 1606, and then disappears until 1775 when it is mentioned in a few more instances, disregarding completely what was going on in the West while the other events (rather small in comparison) were taking place in the East; not even once are the names of Friar Junípero Serra or Bernardo de Gálvez or any of the key Spanish expeditions brought to the reader's attention, as if they never happened. It is all about the history of British America and the Thirteen Colonies, or about one third of what was then the United States.

It is no wonder that after reading such books students continue to profess a total disregard for Spain and anything Spanish. But, fortunately, there are other books that have taken a different view, that have attempted to tell the truth based on actual historical fact.

Here in one of such books. Commenting on the De Soto and Coronado expeditions, American historian Edward Gaylord Bourne wrote:

> These great expeditions of De Soto and Coronado, undertaken for the exploration of the interior of the present United States a century and a half before La Salle, and over two centuries and a half before Lewis and

Clark, were the natural outflow of the marvelous experiences of Cortés and of Pizarro in Mexico and Peru, and mark the highest reach of Spanish energy in our own country; nor have they ever been surpassed as exhibitions of skillful leadership and enduring labor by any similar enterprises by the French or English in North America. Their results were keenly disappointing at the time, but in the record of exploration of the globe they occupy a high and honorable place among the great enterprises of history.[32]

It is also interesting to note that at a major bookstore (in Paramus, N.J, boasting a book inventory of well over 1,000,000 titles, we couldn't find a single book on Spain or on any subject relating to Spain or the Spaniards; not even in the art section—no Velázquez, no Goya, no El Greco, not even Picasso, supposedly America's most admired Spanish painter. When asked about any editions of *Don Quixote*, the young clerk blushed and replied: "Who? No, we don't have it! Try the city! They are more, you know, sophisticated..." Well, we followed his advice. At a world's famous bookstore in lower Manhattan, boasting an inventory of millions of books, we could only find one used paperback copy on "Don Quixote," and in the Americana section only one single title on the Spanish Southwest. Almost at the point of walking out, we were told to inquire at its old and rare book collection where we met similar results. As we were leaving we spotted several tables staked with hundreds of art books, muttering to ourselves: "Well, maybe here we will find a book on the Spanish masters." Nothing was found. Our trip to "cosmopolitan" New York ended up in a total fiasco.

CHAPTER SIX

THE TRUE BEGINNINGS OF UNITED STATES HISTORY

American history did not begin with the landing of the English at Jamestown in 1607 nor with the arrival of the Mayflower in 1620, not even if Sir Humphrey Gilbert had succeeded in his expedition to Newfoundland in 1578. Of course, it did not begin either in 1585 when Richard Greenville, cousin of Sir Walter Raleigh, took his colony to Roanoke. As it is known, pressed by starvation and other calamities the colonists soon abandoned it and went back to England with Francis Drake. American history, the history of the republic, of the United States of America, began one hundred years earlier with the 1513 landing of the Spaniard Juan Ponce de León in Florida. And the great enterprise of the discovery, exploration, and colonization of North America, that is to say, bringing North America into Western culture, did not originate in the northeast but in the southwest, through the Gulf of Mexico, not the Atlantic. Historian Robert S. Weddle explained it this way:

> The vital conduit for the first real European access to the North America mainland—the Gulf of Mexico—has been grossly neglected, never having been treated as the distinct entity that it is ... .Following Columbus' initial discovery of the fringe islands, the Andalusian voyagers groped their way through the maze, seeking a continent.

Running uphill, as it were, they found Central and South America. Not for sixteen years did the first navigator find the crucial passage into the Gulf of Mexico. Another decade passed before the discoverers realized that a second continent lay beyond the Gulf Only then could the actual discovery of mainland North America begin.

Through this "Spanish Sea"—which the Gulf remained for almost two centuries after the first European entry—the discoverers and explorers advanced onto the continent. The Gulf and its environs were the theater for the earliest and most determined efforts to conquer the natives and explore and settle the interior.[33]

In the early 17th century, around the time the British arrived, Florida comprised the eastern half of present-day United States, and not just today's peninsula. The Spaniards called it "país" (country) extending from Mexico to Newfoundland in northeastern Canada. Thus, when reference is made in modern American history books that in the 17th century Florida was under Spanish domain, we now know the territory it comprised, which included the one British America or the Thirteen Colonies would later call home. It is then a fact that British America and later the Thirteen Colonies were thus founded on lands which had been previously claimed by Spain as they fell within the boundaries of the Spanish side of the Demarcation Line. (Spain, by necessity, only recognized England's claim on North America by the Treaty of 1670— 63 years after the landing at Jamestown.) It could then be argued that all future territorial claims and settlements by the British, French, Dutch, Germans, and others, infringed upon the sovereignty of Spain and were thus unlawful and illegitimate, including the founding of Jamestown and the landing of the Mayflower. The only claim England had on the eastern coast of North America were the discoveries made by John Cabot (an Italian) and even that is shrouded in historical uncertainty, especially as it pertains to his second voyage. In any event, having found no gold or riches, his voyages were deemed a failure and only had any relevance many years later when England became Spain's rival and alleged Cabot's discoveries as the basis for her rights in North America.

Commenting on John Cabot's discoveries, historian Edward Gaylor Bourne wrote:

> The date of the land fall, June 24th, does not appear earlier than the so- called Cabot map of 1544. It was probably derived from Sebastian Cabot. In regard to the land fall, controversy has been as busy as with the identity of the San Salvador of Columbus, but the results are not so satisfactory. The Canadian scholars Dawson and Prowse advocate respectively Cape Breton and Newfoundland. Harrisse has been insistent for Labrador, but with slight assent from those familiar with the region. In view of this uncertainty, it has been questioned whether John Cabot's report that he found the main-land should be accepted as final. He may have been as much mistaken as was Columbus about Cuba.[34]

On the same topic, a group of American scholars commented: "The voyages of John Cabot and his son Sebastian in 1497-1498 provided the basis for the English claim to North America, though there was nothing that could be called a British empire in the New World until the settlements of Virginia in 1607."[35]

And regarding how the Demarcation Line dividing the New World between Spain and Portugal was viewed by rival Europe, historian Ainsworth Means had this to say:

> As might be expected, the Pope's demarcation of the New World was far from being universally accepted; even France, a Catholic power, questioned it. Consequently, rivals and foes of the two Iberian powers came to maintain that the sole authentic title to lands in the Americas claimed by European slates was that conferred by "effective occupation." Precisely what was meant by this formula it is hard to say. One interpretation might be the stark one that a given place belonged to a given European power only until a second power managed to wrest it from the first; and, in fact, this interpretation was the one frequently in force among the rival powers. On the other hand, the enemies of Spain, in the sixteenth century and even afterwards down to our own time, often

claimed that little or nothing was being done by the Spanish government and people to explore, settle, and administer the gigantic territories over which they pretended to have a sole right to rule. The falsity of this claim will be frequently demonstrated in this book, and already, in Chapter II, we have seen how ably the Spaniards penetrated wilderness which later became their firmly held dominions.[36]

This is how the English interpreted it when they landed in North America in 1607, even though they were well aware of the fact that Spain had already discovered, explored, and settled half of the continent. Naturally, they did not attempt to wrest the land they occupied directly from Spain, but rather sneaked in stealthily while Spain momentarily winked, which was symptomatic of their modus operandi. Once again, opportunistic England never confronted its adversaries with manly resolve, at least not in America for most of their stay there (over 300 years.)

By the time of the British landfall, the Spaniards had already etched an indelible mark on the North American landscape and laid claim to almost half of the continent for Spain. Coronado, De Soto, Ponce de León, Cabeza de Vaca (the man who in reality discovered ancient North America), Narváez, Pineda, Menéndez Avilés, and literally hundreds more had crisscrossed the immense uncharted territory in one of the greatest and most fascinating epics in the annals of discovery and exploration. In sharp contrast, once on North American soil, the British set up camp on the narrow strip of land along the northeastern coast and never ventured beyond its borders. Not that this should surprise us as they came to North America driven by drastically different pursuits. No dreams of glory, honor, or reverence for king and country ever stirred the passion in their souls. American historian Charles F. Lummis put it this way (translation by the author):

> Jamestown, the first English colony in North America was not founded until 1607, and by that time the Spaniards were permanently

established in Florida and New Mexico, and were absolute owners of a vast territory to the south. They had already discovered, conquered, and largely colonized the interior of the Americas, from northeastern Kansas to Buenos Aires, and from the Atlantic to the Pacific. Half of the United States, all of Mexico, Yucatan, Central America, Venezuela, Ecuador, Bolivia, Paraguay, Peru, Chile, New Granada, and other vast territories, all of which belonged to Spain, when England acquired a few acres in the North American coast nearest to home. The Spaniards were the first ones to observe and survey the depths of the world's largest gulf; to discover the two largest rivers; to see the Pacific Ocean; to learn that there were in fact two continents; to circumnavigate the globe; to open new roads leading to the farthest corners of our own country and of the lands to our south; to found cities thousands of miles inland, and all of this much before the first Anglos landed on our shores. To think that a poor Spanish lieutenant accompanied by twenty soldiers, traversed an indescribable desert contemplating the Grand Canyon three centuries before it was seen by. North American eyes! ... When the reader finds out that the best English book does not even mention the fact that the first navigator who went around the world was a Spaniard; that the first explorer who discovered Brazil was a Spaniard; that the first one to discover California was a Spaniard; that the ones who discovered and founded colonies in what is today the United States were Spaniards... he would realize that the time has come for us to do more justice than our fathers did, in a matter that should be of the utmost concern to all true North Americans.[38]

By the beginning of the 18th century, while Spain was already engaged in a mammoth effort to colonize the New World, she founded two cities in North America and discovered half of today's U.S. states, while other European nations were barely making their presence known. France had but managed to make a few uneventful forays in the continent; Portugal had only settled a few spotted colonies in South America; and England had done even less. Between Cape Horn and the North Pole there was hardly any visible trace of England or the English. Commenting on the French influence in North America, American historian Richard B. Morris wrote:

Culturally, New France lagged behind both the Spanish and the English colonies: no newspaper or book was printed there until the mid-18 century. And since the crown never put its full influence behind an active program of settlement, the French colonies were never adequately populated. By 1763 they had barely managed to settle some 80,000 people from Canada to Louisiana, a stretch of territory more than 2,000 miles in length.[39]

The Spaniards were the first Europeans to marvel at the Grand Canyon, the Rocky Mountains, the Mojave Desert, Lake Utah, the Sierra Nevada, and the mighty Mississippi River. They were the first to give these, and hundreds of similarly natural wonders, colorful Spanish names such as Bahía de los Farallones (San Francisco), Puerto de San Miguel (San Diego Bay), El Llano Estancado (in Kansas), Lago de los Timpanogos (Lake Utah), Río del Tizón (Colorado River), Bahía del Espíritu Santo (Tampa Bay), Madre de Dios del Jacán (Chesapeake Bay) and many, many others. Regarding California's Spanish names, historians Barbara and Rudy Marinacci wrote:

>...Of the State's fifty-eight counties, thirty-two of them have Spanish titles—and three more started out Spanish. They are Alameda, Amador, Calaveras, Contra Costa, Del Norte, El Dorado, Fresno, Los Angeles, Madera, Marin (an abbreviation), Mariposa, Mendocino, Merced, Monterey, Nevada, Placer, Plumas, Sacramento, San Benito, San Bernardino, San Diego, San Francisco, San Joaquin, San Luis Obispo, San Mateo, Santa Barbara, Santa Clara, Santa Cruz, Sierra, Solano, Tulare, Ventura. Kings, Stanislaus, and Trinity are translations of the original Spanish names for the rivers that flow through them: Los Santos, Reyes, Estanislao, and Trinidad... (A number of other titles look Spanish but are actually Indian names recorded in Spanish, like Colusa, Inyo, Modoc, Napa, Shasta, Sonoma, Tuolumne, Yolo, Yuba.) Then there is the matter of cities. Of our sixteen largest metropolitan areas, fourteen have Spanish names, either exclusively or included within their scope: Fresno, Los Angeles, Modesto, Sacramento, Salinas, San Bernardino, San Francisco, San Diego, San Jose, Santa Ana, Santa Barbara, Santa Rosa, Vallejo, Ventura. ... Many of California's bays have Hispanic titles:

San Diego, San Francisco, Monterey, San Pedro, Santa Barbara, Santa Monica; among smaller bays, Bodega, Lunada, Morro, Trinidad. Of the eight Channel Islands, only one-Anacapa—is non-Hispanic. Along the coastline remain many Spanish- derived names for puntas: Points Ano Nuevo, Avisadero, Buchon, Cavallo (from "caballo" or horse), Conception, Delgada, Goleta, Gorda, Lobos...Loma, Lopez, Medanos, Pescadero, Piedras Blancas, Pinos, Pitas, Purisima, Reyes, Rincon, San Mateo, Sur...[40]

If a similar survey would be conducted in North America today, we would find literally thousands of other Spanish names across the nation, especially in the south, southwest, and west, and not only in cities but in many small towns and villages. For instance, a small town in the state of Ohio is called "El Toboso," the name immortalized by Miguel de Cervantes in "Dulcinea del Toboso," the heroine of *Don Quixote*.

The Spaniards were also first to discover the Gulf of Mexico, called for many years the Spanish Sea (also "Seno de México" and "Golfo de México," which was discovered by Sebastián de Ocampo.) This discovery made possible the exploration of the northern continent mainly from the Spanish outposts in Cuba and Mexico, as already explained by historian Richard S. Weddle (see previous endnote [33].)

They were also first to found towns and cities across the continent which would later flourish and become among America's largest and most prosperous, such as San Francisco, Los Angeles, San Diego, Monterrey, San Antonio, and Santa Fe. They were first to discover and/or explore, and in many cases name and settle, almost half of our present-day states; twenty-five to be exact: Alabama, Arizona, Arkansas, California, Colorado, Florida, Georgia, Illinois, Indiana, Kansas, Kentucky, Louisiana, Mississippi, Montana, Nebraska, Nevada, New Mexico, North Carolina, Oregon, South Carolina, Tennessee, Texas, Utah, Washington, and Wyoming. It may startle some to know that in the same year of the signing of the Declaration of Independence (1776), the Spaniard Juan Bautista de Anza discovered the Sierra Nevada, and founded San Francisco; Pedro de Villazur, the Platte River (called by the Spaniards Río del Espíritu Santo); and Atanasio Domínguez Silvestre, Lake Utah, the Silver River, and the Old Spanish Trail; and the venerable Padre Junípero Serra the mission of San Francisco in California.

They were also the first Europeans to interact intimately with the North American natives, to learn and write copiously about their languages, cultures and to teach them the essence of Western civilization, from the sublime to daily chores such as plowing the fields or making bread. They introduced the horse (Gregorio Villalobos and Hernán Cortés brought it with them to Mexico in 1521), cattle (most likely being the descendants of herds brought to Santo Domingo by Christopher Columbus), all kinds of livestock and poultry, the wheel, iron mining, European and South American plants and spices such as cocoa, sugar cane, vanilla, and cinnamon, and the fragrant rose. They were the first ranchers and cowboys, especially in Texas, California, and New Mexico, thus pioneering American agriculture and cattle industries (including the Texas long-horns), which grew so quickly that by 1860 Texas alone had more than three and a half million head of cattle. The reader is urged to read the article by Bruce M. Shackelford on the origins of the Texas long-horns, in which he partially wrote:

> Christopher Columbus brought spotted Castilian range cattle that became the basis of future herds in the Americas. By the 1520s over 8,000 cattle were herded on the Island of Hispaniola. Nearly every expedition of Christopher Columbus brought spotted Castilian range cattle that became the basis of the future northern frontier of Mexico, now Texas. ...In the mid-1500s, ranching exploded on the northern frontier of Mexico in the area called Nueva Vizcaya. Cattle were brought from Spain, the Canary Islands, and the islands of the Caribbean to populate the huge ranches called estancias. A traveler in northern Mexico

reported in 1579 that some ranches had as many as 150,000 cows and that 20,000 cattle were considered a small herd. In 1586, two of the estancias branded a total of 75, 000 calves. ... By 1685 Spanish livestock operations had been established in the areas of present-day East Texas, Arizona, California, and New Mexico. ... The Franciscan missionaries that founded the missions of San Antonio continued to bring cattle to Texas with breeding annually greatly increasing the number of cattle. Each mission operated a ranch manned by Indian converts to Catholicism under the supervision of the Franciscan friars. By the 1760s the ranches contained large cattle herds. An inventory of livestock made in 1762 lists almost 5,500 cattle running on the mission ranches.[41]

They were first to cultivate the land and teach the Indians better methods of farming, to plant maize as well as many other vegetables and cotton (especially in New Mexico), orange and other fruit-tree varieties, and grape vines, all of which later flourished into one of the building blocks of the United States economy: agriculture. They were also the first to transport (on foot or mule) native plants across the continent and to cultivate them everywhere, such as the tomato, potato, even peanuts, and to introduce innovative systems of irrigation still in use today, plus mules, pigs, sheep, chickens, goats, and donkeys. The only domestic animals the Indians knew were the turkey and the dog, especially in the southwest.

Undoubtedly, today's California and Florida's citrus industries are forever indebted to the Spanish Padres of the 17th and 18th centuries, as well as California's wine-growing industry and Georgia's peach-growing industry. The nation is also beholden to Spain (and to Mexico) for its ranching (a derivative of the Spanish word "rancho," or small farm), its first cowboys (the "vaquero," or "cowboy," a boy cattle herder), and numerous other industries, customs, and folklore. If the United States today is the world's leader in agriculture, which indeed it is, it owes it to those beloved Franciscan monks riding on their docile donkeys across the plains in sun-scorched days. Their memory should be etched forever in the nation's history. Friar Junípero Serra was not only the first pioneer of California but also one of North America's first pioneers. Regionalizing the Spaniards while nationalizing the North American patriots is indeed a grave mistake and a historical injustice. They were all "founding fathers" of our great republic with one very big difference: the Spaniards earned this honor 300 years before the others. Regarding the work of the Spanish missionaries in North America, Agnes Repplier, in her book *Junípero Serra*, wrote:

> Considering the absolute and irresponsible authority possessed by the missionaries, their conduct has been marked by a degree of humanity, moderation, and benevolence unexampled in any other situation. There are few instances to be found where men, enjoying such unlimited confidence and power, have not abused them. Yet the missionaries of California neither betray their trust nor show themselves unworthy of confidence. On the contrary, there are many proofs of their zeal, industry, and philanthropy. Since the country has opened up, strangers have found in their missions disinterested hospitality and kindness.[42]

And, in another passage, Ms. Repplier talked about their major contribution not only to California but to the nation at large:

> From the time that the Mexican republic was established, it never ceased its efforts at secularization (of the missions). Two things only stood in its way: the amazing but none the less reluctance of the Indians to be emancipated, and the fact that seven-eighths of the country's produce was raised in the missions. Their dissolution would mean the collapse of industry and trade. ...but Spain's gift to America was one of disinterested benevolence, and Fray Junípero Serra was her almoner. The Atlantic coast knows little but his name, and sometimes not even that but the Pacific coast holds him in reverence, and has atoned, as best it could, for the destruction of his life's work by putting up monuments in his honor. California's historians are united in praising his purity of intention, which is one thing; his fidelity of execution, which is another; and his far-sighted wisdom, which is a third, and which insured the success of everything he undertook.[43]

But much before the continent was discovered, there was an extraordinary figure that initiated it all, Queen Isabella of Spain, whose many virtues as a mother, wife, statesman, and warrior will continue to be an inspiration to men and women throughout the ages. Whatever she was called upon to do, whether willingly or unwillingly, she discharged her duties flawlessly.

Has the United States ever properly recognized the contribution of those pioneers? To some degree it has but we feel it has been hardly enough. Here are some of the recognitions of which we are aware: in 1940 the United States Postal Service issued a 3-cent stamp commemorating the 400th anniversary of the Coronado expedition; a 15-cent stamp honoring General Bernardo Gálvez (issued on July 23, 1980); and in 1935 the United States Government issued a Silver Half Dollar commemorating the 400 Anniversary of Alvar Núñez Cabeza de Vaca's overland trek through much of the southwest. The obverse bears the "head of a cow," which is a literal translation of his name, and the reverse a yucca tree and a map showing the Old Spanish Trail with the name "El Paso" at the end of the Texas map. We also know of the splendid statue at the U.S. Capitol of Friar Junípero Serra; the statue of Bernardo de Gálvez on Virginia Avenue in the nation's capital; the majestic statue of Queen Isabella at the main entrance of the Pan American Union, in Washington; and the magnificent painting of Hernando de Soto in the Rotunda of the U.S. Capitol. And talking about de Soto, on June 18, 1991, the State of Mississippi re-named the Mississippi River Bridge on U.S. Highway 49 the Hernando de Soto Bridge, and also in that same state, May 9th was declared Hernando de Soto Day. In addition, we know that in 1893 the United States government minted the "Queen Isabella Commemorative Quarter," as requested by the Board of Lady Managers of the Columbian Exposition. The obverse has the crowned bust of Queen Isabella, and the reverse features a kneeling female with distaff and spindle. The Coronado

Bridge, in San Diego, opened in 1969, which has become a symbol of the San Diego area, is also a welcoming tribute to the titan of the North American southwest. Yet, mainstream America hardly knows about these great men and their contribution to the nation's history. More education is unquestionably needed on this subject, especially in the schools where the vast majority of students, if not all, know very little about Hispanic history, especially as it relates to their own. This is truly a disgrace and a black eye on the American educational system.

By the time the other Europeans arrived one hundred years later, Western civilization had already taken root in North America. People were already speaking, reading, and writing one European language; worshiping one Christian God in their first churches and temples; building their first towns, cities roads, bridges, and houses; making use of their first tools; farming their own fields; raising their own cattle and breeding other domestic animals; traveling on their first horses, mules, and wheeled carriages; sailing on their first vessels; cooking their first foods; manufacturing and trading their first goods; minting and using their first currency; lumbering their first trees; making their first garments; singing their first songs; hand-crafting their first art objects; writing with their first writing instruments on their first papers; reading their first newspapers; printing their first books; attending their first schools and being trained in their first trades and professions; running their first governments and enacting their first laws; working in their first industries; selling goods in their first stores; mining their first natural resources; enjoying their first forms of entertainment and playing their first sports; doing their first gardening; eating their first bread; seasoning their first foods; drinking their first wines; tending to the sick in their first hospitals by their first doctors and nurses and taking their first medicines; taking care of their elderly in their first institutions; caring for abandoned children and abused women in their first shelters (convents); raising their first families and communities. Thus, saying that American history began in 1607 and that the English, Dutch and Germans were the true builders of North America is as misguided as saying that the Vikings were the first true discoverers of America.

The Spaniards provided the coinage system that would prove invaluable during the American Colonial period, and that would form the basis of today's U.S. currency. It should be noted that the Spanish Doubloon (the double of one escudo, in denominations ranging from ½ to 8 escudos) was freely used by Southerners during the Colonial times, who often had their cash assets in Spanish gold. And during Alexander Hamilton's era, all foreign coins in circulation could be accepted as legal tender for a period of three years. After that, only Spanish silver could be legal tender, a standard that was in effect from 1792 to 1834, and a single Spanish gold standard thereafter until 1857. The United States would not begin production of its own gold until 1795 with the $5 half eagle, but even then the Spanish Doubloon continued to be the preferred currency. Our current dollar sign ($) is also derived from the Spanish Milled or Pillar Dollar (the pillar and scroll design on the coin's reverse), which was first used by a government clerk as early as 1788 and came into general use shortly thereafter. It is known as "America's first Silver Dollar," which was minted at the mines of Mexico, Perú, and Bolivia, and circulated widely during the Colonial and Revolutionary periods and used as legal tender until 1857. The "piece of eight" as it was also called, had a value of 8 reales. Merchants would break the coin into eight pieces or "bits." English-speaking colonists were the first to refer to it as a dollar and, throughout most of the 18th century, it was the standard monetary unit for settling debts and contracts. In 1793 the United States government passed a law making the 8 reales silver dollar part of the nation's monetary system. In this regard, historian Richard B. Morris wrote:

Spain set up a mint in Mexico in the 16th century. For almost 300 years it sent out a stream of silver coins to all the world. A considerable portion reached the colonies, chiefly by way of the West Indies. The basis of this coinage was the "peso" or piece-of-eight, always called in the colonies the "Spanish Dollar." The denominations were the dollar, the half-dollar, the quarter, the eighth, and the sixteenth. The eighth was a "real," known in the colonies as a "real" or "Spanish bit." It corresponded in value to the English sixpence. ... In the period of the Confederation, 1775-1889, the new states were on a paper-money basis, the Continental currency driving out all coins. The issues were in terms of Spanish dollars, constituting the first official recognition of the Spanish coin as the standard of America. ... As early as 1785 Congress had endorsed the Spanish dollar as the standard unit. ... Congress merely redeemed the legal tender of Spanish coins decade after decade. ... The only coins which could circulate were Spanish coins so worn that they could not be sold for gold. ... Actually, the United States was on a Spanish silver-coin standard from 1792 to 1834 and a single gold standard after 1834.[44]

Here is an interesting fact pertaining to Spanish coinage, one, indeed, quite embarrassing to the British. Due to the shortage of silver no proper crowns of England's King George III were struck until 1808. However, prior to that time, the British were in a dire need to have their own silver coinage and, instead of finding their own silver, in America or elsewhere, and minting their own coins, as any resourceful nation would do, they resorted to committing a blatant act of counterfeit, i.e. fraud, by counter- stamping thousands of the "8 reales" Spanish milled or pillar dollar from Spain's Guatemala mint with a small image of King George III. In other words, they seized these silver pieces from Spain, counter-stamped them with the image of their monarch, and put them in circulation. The counter-stamping of these coins was performed in a very crude and tasteless manner, as if the perpetrators were in a hurry to just get them out. An incredible act, but true!

In 1873, the United States was compelled to issue the Trade Dollar in order to compete with the Spanish Milled Dollar and the Mexican Silver Dollar for the trading of goods in Asia and China.

The U.S. companies that bought goods in the Orient had to purchase both silver dollars at a premium so they could pay the Chinese. However, according to the Coinage Act of 1873, these Trade Dollars were only issued by request, which the buyers had to buy at the mint. The Chinese accepted the new United States coin but only temporarily as the production of the Eighth Real increased and the Chinese still preferred to be paid in Spanish currency as they were for long accustomed. On February 17, 1776, the Continental Congress issued a note of 2/3 Dollar to help finance the war. The emission totaled $4,000,000 payable in Spanish Milled Dollars or the equivalent in Spanish gold or silver. This is further proof of how strong the Spanish currency was during Colonial times before, during, and after the U.S. independence.

The Spaniards founded a necklace of far-flung missions with the dual purpose of propagating Christianity and caring for the well-being of the natives. By 1617, in New Mexico alone, the Spaniards had founded a total of ninety towns, eleven churches, twenty-five missions, and one school for the teaching of reading and writing. In the year that the City of Puebla (Mexico) was founded in 1532, it had a population of 32 inhabitants, but by 1678 it had grown to well over 80,000, or 20,000 more than the City of New York had when it was founded one hundred and twenty-two years later.

It was a Spaniard, Lucas Vázquez de Ayllón, who in 1521 discovered the James River (which he called St. John the Baptist) in latitude 33° 30, identified as Georgetown Entrance, in South Carolina. He returned in 1525 and further explored up the coast for some two hundred and fifty leagues and founded a colony near a large river, which may have been Cape Fear, 32 miles from the site where the British would ninety-five years later found historic Jamestown, the birthplace of British America. The colony founded by Vázquez de Ayllón in 1526 was named San Miguel de Gualdape and, although it was short-lived, it was nonetheless the first European settlement in North America. Besides his exploration deeds, his legend of "Chicora" triggered further explorations of the area by other Spaniards and Europeans as well, based on the belief that a new Andalucía existed in North America. In this regard, historian Paul E. Hoffman wrote:

> All the Spaniards must have appreciated the importance of discovering what to then was a previously unknown land north of the Bahamas Islands. But none could have known that their reports about this land would plant the seeds for one of the more important, if neglected, legends connected with North American exploration. Re-located and worked upon by men's imaginations until the discovery assumed the form of a new Andalucia flowing with milk and honey, not to mention laden with pearls, gold, silver, wine grapes, and olives, it was to spawn a legend that, together with another legend about the continent born three years later, would motive Spaniards, French, and Englishmen to explore and attempt to colonize the coast of North America between the latitudes 32° and 39 north.[45]

In other words, he credits both Lucas Vázquez de Ayllón and Giovanni da Verrazano (who claimed that an isthmus existed somewhere in North America allowing for an easy passage to the Orient) with spurring all the ensuing discoveries and explorations of the northeastern coast of North America, precisely the area where the Thirteen Colonies would one day be founded. Yet, Vázquez de Ayllón's name has been summarily forgotten with most people not even having an inkling of who he was and what he did in contributing to the history of the United States.

It may surprise some to know that Spain's presence in North America outlasted both England's and France's. In total, it lasted over three centuries, from the time of the arrival of Ponce De León in 1513 to the time Spain ceded Florida in 1819, outlasting England by sixty-seven years, from 1607 to 1846 when England ceded the Oregon territory. And if one would count Mexico as part of Spain up to its independence and subsequent cession of

California, Nevada, Utah, and Arizona in the treaty of Guadalupe-Hidalgo of 1848, Spain's presence would have outlasted England's by even more. It also outlasted France by seventy-seven years, from the time of the arrival of Jacques Cartier (Newfoundland) in 1534 to its cession of Canada and lands east of the Mississippi to Britain, and its holdings west of the Mississippi to Spain in 1763 (by the Treaty of Paris).

As Edward Bourne states in his book *Spain in America, 1450-1580*:

> In Central and South America Spain tenaciously held its possessions for over 325 years, almost as long as the sway of imperial Rome over western Europe, and longer than the British hold over the American colonies or India. Self-government as it was known in the English colonies was never granted to Spain's American possessions. But that sort of self-government was unknown in Spain itself. The Spaniards left no heritage of freedom but they did leave a permanent cultural imprint.[46]

CHAPTER SEVEN

THE FORGING OF A NEW CIVILIZATION

In the meantime, to the south, in the other America, far more hostile, enigmatic, culturally, and militarily advanced, the Spaniards were immersed in an even greater epic. Like armor-clad mythological gods they tramped through and across the imposing vastness or, as historian Herbert E. Bolton observed:

> The ranks of these armies were filled with eager young fellows who had read in Spain or obtained in the book stalls of Mexico and Lima the romances of chivalry just then being published— *Amadís de Gaula, Las Serges de Esplandián, Palmería de Oliva*, and a dozen others, whose influence in the conquest Dr. Irving Leonard has so convincingly set forth.[47]

The legendary military genius Hernán Cortés, whose exploits have confounded historians and tactical warfare experts for centuries; the tough as nails Francisco Pizarro, whose imagination, resilience, and sense of purpose changed the history of an entire continent forever; the tenacious Francisco de Orellana, who redefined the very meaning of human endurance after sailing for the first time the length of the Amazon river west to east (afterwards he returned to his native town of Trujillo, in Spain, but so longed for America that he went back and died in the Amazon, just like he desired); the fearless and unyielding Pedro de Alvarado, called "El Sol" (the Sun) by the Indians, whose mere presence wreaked havoc among friend and foe alike (this was the same Alvarado who in the siege of Mexico City had 13 brigantines built at Tlaxcala, which were then transported on the shoulders of his soldiers for fifty miles inland and across the mountains to the lake in Mexico City, a heroic, or rather, superhuman deed unmatched in human history, according to many scholars. By the way, the master carpenter who built the ships was a Spaniard by the name of Martin López. Balboa accomplished a similar feat with two brigantines he had ordered to build when discovering the Pacific Ocean); the quintessential explorer, Vasco Núñez de Balboa, whose visionary spirit led to the discovery of the world's largest body of water. These Spanish Conquistadores, or latter-day knights, as they are often called, together with the venerable priests and missionaries, had accomplished the impossible in less than fifty years: The Antilles had been conquered by 1515, twenty-three years after Columbus voyage; the Aztecs by 1521; and the Incas by 1536. Regarding the Spanish conquistador, historian Trevor Davies observed:

> The ambitious part which Spain played in the sixteenth century turned on the fact that Spanish soldiers were the best in the world. For a century and a half no Spanish army was ever defeated in a pitched battle, and in the cosmopolitan armies of Charles V the Spanish contingent was always used as the spearhead of ally specially daring attack—at Pavia or Mühlberg or Gueldres.[48]

Another historian, Archibald Wilberforce, had similar laudable words about the daunting spirit of the Spanish soldier, a true paragon of military life:

> Philip (II) had also the advantage of finding himself at the head of a large standing army in a perfect state of discipline and equipment, in an age when, except some few insignificant corps, standing armies were

unknown to Christendom. The renown of the Spanish troops was justly high, and the infantry in particular was considered the best in the world. His fleet also, was far more numerous, and better appointed, than that of any other European power; and both his soldiers and sailors had the confidence in themselves and their commanders which a long career of successful warfare alone can create.[49]

The Spaniards founded the continent's first cities and universities (the University of San Marcos, in Lima, was founded in 1551, eighty-five years before Harvard, and one-hundred and ninety-five years before the Presbyterian College of New Jersey, later Princeton) totaling twenty-two by the end of the colonial period. Even in faraway Philippines they founded the University of Manila in 1648, substituting the school of San José founded by the Jesuits many years before. They established the first schools and libraries, botanical gardens, newspapers, and hospitals for the elderly and the mentally ill; convents for poor and abandoned women and abused children. They wrote and printed the first books (the Spaniard Juan Pablos, from Seville, was America's first printer), and built the first churches and cathedrals. And it was in Spanish-America where the first scholars and literary figures emerged, among them, the poet Bernardo de Balbuena, born in La Mancha, Spain (1568) but educated in México (where he went with his family at age two), author of *Grandeza Mexicana* (Mexican Greatness), and *Cosmografía Universal* (Universal Cosmography); the dramatist Ruiz de Alarcón, born and raised in México, whose works were imitated by Corneille and Moliére; Sor Juana Inés de la Cruz; Don Carlos de Sigüenza y Góngora; the Inca Garcilaso de la Vega; and the "Lunarejo," an Inca from Cuzco called Don Juan de Espinosa y Medrano, who became one of the best critics and commentators of St. Thomas and Luis de Góngora, to name a few. Thomas Cage, the English traveler and writer, often a harsh critic of Spain, wrote about the high cultural level achieved by the Spanish church in America. In Tlaxcala (México), for example, he observed that the friars had next to the monastery a very nice church, to which some fifty singers, organists, players of various instruments, trumpet players and chorus girls belonged, all of whom were Indians and who accompanied the mass with very soft and harmonious music to the great delight of all present. It is indeed amazing that such giants as Ovid, Petrarca, and León Hebreo were translated by mestizos or Indians, and also that the mestizo Don Bartolomé de Alba translated into the Nahualt two of the plays of Lope de Vega. The Spanish viceroys played a key role in fostering the arts in the New World. By the middle of the 16 century, in just fifty years, they had completed a mission unmatched in human history. By 1554, there were 200 Spanish towns with 32,000 houses, 9,000 Indian communities, two viceroyalties, 10 courts, 29 seats of government, four archdioceses, and 24 dioceses. The Spanish population totaled 140,000 people, or 1.25% of the overall population of 11,229,650. Spanish colonial America had begun. It is worth noting that in 1524 there was not a single Mexican who knew how to read or write, but that twenty years later there were so many of them that bishop Zumárraga ordered the printing of books in their own language for their use.

The love for learning and intellectual fervor were well-rooted in Spain long before America was discovered, and what the Spaniards did was to transplant them to the New World with the same fervor and enthusiasm to which they had been accustomed since the Middle Ages. In this regard, we would like to quote this observation by historian Trevor Davies:

> Side by side with signs of military greatness, the opening years of the sixteenth century showed some earnest of that intellectual ascendancy of Spain which was so marked a century later... The vigour of university life was becoming especially remarkable. Salamanca, of early thirteenth-century origin, was already growing hugely in reputation and in size. Men of other nations came to it, said Pedro de Medina, "as though to a fair of letters and of all virtues." By the middle of the sixteenth century

(1552) its matriculation roll showed a total of 6328 persons—a total which hardly any other university in Europe at the time could equal. It attracted students of all classes, from the wealthy noble surrounded by his attendants to the poor "sopista" who relied on charity for his livelihood. Though conservative and scholastic in its tendencies, it was by no means unreceptive of new ideas. It was here that Columbus revealed the secrets of the New World. Here, too, the Copernican system was taught long before its acceptance elsewhere. Almost along amongst universities, its anatomists were allowed to dissect the human body when such practices were forbidden as impious in most of the medical schools of Europe. It was almost unique, too, in its furtherance of the higher education of women. Men and women were admitted without distinction to its courses of study and degrees; and two women at least, Lucía de Medrano and Juana de Contreras, were in the habit of giving public lectures in the university. It is said, too, that Francisca Lebrija, the learned daughter of Antonio de Lebrija, reputedly the most learned man of his age, sometimes lectured as her father's deputy.[50]

But the University of Salamanca was by no means the only one in Spain. There were others, if not as old and as important, perhaps, equally providing a reservoir of intellectual scholarship and knowledge not only for Spain but all of Europe as well. Historian Davies continued with his observation:

Valladolid, another of the older universities of the Peninsula, was world- famous for its highly specialized surgical work. But the intellectual ferment that was going on may best be gathered from the new foundations that were appearing about the beginning of the sixteenth century. A mere enumeration of the new universities is impressive: Sigüenza (1472), Saragossa (1474), Ávila (1482), Barcelona (1491), Valencia (1500), Santiago (1504), Seville (1516), Granada (1526.) Still more impressive is the University of Alcalá, the greatest of the new foundations, which owed its origin to Cardinal Jiménez (1508.) It was not only a university, but a university city, a large portion of which consisted of houses for students and booksellers. It contained within its walls some of the greatest scholars in Europe and welcomed with enthusiasm the full tide of Renaissance thought and learning. The permanent fame of Alcalá rests upon its Polyglot Bible, which contained amongst other notable things the first Greek Testament ever printed (1514)—two years before the much-extolled Greek Testament of Erasmus and incomparably superior to it in its critical text. Its Hebrew text of the Old Testament was so good that it was copied for centuries all over Europe. It was not, in fact, until the nineteenth century that the labours of Ginsburg, based on those of Kennicott, produced a definitely superior critical text of the Hebrew Bible. The work as a whole, with its grammar, lexicons, editions of Aramaic targums and other aids to scriptural study has justly been described as "the first scientific work of the modern world." (Menendez y Pelayo, 'Historia de los Heterodoxos Españoles.)[51]

And Mr. Davies concluded with this other observation about book printing in Spain, which helps explain the extraordinary production of books of all sorts by the Spaniards in colonial America:

> The art of printing came early to Spain. Even if the date 1468 on the famous "Barcelona Book" is, as many hold it to be, a misprint, there is no doubt that a certain Lambert Palmart was busy printing at Valencia in 1474—almost three years before Caxton set up his press at Westminster. A law of 1480 allowed the importation of foreign books duty free. The growing intellectual activity of Spain was shown by the activity of its printing presses. Habler enumerates no fewer than 720 books printed in Spain at twenty-five different towns before the end of the fifteenth century. These figures become impressive when they are compared with the 358 books enumerated as having been printed in England during the same period. They are a fair index to an increasing intellectual activity that was destined to combine with the wealth and military power of Spain to raise her for a short period to a position of undisputed dominance in Europe. (Habler, *Bibliografia Ibérica del Siglo XV*, E. Gordon Duff, Fifteenth Century English Books.)[52]

Commenting on Spanish American prosperity under Spanish rule, American historian Edward Gaylord Bourne wrote:

> ...but, after all, the general impression derived from the narratives of English residents in New Spain and other early travelers is that they

observed no particular contrast between governmental conditions in Europe and America. It is the opinion of this writer that, all things considered, Spanish America was as well governed as was Spain, and was, on the whole, more prosperous; that the condition of Peru and the rest of South America was below that of New Spain in many aspects; and that at no time in the history of Mexico, up to within the last quarter of a century, has the government been so good as her people enjoyed under the abler viceroys such as Mendoza or Velasco in the beginning, or the younger Revillagigedo at the end of Spanish rule.[53]

On the subject of Spain's contribution to both Americas, a group of American educators wrote these emotion-filled and grateful words in their book *Spanish Gold*, which was written for young adults:

The first explorers in what is now the United States were Spanish. They were the first to bring gifts from across the seas to America, which was then the land of the Indians. These Spanish explorers and settlers were like those who later came from other countries. They hoped to become rich in the new country. They hunted everywhere for gold, but most of them found none. They looked in Puerto Rico, Florida, Louisiana, Texas, New Mexico, California, and other places. In all of these places, which are now a part of the United States, they built towns and left settlers, but they did not find great riches. They did not find gold here, but they brought to the new land something much better than gold—gifts from across the seas.

These gifts brought by the Spaniards were of many kinds— plants, tools, animals, and so on. The Spanish gave us our first towns, our first cattle ranches, our first churches and schools, our first mines. They explored and gave Spanish names to large parts of our country—to mountains, deserts, rivers, lakes, and towns. They brought their language and ways of living, building and farming ideas, crafts, beautiful music, stories, and poems. These gifts have been handed down to us through the years until they have become a part of our American way of life.

We like to think of these gifts as "Spanish gold"—riches that the Spanish brought to our country from lands across the sea. The Spaniards made our country far richer than if they had found gold here and had brought nothing in return.

Spanish explorers and settlers also went to other parts of the New World. They went to Cuba and other islands of the West Indies, to Mexico and Central America, to Perú and other countries of South America. To each one of these places they took their gifts plants and animals, tools, farming methods, music, building ideas, schools, and churches. It is not strange, then, that today we find the Spaniards' gifts in those countries as well as in our own. The gifts from Spain have made us alike in many ways.

People from those other countries of America would feel very much at home in Puerto Rico, New Mexico, Texas, parts of Florida and California, or in any part of our country which the Spaniards explored and settled. They would find many ways of living which would remind them of their own homes. The same thing would be true if we were to visit their countries. Even though most of us do not speak Spanish, we have many of the same gifts which were taken to our neighbors.[54]

A little known fact is that Spain pioneered the first scientific expeditions to the Americas (which continued uninterruptedly for a period of 300 years) to learn about the flora and fauna of the New World. Among the most famous ones were: the expedition of the French scholars Bouguer, Godin, and La Condamine, accompanied by the Spaniards Ulloa and Jorge Juan in 1734-44; the expedition of Hipólito Ruiz, José Pavón and the Frenchman José Dombey to Perú and Chile in 1777-78, at a cost of over 400,000 pesos, which produced two important scientific treatises, "Flora peruana," and "Quinología;" the expedition of Martín Sessé and José Mariano to Mexico, Central America and California in 1791 and 1795-1803; the expedition of Francisco Javier Balmis to introduce the vaccine against smallpox in Latin America, the United States and Asia in 1803; and the expedition of captains Alejandro Malaspina and José Bustamante y Guerra across the Pacific accompanied by the naturalists Antonio de Pineda and Née y Tadeo Haenke in 1789-94, which was perhaps the most important scientific expedition ever undertaken by the government of Spain, because of its many discoveries, collection of specimens, drawings and the creation of over 70 new sea and coastal charts. The Malaspina-Bustamante y Guerra expedition voyaged to all the coasts of the Spanish possessions, including California and the Northwest. The narrative of this expedition was published in Madrid in 1885, under the title "Viaje político y científico alrededor del mundo por las corbetas Descubierta y Atrevida al mando de los capitanes Malaspina y Bustamante desde 1789 a 1794"; the Botanical Expedition of 1783 and subsequent years, which was later transformed into an important institution for scientific research under the direction of Mutis with the collaboration of the great scientists Francisco José de Caldas, Francisco Antonio Zea, and Jorge Tadeo Lozano, all of whom collaborated in the writing of the monumental work "Flora de Bogotá," which is preserved at the Madrid Botanical Gardens. In addition, the Spanish government sponsored numerous expeditions of non-Spanish chemists and mineralogists, such as the one by the Elhuyar brothers to Mexico and New Granada in 1793; the one by Nordenflycht to Mexico in 1788; the one by Peter Loeffling to Guayana in 1755-56; and, of course, the famous Humboldt expedition to Latin America in 1799-1804, sponsored by King Charles IV. We should also take note of the last of these expeditions, the one called Comisión Científica del Pacífico (Scientific Commission of the Pacific) in 1862-1865, under the leadership of Marcos Jiménez de la Espada, accompanied by the renown naturalists Almagro, Paz, and others. The expedition explored the entire Pacific coast of South America, including the Andes and then, traveling by canoes, crossed the Amazon into Brazil.

In this regard, Harvard University historian Robert S. Chamberlain wrote: "A vast body of historical writing, much of it of high quality, was produced during the (Spanish) colonial period, and important anthropological and linguistic studies were made."[55]

However, America was but one of Spain's many world endeavors. At the same time that the Western Hemisphere was being discovered, explored and colonized, the Spaniards were also sailing feverishly around the globe reaching as far as China and Japan. They discovered and/or explored most of Oceania, including Micronesia, Melanesia, Polynesia, and the Philippines where they founded Manila in 1571, as well as New Guinea. In fact, during the entire 16th century, Spain was the dominant exploring nation in that part of the world.

The Spaniards were first to complete the circumnavigation of the world, not once but twice, and to find a new sea route from Mexico to the Philippines. They made the first map of the Americas in 1500, the first historical atlas (1560) and were first to observe the currents of the Gulf of Mexico. It must also be noted that Amerigo Vespucci came to America on the expedition of the Spaniard Alonso de Ojeda in 1499. John Cabot was also in Spain in 1492-93, seeking the favor of King Ferdinand for his expeditions and learning about the art of navigation. His son, Sebastian, also won the favor of the Spanish Crown and was under its service for thirty years. He led an expedition to South America and discovered Paraguay and was the first to navigate the Parana river. Charles V appointed him Captain of the Seas and he later married a Spanish widow, Catalina Medrano. Last, but by no means least, Magellan's expedition was sponsored by Spain and financed in part by Charles V himself. Thus, the glory of all of his great exploits, including his first circumnavigation of the globe (which was completed by the Spaniard Juan Sebastian Elcano), the discoveries of the strait bearing his name, Oceania, the Philippines, and many other Pacific islands, must be equally shared between him, Spain, Charles V, as well as his experienced Spanish crew, among whom were Elcano (who completed the voyage), Gómez, Quesada, Mendoza, Barbosa, and many others. Between Magellan and Columbus, both of whom were in the service of Spain, almost half of the unknown world at the time was discovered. Saying that Spain discovered America is only half of the truth for she discovered that plus half the world.

CHAPTER EIGHT

EUROPE JUMPS ON SPAIN. ENGLAND LEADS THE WAY.

At home, right on her own backyard, Spain was battling on another front, archenemies England, France and the Lower Countries, on the one hand, and the spread of Protestantism on the other. The tormented queen, Elizabeth I of England (whose own father Henry VIII had declared illegitimate and unfit to rule) became enraged over Spain's sudden rise to fame and fortune and her Catholic crusade and vowed revenge on land and sea. Fearing Spain's power and confronting her openly, she opted to unleash furtive acts of terrorism and piracy through her cohorts, the pirates Drake, Hawkins, Cavendish, Raleigh, Morgan, and many others who systematically ravaged, ransacked and plundered America's Spanish possessions at will, reveling in their onslaught. Regarding Queen Elizabeth and her reign of terror, historian Trevor Davies observed:

...The change to a bolder policy was partially due to the increase of English piracy in the New World, which, after Drake 's return from his highly profitable journey of circumnavigation (October 1580), was being planned on a gigantic scale, the queen making no secret of her share in the profits. The increasingly severe persecutions of Roman Catholics in England acted as further goad to action. "The priests they succeed in capturing," wrote Mendoza (August 12"', 1581), "are treated with a variety of terrible tortures; amongst others is one torment which people in Spain imagine will be that which will be worked by Anti-Christ as the most dreadfully cruel of all." Elizabeth was, seemingly, able to shock even the supporters of the Spanish Inquisition by her torture-chamber in the Tower.[56]

After his four-year shameful voyage, Francis Drake brought back to England ships laden, or rather bulging, with the coveted Spanish gold and treasures (estimated to have been over 1,200,000 English pounds) to an euphorically grateful queen who, after a sumptuous banquet immediately dubbed him a knight and appointed him admiral of the English navy. It is a well-known fact that the Bank of England was founded with the gold hauled in by the Golden Hind, and so were the East India Company and much of England's future economic prosperity. Drake's loot was so enormous that he used some of it as ballast. Back in England he paid off his many sponsors (among whom was the queen herself and most of the nobility) with a dividend of over 5,000 per cent on their investment! Although a skillful seaman, Drake was above all the consummate pirate and profiteer. As far as his celebrated circumnavigation of the world is concerned, this was nothing more than a fortuitous event for he chose to sail back to England via the Strait of Magellan to avoid confronting the heavily guarded Spanish Atlantic coastline. In any event, his voyage around the world was not the first or the second but the third. By the way, Mr. Francis Drake himself snatched the statues of two apostles, St. Peter and St. Paul, plus four more from inside the niches which are on each side of the main gate of the Basilica Menor de Santa María, Primada de América, in Santo Domingo, Dominican Republic. Where are they? They should have been returned to Santo Domingo long ago...

Further on the topic of the impact that the Spanish gold and silver had on the English economy, Lord John Maynard Keynes wrote (translation by the author):

Mr. Phipps' expedition to salvage a Spanish galleon thought to have sunk about fifty years earlier off the cost of Haiti, is one of the most extraordinary cases of improbable success. On its return voyage to London in 1680, it had recovered from the sea a treasure estimated at between 250,000 and 300,000 sterling pounds, yielding a dividend of 10,000% to its investors, the largest ever. The excitement and stimulus prompted by such an event were the immediate cause of the prosperity movement of the London stock exchange, which reached its climax in 1692-93, setting the basis for the establishment of the Bank of England, the official list of the stock exchange (with 134 quoted securities or stocks) as in modern times, and the currency reform made by Locke and Newton.[57]

One of Drake's counterparts (and also a relative), the pirate John Hawkins, was not as fortunate as he was beheaded by his own King Jacob I in 1618 for "horrific acts of piracy against Spain." In his book, "Discoverers of America," American historian Charles Norman wrote:

The ships turned out to be English (he refers to the time when the French were planning their departure [to] their first outpost in Florida after being defeated by the Spaniards in 1565, when suddenly they spotted four vessels approaching from the sea) under the command of Master John Hawkins, afterward knight, captain of the Jesus of Lubeck— a galleon of 700 tons belonging to Queen Elizabeth—and "general of the Salomon, and two other barks going in his company," the Tiger and Swallow. He had left Plymouth October 18, 1564, "with a prosperous wind, " sailed to Guinea on the African coast, loaded his ships with slaves, and having sold them in the West Indies under threat of bombardment if the Spaniards refused to buy, was now proceeding up the America coast on the return voyage to England, "with great profit to the ventures of the said voyage, as also to the whole realm, in bringing home gold, silver, pearls and other jewels great store." The queen was one of the venturers—that is, a shareholder.[58]

But Thomas Cavendish, another English pirate, was more fortunate. For years he patrolled the Pacific sea route stalking Spanish galleons. Over time, he managed to seize nineteen of them, including the gold-rich Santa Ana on its return voyage from the Philippines in 1587. Another one was the corsair John Anson, who, commanding the Centurion, seized the Spanish galleon Nuestra Señora de Covadonga on a return voyage from the Philippines in 1743 laden with Spanish gold, estimated to have been over $100 million in gold and virgin silver. His reward was being appointed "first lord of the admiralty" by the English Crown. Obviously, all of these treasures greatly impacted the English economy; in fact, it transformed England from a poor nation of farmers into one of the world's wealthiest. Then, there was Henry Morgan who scourged the Spanish possessions in the Caribbean for three years ravaging every town on his path, including the city of Panama in 1671 where he committed some of the most barbaric acts of piracy ever recorded. Historian Mendel Peterson lets Exquemelin narrate the plunder by Morgan, but first he says (Peterson):

> Behind him Morgan left complete devastation and ruined fortunes. With him he carried the greatest quantity of loot ever taken from a Spanish city, exceeding even the wealth extracted by Drake almost a century before; and then he quotes Exquemelin: "He carried with him one hundred and seventy-five beasts of carriage, laden with silver, gold, and other precious things, besides six hundred prisoners, more or less, between men, woman, children and slaves."
> The strange assemblage made its way slowly over the trails toward the Atlantic coast. The clanging of the loaded mules and the tramp of the marching men was drowned out by the weeping and cries of the women and children among the prisoners, who suffered terribly during the journey.[59]

Spain quickly protested and Morgan was detained and summoned to England by King Charles II who, instead of punishing him as he had promised Spain he would do, knighted and appointed him lieutenant governor of Jamaica. Previously he had won the favor of the governor of Jamaica, Thomas Moodyford for his onslaught on Portobelo (1668), the emporium of Spanish commerce in America. And, historian Philip Ainsworth Means joined a long list of noted historians in denouncing Morgan's callousness. Here are his own words:

> Early in 1668 rumors reached Modyford (the English governor of Jamaica) that the Spaniards were about to attack Jamaica in order to recapture it. He sought to protect his island by using Morgan as a weapon, and accordingly he appointed his young friend as "Admiral " of the buccaneer fleet. An attack upon Cuba was planned. Morgan 's boldness was seasoned with caution so that, instead of assaulting the strongly fortified city of Havana from the sea with his fleet, or of investing it from the landside with his small army of 500 men, he contented himself with a naval demonstration outside the harbor and then, with a great deal of cruelty, swooped down upon a poor little town near the eastern end of Cuba. The inhabitants did what they could to defend themselves and the mayor of the town was slain in the combat. Morgan, however, triumphed. Persons who might pay ransoms were taken prisoner and tortured until they disgorged their gold. Humbler, folk were merely murdered. Women and children were crammed into the church where they we subjected to every sort of indignity and terrorism. All this befell in Holy Week, late March, 1668.[60]

Acts of despicable criminality, torture, and barbarism were thus so routinely rewarded by the English Crown. Robert Sedgwick, the English colonizer of New England, summed it up this way (translation by the author): This kind of business in the Western Indies, consisting of being a corsair plundering and burning cities at will, and although for a long time practiced, is not honorable to the navy of a prince.[61]

It must also be remembered that William Paterson, the founder of the Bank of London, organized time and again smuggling expeditions in the Spanish possessions up to 1700, when a Spanish fleet of 11 ships put an end to his illicit operations. The British, French and Dutch pirates devastated some of Spain's most cherished possessions in the New World, such as Cartagena, Panama, Portobelo, Santo Domingo, Havana, San Juan (Puerto Rico) and 25 more, exhibiting bone-chilling acts of violence and cruelty, including burning those cities to the ground, lynchings, tortures, rapes, desecrating temples of worship, and carrying with them as much gold and silver as they could, leaving behind the ashes of once beautiful towns populated by peaceful and innocent people.

In comparing the English pirates with the Spanish conquistadors, Spanish historian Salvador de Madariaga wrote: (translation by the author)

> All of these men—Hawkins, Drake, Raleigh, and others—differed from the Spanish conquistadors in a very important aspect: they were less creative aesthetically and far more economically inclined. None of them, including Raleigh who was something of a poet, would have been able to imagine the kingdoms of the Indies which, under the spell of the prolific inspiration of Cortés and the Pizarros, illuminated the continent with a constellation of magnificent cities and turning Chile, Peru, New Granada and above all New Spain into cities as beautiful as those of Spain built under Roman influence.[62]

On this same subject, English economist Lord Maynard Keynes wrote (translation by the author):

> But in the rest of Europe, the new buying power originated through private enterprise, including that of the corsairs. Because, regarding England, a considerable share of its income was due to the capture of Spanish treasure ships and to similar military deeds. These expeditions were organized by trade unions and corporations that provided the capital, and represented business speculations whose success and gains helped stimulate the enterprise spirit of other ventures. The period of maximum English prosperity began really upon the return of Drake 's first important voyage in 1573, and was reaffirmed with the immense

riches he brought in after his second of 1580, and without disregarding his third of 1586. The value in gold and silver of this combined treasure has been estimated at between 300,000 and 1,500,000 sterling pounds, although professor W.R. Scott thinks that it was much larger. The effect of these great sums of money had to be a predominant factor in England's eleven years of prosperity from 1575 to 1587.[63]

We would also like to include this observation by noted Mexican historian José Vasconcelos (translation by the author):

During the time we have lived under the moral influence of strangers, the writers coincide in affirming that the thirst for gold was the dominant factor of the Spanish conquerors who, consequently, are presented as rough and greedy men whose undeserved good fortune allowed them to achieve deeds which not even the harshest of critics can but be amazed at them. When Bernal Díaz del Castillo wrote his book, no one had dwelled on such criticism; thus, in his writings, he finds no need to confess any charges which did not yet exist. However, in sincere and truthful words, Bernal Díaz recognizes that they were "searching for gold to trade," meaning what to give in exchange for heeds and other objects. And it is precisely such manly openness of which Spain's enemies have made the most use as proof of their charges while saying nothing about the sublime forces that drove them to that great enterprise. On the other hand, they glossed over the infamous deeds perpetrated by the English pirates who came afterwards, many of whom were of nobility and who, incapable and unwilling to work for the gold, dedicated themselves to plundering unprotected cities.[64]

The French corsairs were also busy carrying out their own infamous deeds, ransacking and plundering Spanish cities and towns, such as the corsair Jacques de Sorie who sacked and burned Havana and murdered thirty- four prisoners in cold blood, and the pirate Gramont who seized La Guaria (Venezuela) in 1680. And the Dutch too, like the pirate Piet Heyn, an admiral of the Dutch fleet, who captured an entire Spanish treasure fleet in the 17th century, or Cornelius Holz, "wooden leg," who plundered Campeche in 1633, or the seizure of Curaçao in 1634, which soon became a focus of contraband. The Chinese were not too far behind with Limahon ransacking Manila at his pleasure. Even the Scots colonists, organized under the leadership of William Paterson, the same founder of the Bank of England, attempted in 1700 to plunder Spanish gold but were defeated by a Spanish fleet.

England was not a builder of nations in the classical sense, like Rome or Spain were, despite the fact that at one time her empire extended some 18 million square miles around the globe, but it was an empire floating on air, with no solid foundation whatsoever. Some may rebuff the argument putting forth as an example her many "offerings" in the founding of British America, to whom we would reply by saying that the United States was founded by distraught English expatriates who repudiated their own tyrannical government and who sought above all else to sever all ties with their homeland. Their quest of freedom was inspired in part by John Locke and the Spanish Jesuit Francisco Suárez, two of Europe's greatest philosophical and political theoretical thinkers of the time. In other words, England, the nation, had very little to do with the birth of the great northern republic. In fact, it sought nothing more than to subjugate it and exploit it for self-gain.

For instance, the Sugar and Stamp Tax, which spurred the final chapter of American independence, was imposed in order to liquidate England's alarming rise in its national debt which had increased to 130,000,000 sterling pounds. In sharp contrast, few, if any, Spaniards left Spain with equal feelings. Quite the contrary. Wherever they voyaged they took Spain with them keeping her close to their hearts and fresh in their memories, and always striving to transplant it wherever fate may have led them. Here is an interesting fact which further demonstrates the major differences between the English and the Spanish: The Thirteen Colonies declared their independence from England exactly 169 years after the first English settlers reached North America (1607-1776.) On the other hand, the nations of Spanish-America declared their independence from Spain 333 years after being discovered (1492-1810-1825) and, in the case of Cuba 406 years after. It is also interesting to note that the Dominican Republic, after declaring its independence from Haiti in 1844, was re-annexed to Spain lasting from 1861 until 1865. In other words, for England British America was nothing more than a colony whose only purpose of existing was to serve the metropolis and enrich it. No city, no town in British America could possibly be compared to the magnificent cities and towns that Spain built in Mexico, Perú, Cuba, and in many other places.

And what was ultimately England's motives in traversing the ocean? Historians Bruce Catton and William B. Catton explained it this way:

> And on the national level, people in high places were still aware of the cluster of imperial ideas so ably put forth by publicists like the Hakluyts. They had devised a formula which no later arguments in favor of colonies would improve upon: discovering gold and a Northwest Passage to the Orient, converting the North American Indian to Protestant Christianity; planting overseas settlements that would assist the navy and provide raw materials, new markets, and home and opportunity in safely distant spots for England's restless poor. There was something here for everybody. Religious, social, and commercial motives had been neatly blended in a plan designed to benefit individuals while enhancing England's strength and strategic position in her struggle with Catholic Spain ... The formula that finally began to produce results combined the essential elements—land, profits, religion, and the national interest—in ways that said a good deal about the kind of empire the English were going to build and the kind of society that would gradually take shape in their new overseas dominion. The key element, by which the needs and aspirations of prospective colonists were yoked to those of the nation, was land.[65]

Were the English pragmatic? Yes, a nation of farmers needed to farm and the Elysian fields of North America were to their eyes far more than they could have dreamed of finding in their motherland.

What the English sought as soon as they set foot on North America was to go about the business they knew best: to farm the land, both for their own subsistence and as a future business base. Simple folks in pursuit of simple goals—live, let live, work, and make money. The America they encountered (Virginia) allowed for that simplicity of life with no big barriers to overcome or having to face any major menacing forces posed to strike from within or from without. Such peacefulness facilitated their labor, organization, and prosperity. No big wars, no formidable foes or empires to subdue, no mighty rivers and natural barriers to tame but just the open, fertile fields of a generous new land. Contrast this with the America found by the Spaniards one hundred years earlier and you could gain instant insight into the major differences affecting the future development of the United States and Spanish America.

Regarding England's other colonies, she sought above all else their sheer subjugation and exploitation for self-national gain. In the case of India, where she established several trading stations at Surat in 1613, her main objective was to transform that country into a vast agricultural reservoir and market for her duty-free goods. From the defeat of Nawab of Bengal at Plassey in 1757, which marks the beginning of English rule over that country, through 1949 when it adopted its own constitution, or a span of 192 years, and 336 years if we count from 1613, India has remained to this day a nation besieged by staggering misery and poverty and a stagnated national economy. While we do see how England's economy prospered during her reign in India, we fail to see how India prospered under her rule after so many years.

In New Zealand, from the first English settlement in 1840 through is independence in 1931, or ninety-one years later, not much transpired other than the usual one-sided economic gain. In Jamaica, once a possession of Spain, it was turned into a pirate and smuggling haven for a period of 100 years, serving also as an outpost for the callous pirate Henry Morgan. Black slaves were imported in such large numbers for the production of sugar cane and other crops, that they soon outnumbered the whites who ultimately left. Today, after 300 years of English rule (it was ceded by Spain to England in 1670 becoming a part of the British Commonwealth in 1962) it remains little more than a paradisiacal resort for Western tourists. It is interesting to note that England moved on Jamaica following the publication of the book *The English American*, by Thomas Cage. The book caused a sensation as the first comprehensive account of Spanish America, and Cage's suggestion of Spanish weakness is universally credited with encouraging the British to lay siege to Jamaica in 1654. In British Guiana, where the English established a colony in 1796, it has remained just that through today. In Australia, where the English established a settlement in 1788 on the shores of Port Jackson, (precisely where Sidney now stands) it was quickly turned into a penal colony. After that, and for many years until about the middle of the 19 century, it served exclusively as a dumping ground for criminals and undesirables from the British Isles. Then sheep raising was introduced and wheat exported in large quantities to England. It was not until gold was struck at Victoria in 1851 that Australia developed quickly. From a penal colony to sheep raising and wheat farming to mining gold, what else did the British do in Australia worth noting until it became independent in 1901? In Kenya, in a span of 77 years (from 1887 when a British association was granted concessionary rights to the Kenya coast by the sultan of Zanzibar to 1965 when it was granted independence from England) the only contribution made by the English to that country was the railroad built in 1895-1901 from Mombasa to Kisumu on Victoria Nyanza for the sole purpose of facilitating trade with Uganda. And finally, South Africa. What can be said that has not already been said by contemporary history and world opinion? Who can come on England's defense regarding her conduct in South Africa? No intended human suffering is ever justified, regardless of time or circumstances, but in the 20ᵗʰ century, in the Age of Reason, and inflicted not by a barbarous state but by Mother England, the land of Chaucer, Shakespeare, Locke and Spencer? Apartheid, one of history's most blatant and callous disregard for human decency, it is thus defined by the Oxford Dictionary: "The policy of strict racial segregation and discrimination against the native Negroes and other colored people as practiced in South Africa."

The ghastly seizure of the native Bantus's lands (comprising about 14% of the country) and their displacement (between 1950-1968 in the hundreds of thousands) to concentration camps, far away from city limits so the whites (the British) could occupy them and profit from their vast mineral resources, is but one episode in the plight of so many innocent lives against a tyrannical government so obsessed in capitalizing on their misfortune. But prior to Apartheid, when gold was discovered in South Africa in the late 1800s, more than 100,000 Dutch nationals, mostly women, were routed and placed in concentration camps where over 22,000 children suffered unimaginable squalor and perished of starvation. (It is interesting to note that the term "concentration camp" was first coined by the British themselves during that time.) The British sought to force the Dutch out to seize the land and exploit it, which they ultimately accomplished. They showed absolutely no mercy with the Dutch or the natives just to gain control. In sharp contrast, Spain, at the end of her rule in America, had mothered a total of eighteen nations, not colonies, as so named by England and the other countries. In fact, Spain never referred to her America's possessions as "colonies." There were not colonies but "reinos" (kingdoms), as part of Spain as Castile or Aragón, or as historian Sir Arthur Helps said: "Colonies is a convenient term to describe the Spanish American possessions, but it is hardly a correct one; they were really attached to the Crown..."[66] And historian Salvador de Madariaga added (translation by the author):

> The Spanish concept of the Indies could not be "colonial." The territories discovered, conquered and settled by the Spaniards could in no way be considered as the property of Spain. They came to be "these kingdoms," on an equal footing with the kingdoms of the Peninsula, some other Castiles, Leones, and Valencias, collective unities of Spanish life bound among themselves and to those of Europe by the King.[67]

There was pain, suffering, injustice, conflict, and blood. The price of civilization is always high. But, in the end, two distant worlds became ever so close and a new civilization emerged. And, if Bolivar's dream of a unified America had borne fruit, as set forth in his Letter from Jamaica in 1815, and which he thought would be so recognized and approved at the Congress of Panama in 1826, those eighteen nations, by right of a cultural heritage once predominantly superior, would have become one in which case America's preeminent republic would have been the one to the south instead of the one to the north.

But what about tomorrow? What would America be in another 50 or 100 years?

The United States has remained the world's leader for almost 100 years. But nations, even the mightiest ones, as history has repeatedly shown us, must at one time or another face their inevitable demise. The mighty legions of Rome, once unstoppable across Europe and Asia, were eventually stopped, and Spain, with an empire sprawled around the globe, crumbled like a deck of cards.

Could the same happen to the United States? We hope and pray that it does not but it could and, if it does, it would come not as a result of an invading foe but from within due mainly to these factors: 1) the gradual cultural, political, and social fragmentation of the Union; 2) the constant stream of foreign nationals who to this day refuse to assimilate to what once was the all-revered American Dream; and 3) by the erosion of the nation's democratic principles, values, traditions, and institutions.

The truth is that no nation can survive, much less endure, the overwhelming influx of foreigners whose only purpose of integration revolves around economic opportunity. Yes, the United States is the land of opportunity and opens its arms to all those willing to participate in that endeavor to make the nation stronger. However, the United States is far more than that; It is also the land of many dreams, of an ideal that has turned the entire world around, of a quest that ennobles the human spirit and promises to eradicate human ills and suffering forever. Those coming to its shores must also subscribe to that other United States and strive to look deep into its soul to learn, understand, and appreciate its true greatness. No one can claim to be an "American," a citizen of this nation, not being eager to embrace those principles and ideals and without fully knowing its culture, history, language, and people.

Back to Spain in America. Unquestionably, England was a major predator of Spanish gold and silver, extending its reach not only to the Americas but to Europe as well as the world. In 1568, by direct orders of the queen, a Spanish vessel was seized off the coast of England where it had taken shelter after running into a major storm. The ship carried a large cargo (one million gold ducats) of gold earmarked for paying the wages of the Duke of Alba's army stationed in the Lower Countries. More Spanish gold and silver for England's coffers. Unspeakable cruelty was also evidenced by the English in 1580 after capturing a contingent of Spanish and Italian soldiers sent to Ireland by Philip II in support of the Irish rebels. All 300 men were unmercifully strangled one by one.

But England's voracious appetite was not limited to Spanish gold and silver. Time after time the British smugglers prowled the Atlantic and Pacific coastlines seizing tons of precious lumber (cedar, oak, and especially logwood) estimated to have been ten million pounds per year. Smuggling became so prevalent that the Spanish viceroy Fernando de Alencastre Norena y Silva turned to

Madrid for remedy. After the Treaty of Utrecht (1713), the situation greatly deteriorated and the British intensified their clandestine operations. It should come as no surprise if most of England's fine furniture of the 18th and 19th centuries, as well as its ships, buildings, and houses were fabricated using the contraband lumber seized from Spanish possessions in South America.

From the 17th to the 19th century, England never ceased to harass Spain whether through piracy, smuggling, or by advocating and supporting South American independence. In 1806 and 1807 it attacked Buenos Aires, and in 1817 dispatched thousands of English volunteers and large sums of money to Venezuela to help finance its independence from Spain. Ultimately, what she sought was to control the Southern Hemisphere or, at the very least, to form partnership with the United States.

The intervention of the Holy Alliance and the Canning-Polignac memorandum of October 9, 1823, forbade any intrusion in the internal affairs of the Americas by all European powers. Early on, the Spanish American patriots sought England's support in their cause for independence but, at the same time, they feared England's ultimate motives and thus decided to wage war against Spain on their own. In 1825 England officially recognized the new South American States (the United States a few years earlier, in 1822.)

The Spanish empire in America was nearing its end. But England was persistent. South America was too huge of a market to pass it up, especially at a time when her own empire was showing signs of disintegration. Toward that end, and as a first step, she set her eyes on the Falkland Islands. Her only obstacle would be Argentina but that was no big sweat. Who were the Argentinians to pose a challenge to mighty England, especially when having the United States as an ally? Thus, she proceeded to seize them once and for all in 1982, and when Argentine defiantly stood in the middle, England, aided by the United States, put forth its naval might inflicting a humiliating defeat on the South American nation. Perhaps a brief account of the history of the Falkland Islands would help the reader understand the succession of events.

The islands were discovered by the Dutch in 1600 and visited anew by the Dutchmen Lemaire and Schouten in 1616. (It is interesting to note that the Spanish mariner Esteban Gómez, of the Magellan expedition, may have sighted the Falkland Islands long before the Dutch.) In 1690 the English John Strong discovered the strait between the larger islands which he called "Falkland." In 1701 the French arrived, claimed the islands but later abandoned them. In 1764 they went back and the famous French mariner Bougainville founded a factory at Port-Louis. A year later, the English arrived and founded another factory which he called Port Egmont in the western island. Spain protested to France for the intrusion into her territory as set forth in the Treaty of Tordesillas (1494). An accord was reached in 1766 in which Spain agreed to indemnify France while taking possession of the eastern island. Here the Spanish established the Puerto Soledad factory and named its first governor, Felipe Ruiz Puente. Although illegally, Port Egmont remained under English control until the new Spanish Governor Ruiz Puente found out and notified Madrid. A Spanish fleet was immediately dispatched to throw the English out. At this juncture, the English argued that the island had been discovered and settled by them (which was untrue) but such claim was rejected by Buenos Aires' governor Bucarelli who dispatched another fleet to take it back. The English finally capitulated on May 10, 1770, but not without demanding the return of Port Egmont. Spain turned to France for support but France refused to help and Spain had no choice but to cede the island back to England by the Rochford-Masserano Agreement of 1771. In 1774 England abandoned both the island and the factory and Spain regained its sovereignty over the disputed territory. In 1806 a governor was named in Patagonia with jurisdiction over the Falklands. In 1820 the Falklands were occupied by Argentina but in 1830 the English returned and again seized control. For 152 years Argentina has repeatedly claimed her rights over the islands to no avail. In 1982 it lost them perhaps forever in the disastrous Falkland War.

As it can be clearly seen from the foregoing, England never had any rights over the Falklands. Until 1820 they belonged to Spain and later to Argentina. But there is another issue. Was not England a European nation and thus forbidden to intervene in the internal affairs of the Western Hemisphere and much less to occupy a piece of its territory? Was this not a blatant violation of the Monroe Doctrine? And how did the United States, the nation who proclaimed it, decide to form an alliance with a foreign power against a Western Hemisphere nation?

CHAPTER NINE

SPAIN AND THE AMERICAN GOLD

As we have already stated, little of America's treasures reached Spain; besides, only the gold was remitted to Spain while a large quantity of the silver remained in America to be used for exchange. Regarding the flow of gold and silver into Spain, Spanish historian Ramón Trías Fargas explains: "Up to 1520, the American treasure consisted of 100% gold; from 1531 to 1650 it was down to 15%; and after 1650, 99% of the total was silver, not counting contraband."[68]

The truth of the matter is that other nations, not Spain, profited greatly from that bonanza, and that whatever portion made its way into Spain ended up somewhere else, whether for financing multiple wars, paying the long list of international bankers and debtors, such as the Fuggers of Augsburg, or Genovese and Spanish financiers, such as Nicolás Grimaldi, Ambrosio Spínola, Simón Ruiz or the Ximenes (often paying up to 50% of interest on those loans.) By the time of Philip II's death (1598), the consolidated Spanish national debt, not counting her floating debt, was estimated at over 76,540,000 Ducats. In 1639, King Philip IV had to pay 70% interest on the loans he received, or purchased an endless supply of badly needed goods and services for national consumption. (The Fuggers of Augsburg lent money to kings and the church, a practice that led to the establishment of government banks, the most important of which was the Bank of England, founded in 1694.) In this aspect, historian Ainsworth Means commented:

> The fundamental weakness of the Spanish system ... arose largely from the fact that the anciently flourishing industries of Spain had been ruined by taxation and other factors, and also from the fact that gold and silver were needed to pay for imported goods of kinds which Spain had once manufactured but which she no longer produced. In a word, Spain was far inferior to all her rivals in commercial sagacity and consequently in commercial strength.[69]

On the same subject, a group of noted American historians wrote:

> Massive imports of silver from the mines of Mexico, Bolivia, and Peru produced such a depreciation in the value of silver that quantities of gold had to be hoarded for the critical transactions. Henceforth, for about eighty years, the European economy ran on silver. The result was a tremendous inflation. Prices and wages rose to fantastic heights in what may be considered an artificial prosperity. It did not affect all parts of Europe alike. The German silver-mining was ruined by the flood of silver from the Americas. As a consequence, the position of Germany declined, while England and the Netherlands rose to preeminence. For a brief period Spain shared this preeminence, but it was ill-fitted to continue it. Spanish industrial development was too feeble to supply the demand for manufactured products from the European settlers in the Western Hemisphere. Accordingly, they turned to the north of Europe for the textiles, cutlery, and similar products they urgently needed. By the sixteenth century the Spanish economy, which had first seemed to be prospering greatly from the discoveries, lay almost completely in ruins.[70]

The rest of the treasure either remained in America, was seized by pirates and privateers, or sunk to the bottom of the sea. In the words of historian Américo Castro: "Her (Spain) political empire extended over large and rich lands, lasted over three centuries and, yet, Spain did not enrich herself nor did the Spaniards kept up with the scientific and economic culture of their other neighbors."[71] It is ironic that Spain so contributed to the future prosperity of England, France, and the Netherlands, to the degree that it has been established that Americas' gold and silver set the basis for modern capitalism in Europe and sparked the industrial revolution (Sombart, Weber). In this regard, Spanish historian Emilio Fernández Fuster stated (translation by the author):

> The most notable economic centers of the time (England, France, and the Lower Countries) were the definite receivers of the treasure conquered by Spain in America. Of that extraordinary accumulation of benefits evolved the idea and almost the necessity to invest in order to gain larger yields. The big companies of America (English and Dutch) obtained extraordinary benefits and, as mentioned by Max Weber, developed and made popular the stock capital system which then extended to all the other European nations. The importance of this fact is undeniable. During the 17th century the capitalists who increased enormously the wealth of their countries were British and French, not Spariards.[72-]

English historian A.L. Rowse wrote extensively on this topic, which said in part:

> The Elizabethans awoke to the new world to find the Spaniards and Portuguese already entrenched in it ...It is rewarding to investigate how the shift of power came to rest with England, when Spain had such a lead... The contrast between the economics of the two countries, the policies followed in one and the other and their subsequent fortunes, is exceedingly instructive... The most striking of these new economic forces, by its very newness, was the rise in prices throughout Western Europe consequent upon the immense import of treasure from the American mines into Spain from the middle of the century. The amounts went on increasing with each decade until 1600, when their reached their apogee ...The stream of silver pouring into Europe had consequences unsettling, stimulating, uncontrollable: upsetting old ties and established relationships of value, stimulating new enterprise, reinforcing pressures

creative of a new order. The rise in prices differed from one country to another; there was a different time-sequence. In Andalusia prices increased fivefold during the century; in France two and a half times; in England the threefold rise did not culminate until 1650... "Never in the annals of the modern world has there existed so prolonged and so rich an opportunity for the business man, the speculator and the profiteer." So thought Lord Keynes: one may wonder whether the nineteenth century was not as good a time for them. Some people have thought that the earlier period saw the birth of modern capitalism.[73]

Commenting on the stream of Spanish gold and silver flowing into Europe, American historian Richard B. Morris wrote:

> The resultant flood of precious metals into Europe precipitated a price revolution, during which prices rose more than 100 per cent in Spain. The vast increase in the quantity of money transformed western European society. The feudal structure was weakened, the insecurity of the working class was increased, capitalist activity was spurred and the less wealthy nations were aroused. Moreover, the expanded supply of money paid for the European conquest of the Americas as well as the transportation and resettlement of countless emigrants from the teeming Old World to the empty spaces of the new.[74]

It would be quite fitting to do an analysis of the value of America's treasure. We will start by quoting these words from historian Mendel Peterson:

> The sum total of treasure which the Spanish extracted from the New World was enormous. Not, perhaps, as great as the gossip of the time proclaimed or the latter writers were wont to believe, but sufficient to alter materially the economy of Europe: Increasing production of gold and silver was the most important cause of the price revolution of the sixteenth and seventeenth centuries. As by far the greater part of this metallic wealth came from America, the function of Spain in the movement was a very significant one. She became the distributor of the precious metals to the rest of Europe. And since she "produced little and manufactured less," she performed this function with an efficiency which

startled even the Spaniards. (Clarence H. Haring, "Trade and Navigation Between Spain and the Indies," pp.177-178.)[75]

Later, discussing the huge quantity of that treasure that remained in America, historian Peterson liberally quotes the English Dominican friar Thomas Cage who lived in Guatemala between 1625 and 1637. First, he said (Peterson):

Travelers to the New World were quite overcome by the richness of the ornamentation in the churches and in the homes of the wealthy. "There is in the cloister of the Dominicans (in Mexico City) a lamp hanging in the church with three hundred branches wrought in silver to hold so many candles, besides a hundred little lamps for oil set in it, every one being made with workmanship so exquisitely that it is valued to be worth four hundred thousand ducats [Ducat= 8 reales, or 375 maravedís in the mid-1500s]." The goldsmiths' shops and the richness of the objects displayed were a source of wonderment to the Englishman: "The streets of Christendom must not compare with those in breadth and cleanness, but especially in the riches of the shops which do adorn them. Above all the goldsmiths' shops and works are to be admired... " "To this I may add the beauty of some of the coaches of the gentry, which do exceed in cost the best of the Court of Madrid and other parts of Christendom; for there they spare no silver nor gold, nor precious stones, nor cloth of gold, nor the best silks from China to enrich them." The wealth of Guatemala, while not comparable to that of Mexico, was enough to continue to impress Cage. In one church in the southern colony he describes two treasures: "... a lamp of silver hanging before the high altar, so big as requires the strength of three men to hale it up with a rope; but the other is of more value, which is a picture of the Virgin Mary of pure silver, and of the statue of a reasonable [sic] tall woman, which standeth in a tabernacle made on purpose in a Chapel of the Rosary with at least a dozen lamps of silver also burning before it. A hundred thousand ducats might soon be made up of treasure belonging to that church and cloister."[76]

The news of the discovery of land to the west swept Europe. As the wealth of the Americas began to flow during the succeeding decades, news of the wealth spread by word of mouth through sailors and merchants. It was common talk in the taverns of the seaports of France and England and the legend began to grow. Not only did the swift wind of rumor carry the news, those bankers of the Spanish Crown, the Fuggers, with a direct interest in the Indies trade, regularly spread the word of the arrival of the Indies fleets through their newsletters and gave details of the treasure and other cargo aboard. Soon, very soon, after the trickle became a respectable stream, French corsairs began to appear on the coast of Spain when the fleets from America were due. The years of war between Francis I of France and Charles V of Spain saw the Spanish coast swarming with French letters of marque threatening the golden route. Even in times of peace the enemies of Spain were a danger. French and English authorities looked the other way as private armed ships left their ports to sail the treasure route.

Almost as soon as French corsairs threatened the safe arrival of the treasure ships on the Spanish coast, bolder spirits invaded the Indies themselves. John Cabot met a French corsair off the coast of Brazil in 1526. The next year an English ship appeared in Santo Domingo, throwing that colony into an uproar. In 1540 an English ship captured a Spanish laden with hides near Santo Domingo. By the time Peru had been opened and her gold and silver were flowing toward Spain, the French and English had developed an insatiable taste for Spanish treasure. Thus, almost as soon as Spain had located the treasure they sought, she was called on to defend it.[77]

With regard to the total value of the treasure extracted by Spain in America, Salvador de Madariaga provided the figures based on Humboldt's own account (translation by the author):

Humboldt estimated the total extracted from America's mines from 1492 through 1803 at 4,851,156,000 pesos fuertes (hard pesos.) The value of both metals that stayed in the Indies was calculated by Humboldt at 153 million piastras, possibly an insufficient figure; while he calculated the amount that went to Asia at 133 million pesos. What remained, or the total amount of the importation of both metals to Europe was (and not only to Spain) from 1492 to 1803 5,445 million pesos fuertes, which included the gold and silver produced in the mines of the New World by the Portuguese Crown, and which value in the same period amounted to 855,544,000 pesos.[78]

And historian Dave Homer, in his magnificent work *The Treasure Galleons*, estimated the treasure's total between 1495 to 1820 at $10,438,000,000, with the bulk of it from 1556 to 1920. Of this total, he calculated that about 10% was "lost to enemy attack, pirates and privateers, or to storms at sea or shipwreck," (which we find very low indeed). What he did not tell us is the amount of the treasure that stayed in America or the other amount that was funneled into Europe, which must have accounted for at least half of that total. In other words, based on our own calculations after having consulted the figures provided by numerous sources, of that treasure's total about 20% to 25% actually reached Spain and remained there. Regarding this European bonanza of the America's treasure, Horner added:

> The great value of treasure that the galleons brought to Spain was the main factor contributing to the country's rise, as well as to her decline. Spain's bullion imports soon exceeded the money supply in all of Europe, which catapulted financial investments of Castilian merchants into fortunes overnight. But the accompanying rise in prices, as well as taxes, and a lack of a fully integrated economy, soon made Spain a good market place for the goods and services of other countries: "the inrush of bullion into the country was bound in the long run to destroy its export trade with the rest of Europe. For prices would always be higher in Spain than elsewhere. After acting as a temporary stimulus to internal trade, they would make her, in international trade, a bad market to buy from and a good one to sell to ... "(R. Trevor Davies, *The Golden Century of Spain 1501-1621*, p. 71).

Because of Spain's financial commitments beyond her borders, her imported gold and silver did not remain long in the vaults of the crown or in the pockets of her people. Her fiscal solvency continuously depended on the treasure shipments from Cartagena, Veracruz, and Callao. As long as the treasure shipments arrived regularly, Spain could afford to purchase goods and services from other European nations, and she did so with little concern for developing a more fully unified economic environment of her own. But when galleons failed to arrive, when storms and reefs and enemy privateers began to take their toll, it was a different story.[79]

Also, in this regard, Spanish historian Pedro Aguado Bleye had this to say about America's treasures and Spain (translation by the author):

Neither the monopoly nor the part of the precious metals (especially silver) which corresponded to the royal treasury benefited Castile, but, rather, the industrialists and businessmen who advanced to the kings large sums of money at high interest, money and interest which were paid largely with the remittances coming from America.[80]

Let us see now how the treasure extracted in the year 1804 was dispersed. Again, Madariaga quotes Humboldt's figures:

Humboldt estimated the total income from the Indies in 1804 at 36 million hard pesos, and of all the overseas Spanish possessions at 39 million hard pesos. Of this amount, 31 million were spent overseas. Admitting a similar proportion from gross to net income in the three continents (Asia, Africa, and America), the Indies absorbed 28,615,384 pesos, leaving as net income for the Crown 7,384,316 pesos. We can be sure that this official income of the State, based on Humboldt's estimates for 1804, was far greater than the average income up to the time of the Bourbons, whose financial administration left much to be desired. "The vast majority of the writers of political economy who have dealt with the treasury of the Peninsula—writes Humboldt—have founded their estimations on false bases, exaggerating the treasures that the Court of Madrid received annually from its American possessions: even in the most abundant years, those treasures never exceeded nine million pesos [...] a fifth of the total income of the State." However, despite the aforesaid, Humboldt estimated excessively these figures according to the most reliable modern sources. Professor Hamilton estimates the total importations of gold and silver from the Indies to Spain between 1503 and 1660 at 117,386,086,5 pesos on account of the State, and at 330,434,845,8, on account of private individuals for a grand total of 447,820,932,2. This equals for that period of 157 years an average of 2,852,362 annually. From that moment forward, the remittances of gold and silver to Spain diminished quickly. According to the same source, among the causes were: an increase in the illegal trade of those metals;

contraband of a million pesos annually that filtered from the Andes to Buenos Aires; a higher cost of mining; ...a rise in the trade with the Orient; and others.[81]

It is also worth noting that Spain's revenues from the Indies declined sharply from the five-year period of 1591-1595, being 35,184,000 pesos, to those of 1656-1660, being 3,361,000.

For Spain, the America's glimmering treasure was a mirage, a chimeric pursuit of foolhardy dreamers, and although she extracted it from the mines (which she had to locate) and was its custodian at first and soon after its conduit, it quickly slipped away from her grip and was immediately grabbed by other nations dying to bring it home. In terms of effort, time consumed, the loss of human life (Spanish), and overall cost at home and abroad (including America) the American enterprise, from beginning to end, was for Spain an insane and painfully prolonged venture of catastrophic consequences from which it took her hundreds of years to recover, if in fact she ever did or has. Moreover, the American enterprise totally bankrupted Spain. And, as another group of American historians stated: "The very foundations of capitalism were shaken by the massive bankruptcies of the Spanish government in 1575, 1596, 1607, and 1647."[82] If she would be called upon to do it all over again, it is most certain that she would bow out and pass it on to other nations, perhaps England, France, or Holland, so they could experience themselves the enormous hardship Spain was forced to endure for so many centuries. Of course, knowing all of these nations well, we could anticipate their reaction which would be none other than to step back and pass the honors to someone else. Why? Because, among many other things, they would do the numbers and soon realize that it was not worth it in time, effort, and potential financial gain.

Back to Spain in America. This anti-Spanish sentiment quickly took hold throughout Europe and found fertile grounds in the

French zealot William of Orange, whose libelous "Apology" originated and fueled the now infamous and totally discredited Black Legend. The Amsterdam edition of Friar Bartolomé de las Casas, published a few years later (1620), also contributed greatly to making Spain and King Philip II the target of so much harsh criticism and calumnies, especially when falling into the hands of their many enemies, among them Antonio Pérez, secretary to the king, and later the German poet Friedrich von Schiller in his dramatic work *Don Carlos.*

Regarding Friar Las Casas, historian Philip Ainsworth Means had this to say comparing him to another friar and compatriot, Francisco de Vitoria:

> Today he is all but forgotten (Friar de Vitoria) by most of us, but in his own time and for more than a century afterwards he was honored most greatly both in Spain and elsewhere in Europe because of his wisdom tempered by compassion in many fields of thought. Vitoria did by logical reasoning and by quiet analytical exposition all that could be done to save the Indians in America from injustice and oppression, and to him must go a last share of the credit for the fact that a desire for mercifulness became the central feature of Spanish colonial power. It is one of history's sardonic jests that a much less intelligent and much less noble man, Friar Bartolomé de las Casas, the over- advertised "Apostle of the Indies," should have captured a great part of the credit that Vitoria ought to have received.[83]

Francisco de Vitoria was a Dominican friar born in Vitoria (Spain) or possibly in Burgos in 1483 or 1486 and died in Salamanca in 1546. He received his doctorate in 1522 in Art and Theology from the Colegio de Santiago in Paris. His 15 "Doctrinas" (of which only 13 remain) were published in Lyon in 1557 and in Salamanca in 1565. Today he is widely recognized as the founder of International Law.

The widely read book series and engravings by Theodur de Bry on Exploration of the Americas by the Europeans in 1595, in which he depicts the much cruelty committed against the Indians by the Spanish also contributed to exacerbate this anti-Spanish sentiment in Europe; after all, it was the first view Europe had of native Americans. And Catherine de Medici also added fuel to the fire, primarily through confrontations with Philip II. In this regard, here are the words of historians Danniel P. Mannix and Malcolm Cowley:

> What was originally the "Black Legend" of Spanish ethnocentrism and genocidal cruelty spread quickly throughout Europe as political, economic, and religious sentiment fueled colonial expansion. Though initially shocked by Sir John Hawkins' first slavery venture in 1562-63, Queen Elizabeth quickly changed her mind Not only did she forgive him but she became a shareholder in his second slavery voyage.[84]

Historian Trevor Davies put it this way:

> The character of this man (Philip II) has been the source of age-long controversy. From his own day almost to the present one he has been represented as a monster of iniquity... The "Black Legend" had its beginnings with the famous "Apologia" of William the Silent, which was published for purposes of anti-Spanish propaganda in 1581, and in the "Relaciones" of Philip's traitorous secretary Antonio Pérez, which were published with a like purpose in London in 1594. It rolled on through centuries, gathering volume like a snowball. For most of the memoir writers, historians and dramatists approached the subject of Philip II with a violent prejudice. Frenchmen, Dutchmen and Englishmen were the inheritors of national hatred Protestants had even stronger grounds for dislike; and to nineteenth century liberals Philip was apparently the incarnation of everything they hated—bigotry, autocracy and the oppression of small nations. The hostile presentation of Philip II had not exhausted itself till the end of the nineteenth century. For two centuries after his death few were found to take up the pen in his favour.[85]

Further on the subject of America's gold, it must also be noted that only a fourth of Atahualpa's treasure, which totaled 1,528,500 pesos reached Spain (it is interesting to note that of this treasure,

Pizarro himself put aside 100,000 gold pesos earmarked to build the first church of Perú, which he later called San Francisco); that most of the famous Moctezuma treasure, estimated at 2 million pesos partially sunk to the bottom of the lake as the Spaniards were being driven out of Tenochtitlán and what remained (which was shipped by Cortés to Charles V in three caravels under the command of Alonso de Avila and Antonio de Quiñones) was seized by the French corsair Jean Florin near the Azores; that over 2,000 Spanish treasure ships sunk at sea, such as the Nuestra Señora de Atocha sunk with a Spanish fleet off the Florida Keys in 1622 and recently salvaged by Mel Fisher, and the Nuestra Señora de la Maravilla, sunk off the Bahamas in 1654 which, among other treasures, carried a solid gold statue of the Virgin Mary; that pirates, British, French, Dutch, Chinese, Arabs, and others, such as the dynasty of the Red Beard in the early 15 century, seized huge amounts of it which they in turn shared with their respective monarchs; that incalculable amounts of contraband Spanish gold flowed incessantly from America to Europe, filling the coffers of royalty and spurring the prosperity of those nations; that non-industrial Spain had to purchase from other Europeans countries (often paying highly inflated prices) most of what it consumed; that most of the gold kept by the conquistadores as their share (less the royal fifth or quinto) never reached Spain as it was invested in the construction of cities, towns, and splendid cathedrals, churches and palaces still standing today. In short, America was, from an economic standpoint, a catastrophic venture for Spain making her by no means the wealthiest nation in Europe (as it is often claimed to have been) but the poorest. Following her defeat in the Spanish-American War of 1898, which marked the decline of the Spanish empire in America, it took Spain almost a century to heal the wounds from her long struggle beyond the seas. On the other hands, the other European nations, France, the Lower Countries, and in particular England, did become the wealthiest of nations. In retrospect, King Ferdinand was right after all when he stated that the future of his new nation was to be found closer to home, in Africa, and not in faraway America.

By 1504 Spain's national revenue totaled 547,000 sterling pounds a year, while England's under Henry VII totaled a fifth of that, or 100,000 sterling pounds. This clearly shows that just a few years after discovering America Spain was financially sound, much richer than rival England.

As far as the other myth, the Potosi mine in Bolivia, it is true that between 1545 and 1705 it yielded 3,200,000,000 silver pesos, but it is also true that most of that treasure found its way not to Spain but to the rest of Europe and Colonial North America, greatly impacting and transforming their respective economies.

We said before that the Spaniards spent a large share of the gold and silver they found in America in building it. The Atahualpa treasure was distributed as follows (figures are given in equivalent U.S. dollars as of the first part of the 20th century, one gold peso=$5): Royal Fifth (Spanish Crown): 1,553,623; Francisco Pizarro: 462,623; Hernando Pizarro: 209,100; Hernando de Soto: 104,628; each horseman: 52,364; each foot soldier: 26,182. We already said that Pizarro put aside 100,000 gold pesos to build the first church of Perú, which in today's dollars would amount to $500,000 (the conversion for William Prescott was $1 1 for a gold peso but many scholars disagree putting it at $5.) Now let's see what Pizarro and the Spaniards did with a lot of that treasure in Perú. We will let historian Charles F. Lummis tell the story (translation by the author):

> In his brief administrative career Pizarro obtained notable results. He founded several cities on the coast and named one of them Trujillo in memory of his own native town. But, above all, he took great pleasure in urbanizing and beautifying his dear Lima and in fostering commerce and other areas needed to develop the new nation. There is a notable contrast that evidences his great managerial skills. When the Spaniards arrived in

Cajamarca two spurs cost 250 gold pesos. A few years before Pizarro's death, the first cow taken to Perú cost 10,000 gold pesos; and two years later the best cow could be bought for less than 200 gold pesos. The first wine barrel sold for 1,600 gold pesos; but three years later domestic wine was available in Lima at a very modest price. The same could be said about everything else. A sword sold for 250 gold pesos; a cape for 500; a pair of shoes for 200; and a horse for 10,000. But two or three years later, due to Pizarro's extraordinary managerial skills, all goods produced or available in Lima were within everybody's reach. Not only did he foster commerce but the country's industry as well as developing agriculture, mining and the mechanical arts. In short, he was putting into practice very successfully the general principle of the Spaniards that the main wealth of a country is not its gold, forests, or lands but its people. The Spaniards sought everywhere to educate, to christianize and civilize the Indians for the purpose of making them worthy citizens of the new nation, instead of eliminating them from the face of the earth so the newcomers would take their place, as it has mostly happened with the conquests undertaken by other European nations.[86]

So did Cortés in Mexico, Velázquez in Cuba, Ponce de León in Puerto Rico, de Soto in North America, and many more Spaniards throughout the vast empire. We are maintaining that at least two thirds of Atahualpa's treasure was used for that purpose, and that most of the royal fifth eventually went back to its original source, meaning America. It is also worth noting that Juan Pizarro, brother of Francisco, before he died, donated the lot of the Temple of the Sun in Cuzco, which he had received after the conquest, to the Dominicans to build there the church of Santo Domingo. The British built little or nothing wherever they went and, if they did, it was for the sole purpose of facilitating a larger return on their investment, like bridges or roads leading to exploitable resources. The Spanish gold and silver seized by the English pirates, Drake, Hawkins, and company, went straight into the coffers of Queen Elizabeth and the English royalty and to foster England's own economy.

CHAPTER TEN

SPAIN AND SLAVERY

On the subject of black slavery, the first nation to raise its voice against it was Spain. In this regard, historian Salvador de Madariaga stated (translation by the author):

> Friar Las Casas himself was the one who advocated it in order to help the Indians, although later he admitted having erred, and Father Avendaño fought hard for abolishing it. But the vigor of the human spirit did not go any further at the time. A great victory had been won saving the Indians from slavery—a victory in which Spain showed to be superior to its time; but eventually she had to pay for that victory by bringing to the Indies another human race to carry on stronger shoulders the weight of slavery imposed by the era and circumstances.[87]

And the Spanish king, Fernando VII, was the first to urge the abolishment of the trade and, to this end, asked England to join him in convening the treaty of September 23, 1817, signed on behalf of Spain by García de León y Pizarro and of the king of England, George III, by Henry Wellesley. However, England did not abolish it in its colonies until 1834. In the Spanish possessions in America it was abolished many years before it was finally abolished in the United States by President Lincoln in his Proclamation of September 23 of 1862 and January 1 of 1863. In Mexico, for example, it was abolished in 1825.

It is true that Spain imported black slaves to America and that abuses were often committed. What is not true is that Spain was the only nation so doing. In fact, contrary to the others, she sought early on to remedy their condition and protect their wellbeing. For example, by royal decree of 1503, Spain's Catholic monarchs forbade slavery and ruled that all Indian slaves be set free and be paid wages for their work. Excluded from working were children, women, the sick, and the elderly. In this regard, Sir Arthur Helps, the distinguished historian referred to the orders personally given to Ovando by Queen Isabella and King Ferdinand prior to his departure for the Indies:

> ... That all the Indians in Hispaniola should be free from servitude and be unmolested by anyone, and that they should live as free vassals, governed and protected by justice, as were the vassals of Castile. ... The Indians should be treated with much love and kindness, so that no wrongs done to them should hinder their reception of our holy Faith by creating an abhorrence of the Christians ... that he should take care that natives and Spaniards lived in peace, administering justice with an equal hand, since this will be the best way to ensure that no violence is done to the Indians.[88]

Even in her will, Queen Isabella urged the King and her daughter to treat the Indians with benevolence:

> Wherefore I very affectionately supplicate my lord the King, and charge and command my said daughter (Juana) that they act accordingly, and that this (the conversion of the Indians) should be their principal end, and that in it they should have much diligence, and that they should not consent or give occasion, that the Indians who dwell in those islands or on the Tierra Firme, gained, or to be gained, should receive any injury in their persons or goods, but should command that they be well and justly treated. And if the Indians have received any injury, they (the King and her daughter Juana) should remedy it, and look that they do not infringe in any respect that which is enjoined and commanded in the words of the said concession (of the Pope).[89]

Later, by the royal decree of 1520, King Charles V declared the unconditional freedom of all Indian slaves. The royal letter of 1523, addressed to Hernán Cortés, banned all forms of oppression so the Indians would be converted to Christianity with kindness. And Cortés himself, a devout believer, often exhorted his followers to seek fame and fight with courage like the Romans, but he also instilled in them a deep sense of Christian zeal and crusading. Before every battle, he celebrated mass and had his men pray to St. Peter and St. James. With regard to the black slaves, as early as 1517, and on the advice of Friar Bartolomé de Las Casas, King Charles V had reluctantly agreed to their importation, a decision he would later regret deeply when learning how they were hunted down and treated by the British and Dutch trade profiteers. In this regard, Charles F. Lummis wrote:

> The Spaniards did not exterminate any Indian nation, in contrast to the hundreds of them that were exterminated by our ancestors (the English). And besides every first and necessary bloody encounter was immediately followed by the education of the natives and their humanitarian care. The fact is that the Indian population that was once under Spanish domain is today larger than it was during the conquest, and this amazing contrast in conditions, and the lesson that it entails regarding the contrast of methods, is the best possible answer to those who have corrupted history.[90]

And, regarding the conquest of Peru by Pizarro, Mr. Lummis offered this observation:

> The shedding of blood in the conquest of Peru was much less than that of the final siege of the Indian tribes in Virginia. It hardly had as many Peruvian victims as the war of King Philip, and it was less bloody because it was more open and honorable than any of England's conquests in the Eastern Indies.[91]

Also on the same topic, American historian Robert S. Weddle wrote these truthful words commenting on the discovery:

As is almost always the case with tremendous government undertakings, the effort was mismanaged. Fraud and callous disregard of human life were its concomitants, as were hypocrisy and deceit. But no one has dared suggest that such abuses were confined to the great Spanish adventure, or to the colonial period.[92]

And in another passage he added:

Much has been written concerning the motivation for risking such hazard and hardship: lust for gold and glory; missionary zeal for converting the savage; or merely the restless conquistador spirit, the Ulyssian itching foot, that caused the hardy Extremadurans to forsake the connubial bed for a life of wandering. But there was another, perhaps allied, factor that has been given less consideration, one often expressed in royal orders and in the letters and reports of the conquistadores themselves in reference to exploring the unknown land: "To know its secrets. " Such a quest has propelled man into the unknown since his very beginning. The discoverers, the explorers, and the conquerors, then, came for multiple reasons: for glory, God, and gold, yes—but also for knowledge.[93]

And, also on the same subject, Professor Robert S. Chamberlain had this to say:

The motives which inspired the Castilian sovereigns to create a vast empire in the Americas were the desire to achieve more extensive realms, propagate Christianity, and obtained increased revenues. The early conquistadores were impelled by several motives which varied in intensity with regard to individuals, time, and place: desire to gain wealth and position, desire to add to the glory of the Castilian Crown, zeal to propagate Christianity, and love of adventure ...In this manner, Cortés conquered Mexico, Alvarado Guatemala, Pizarro Peru, Jiménez de Quesada New Granada, and Montejo, Yucatan... The military triumphs of the Spaniards over incredible numerical odds were the triumph of indomitable representatives of a more highly developed society over those of a lesser. The conquest was accompanied by great cruelty, but it was no greater than that of contemporary conquest elsewhere. Ruthless exploitation of the natives followed colonization, but such was the common lot of subject peoples during the period. The intent of the

Castilian crown toward the Indian masses, if not the actual practice, was beneficent. While the production of gold and silver was the chief source of crown revenues in the Indies and became the basis of much private wealth, agriculture, grazing, and commerce were soon highly developed and local industries of various types came into existence. Certain colonies like Chile, Tucatan, and the Rio de la Plata, were almost exclusively agricultural and pastoral. The existence of a large Indian population, many groups of which possessed high cultures of long standing, and the impact of European culture and Christianity on the New World civilizations led to fundamentally important social, cultural, and racial developments.[94]

Further on this subject, with regard to the Encomendero, historian Sir Arthur Helps wrote:

The laws enacted for the treatment of the Indian slaves—were equally emphatic in intention. It was laid down that it was "the inseparable duty" of the Encomendero to defend the person and property of the Indian client and to see that he was in no way aggrieved (Recop. de Leyes, 10th May 1554.) If this duty was not fulfilled the Encomienda was to be confiscated. [95]

Moreover, historian John McManners asserted:

"Yet the crudeness of crusading self-interest does not detract from the genuineness of the zeal to spread the Christian faith—the self-interest and the zeal coexisted without contemporaries being conscious of their incompatibility. Prince Henry the Navigator, who inspired the Portuguese voyages, had as his objectives (solemnly affirmed for him in a papal bull) to spread Christianity and to join forces with fellow Christians—a reference to the hope of finding the mysterious kingdom of Prester John, a legendary Christian king in Ethiopia or Asia. When Vasco de Gama landed at Calicut, he said his quest was for fellow Christians and for spices. The official policy of the Spanish Crown put the conversion of the native population as first priority. ... Without the peculiar force of religious certainty, it is hard to see how the conquistadores could have triumphed; steel blades, thirteen muskets, sixteen horses, and intrigues with dissatisfied tribes are hardly sufficient explanation. ... Bernal Díaz del Castillo, that literate soldier of fortune, summed up his reasons for going to the Indies: "to serve God and His Majesty, to give light to those who were in darkness, and to grow rich, as all men desire to do."[96]

And, commenting on Spain's achievements in the New World, American historian Edward Gaylord Bourne wrote:

If now we review the same events with the eyes of the old campaigner of the conquest, Bernal Díaz, as he looks back forty-seven years, we see that first there come to his mind the wonderful changes in the life and condition of the Indians, changes in range and character perhaps not equaled before in the history of the race in so short a time. Instead of the fearful temples of Huitzilopochtli and Tezcatlipoca, smoking with human sacrifice and dripping with blood of victims, there are Christian churches; while upon the Indian themselves have been bestowed the hardly won prizes of ages of slow progress, the developed arts, the various domestic animals, the grains, vegetables, and fruits, the use of letters and the printing press, and the forms of government. As the child physically and mentally passes rapidly through the earlier stages of the development of the race, so the natives of New Spain in a generation and a half were lifted through whole stages of human evolution. If these gifts came through war and conquest, so Roman culture came to Gaul and Britain.[97]

Finally, on the subject of Spain's ill-treatment of the Indians, Mr. Gaylord Bourne added:

Ovando had been ordered to treat the Indians as free men and subjects of the king and queen, but he soon had to report that if left to themselves they would not work even for wages and withdrew from any association with the Spaniards, so that it was impossible to teach or convert them. To meet the first of these difficulties, the sovereigns instructed him, March, 1503, to establish the Indians in villages, to give them lands which they could not alienate, to place them under a protector, to provide a school-house in each village that the children might be taught reading, writing, and Christian doctrine, to prevent oppression by their chiefs, to suppress their native ceremonies, to make efforts to have the Indians marry their wives in due religious form, and to encourage the intermarriage of some Christians with the Indians, both men and women.[98]

Humboldt was also a great observer of the condition of the Indians in the Spanish possessions and wrote extensively on this subject. Historian Salvador de Madariaga quoted many of his observations. Here are a few (translation by the author):

"Nowhere does the Indian enjoy more perfectly the fruit of his work than in the mines of México, no one can force the Indian to dedicate himself to this kind of work or to prefer this exploitation over another; unhappy with the mine's owner, the Indian goes elsewhere to offer his services to another patron willing to pay him more regularly or in real currency. These exact and comforting facts are little known in Europe. "

And what about the Indian's pay? Again, Humboldt offers this observation:

"...the Mexican miner is the best paid among all miners; while in a Saxon country the miner earns 4 or 4 and a half Francs for a five-day week of work, the Mexican miner earns 25 to 30 Francs, and there are cases of 9 and a half Francs per day. A carpenter of New Andalucia earned in his time 5 to 6 Francs, that is to say, more than a Saxon miner in a whole week."

Regarding the work in the fields, here is Humboldt again:

"The Indian worker is poor, but he is free. His condition is preferable to the field worker of most of northern Europe. No servitude exists in New Spain, and the number of slaves is almost nil. For the most part sugar is the product of free hands."

Regarding the Indian's pay in the fields, he finds the salaries paid in México superior to those paid in France and the United States, commenting that the Mexican field worker earns five times as much as the one of an English colony, adding:

"New Spain, with a population of about 6 million, gives to the treasury of the king of Spain twice as much net income as England gets from its many possessions in India with a population five times as large."[99]

127

As stated by the above historians as well as by many others, no one can dispute the fact that Spain endeavored to protect both the Indians and black slaves from the very beginning although, admittedly, not always successfully. Wrestling with such complex problem thousands of miles away was an overwhelming task for the well-intended Spanish Monarchs.

In this regard, Charles F. Lummis observed:

> The affirmations of the office historians that the Spaniards enslaved the people or other natives of New Mexico; that they had to choose between Christianity and death; that they were forced to work the mines and similar things, are totally inaccurate. Spain's policy toward the Indians of the New World was one of humanity and justice, of education and moral persuasion, and even though some individuals violated the strict laws of their country with respect to the treatment of the Indians, they were justly punished.[100]

In this regard also the following comments should be made: Hernán Cortés was quoted as saying about his illegitimate son, Martín, that "... because of who he is I profess for him as much love as I do for the other son I had with the Marquise." According to a 1515 law, Indians were declared free to marry with an Indian or an American-born Spanish woman provided she would be of age. This Indian woman was the subject of a very special care, for example, not being allowed to work while pregnant, to breast-feed a white woman's child while breast-feeding her own, and by being also exempt from paying taxes. It must also be said that if there was any bigotry toward the Indian or black it was not due to race with the connotation that the term carries today, but to the fact that they were not yet duly converted to Catholicism. In other words, Spaniards did not discriminate against native Americans or blacks on the basis on ethnicity, culture, background, social status, or beliefs.

In contrasting Spain's and England's treatment of America's natives, historian Salvador de Madariaga wrote (translation by the author):

When judging the work done by the Spaniards in America, one naturally thinks of the later work of the English in North America. Points of contrast at once leap to the eye. As the first permanent Spanish settlement dates back to 1493, and the English settlement to 1607, both countries having been in the New World, the England so produced is the England of the Stuarts and the Commonwealth, whereas that (of) Spain was the Spain of the Catholic Monarchs and of Charles V. The Spanish colonization coincided with the period of adventurous exploration; the English colonization followed the period of adventures. When the Spanish Conquistadores are accused of being inhuman, this difference of time should be borne in mind. All that has been said—and the first to say it have been the Spaniards—about that cruelty may well be true, but it is not the whole truth. It should not be forgotten, for instance, that during that same period the English were also conquering and colonizing, but they were doing so in Ireland; and their conduct cannot be said to have been any more effective or humane. So, the two movements differ in the world they took with them. And even more so in the world that they found, for the English did not find a Mexico, a Peru, or Bogota.[101]

But in America, centuries before the Spanish arrived and up to the time of the conquest, slavery was also a widespread practice among the native Indians. The three major South American indigenous cultures, the Aztecs, Incás and Mayas indulged in slavery and routinely committed multiple acts of unimaginable cruelty toward their own people. In this regard, Edward Gaylord Bourne had this to say:

The Aztec power was a military despotism exercised by three confederated warlike tribes, who lived upon the plunder of their enemies and the tribute of their subjects. War for food and war for victims for the sacrifices was their chief occupation. The lack of domestic animals for suitable food had contributed to the survival of the custom, partly religious and partly utilitarian, of eating the flesh of the sacrificed victims. The mass of the outlying Indian population were oppressed by their predatory rulers and not disinclined to a change when once the new-comers showed themselves superior.[102]

And the distinguished historian John Fiske offered his own observations on the same subject:

...Yet if we are to be guided by strict logic, it would be difficult to condemn the Spaniards for the mere act of conquering Mexico without involving in the same condemnation our own forefathers who crossed the ocean and overran the territory of the United States with small regard for the proprietary rights of Algonquins, or Iroquois, or red men of any sort. Our forefathers, if called upon to justify themselves, would have replied that they were founding Christian states and diffusing the blessings of a higher civilization; and such, in spite of much alloy in the motives and imperfection in the performance, was certainly the case. Now if we would not lose or distort the historical perspective, we must bear in mind that the Spanish conquerors would have returned exactly the same answer. If Cortés were to return to this world and pick up some history book in which he is described as a mere picturesque adventurer, he would feel himself very unjustly treated. He would say that he had higher aims than those of a mere fighter and gold-hunter; and so doubtless he had. In the complex tangle of motives that actuated the medieval Spaniard ... the desire of extending the dominion of the Church was a very real and powerful incentive to action. The strength of the missionary and crusading spirit in Cortés is seen in the fact that where it was concerned, and there only, was he liable to let zeal overcome prudence.

There can be no doubt that, after making all allowances, the Spaniards did introduce a better state of society into Mexico than they found there. It was high time that an end should be put to those hecatombs of human victims, slashed, torn open, and devoured on all the little occasions of life. It sounds quite pithy to say that the Inquisition, as conducted in Mexico, was as great an evil as the human sacrifices and the cannibalism; but it is not true. Compared with the ferocious barbarism of ancient Mexico the contemporary Spanish modes of life were mild ...[103]

Respecting this very same subject, historian Philip Ainsworth Means had this comment:

With all its shortcomings Spain's rule in those parts of America (the Spanish Main) which she occupied most intensively, and held against all foes for three hundred years, resulted in a more perfect preservation of the ancient native race of America than in the parts ruled by any other European nation. It so happened that none of the regions where the Spanish-Indian colonial culture grew to greatest strength is suited by nature to wholly White Race occupation ... In Mexico and throughout the Andes region the native element of the population remained a large proportion of the whole and, under Spanish rule, the Indians not only survived but increased and formed an integral part of colonial society under conditions which permitted the most capable of them to hold respectable positions. In this respect Spanish American differed from and was superior to those parts of America held by other European nations. One can only guess what the results would have been if France or England had taken the regions held by Spain, but all things considered it is likely that the English would have pushed the Indians into the eastern jungles and replaced them with Negro slaves...[104]

And, as far as slavery in North America is concerned, much before the arrival of the Spaniards, the Mariame Indians also practiced slavery and often committed barbaric acts of cruelty particularly toward their women, as told by Alvar Núñez Cabeza de Vaca.

Another noted American historian, David J. Weber, had this to say comparing the Spanish and the English treatment of the Indians:

In contrast to the Anglo-American frontier in North America, which largely excluded natives, Spain sought to include natives within its new world societies. Thus, Spanish missionaries labored to win the hearts and minds of Indians in what might be defined as a spiritual or cultural frontier—a frontier that some natives resisted with a fervor that matched the missionaries zeal to convert them.[105]

On the other hand, as soon as the demand for black slaves arose, and seeking only to capitalize on their trade, England immediately stepped in and became the World's Dominant Slave Trading

Nation. In 1672 England established the Royal African Company, which became so successful that by the Asiento of 1713 (prior to that, in 1528, an Asiento was granted by Charles V to the German traders Ehinger and Sayler) it was granted a 30-year monopoly for the sale of 144,000 black slaves per year to the Spanish possessions in America, or 4,320,000 slaves in total. The price paid for slave at the time was between 80-100 pesos (about $100 of today's U.S. Dollars); thus, in that deal, mother England grossed an estimated $432,000,000, an astronomical sum at the time. Once again, England derived huge profits from America's gold...without having to conquer any empires. Regarding the slave trade, it should be mentioned that it was Portugal, not Spain, the nation that started it and that profited greatly from it. The first Asiento (different from the licenses that were granted in the 16th century) for the importation of black slaves was granted to the Portuguese Pedro Gómez Reynel, whereby he was obliged to deliver 4,250 slaves annually up to a total of 38,250 for which he would be compensated 900,000 ducados payable at the rate of 100,000 per year. The other slave nations, besides England, were Holland, Germany, and France. Although Spain granted licenses and asientos (about 6,000 to private profiteers) for the importation of black slaves to America, she refused to get directly involved in the actual trade—hunting them down, transporting them, and selling them—preferring to leave such a task in the experienced hands of the true masters of the trade. The amount of money collected by all of these nations, headed by England, for the slave trade made them rich beyond belief. In terms of the number of imported black slaves, it must be noted that there were far fewer black slaves in all of Spanish South America than in the other European possessions, even though these covered a much smaller territory. In fact, the largest concentration of black slaves were in the Antilles, Brazil and, yes, Louisiana, U.S.A. In this regard, historian Salvador de Madariaga provided the following startling figures based on Humboldt's account:

First, with regard to the number of black slaves, here's Humboldt's testimony: "In all of the Spanish colonies, without excluding Cuba and Puerto Rico, which together comprised a territory far larger than Europe, there are fewer black slaves than in the state of Virginia." ... Humboldt provides figures that demonstrate the monstrous consumption of black slaves in the New World, particularly in the French and English colonies, despite the fact that they were much smaller than those of Spain. Of the 70,000 slaves traded annually, the British colonies consumed 38,800 and the French ones 20,000, leaving 11,200 for the Spanish and Portuguese territories, incomparably larger. In the 106 years preceding 1786, the British West Indies traded 2,130,000 black slaves. In total, the West Indies, including the Spanish Islands which had a population of 2,400,000 blacks, traded between 1760 and 1825, [approximately] 5,000,000 black slaves. Humboldt concluded that in all of the New World the most honorable nation regarding slavery was New Spain where such trade was almost non-existant.[106]

But there is more, much more. England, as well as Holland and others, not only traded unscrupulously in slavery and eventually monopolized the trade, but also tortured the slaves unmercifully and abominably inflicting on them mental and physical harm never before experienced by humans. Their own historians expressed horror when writing about this barbaric behavior from nations considered to be among Europe's most civilized. Here are some revealing comments by well-established historians on British, French, and Dutch torture practices routinely inflicted on their innocent victims (translations by the author): " ... the mutilation of criminals, the branding with a hot iron of incorrigible rogues, and the methods of torture to force confessions were commonly practiced by the English... (Jackson Harlow).[107]

When several Spanish prisoners refused to divulge the information sought...

...the French or Dutchman (called the "Olonés") exploded into a rage to the point that he took out his knife and plunged it into the chest of one of the prisoners; he then yanked out his heart with his own sacrilegious hands and started biting into it with the frenzy of a starving wolf yelling to the other prisoners: "I will do likewise to you if you fail to show me the way." (Exquemelin, A.O.)[108]

Also, in another passage, the same historian Exquemelin described in horrifying detail the torture of a prisoner by the pirate Morgan:

Seeing that the man was unwilling to talk, they put him on a horse dislocating his arms with much cruelty. Then, they twisted a rope around his forehead, tightening it so hard that his eyes bulged like eggs as if they were to fall out of his skull; ...then, they hanged him and started hitting and belting him while in a posture of excruciating pain. They then cut off his nose and ears and burnt his face with hot straw until he collapsed.[109]

Later, in another passage, the same historian described some of the other atrocities committed by Morgan after seizing Portobelo, this time against women and children:

Once this was accomplished, they ate and drank as they customarily did, that is to say, indulging in all sorts of abuses and excesses. Following these two vices, they immediately. proceeded to rape and commit acts of adultery with many honorable women, whether married or not who, fearing for their lives, were forced to give their bodies to those lustful and heartless men.[110]

And historian Varinas, upon his return to Madrid in 1675, wrote (translation by the author):

Who would dare see, as I have, for lack of government and not power, the heretic pirates of the Indies desecrate the temples and turn them into jails and dungeons worse than those of Algiers to lock up the captives; for the temples of the Indies are used as stables and filthy places. Who would dare see also the images of Christ and his holy mother violated and dragged on the floor; the sacred glasses and ciborium of the Holy Sacrament turned into urinals, and other religious ornaments equally desecrated; the women, widows, maidens, and those married raped and disgraced in the temple in front of their horrified husbands and parents ...[111]

We should also mention that after returning to England from his second voyage, the English pirate Hawkins proudly chose for his crest a chained arab or negro as a symbol of his human trade.

We are merely mentioning the name of the English Blackbeard, a privateer turned pirate in the early 1700s, preying along the Atlantic coast of North America and the West Indies, for to enunciate his cruelty and many atrocities committed on ships and settlements would require several pages. Blackbeard's headquarters were both in the Bahamas and the Carolinas and he is known to have shared much of his Spanish booty with the compliant governor of North Carolina.

Regarding the treatment of black slaves by the English, Charles Wesley, the noted English evangelical reformer who lived and preached among the English settlers in North America wrote (translation by the author):

> It would take a very long time to relate the scandalous cases of diabolic cruelty inflicted on the black slaves by the English colonizers. Here is one of those cases: Mr. Hill, a dance teacher in Charlestown, whipped a woman slave until she dropped lifeless to his feet. Then, after a doctor revived her, he whipped her again several times with equal vigor and then poured hot sealing wax on her. The crime the poor woman had committed was simply to overfill a cup of tea.[112]

It is worth noting that in the census of 1790, the United States (the Thirteen Colonies) population totaled 3,929,625, of which only 59,557 were free blacks while an astonishing 697,624 still remained slaves, or about a sixth of the total population. On the other hand, as early as 1753 the Spanish king, Charles III, abolished the trading of black slaves in the Spanish possessions and set them free in 1789, seventy-three years before the Emancipation Proclamation by President Lincoln (1862) and seventy-six years before the ratification of the 13th Amendment to the United States Constitution (1865.)

The following breakdown shows how the South American population shifted from 1492 through 1825 among Indians, whites, blacks and mixed races:

1492 - Total indigenous population: 13,385,000.
1570 - Indians: 10,827,150; whites: 140,000; blacks, mestizos, and mulattos: 262,500. Total population: 11,229,650.
1650 - Indians: 10,035,000; whites: 849,000; blacks: 857,000; mixed races: 670,000. Total population: 12,411,000.
1825 - Indians: 8,634,301; whites: 13,474,835; blacks: 6,046,000; mixed races: 6,252,000. Total population: 34,531,536.115.

The above clearly illustrates the rapid growth of the black population and mixed races and the decline of the Indians, mostly due to mixed marriages with whites and blacks. It also illustrates that by 1825 the entire black population, or 6,046,000 souls, were legally free.

In 1708, the English historian Hans Sloane witnessed the treatment of slaves while traveling in Jamaica, which he described this way (translation by the author):

> The punishment inflicted for crimes committed by the slaves in cases of rebellion is burning, nailing them first to the ground with hooks in all four limbs, and then gradually burning their feet and hands all the way up to their head, causing unimaginable pain. ... These punishments are such as well-deserved at times by the negroes, who are an evil generation ... [On the way slaves were generally treated by the English] After whipping them continuously, they threw on them hot pepper and salt as to make the wounds sting, and also at times melted hot wax and other very exquisite torments.[113]

He also tells us that the punishment for negligence was to whip the slaves using pointed spears until they bled to death. Nor did the English show any mercy in the treatment of United States' prisoners during the War of 1812.

And, regarding the other myth of the Spaniards' genocide of the America's Indian population, it is Humboldt himself who denies it in the strongest terms. According to historian Salvador de Madariaga,

> Humboldt demonstrated that there was not such a thing. Concerning the Indians of New Spain (Mexico) Humboldt arrived at the following conclusion: Not only is the Indian population increasing from one century to another, but also the vast region designated with the name of New Spain is now more populated (1803) than it was before the arrival of the Europeans.[114]

And then Madariaga continued:

> This increase in the population of New Spain was due, according to Humboldt, to an increase in prosperity. The work in the mines— Humboldt noted—is totally free throughout the kingdom of New Spain; no Indian, no mestizo can be forced to work in the mines.[115]

It is also worth noting that in his report to the king, Velasco mentioned that of Lima's four hospitals the only one that prospered was that of the Indians, because those designated for the Spaniards were always too full with patients. In this regard (the systematic extermination of the Indian race by Spain as alleged by the English and others), historian Philip Ainsworth Means wrote also these revealing and truthful words:

> True, in many of the wars which Spanish conquerors waged against Indian nations in order that a Christian and Spanish empire might be built up, there were countless cruelties committed, sometimes on one side, sometimes on the other. But as often as not, these were the result of military necessity rather than of innate ruthlessness. Inevitably, when a

people of advanced civilization sets out to found a colony in a land of a people less advanced, that colony is raised upon blood, grief and shattered freedom. Any other European people placed in the situation of the conquering Spaniards would have behaved both as well and as ill as they did. There is a word of truth in the couplet: "Estas maldades fueron la saña—de todo un pueblo y no de España" (These wickednesses were the fury—Of a whole age, not of Spain only.[116]

CHAPTER ELEVEN

ON THE SPANISH INQUISITION

And, with regard to the other myth, the Spanish Inquisition, the institution itself, as well as its practices, was not founded by Spain but by Pope Gregory IX in 1233 against the heretical sect Albigenses, and then introduced in Spain (Aragón) two years later. In Castile, King Alphonse the Wise refused to allow it and it was not until the reign of the Catholic Monarchs that it was finally permitted. However, with all of its alleged evil practices, the Spanish Inquisition pales in comparison with the excesses of the British tribunals of the 16th and 17th centuries as we shall see below.

First of all, the percentage of executions for heresy by the Spanish Inquisition was less than 1% of all the cases tried. On the other hand, the executions for witchcraft and sorcery in England were 19% of all the cases tried and, during the first four years of the reign of James I, it increased to 41%. And, the executions of witches in continental Europe has been estimated at over 300,000, of which at least 200,000 were performed in Germany and over 8,000 in Scotland between 1560 and 1600. On the other hand, in England it toppled 70,000 (see Robert Steele, *Social England*, 1931.) And how were these witches tortured to force out a confession? Through the use of a horrendous instrument called "bootikins," or a small boot, which was placed between the ankle and the knee and then hit with a hammer causing excruciating pain. In 1645, the infamous Hopkins alone hunted down a total of 29 witches of whom 19 were executed. In America, in over 300 years, the Spanish Inquisition executed some 100 heretics, while in North America alone, in the middle of the 19th century, a total of 3,839 persons who had been convicted of witchcraft were executed. But these executions were not only for witchcraft. There was the case of a Mrs. Gaunt, whose execution was witnessed by William Penn, the founder of Pennsylvania, as was then the custom. Mrs. Gaunt, an old lady, known for her charity and mercy, was being tried for having sheltered a fugitive. Although historian Grahame claimed she was burned, according to historian Trend she was tortured first and then executed along with others. Here is his description of the execution (translation by the author):

> All of you (referring to all those to be executed along with Mrs. Gaunt) have to return to the towns you come from; from there you will be dragged to the execution site, where you will be hanged until death nears; then, while still alive, we will cut open your bodies and yank out your entrails (intestines) which we will burn before you; then we will cut off your heads and will mutilate your bodies, and dispose of the remains as ordered by the king.[117]

It is also interesting to note these remarks on the Spanish Inquisition brought forth by historian Trevor Davies (an Englishman, professor at Oxford):

> Popular tradition dies so hard that it is still necessary to point out that the Spanish Inquisition, judged by the standards of the time, was neither cruel nor unjust in its procedure and its penalties. In many ways it was more just and humane than almost any other tribunal in Europe. Thus, for example, a conviction could not be obtained without the testimony of seven witnesses, two of whom had to be in substantial agreement. Again, the accused was allowed the assistance of trained lawyers and an advocate to save him from making any false step through ignorance. He

had also the right to recuse any judge whom he suspected of prejudice; the judge successfully recused having to abandon the case to his colleague. To protect him from the effects of private animosity he was allowed to make a list of all persons whom he believed to be his enemies, and should any of his accusers be found to figure on the list their evidence would be completely rejected. With the same intention, false accusations were subjected to the severest penalties. Prisoners awaiting trial were supported with every care for their material comfort, their prisons frequently inspected and their complaints carefully considered. Furthermore, unlike almost all other tribunals in Europe at this time, the Inquisition was very sparing in the use of torture, and adopted methods of torture far more humane than was customary, special care being taken to do the accused no personal injury. It should be remembered also that the Inquisition did much to save suspects from the violence of fanatical mobs and much to combat ignorant superstitions, and so—to give one example— saved Spain from those hideous witch-hunts that were a common feature of life in Northern Europe as late as the eighteenth century.[118]

With regard to religious tolerance, or rather intolerance, in North America, we must remember the "Tolerance Act" of the state of Maryland in the middle of the 17th century, which prescribed death and seizure of the estate of all those convicted of negating that Jesus Christ was the son of God or the Sanctity of the Father, the Son and of the Holy Spirit, or the divinity of any of them, or the unity of divinity, or the use of adverse words when referring to the Trinity or to either one of the three persons.

Finally, with regard to the other myth that Spain destroyed the Indies, our discourse in the previous pages should have sufficed to render invalid and baseless that long-held calumny by Spain's foes. Modern scholarship and a long list of distinguished historians have put that theory to rest for good, including Salvador de Madariaga who had this to say:

Modern research has proved that the Spaniards destroyed much less than it is commonly said, although there was indeed a systematic and general destruction of Aztec temples and documents. However, was there anything else possible? The primary objective of the 15th century Spaniard was the Christianization of the Indies, and therefore the criteria could not have been anthropological, that is to say, indifferent to the matter of religion. Much less of an excuse before civilization and history was the general destruction of works of art that was made both in Edward VI's and Queen Elizabeth's England by the Iconoclasts.[119]

In this regard (as well as in others) the serious reader will find it to his or her advantage to read the works by Charles F. Lummis, Salvador de Madariaga, José Vasconcelos, Philip Ainworth Means, Edward Baylord Bourne, Sir Arthur Helps, Mendel Peterson, Carlos Pereyra, Charles Gibson, Américo Castro, Davies Trevor, Richard B. Morris, John Fiske, all of which are mentioned here.

CHAPTER TWELVE

WESTERN CIVILIZATION TAKES ROOT IN THE AMERICAS. THE SPANISH MISSIONARIES AND THEIR LABOR OF LOVE.

Back anew to Spain in America.

Undaunted by the prevailing adverse circumstances, and although somewhat weakened by the forces of time and the enormous weight of her vast world empire, Spain kept pressing forward to complete her mission.

The men of the sword, now legendary, became the men of the cloth and the pen—the saintly missionaries and monks who took upon themselves the redemption of the heathen on the one hand and the propagation of Western civilization on the other. Like the conquest, the conversion was swift and decisive. By the end of the 16th century, in little more than one hundred years, America's 7,000,000 Indians were converted to Christianity. According to a letter written by Friar Martín de Valencia, the head of the "twelve apostles" (a group of twelve Franciscan friars sent to Mexico on

May 12th, 1524), by 1531 the Franciscans had baptized in Mexico alone over 1,000,000 Indians. The three main religious orders responsible for this extraordinary achievement were the Franciscans, Dominicans, and the Jesuits. During the 17th century, the Franciscan Order had established 700 convents with 3,000 priests; in the same century, the Dominican Order had set up nine provinces, three of them in Mexico with 2,000 priests; and in 1580, the Jesuit Order totaled 217 priests, jumping to 1,020 in 1616 and to 2,617 in 1767. Indeed, the Americas' 800 million Catholics are forever indebted to these Spanish missionaries for laying down the foundations of their religion in so vast a land. Yet, their names have been, for the most part, forgotten and are rarely mentioned anywhere.

With regard to North America, the Spanish conquistadors, explorers, and very especially the saintly missionaries, planted the seeds of Christianity very early on and worked tirelessly to erect hundreds of churches across the vast territory. To illustrate this, we will mention just a few. North America's first church was founded in 1560 in Saint Augustine, Florida, by friar Francisco de Pareja, but many years before the missionaries who accompanied Coronado in 1540 founded also many others, and in 1598 the ten friars who marched with Juan de Oñate founded North America's second church named Chamita, in the town of San Gabriel, and in 1606 the third church was founded in the city of Santa Fé becoming a parish in 1627, built by the historian Friar Alonso de Benavides. The temple of San Miguel was built in the same city in 1636 and on that same site stands today the magnificent Santa Fe Cathedral. In New Mexico, a few years before the landing of the Mayflower, eleven churches had been founded, and by 1629 another six in the region of the Zuñi, in six of the "Seven Cities of Cibola." In 1629 Friar Antonio de Arqueaga founded a church in the old town of San Antonio de Senecú, below the Rio Grande, and a year later founded another in the town of Nuestra Señora del

Socorro. Then in 1635 the Church of Isleta in center New Mexico was founded. The list goes on and on; in fact, it is endless. No other nation in the history of humanity founded so many churches across such a vast domain, both in North and South America and against so many odds as Spain and the Spanish missionaries did in less than one hundred years, and we are not counting the many hundreds more that they founded around the globe, especially in Asia, including China, Japan, Cochin China, Tonkin, and Formosa (Taiwan). It is worth noting that in Tonkin (now North Vietnam) the Spanish and French joined forces and fought side by side against the local rulers, and that had it not been for the bravery and loyalty of the Spanish the territory would have been lost. However, in a surprise move at the end of the conflict, the French disposed of the Spanish army sending it back to Manila and seizing absolute control on April 1, 1863.

John McManners had this to say:

About 1630 the far eastern scene had been reconnoitered. At the cost of his life, the Jesuit Bento de Goes had travelled from India to China disguised as a Persian trader, but taking a name proclaiming his allegiance, Abdullah Isai, the servant of God. His five-year journey in 1602-7 across the roof of the world proved there was no kingdom of Prester John and no Cathay but China. Franciscans, Dominicans, and Jesuits had pushed into Burma and Siam in the wake of Portuguese mercenaries who took service with local kings. From Portuguese Malacca and Spanish Manila the friars went to Cambodia and Cochin China, and adventured through the network of the powerful Islamic presence in the Malay archipelago. Of the Jesuits, Antonio de Andrade had crossed vertiginous gulfs on rope-bridges and arches of snow to enter Tibet, and built the first Christian Church there in 1626. Five years later, Francisco de Azevedo was drinking buttered tea with the king of Ladak, a scruffy figure with a necklace of skulls who nevertheless gave him a skeletal horse and two jak's tails as a present. By contrast, other members of the order were deep in sophisticated liaison with the imperial court of China. Around the coasts of India there were solidly established communities of Christians, and in Ceylon, where the Portuguese had successfully intervened in wars between rival kingdoms, the Franciscans had 80 establishments and the Jesuits 16. The Church of St. Thomas was now incorporated in the Roman communion.[120]

Regarding the work and sacrifices the typical Spanish missionary had to endure in North America, Charles F. Lummis had this observation (translation by the author):

> The missionaries who went to New Mexico had to leave, naturally, from Old Mexico, and before that from Spain. Some of those peaceful men, who dressed in gray habits, made long journeys and confronted such dangers unknown by the Stanleys of our time. They had to procure their own garments and church ornaments and pay for the trip from Mexico to New Mexico...The tariff was two hundred and sixty-six pesos, a big hardship for a man whose salary was fixed at one hundred and fifty pesos per year (they were not increased until 1665 when they went up to three hundred thirty pesos, payable every three years.)... With that meager pay, which was all the synod was able to afford, they had to take care of their own personal expenses as well as those of the church.
>
> Once in New Mexico, after completing the dangerous journey... the missionary headed first to Santa Fe. There, his superior immediately assigned him a parish and, turning his back to the settlement of his compatriots, travelled by foot fifty, one hundred, or three hundred miles to his new and unknown post. Sometimes he was accompanied by an escort of three or four Spanish soldiers; but very often he had to make the dangerous journey alone. His new parishioners sometimes welcome him with a thrust of arrows and others with sullen silence. He was unable to speak to them as they were unable to speak to him, and the first thing he had to do was to learn from those reluctant teachers their strange language; much harder to learn than Latin, Greek, French, or German. Totally alone among them, he had to depend on himself and on the favors of his unwilling followers for the bare necessities of life. If the plan was to kill him, there was nothing he could do to defend himself If they refused to feed him, he would starve to death. If he became ill or was unable to function, he had no other nurses and doctors than those treacherous Indians. I do not believe that there is in history any other cases presenting such absolute loneliness, abandonment and despair as

was the life of those unknown martyrs and, insofar as the danger they faced, no other man has ever encountered them to such a high degree.[121]

These words by historian Trevor Davies are also quite appropriate:

> Spanish missionaries, such as St. Francis Xavier and Cosmo de Torres, were to be found in almost every heathen land from Morocco to Japan. It was they who first made known to Europe the most inaccessible parts of Asia and Africa as well as the American continents. At the same time, Spain was the land towards which every Roman Catholic in the world looked for support in time of persecution. Irishmen, especially, fled from the tender mercies of Elizabeth to colleges founded for their benefit by Philip II at Seville, Salamanca, Alcalá and Valladolid...It is probable that no other part of Christendom, Papal or Protestant, had such a high proportion of its clergy notable for learning and sanctity of life. It was chiefly from the ranks of the Spanish clergy that the fearless and devoted Spanish missionaries, already mentioned, were recruited.[122]

One of those missionaries, Saint Pedro Claver, once an aristocrat in his native Spain, personally baptized over 300,000 Indians during his thirty years of service in America and ministered to the blacks in the slave ships docking at Cartagena. His pious hand tended to the suffering of Indians and black slaves alike for which he was also called "The Apostle of American Slaves" (the other one being the Spanish Saint Francis Solano, named patron of Lima and other cities. He was canonized in 1726.) Saint Pedro Claver was canonized in 1888. In North America, the Spanish missionary Friar Junípero Serra founded nine missions in California, dedicating his entire life to converting and teaching the natives. United States historian Francis Bret Harte, in his book *Tales of the Argonauts*, offered this description of the saintly Padre whom he called "the first known pioneer in the history of California":

He approaches us laboriously across a southern plain. He is old and thin, too thin, friendless, alone. He has left his tired muleteers a league behind, and has walked on ahead without a knapsack or wallet, carrying no more than a bell and a crucifix. The plain is typical of the region, one of those that tourists do not like. At once, sun-scorched and glacial, windswept, seared to its very core, cracked with open crevices. As the cruel sun sets the old man falters, bends forward and falls to the ground in exhaustion. There he lies all night long. The following morning, some Indians find him there; they belong to a weak and simple race, and with clumsy friendliness they offer him food and drink. But, before accepting these, the old man kneels, says matins and baptises them into the Catholic faith... This was Fray Junípero Serra, and the sun rose this morning over Christian California... There is no more heroic figure than that of the Franciscan monk, thin, consumed by his journeying, independent and self-denying.[123]

Such was Friar Junípero Serra, on whose memory the "Serra Monument" was erected by the Order of Panama at Old Town in San Diego on July 16, 1759. Also, in 1963, by Act of Congress, the United States minted five National Commemorative Silver Medals honoring Friar Serra as "The Apostle of California." With regard to the Serra Monument it should stand today not in San Diego but across the Potomac, cuddled between the Jefferson, Washington, and Lincoln Memorials. What these great patriots did for the east Friar Serra did it for the west, if carrying with him not a sword but a cross and a book. We should also mention that in 1988 Pope John Paul II declared Father Serra "Blessed." The revered Franciscan, who died on August 28, 1784 at the Mission San Carlos is buried there. When talking about father Serra we must never forget his faithful companion and right arm Friar Francisco Palau, who wrote his biography, *Relación histórica de la vida y apostólicas tareas del venerable padre Fray Junípero Serra*, (Historical Relation of the Life and Apostolic Deeds of the Venerable Father Friar Junípero Serra), published in Mexico in 1787 and in 1944 in Madrid. It is also interesting to note that the successor of padre

Serra, Friar Fermín Francisco de Lasuén founded himself ten more missions in California.

Also in North America, the Jesuit missionary Eusebio Francisco Kino (a distinguished mathematician in Spain and author of the important work *Exposición Astronómica del Corneta*, published in 1681), made more than 50 journeys from his mission Nuestra Señora de los Dolores in Sonora accompanied only by a few Indians guides. He established husbandry at the missions he founded and brought to them cattle, horses and sheep and distributed cattle and seed grains among the Indians. Moreover, he made two expeditions down the Colorado River, reaching on the second the Gulf and reaffirming that California was not an island. He was also the first to map Primería Alta (now northern Sonora and southern Arizona) published in 1705. Until the 19th century it remained the basis for all other maps of the region. Another great missionary was the Franciscan Francisco Garcés as a missionary at the San Javier del Bac Mission, in Arizona, where he remained for twelve years. He later journeyed to New Mexico, Nevada (being the first white man to enter the region) and other distant areas preaching the gospel, founding missions (mainly in Colorado) and converting and teaching the Indians. While in North America he had trekked over 2,000 leagues in an immensely vast area. On July 19, 1781, the Indian chief Salvador Palma (his new Christian name) assassinated padre Garcés and two other missionaries, along with Captain Rivera y Maldonado, one of the founders of California.

Another Spanish missionary, the Jesuit Juan María Salvatierra, while exploring California founded five missions. And another, Friar Bernardino de Sahagún, wrote the first trilingual dictionary in the Americas in Latin, Spanish and Quechua, as well as the first grammar book for the learning of the Nahualt language— *Vocabulario y gramática del Nahualt* (Nahualt Vocabulary and Grammar)—and various studies on Nahualt literature. Today he is widely recognized as the founder of modern ethnology. Another missionary and a relative of the Emperor Charles V, Pedro de Gante, built more than one hundred churches in Mexico where he baptized thousands of Indians and a hospital for the sick who flocked to him seeking comfort and healing. He later wrote the important work *Doctrina cristiana en lengua mexicana*, (Christian Doctrine in Nahua), published in 1528. The Jesuit missionary Alonso Barzana was fluent in eleven indigenous languages and wrote numerous catechisms, grammar books, and dictionaries.

Another Spanish Jesuit missionary, José de Anchieta, did so much good in Brazil that it would take many pages to describe all of his great deeds. He dedicated his whole life to evangelizing and teaching the Indians, especially the children, and founded many schools and missions in the impenetrable jungles of Brazil. He mastered the Tupi language and composed many songs in it for his various teachings and wrote several grammar books and dictionaries. Moreover, he introduced numerous European plants and animals in the region and is credited with the founding of the city of Sao Pablo, today Brazil's largest. He was declared a Venerable of the Catholic Church in 1736.

Much could also be said about two other honorable missionaries, Friar Juan de Zumárraga and Toribio Motolinia, and about literally thousands more who crossed the Atlantic with equal religious fervor and zeal. Another of these dedicated monks deserving very special mention was Florián Baucke, a Jesuit missionary who spent many years in Paraguay. He imbued in the natives of the region (whom he loved dearly) a great passion for music and even organized a small orchestra, teaching them also how to cultivate the land and carve wood for the building of altars, to paint religious images, to make soap, to weave and dye wool, to work iron and silver, to forge bells, and to make missals that looked as if they had actually been printed. And there was Saint Toribio de Mogrovejo, Archbishop of Lima, who upon arriving from Spain in 1581 traveled by foot from Panama to Lima, and in the years he spent in Perú traveled also by foot over 3,000 kilometers, staying in each town some three years until his mission was accomplished. He founded this city's first seminary and contributed to the founding of the Santa Clara convent for poor maidens plus another one for abandoned women. He spoke and wrote Quechua fluently and wrote a catechism in this language. Father Mogrovejo was canonized in 1726 and his day is celebrated in Perú March 23rd. Finally we should mention father Bartolomé Olmedo, who accompanied Hernán Cortés to Mexico, generally considered the first Apostle of New Spain (México) and who it is believed baptized over 2,500 Indians, including Doña Marina.

Every year, over a period of three centuries, the Spanish Crown sent to America over two hundred missionaries at a cost of sixty million pesos. Once the missionaries reached their new American destination, the king was obliged to provide for all basic necessities as well as pay them a salary or "situado" of between 200 and 300 pesos. In 1687, in Perú alone, the Crown had spent over 200,000 pesos in repairs to the churches. All of this clearly evidences Spain's strong commitment to her Christian mission in the New World.

It is interesting to note that when the need arose to establish a single language to facilitate the teaching and conversion of the America's natives, the Spanish clerics firmly and unanimously proposed and advocated not for the use of Spanish or Latin (always the preferred language over Spanish) but for one of the two predominant native languages, the Nahualt for Mexico and the Quechua for Peru, even though the Crown had voiced its concern over such usage. But so they did and quickly began to learn diligently those two languages (plus many others), to use them in their daily teachings, and to write numerous grammar and vocabulary books in them.

Respecting the labor of the missionaries in America, there is an interesting passage by John Gilmary Shea in his book *History of the Catholic Missions among the Indian Tribes of the United States, 1529-1854*, in which he observed:

> A few years since the labors of the Catholic missionaries were ignored or vilified, now, owing to the works of Bancroft, Sparks, O'Callaghan, Kip and others, they occupied their merited place in our country's history...One remarkable fact will, at all events, appear in the course of this work, that the tribes evangelized by the Spaniards and French subsist to this day, except where brought in contact with the colonists of England and their allies or descendants; while it is notorious that the tribes in the territory colonized by England have in many cases entirely disappeared and perished without even having had the gospel preached to them. The Abnaki, Caughnawagas, Kaskakias, Miamis, Ottawas, Chippeways, Arkansas, and the New Mexican tribes remain and number faithful Christians, but where are the Pequods, Narragansetts, the Mohegans, the Mattowas, the Lenape, the Powhatans? They live only in name in the rivers and mountains of our land.[124]

These missionaries devoted their entire lives to evangelize and convert the non-believers into Christianity, the only path, so they thought, to save their poor souls, meaning that they cared deeply for them and thus sought their salvation as well as their general wellbeing. On the other hand, it is quite evident that the English were not in the least preoccupied with such spiritual concerns and it is for this reason that all of the Indian tribes with which they came in contact ultimately vanished. A harsh condemnation indeed. We should also take note here of one Spaniard, José de Escandón, colonel of the militias in New Spain (Mexico) under whose leadership the Franciscans founded a total of 57 missions and the Dominicans 30 in that region; in addition, he also founded 21 towns populated with Spaniards and Indians from Tlaxcala.

Half the world away the Spanish missionaries converged on Asia with equal zeal and perseverance. The Basque Jesuit St.

Francis Xavier, a close friend of the Spaniard Ignatius of Loyola (the founder of the Jesuit Order) at the University of Paris, journeyed to the farthest confines of Ceylon and Japan to propagate his Christian faith. He died in 1552 just before he could fulfill his dream of evangelizing China. In 1575, the priest Martín de Rada made the first Spanish expedition to China. And another Jesuit missionary, Antonio de Andrade, after overcoming unimaginable odds, built the first Christian church in Tibet in 1626. In the Philippines, by 1750, the Augustinian missionaries alone had founded fifty-eight missions with one hundred and eight priests.

One of these missionaries was San Juan de Rivera. After completing his studies at the University of Salamanca, he journeyed to the Philippines and later (1678) to Japan. Back in the Philippines he was appointed Prior of Guadalupe and soon after left for China, where he remained dedicated to propagating the Catholic faith for over thirty-two years, founding there many schools, churches, and hospitals. Although he lost his sight, never did he abandon his evangelical task in China, where he died.

With the missionaries came the colonizers, men of all trades and professions who built the first cities and towns, roads, and bridges, and established the first industries, businesses, and governments. Spain's mission had thus been completed. First came the conquistadors, whose mission was to discover and explore the New World. Then came the missionaries to educate America's native population and to teach them all the virtues of Western civilization. And, finally, came the builders or colonizers to complete the task. Whether she did it right or wrong is not the issue. The issue is that she did it in the best possible way she could and knew how and, with regard to North America, aided by some of her offspring— Mexico, Cuba, the Dominican Republic, Puerto Rico, and others.

The Spaniards, in contrast to other colonizers, and in particular to the English, habitually intermarried with the Indians and Blacks, never professing racial prejudice or bigotry. Hernan Cortés himself married a daughter of emperor Moctezuma, Isabel Cortés de Moctezuma, whose maiden name was Tecuichpochtzin and who bore him a daughter, Leonor Cortés de Moctezuma. He also had a son, Martín Cortés, with his beloved and inseparable companion the princess Doña Marina, daughter of an Aztec chief. At age six he sent him to Spain to be raised as a Spaniard. And he had another daughter, Catalina Pizarro with a Cuban Indian woman. Many of Cortés' captains did the same, including Cristóbal de Olid. José Sarmiento de Valladares, viceroy of New Spain (Mexico, 1696-1701) was married to Doña María Andrea Moctezuma Jofre de Loaisa, fourth granddaughter of the Emperor Moctezuma through his son Pedro Pohualicahualt. Francisco Pizarro, although never married, had four children from two Inca princesses and set the example for wide interracial marriages throughout Peru. His brother, Gonzalo Pizarro, also mixed his blood with one or two Indian women who bore him four or five children. In addition, the Spanish conqueror Hernando de Guevara married Higuamota, the daughter of the Haitian Indian chief Anacaona in 1500. There was another Spanish conquistador named Francisco Fajardo, the son of a Spanish nobleman and Isabel, an Indian princess from the Guaiquerí tribe, whose grandfather was an Indian chief or cacique of the Valley of Mayo in the province of Caracas. Also Diego de Almagro, the Young, the son of one of the conquerors of Perú, who married his servant, an Indian woman by the Christian name of Ana Martínez. And the colonist Juan Betanzos (who learned the Quechua language and became an interpreter for Pizarro) married in Perú the sister of the emperor Atahualpa. Of course, one of the most notorious of such marriages was that of the Inca Garcilaso de la Vega, the son of a Spanish conquistador, Sebastián Garcilaso de la Vega and an Indian princess, who became a noted historian and whose book, *The Royal Commentaries of Peru* (1609-1617) is a valuable source of information for the study of Peruvian history.

Similarly notorious was Saint Martín de Porras (canonized in 1962), born in Lima of a Spanish father and a black creole of Panama. It is most interesting to note that the Spanish brigadier general Félix María Calleja del Rey, who fought against the Mexican independence leaders Hidalgo and Morelos (and was later appointed viceroy of Mexico) married a native Mexican woman for which he was widely respected and praised. As early as 1503, the Spanish viceroy Francisco Roldán had promulgated the assimilation of the Spaniards with the Indians. It is interesting to note that by royal ordinance of 1768, at least one fourth of the students admitted to priesthood seminaries were to be Indians or mestizos.

Nor did the Spaniards discriminate against members of the opposite sex in attaining positions of worth. As a matter of fact, women in general played an important role in advancing Spain's mission in America. The first European women came to America on the expedition of Nicolás de Ovando in 1502. Among America's most famous women was the above-mentioned Doña Marina, known for her extreme beauty, intelligence, and shrewdness. Always by Cortés' side, off as well as on the battlefield, she participated in all phases of the conquest and was Cortés' closest advisor and confidant. Her command of the Mayan, Nahualt, and Spanish languages, coupled with her extraordinary diplomatic skills, strong will, and decisiveness was a key factor in subduing the Aztecs. It must also be remembered that a grand-daughter of the Indian chief Xicontécatl became the governor of Guatemala.

Also, on leaving Havana for Florida in 1539, Hernando de Soto named his wife, Isabel de Bobadilla, governor of that island. Another woman, Beatriz de la Cueva, wife of the conqueror Pedro de Alvarado took over the reins of power upon his death in Guatemala in 1541. Another, María de Toledo, after the death of her husband Diego Colón (Columbus' son) was named to Spain's highest post in America—Vicereine of Hispaniola in 1536. And another, the Haitian princess Anacaona so impressed the Spaniards with her courage and leadership that upon the death of her husband, Caonabo, and later of her brother, Behechio, in 1503, was allowed to rule over her people until she died. Also among the most notable of these women was Isabel Barreto y Quirós, the wife of the famous Spanish navigator Alvaro de Mendaña. Upon his death, right after discovering the Santa Cruz Islands in Oceania in 1595, she took over as commander of the fleet of six ships and 280 rugged conquistadores and brought them to safety. And another, María de Peñalosa, daughter of the Spanish conquistador Pedrarias Dávila and wife of the Spanish governor of Nicaragua, Juan Contreras, gallantly defended her husband's governorship in the civil wars that broke out in 1544 while he was away in Spain. And yet another, Ana Francisca de Borja, wife of the Spanish Viceroy of Peru, Pedro Antonio Fernández de Castro, governed splendidly in his absence for six months (the second half of 1668) and even dispatched troops to stifle a revolt that had just erupted at Portobelo.

In North America, the Spanish Friar Junípero Serra, among others, appealed vigorously for the total assimilation of the Spaniards with the Indians. Such practice continued uninterrupted until the very last day of the Spaniards' presence in America resulting in one of Spain's greatest achievements: the creation of the Mestizo race or La Raza as it is called today. Compared to the British or the Dutch in this regard, or even to the French, the Spaniards showed far greater racial tolerance, sensibility and humanity despite the enormous differences between both cultures. Even in today's Spanish America the British, Dutch, and German nationals live in self-designated enclaves totally oblivious to the rest of society. In North America, first the British and later the Colonists, rarely mingled with the natives and much less with the blacks, and no woman, during that long period of time ever held any position of worth, despite the democratic ideology that was already germinating and taking root in the future United States. It took the United States two hundred years to tear down the barriers of racial and gender inequality and to allow all of its citizens to share jointly in pursuing the American dream.

CONCLUSION

Thus, after 500 years in America, Spain finally departed both exhausted and economically bankrupt and bearing the burden of an unjust world. Historian Salvador de Madariaga was indeed right when he said that Spain bled to death in America. Her only consolation, perhaps her only recompense, was the belated realization that she had contributed like none other to the creation of a new civilization. An America without Spain? Possible. Today's America without Spain? Impossible.

Europe, all of Europe, but especially England, France, and Holland owe an apology to Spain for inflicting so much harm on her both in words and deeds for so long, and for conspiring to re-write history in their favor. And the United States must recognize the immense gratitude it owes to Spain, Mexico, and other Hispanic countries, for having contributed so notably to its history and to being what it is today. In the 18th century the United States was just a little piece of land, hardly noticeable on a world map. One hundred years later it turned into a sprawling superpower commanding an entire continent, two oceans, a gulf, and a sea. Similarly, in the 17th century, Europe was a cluster of tiny kingdoms politically and economically bankrupt. A century later the winds of fortune suddenly swept across the ancient lands and turned them into mighty empires. We now know how and why it happened on both counts.

On the other hand, Hispanics here, there, everywhere, should stop whining, put their house in order and take hold of their lives, looking ahead to claiming their place in the sun which has long been waiting for them.

MAIN HISTORICAL
FACTS BY DATE

Introduction

This appendix includes a chronological listing of main historical facts and events relating to Spain and Hispanics in North America from the 15ᵗʰ to the 20ᵗʰ centuries. Each century is introduced by a brief general topic of interest.

About the name "America."

There is generally widespread confusion when using the name "America." To the North American, America means The United States and "Americans" its inhabitants. Thus, referring to the Declaration of Independence, the Bill of Rights, and the Constitution, we say "America's Charters of Freedom," or the "American Revolution," "American Democracy," the "American Way of Life." When a student in the United States is asked "what are you?" he or she unequivocally replies "I am an American." This is technically incorrect, as we shall see. The word "America" comprises two continents: North America, including Canada and Mexico, and South America, plus Central America and the Caribbean, or the Western Hemisphere. This is what it meant when the name "America" was first coined in 1507 in honor of one of its explorers, Amerigo Vespucci (an Italian) which was totally undeserving. A far more proper name should have been "Columbus" or "Columbia" or, even more appropriately, "Colón," or perhaps "Colombo." But America? Mr. Vespucci owes such recognition to a German publisher. As soon as the name appeared it was popularized by protestant Europe vying against the emerging powerful Spain. Some historians have gone so far as proposing that the etymology of the word derives from a region in Nicaragua called "Amerique", which is totally unfounded. Not even Vespucci himself called it America. In a letter to Lorenzo di Pier Francesco de' Medici from Lisbon dated 1502, he referred to it as "Mundus Novus." The letter was published as a pamphlet circa 1504 and in that same year 12 editions were published, totaling 50 by 1550, and then was quickly translated into several languages. There is another letter containing a narrative of his supposed four voyages addressed to Piero Soderini, dated in Lisbon September 4th, 1504, and published in Florence circa 1505-1506 titled "Lettera di Amerigo Vespucci delle isole nuovamente trovate in quattro suoi viaggi." In 1507 it was translated into Latin by Jean Basin with the title "Quatuor Americi Vesputti Navigationes" and included in "Cosmograhiae Introductio" as a preface or preliminary to an edition of the works of Ptolemy published by Martin Waltzemüller in 1507.

Throughout his book Waltzemüller hails Vespucci as the discoverer of a new world, and in chapter IX foists that fourth part of the world in honor of its discoverer, "Amerigen quasi Americi terram sive Americam" and, thus, coins the name "America" in the map made for that book (which remained unknown for several centuries until it was discovered and re-published by Father Fischer and F.R. von Wieser in 1903.) These were his exact words in translation:

But now that those parts (i.e., Europe, Asia, and Africa) have been more extensively examined and a fourth part has been discovered by Americus (as will be seen in the sequel), I do not see why we should rightly refuse to name it Amerigen or America, namely, the land of Americus, after its discoverer Americus, a man of shrewd intelligence, since both Europe and Asia took their names from women. (*Early American Books and Printing*, by John T. Winterich, Dover Publications, Inc., New York, 1981.)

In a later edition of that book Waltzemüller recognizes his mistake and acknowledges Columbus as the true discover of America; however, it was already too late and the name stuck. Indeed Columbus should have been afforded the honor for being the true discoverer. Additionally, the name "America" should be one encompassing all of the Western Hemisphere, from the tip of northern Canada all the way down to tip of Patagonia, and not only to indicate the United States.

And what about the other terms Hispanics, Latins, Latinos, when referring to the people of South America? Are any of those names correctly used? This is a very puzzling and sticky subject, only because South America is a myriad of cultures and races including both foreign and indigenous. Calling them Hispanics or Latins leaves out all of the native inhabitants such as the descendants of the Incas, Mayas, Aztecs, and others, as well as the Blacks and other European cultures, Portuguese, Germans, Italians,etc. The problem is further aggravated by the fact that all of these cultures have not yet been fully assimilated into what we may call a national culture or race. In other words, culturally speaking, just as in the United States, South America is still "being melted" and we do not yet know if that melting process would ever crystallize. Of course, we cannot call it "The Indies" as Spain once called it ("Las Indias") because it would exclude all of the other races. Besides, in calling them Latins or Latinos we should include also part of the Canadians for their culture is basically Latin as well. Another term that has been used, adding to the confusion, is "Ibero-Americans," but this would also be inappropriate because it would exclude all of the inhabitants from non-Peninsular (Spain and Portugal) extraction.

> *The honor of giving America to the world belongs*
> *to Spain; and not only the honor of the discovery,*
> *but also of its exploration which lasted several*
> *centuries and which has never been matched in*
> *any other region of the globe.*
> *To one nation only belongs the glory of discovering*
> *and exploring America, to changing the geographical*
> *knowledge of the world, and to capturing the*
> *knowledge and trade for a span of one and a half*
> *centuries. And that nation was Spain.*
> *A Genovese, indeed, was the discoverer of America,*
> *but he came as a Spaniard; he came because of*
> *the faith and money of the Spaniards; he came on*
> *Spanish ships; and he took possession of all the*
> *discovered lands in the name of Spain.*
> —Charles F. Lummis

The idea of finding a new, more direct route to Asia by sailing west had been floating around Europe since ancient times. Following Marco Polo's voyages during the 13th century, his vivid accounts (which he dictated while being a prisoner for two years in Genoa) of the wonders of the East triggered a feverish interest in finding the wondrous Asia in all of Europe. Of all the European countries, Spain and Portugal catapulted into prominence and led the way in finding such a route.

In the late 15th century, a seaman called Christopher Columbus appeared on the scene and became the discoverer of what he thought was Asia, or India, but that in reality was America. In other words, he bumped accidently into America on what he thought was his way to Asia. Such a discovery did not come easy for him. Being repeatedly rebuffed first at the court of John II of Portugal and later at the court of the Spanish Monarchs, Ferdinand and Isabella, and after more than eight years of supplication, the Spanish Kings finally granted him his wish. From that moment forward Spain became the Mecca of navigational theory and practice, of cosmography and astronomy, while the rest of Europe scratched its head wondering how all of this could have happened. Columbus sailed from Spain in 1492 and stumbled upon America which he, of course, thought to be Asia.

For the next 100 years, Spain would become the nation to beat, as rival Europe sought desperately to share in the glory. But it was not to be, as Spain accelerated to the head of the pack. By the time the others dared to cross the waters of the Atlantic (following the route that Spain had marked), Spain had single-handedly discovered, explored, and settled most of both continents (with the exception of Brazil), meaning the one to the south as well as the one to the north, for it is erroneously believed that Spain accomplished much in the former and very little in the latter.

As it can be seen from the foregoing, Columbus provided the idea and Spain the means. But, rather than providing the idea (for he was by no means the only one to espouse the idea of reaching land by sailing west) his uniqueness really lay in his unwavering persistence to see his long-held dream come true. In fact, much of that idea must be shared with his brother, Bartholomew (who lived in Portugal when Columbus was shipwrecked off the coast of Portugal in 1476) and with the Spaniard Martín Alonso Pinzón, the pilot who commanded the "Pinta" in 1492. These two men greatly influenced Columbus in the realization of his quest.

The 15th Century

1492

*Columbus discovers America for Spain. Christopher Columbus, Christoforo Colombo, or Cristóbal Colón, a Genovese mariner, discovers America (or the Indies as it was then called) and claims it for Spain. However, it was Spain, and Spain alone, the nation that sponsored the voyage as well as the other three voyages that ensued. This sponsorship was total in every aspect, as Spain provided whatever means were needed to carry out all four voyages—ships, crew (including the Pinzón brothers, whose navigational knowledge and experience proved seminal in their success), money, provisions, etc. Without Spain's support (and vision) in all probability America would not had been discovered at that time, nor would Columbus have been its discoverer. It should be noted that Martín Alonso Pinzón (the Spanish pilot who commanded the "Pinta") contributed 500,000 maravedís of his own money to help finance the voyage, and that two of the ships were owned by the Pinzón brothers—Martín Alonso, Francisco Martín, and Vicente Yáñez. It should also be noted that it was Martín Alonso who convinced Columbus to sail in a southwest rather than in a west direction as Columbus had planned. Eventually he agreed, and half-way into the voyage turned southwest after leaving the Canary Islands.

With the discovery, Spain had paved the way for all future voyages to the New World and, in so doing, gained enormous insight in cosmography, meteorology, sailing, and navigation, which she willingly passed on to the other European nations.

Europe's acquisition of this knowledge was mostly due to the book by the Spanish friar Pedro de Medina, titled *Arte de Navegar* (Art of Navigation), published in Valladolid in 1545, being the very first treatise to provide reliable navigational information on American waters. It was intended to be an instructional manual for voyaging to the New World. So impressed was the Emperor Charles V with Friar Medina's work, that he named him Cosmógrafo de Honor in 1549 (Medina was a teacher of mathematics and a founder of marine science, as well as a librarian of the Duke of Medina-Sidonia.) In addition to charts and sailing directions, Medina made astrolabes, quadrants, mariner's compasses, forestaffs, and other navigational instruments. His "... table of the sun's declination was straightforward and his illustrations of how to hold instruments and apply the rules for finding latitude by celestial observations were excellent (Waters, *Art of Navigation in England*, p. 163)."

As might have been expected, the other European nations swiftly translated Friar Medina's book into their respective languages. The French translation by Nicolas de Nicolai, published by Guillaume Roville, Lyons, 1553 (four years after it was first published in Spanish) proved particularly useful to the wave of French explorers who crossed the Atlantic during the latter half of the 16th century and early 17th century, all of whom won the favor of the French monarchy seeking also to establish a presence in the New World that would rival that of Spain. A total of six French editions of Friar Medina's book appeared before 1600, while the Italian translation was first published in 1554. Thus, by the middle of the 16th century, the route to America was opened to one and all thanks to Spain, to Friar Medina, and to a large contingent of Spanish pioneers.

It is often claimed that the Vikings, led by Eric the Red, reached Greenland in the year 982 A.D., and that Leif Erikson (his son) reached the northeastern coast of North America in the year 1000, being immediately followed by many other such voyages. The only historical record known of such voyages was the one left by Leif Ericson, while the others were never found. However, suffice is to say that none of those voyages had any historical significance as far as the discovery of America was concerned, nor were they acted upon by navigators. In other words, they were simply ignored, becoming nothing more than a saga. The Vikings made camp on the lands they so fortuitously reached and left them exactly as they were found, contributing nothing to their discovery. The noted American writer Washington Irving said it best in his book, *The Life and Voyages of Christopher Columbus*:

> Or if the legends of the Scandinavian voyagers be correct, and their mysterious Vinland was the coast of Labrador, or the shore of Newfoundland, they had but transient glimpses of the new world, leading to no certain or permanent knowledge, and in a little time lost again to mankind.[125]

Further on this issue, major events must be recorded by history, otherwise they simply become a theory or a myth No such event was ever recorded.

1493

*Pope Alexander VI issues a bull dividing the New World (the Americas) between the two reigning powers at the time: Spain and Portugal. Spain was granted rights to the area within 100 leagues (300 miles) west of the Azores and the Cape Verde Islands, while those to the east of that line were granted to Portugal. This is known as the Demarcation Line. However, in 1494, by mutual agreement, the two nations agreed to move the line of the demarcation 370 leagues west of the Cape Verde Islands. Thus, the region that would six years later become Brazil (which was officially discovered by the Portuguese Pedro Alvares Cabral in 1500, although it was visited earlier by the Spaniard Vicente

Yáñez Pinzón who discovered the Santa Marta Cape and the Amazon River, and later by another Spaniard, Diego de Lepe) remained under Portugal's domain while the rest of the New World belonged to Spain, including all of North and South America.

1494

*Signing of the Treaty of Tordesillas (at Tordesillas, Spain) between Spain and Portugal, by which the two nations divided the non-Christian world. In essence, the treaty followed the 1493 papal bull of Pope Alexander VI, which fixed the demarcation line along a circle passing 100 leagues west of the Cape Verde Islands and through the two poles. Thus, Spain was granted the entire New World (with the exception of Brazil), and Portugal, was granted Africa and India.

*Second voyage of Columbus in which he discovers the Greater Antilles (West Indies) Bahamas, Cuba, and Haiti, and the Lesser Antilles, Puerto Rico and Jamaica, claiming them for Spain. Also, he founds Isabela (in honor of Queen Isabella), first city of the Americas (today Santo Domingo.)

1497

*John Cabot, or Juan Caboto, was not English, as it is generally believed, but Italian, born in Genoa in 1461 (as confirmed by the Spanish ambassador to London in 1476.) Although it is claimed that he resided in England before Columbus' discovery, the truth is that he was in Valencia, Spain, in 1492-1493 seeking the support of King Ferdinand for the construction of a port. His second family name was Spanish, Montecalunya ("Juan Caboto en España," "Revista de Indias," 1943.) Upon learning of Columbus' discovery, he thought of sailing on his own voyage following Columbus route in Seville and Lisbon. In 1496 he settled in Bristol, England, and was granted a patent by King Henry VII for his voyage sailing from that city in 1497. Although it is believed that he discovered the coast of North America in that year (Cape Breton Island or Newfoundland), the fate of his expedition is unknown, although there is presumptive evidence that he ultimately reached the continent and that some of his crew returned back to England. It should be noted that on learning of Cabot's plan and of the English king's acquiescence, the Spanish ambassador to London, Ayala, formally protested and notified Spain's Catholic Kings of the intrusion in their New World domain. Cabot's second voyage in 1498 was totally fruitless and forgotten, until England became Spain's rival and alleged Cabot's discoveries as the basis for her rights in America. From this moment forward, England unleashed a scheme of systematic covert operations in the New World, seeking to gain the most by risking the least, which ultimately proved very beneficial to her future economic and political expansion. John Cabot's son, Sebastian, whose birthplace remains unknown to this day (it could have been Venice or England), spent 30 fruitful years in Spain, during which time he married a Spanish woman, Catalina Medrano, the widow of a Mexican settler. He was held in high esteem by Emperor Charles V for his navigational knowledge, naming him chief pilot in 1518.

1498

*Third voyage of Columbus, in which he discovers the South American continent (Land of Paria, Venezuela) and sights the Andes Mountains, claiming all such discoveries for Spain.

1499

*Alonso de Hojeda (or Ojeda) sails from Puerto de Santa María and is accompanied on his voyage by the pilot and cosmographer Juan de la Cosa and Amerigo Vespucci, the Italian navigator in whose honor America was named. This voyage is important not only because of Hojeda's discoveries along the South American coastline following Columbus' route, but also because among its crew were the two famous navigators aforementioned, each of whom had a profound impact in the exploration of the New World.

*Vicente Yáñez Pinzón discovers the coast of Brazil and the Amazon River, and Diego de Lepe ventures further south into the region.

The 16th Century

How could a tiny little country with a population of less than eight million people, barely out of the Middle Ages, poor and politically unstable, and still reeling from 800 years of Arab domination have accomplished so much in so little time thousands of miles away from its shores? This is the question that has baffled the serious historian for centuries, and for which there are not yet clear-cut and convincing answers. In a span of less than fifty years that small country, acting all alone and by its own enterprise, had achieved the unimaginable: the discovery, conquest, exploration, and settlement of two distant continents inhabited by peoples as different from its own as those from an alien planet would be to us today. Spain sent no organized armies and no royal fleets to carry out its mission in America as it did many years later when it sought to silence rival England forever. Quite the contrary. Those Spaniards who voyaged to the New World were ordinary folks who ventured far beyond the sea by their own volition, spurred by dreams of glory and adventure into the unknown. Almost 800 years of combating the Moors in a relentless struggle to drive them out had spawned a new race of titans, a new breed of Amadises, a thousand Don Quixotes capable of grappling with the most awesome task. How else could it be explained? Think for a moment of Francisco de Orellana traversing the Amazon river from its headwaters to its mouth in the Atlantic Ocean, covering an area of over 3,900 miles; of Gonzalo Pizarro making headway on foot through the infested Amazon jungle up the Andes, an area even feared by the Incas themselves; of Francisco de Coronado, trudging thousands of miles across the North American prairies, and of thousands more just like them. Fables of golden cities, of fountains of eternal youth, of ghostly fairy lands and enchanted kingdoms, the fictional world of Amadis of Gaule, now re-enacted in real life. That was the dream that flowed through their veins and that stirred their passion to do so many spectacular deeds, their lofty undertaking. Yet, sad as is to say, for some it was none of the above but simply the cold, calculated, frenzied pursuit of gold and riches and the human tragedy that according to them ensued. For them, the discovery of America was a hecatomb. For us, it was the birth of a great new civilization that may one day rise to true greatness.

The 16th century belongs to Spain and to Hispanics, not only in America but in Europe, Asia, and even in Africa when Portugal became a part of her far-flung empire. And that small country, with its legions of Don Quixotes and Amadises, met her challenge gallantly and showed the world the path to a new beginning in remote but promising lands. A golden age indeed of unsurpassed accomplishments in the great tradition of mothers Greece and Rome.

1500

*The Spanish cartographer Juan de la Cosa draws the first map of the world as it was then known. It is interesting to note that the map disappeared from Spain, and that in 1832 it re-appeared in the library of Baron Walckenaer in Paris, at which time it was published for the first time by Humboldt. In 1853 the Spanish government bought it at auction and returned it to Spain where it is now on display at the Naval Museum in Madrid.

1501

*First European women (Spanish) come to America in the expedition of the explorer Nicolás de Ovando.

*Founding of the first charitable organization in the Americas, "San Nicolás," in Santo Domingo, by a pious black woman.

1503

*Sugar cane is first introduced in the Americas (Dominican Republic.) *The horse, the pig, bovine cattle and fowl are first introduced in the Americas (Dominican Republic.)

*Juan de Quevedo becomes the first Catholic bishop in the Americas (Panama.)

*Fourth voyage of Columbus, in which he explores the coast of Central America from Honduras to Panama.

1504

*Amerigo Vespucci returns to Spain following his successful trip to South America (in which he was accompanied by Alonso de Hojeda and Juan de la Cosa) and is granted citizenship of the kingdoms of Castilla and León. From this year forward he is in the service of Spain and is awarded the prestigious title of chief pilot of the Casa de Contratación, which he held until his death in 1512. He married a Spanish woman, María Cerezo, and his nephew, John Vespucci, is named royal pilot of the Spanish Crown. It should be noted that in 1492 Vespucci was in Seville as an agent of the Medicis, and that he was responsible for organizing Columbus' third voyage. Thus, contrary to common belief, Vespucci, an Italian, spent most of his adult life in Spain where he served the Spanish Crown in all of his explorations. It is believed that on his return voyage from South America he may have discovered Florida (Levillier.)

1505

*Friar Hernán Suárez founds America's first school and Franciscan convent in Santo Domingo, which he called San Francisco.

*Juan Ponce de León conquers Puerto Rico and in 1510 becomes governor of the island.

1508

*Juan de Esquivel conquers Jamaica.

1509

*Founding at Darién (Panama) of the Western Hemisphere's first city, Santa María de la Antigua, 100 years before Jamestown (Virginia) by the British.

1510

*By royal decree the first "Audiencia" (High Court) in the Americas is established in the Dominican Republic.

*Diego Velázquez de Cuéllar conquers Cuba.

1512

*Friar Bartolomé de las Casas celebrates the first Catholic mass in the Americas at Ciudad de la Vega, Dominican Republic.

*America's first cathedral is built in Santo Domingo, Dominican Republic.

1513

*Sailing from Puerto Rico, where he was governor, Juan Ponce de León discovers Florida, so called because it was discovered on "Pascua Florida" (Easter feast.) After landing near the site of St. Augustine, he then turns south exploring the coast to Key West and continuing up the west coast as far as Cape Romano. He then retraces his route and goes back to Cuba via Miami Bay. Although

Ponce de León was not the first navigator to sight Florida, he was indeed the first to land on it thus becoming the first European to set foot on North American soil. On this same voyage, the Spanish mariner Antón de Alaminos observes and records for the first time the currents of the Gulf of Mexico (Gulf Stream.)

*Vasco Núnez de Balboa discovers the Colombian side of the Andes Mountains and, on September 25th, the Pacific Ocean which he names "Mar del Sur" (South Sea.) Soon after he builds two brigantines on the waters of the Pacific, the first two ships built in America.

1515

*Francisco Montejo founds San Cristóbal de la Habana (Havana, Cuba.) *1516*

*Publishing of the first chronicle or history of America (the Indies) titled *Décadas*, written by Pedro Mártir de Anglería.

1517

*Ferdinand Magellan (a Portuguese) arrives in Seville and a year later marries Beatriz Barbosa, daughter of his protegé in Spain Diego Barbosa. He will never again return to his native Portugal, and all of his future expeditions and discoveries will be made in the service of Spain and under the aegis of Emperor Charles V who, jointly with a group of investors, finances Magellan's famous expedition at a cost of 8,751,125 maravedís. Magellan sought to find a sea route to the Moluccas traveling west through the Spanish hemisphere as delineated by the Demarcation Line.

*Francisco Hernández de Córdoba discovers the Yucatán Peninsula and the Mayan Civilization.

1518

*Juan de Grijalva, sailing from Cuba, discovers the island of Cozumel (which he names "Santa Cruz"), the Mexican coastline, and establishes the first European contact with the Aztec Civilization.

1519

*Magellan's expedition sails from Seville on five ships: Trinidad, Concepción, San Antonio, Victoria, and Santiago, carrying a crew of 239 men, most of whom are Spaniards with 44 Portuguese. Magellan commands the Trinidad, and all of his pilots and mariners are Spaniards: Esteban Gómez, Gonzalo Gómez de Espinosa, Francisco Albo, Ginés de Mafra. The chief pilot of the Concepción was Sebastián Elcano, who completed the voyage.

*Alonso Alvarez de Pineda (a pilot of Francisco Garay) discovers the northern coast of the Gulf of Mexico and the coast of Texas, both of which he claims for Spain while ascertaining that Florida is not an island but part of a continent. Following his discovery, he proceeds to Mexico where he meets Cortés at the very moment he is sinking his ships and setting out for Mexico City. He then retraces his route and sights the mouth of the Mississippi River (sighted earlier by Pánfilo de Nárvaez) which he names "Rio del Espíritu Santo." Neither Pineda or Narváez had realized the importance of their discovery until it was in fact discovered by Hernando de Soto.

*Publishing of the first geographies of America—*Summa de Geografía*, written by Martín Fernández de Enciso, and *Geografía y descripción universal de las Indias* (Universal Geography and Description of the Indies), written by Juan López de Velasco.

1520

*Francisco Gordillo and Pedro de Quejos land near Cape Fear (North Carolina), then called Chicora by the natives.

*Sailing on three vessels, Magellan and his Spanish crew reach the "Mar del Sur" which he re-names the Pacific Ocean (the Peaceful or Tranquil Ocean, November 27), and becomes the discoverer of the strait bearing his name—Strait of Magellan (although he named it "Estrecho de Todos los Santos") opening the great ocean separating America from Asia. He then sails in a northwest direction across the vastness of the Pacific Ocean and, on March 21, 1521 reaches the Marianas, and ten days later the Philippines where he is killed by the natives.

1521

*Sailing on the Victoria, Sebastián Elcano traverses the Indian Ocean and rounds the Cape of Good Hope finally reaching Seville on September 9, 1522. Elcano had thus completed the first circumnavigation of the world began by Magellan in 1519.

*Hernán Cortés (Hernando or Fernando Cortez, as he is called in English) conquers Tenochtitlán (Mexico) and claims it for Spain. This event will eventually have a tremendous impact on the discovery and exploration of North America and in the future making of the United States.

*Sailing on the Victoria, Gonzalo Gómez de Espinosa reaches Borneo, the largest island of the Malay Archipelago and the world's third largest island.

1522

*Publishing of the first "Carta de Relación" (Letter to the Emperor Charles V) by Hernán Cortés from Mexico.

*In completing the first circumnavigation of the world, Juan Sebastián Elcano measures its circumference based on which it was proven that the world was indeed round. In addition, he establishes that the other side of the world was habitable, a most remarkable discovery for future explorations.

*Juan Bermúdez discovers the Bahamas (named after him), which were ceded to the Virginia Company in 1612. The company was dissolved in 1679 and in that year it became part of England.

1524

*Esteban Gómez (a Portuguese in the service of Spain) reaches New Brunswick (Canada), and proceeds south along the coast to Florida. On this voyage he sighted the Penobscot River, Cape Cod, the Massachusetts Bay, Narragansett Bay, and the mouths of the Connecticut, Hudson (named "San Antón") and Delaware Rivers. It is worth noting that on the Ribeiro map the entire coastline stretching from New Jersey to Rhode Island was called "Land of Esteban Gómez." On the map of Ribeiro in 1529, that part of North America now New York and New England is inscribed: "Land of Stephen Gómez, who discovered it by his majesty's command in 1525. Trees and fruits like those of Spain abound, and turbot, salmon, and pike." Thus, Gómez is a co-discoverer of that region, together with John Cabot, Verrazano, and the Corte-Real. Edward Gaylord Bourne, in his book, *Spain in America, 1450-1580,* notes the following:

> Spanish explorers had now minutely examined the coast of North America, from Mexico to Labrador, with results of great importance for the history of geography, but of little importance to the building of their colonial empire. That they should have neglected that region where the English where to lay the foundations of a great nation and to embody on a grander scale their most valuable contribution to the political life of mankind, may seem strange, yet it was wholly natural. No empire of plantation appealed to Spain, for she had little surplus population, and too many political irons in the fire to do everything for which opportunity offered.[126]

1525

*Pedro de Quejos explores the eastern seaboard of today's United States and reaches New Jersey.

*The emperor Charles V appoints Lorenzo Galíndez de Carvajal, Postmaster General of the Indies, who establishes the first postal system in the Americas.

1526

*Lucas Vázquez de Ayllón founds the colony of "San Miguel de Gualdape" (or Guandape) near the Saint James River, where many years later the English would found Jamestown. Thus, San Miguel de Gualdape was the very first colony founded by Europeans in North America. (For more about this important historical fact consult, among others, the *Concise Dictionary of American History*, edited by Wayne Andrews and published by Charles Scribner's Sons, New York, 1962; or historians Navarrete, Bolton, and Shea, and also Paul E. Hoffman's, *A New Andalucia and a Way to the Orient*, already quoted.)

*Publishing of the *Sumario*, by historian Gonzalo Fernández de Oviedo. In 1535 he would publish the first part of his celebrated work, *Historia natural de las Indias* (Natural History of the Indies).

1528

*Pánfilo de Narváez reaches Tampa Bay and one of his crewmen, Alvarez Núñez Cabeza de Vaca marches inland reaching Apalache, near today's Tallahassee. Narváez and his men continue along the coast (sailing on five small barges they had built), cross the mouth of the Mississippi River and are shipwrecked by a storm on present day Texas (possibly Galveston or Mustang islands) where he perishes. After the shipwreck, Alvar Núñez Cabeza de Vaca and three other survivors become the protagonists of one of the most remarkable adventures in the annals of exploration. Fleeing from the natives who had held them captives and where they had endured much oppression, they set out on a long journey overland. The names of Cabeza de Vaca's companions were Alonso del Castillo Maldonado, Andrés Dorantes, and Estebanico, an Arab from Morrocco. The foursome continue westward and after wandering over a vast territory finally reach Texas, New Mexico and Arizona, and possibly even California. In the long 8-

year journey (1528-1536) they had trudged over 10,000 miles across the North American southwest, or crisscrossed the southern part of the continent almost from coast to coast! Their amazing story spurred the expeditions of Friar Marcos de Niza and Francisco Vázquez Coronado to the North American west. It should be noted that Cabeza de Vaca was the first European to sight the North American bison ("vacas corcobadas" or hunchback cows) and to write an account of his journey. His *Naufragios*, stands today as the first narrative of North America. De Vaca, together with Andrés Docampo, of the expedition of Friar Juan de Padilla, were the first European explorers to journey an immense territory in North America. Docampo trudged the longest distance, from northern Kansas to the south of Mexico in a span of 9 years!

*Alvaro de Saavedra discovers the Carolinas Islands, which he names "Islas de los Reyes" in western Micronesia, and possibly Yap Island. On his return voyage to Mexico he also discovers the "Islas de los Barbudos" east of the Carolinas.

*Alvaro de Saavedra Cerón, who had been sent to the Molucas by Hernán Cortés to look for the Loaisa expedition, explores the northern coast of New Guinea, and on his return voyage to Mexico discovers the "Oro" (Jobi) island in the Geelvink Bay and the "Almirantazgo" islands in the Bismarck Archipelago.

1530-1531

*Nuño de Guzmán conquers Nueva Galicia (in northern Mexico), which soon becomes the focal point for future northern expeditions, and establishes a government in Guadalajara within the kingdom of New Spain, naming Compostela as its capital.

1532

*Diego Hurtado de Mendoza enters the Gulf of California.

*Francisco Pizarro conquers Peru after defeating the Inca Atahualpa at Cajamarca on November 16. The conquest comes to a close when the Spaniards entered Cuzco in November 1533 and when they found the city of Lima on January 18, 1535. As with the conquest of Mexico, the conquest of Peru marks also a milestone in the future making of the United States for three main reasons: one, because many future expeditions to the north were launched from there; two, because much of the gold and silver mined in that region ended up in colonial America and was used in financing the American Revolution; and three, because many of the future North American explorers, principally Hernando de Soto, honed their skills there and where they made their wealth to later finance their expeditions to North America.

1533

*Ortún Ordóñez discovers Baja (Lower) California on an expedition sent by Hernán Cortés.

*Hernando de Grijalva discovers the "Isla de Santo Tomás" (St. Thomas Island, W.I.)

1534

*Printing is introduced for the first time in America. According to José Toribio Medina (who studied and wrote copiously about printing in the Americas), the first printed book was *Escala Espiritual*, written by San Juan Clímaco and printed by Esteban Martín, under the auspices of Juan de Zumárraga, bishop of Mexico. However, the first known printed book was *Breve y más compediosa doctrina christiana en lengua mexicana y castellana*, printed in Mexico by Juan Pablos in 1535, by order of bishop Zumárraga. The only known copy was found by M. Jiménez de Estrada in 1877. Juan Pablos worked for the German printer John Cronberger in Seville and was sent to Mexico to set up printing there. In 1558, the Cortes abolished the printing monopoly held by Juan Pablos, and Antonio Espinosa set up the second printing shop in Mexico. Engraving first appeared in 1547. During the 16th century a total of 251 works were printed in Mexico, and during the Spanish colonial period over 11,652. In Peru (Lima), printing was first introduced in 1584 by Antonio Ricardo with his work *Doctrina christiana y catecismo para instrucción de los indios*, later translated into Quechua and Aymara. In the North American colonies (U.S.), printing was introduced in Cambridge, Massachusetts in 1638, over 100 years later! The first two productions were printed by Stephen Daye or Day, near the end of 1638, titled: *The Freeman Oath*, and William Peirce's *Almanack*, for 1639. However, the first production in book form ever printed in North America was, *The Whole Booke of Psalmes Faithfully Translated into English Metre*, issued sometime in 1640, by Stephen Daye in the press he called Glover Press, at Cambridge. The authors of the translation were the Reverend Richard Mather, of Dorchester, and his fellow clerics Thomas Welde and John Eliot, of Roxbury.

After Mexico, printing was established in the Americas as follows: Paraguay, 1700; Cuba, 1707; Nueva Granada (Colombia), 1738; Quito, 1754; Venezuela, 1764; Río de la Plata (Argentina), 1766; Nueva Orleans (US), 1769; Buenos Aires, 1780; Santo Domingo, 1782; Montevideo, 1807; and Puerto Rico, 1808. In Manila (Philippines) printing was first established in 1593. During the 16th century, there were a total of 251 books printed in Mexico, and during the Spanish colonial period, the total of books printed was 3,948 titles.

1535

*Emperor Charles V creates the viceroyalty of New Spain (Mexico.)

*Possibly in this year, Friar Bernardino de Sahagún writes the first dictionary of the Americas—*Vocabulario trilingüe en castellano, latín y mexicano* (Trilingual Vocabulary in Spanish, Latin, and Nahualt), as well as the first grammar book—

Vocabulario y gramática del Nahualt (Nahualt Vocabulary and Grammar). He is widely considered the founder of modern ethnology.

*Antonio de Mendoza is appointed viceroy of New Spain (Mexico), thus becoming not only the first administrator of Mexico, but of the New World. His accomplishments were numerous, to the point that he is widely recognized as one of the best administrators, if not the best, of New Spain and perhaps of all of America. Among them were the establishment of the first mint (Casa de la Moneda) in 1535; the first printing press with the publishing in 1539 of Bishop Zumárraga's *Doctrina christiana*, in Spanish; the founding of the Colegios of Tlaltelolco for the education of the Indians (1536), and San Juan de Letrán for the mestizos (1537). He also fostered cattle-ranching, expanded the cultivation of lands, favored the silk and wool industries, and opened new roads and many other public works. Further, he was able to establish a stable government and organize the social, political and economic life of New Spain. Moreover, he sponsored many important expeditions to North America, including: the ones by Hernán Cortés and Francisco de Ulloa to the Gulf and the Peninsula of California in 1535 and 1539 respectively; Marcos de Niza to Cíbola (New Mexico) in 1539; Francisco Vázquez de Coronado in 1540-1542; Hernando de Alarcón to the Colorado River in 1540; Rodríguez Cabrillo to Upper California in 1542; and Villalobos to the Philippines and the Pacific beginning in 1542. Unquestionably, Viceroy Mendoza must be considered a great figure not only of the history of Mexico but of the United States as well.

*Viceroy Antonio de Mendoza establishes the Americas' first mint in Mexico.

1536

*Archbishop Zumárraga founds the first school for Indians in the Americas called "Colegio de Tlaltelolco" and the first for "Mestizos" (Indian and white parentage) called "San Juan de Letrán."

*After voyaging for eleven years, the Spaniard Andrés de Urdaneta completes the second circumnavigation of the world.

1537

*Hernando de Grijalva and Hernando de Alvarado discover the "isla de Guedes" (San David) in the Marshall Islands.

1538

*Francisco de Ulloa explores the Gulf of Mexico.

*America's first university, Santo Tomás de Aquino, is founded in the Dominican Republic. However, it did not open for classes until several years later. America's first functioning university, the University of San Marcos, was founded in Lima in May, 1551; Mexico also in 1551 (September). Many other universities were founded as follows: San Fernando and Gregorio Magno, both in Quito in 1620, and then Real Universidad de Santo Tomás in 1786; Mérida and Yucatán, 1621-1623; Córdoba, Argentina, 1622; Santo Tomás, Nueva Granada (Colombia), 1624, but opened for classes in 1639; Guatemala in 1625, and later San Carlos in 1676; Santo Tomás in Philippines, in 1645; Huamanga in Cuzco, in 1677; Havana, Cuba, 1721; Caracas, 1721; San Felipe, in Santiago de Chile, in 1738; Guadalajara, Mexico, 1791. The first school of medicine was founded in 1768; the first mining college in 1792; the first academy of fine arts in 1785; the Carolina Academy of Law in 1780; the first astronomical laboratory (Bogotá) in 1803; the first botanical gardens (Mexico) in 1788; the first anatomical amphitheater (Lima) in 1753; the first academy of arts and sciences (Santiago, Chile) in 1797; the first nautical and drawing school

(Buenos Aires) in 1799; the first college of jurisprudence (Córdoba, Argentina) in 1791, and the first school of mathematics at the same university in 1808; also the first museum (Guatemala) in 1796. It must be pointed out that during the 16th and 17th centuries, there were 28,000 graduates at the University of Mexico, of which 1,400 received doctoral degrees. Both the universities of Mexico and San Marcos were granted Pontifical status in 1595 and 1571 respectively.

1539

*Hernando de Soto, sailing from Havana, Cuba, where he was governor, lands in Tampa Bay, Florida (named by the Spaniards "Bahia del Espíritu Santo.") He then proceeds inland and in 1540 crosses today's Georgia to the Savannah River. From the Appalachians he marches south along the Coosa Valley toward the coast. Crossing Alabama he reaches Mauvilla, capital of the Indian chief Tascalusa. He then proceeds in a northeastern direction wintering at Chicasa. In 1541 he crosses Alabama and then reaches the Mississippi River (named "Rio del Espiritu Santo"), thus becoming its first official discoverer (Alvarez de Pineda and Pánfilo de Narváez had sighted the river earlier but did not realize the magnitude of their discovery). He then continues west through Arkansas and Oklahoma, reaching the Arkansas River. He is also the discoverer of the Suwanee River which he called "River of the Deer". He dies on the bank of the Mississippi on May 21, 1541. The United States gained possession of the Mississippi through the Louisiana Purchase in 1803. Thus, de Soto, during his 4-year expedition and after trudging over 4,000 miles, discovers and/or explores today's Florida, Georgia, the Carolinas, Tennessee, Alabama, Mississippi, Arkansas, Oklahoma, and Texas. But his discoveries and explorations did not stop there. Modern historical records have revealed that he journeyed farther north crossing the Wabash River to what is today El Dorado, Illinois, and reaching as far as Lake Michigan in today's Chicago. Therefore, his discoveries must include also today's Illinois, Indiana, Tennessee, and Missouri. In addition, he discovered the Ohio River at Henderson, Kentucky, and the Ozark mountains of Arkansas as well as the Missouri mountains. He recorded in minute detail all of his discoveries and explorations thus opening North America to future European explorers. What De Soto really had envisioned was to establish absolute Spanish domain of the land he thought was an island, with the ultimate purpose of finding a shorter trade route to the Orient via the Mississippi, to the Pacific Ocean already discovered by Balboa and sailed by Magellan. With this purpose in mind, he brought with him many skillful explorers, in essence North America's first pioneers and colonizers, including carpenters, ship builders, farmers, blacksmiths, merchants, navigators and engineers, as well as domestic animals and great number of supplies such as seeds, pigs, axes, saws and nails. With De Soto, and later with Coronado, Cabeza de Vaca, and many others, the building of North America, the future United States, had thus begun. It is interesting to note that the De Soto expedition in North America lasted a total of four years, three months, and eleven days, finally reaching Mexico September 10, 1543.

*Francisco de Ulloa ascertains that Lower California is not a country but a peninsula and also discovers its west coast. This is the first time that the name California was used; it was taken from the chivalric novel, "Las Sergas de Esplandián," a continuation of "Amadis of Gaul" (the name had been used before in the "Chanson de Roland", v. 2,924).

*Marcos de Niza sets out from Sinaloa (Mexico) and crosses Sonora. He then sends out the Arab Estebanico to explore the area reaching the Zuñi Pueblos. Estebanico is killed in Cíbola and Niza returns to Mexico after contemplating the Pueblos from afar, which he finds larger than Mexico or Seville. His lead traversed diagonally Arizona, southeast to northeast, and crossed the Gila River.

1540

*Dazzled by Niza's account, the Mexican Viceroy Mendoza organizes an elaborate expedition and names as its commander Francisco Vázquez de Coronado. On February 23rd, Coronado sets out from Compostela, Mexico, taking with him Marcos de Niza, 239 Spaniards and many missionaries. While Coronado marches inland, Hernando de Alarcón sails on several vessels along the coast. Two months later, Coronado reaches Cíbola where he finds a desolate town, a far cry from Niza's exuberant description. On July 7th, he reaches the first Zuñi pueblo, Abiquiú or Hawikuh, which he names "Granada." Here he hears about seven other cities farther north, those of Tusayan (Moquis). Twenty days later, one of his soldiers, García López de Cárdenas, discovers the Grand Canyon which he names "Río del Tizón" (it was re-visited for the first time 200 years later!) In the meantime, one of Coronado's soldiers, Hernando de Alvarado, voyages eastward and climbs up the city of Acoma atop a steep crag; he reaches Tigüex, on the banks of the Río Grande (New Mexico) and discovers many pueblo towns. Another of Coronado's soldiers, Melchor Díaz, founds the village of "San Jerónimo" in the Valley Yaqui (Sonora), while Alarcón, with his fleet, explores the Gulf of Lower California, soon after renamed "Sea of Cortez."

1541

*While wintering in the Río Grande Valley, an Indian informs Coronado of the fabulous country of Quivira and, dazzled by his description, he sets out to find it. In April of this year Coronado and his troops trekked a vast isolated region and after a month realize that they have been tricked. Coronado then sends his troops back to the Río Grande and with 30 horsemen continues inland until they reach Quivira, 42 days later, where they find nothing more than a tribe of poor Indians called Wichitas, in today's Kansas, farther from the Arkansas river and toward the north near

Nebraska. Here they rest for a few days and return to Tigüex after trekking thousands of miles through today's Texas, Oklahoma and Kansas. In total, Coronado and his men had discovered the Far West, the Praderas, the Rocky Mountains, the Colorado River, the Grand Canyon, the depth of the Gulf of California, the culture of the Pueblo Indians, New Mexico, Arizona, the Llano Estacado, and Kansas.

*Gonzalo Pizarro (brother of Francisco Pizarro) discovers cinnamon in the Andes Mountains.

1542

*First North American martyrs—Friar Juan de la Cruz is killed by the natives at Tigüex, New Mexico, and his brother Luis de Escalona at Pecos, also in New Mexico.

*Juan Rodríguez Cabrillo, a Portuguese mariner in the service of Spain, discovers Upper California at Puerto de San Miguel (San Diego Bay, September 28) and the islands of the Santa Barbara channel. He also sights Sierra Nevada. Upon his death, his pilot Bartolomé Ferrelo takes command of the expedition and discovers Mendocino Cape (which he named in honor of the viceroy of Mexico, Mendoza) and western Oregon.

1543

*López de Villalobos discovers the "islas del Coral," "isla de los Jardines" (Marshall Island), "Matalotes" (western Carolinas), "Arrecifes," and "Málaga" (Palau.)

*The first emancipation of Indian slaves in North America takes place when Luis de Moscoso, now in-charge of De Soto's expedition and on his return back to Mexico, liberates some five hundred Indian slaves, men and women, taking only with him about one hundred more slaves who were subsequently emancipated like the others by royal orders.

1544

*Emperor Charles V creates the viceroyalty of Peru.

1545

*Íñigo Ortiz de Retes explores and names New Guinea (because of the black skin color of the "Papuas," the inhabitants of the island.) Although the island was discovered by the Portuguese Diego Rocha y Gomes de Sequeira in 1525, during the 16th century, it was mostly explored by Spain.

1546

*The Americas' first workers union is organized in Mexico.

1548

*Juan de Tolosa, one of Pedro de Alvarado's captains, discovers the silver mine of Zacatecas in Mexico, one of the richest in the Americas. Much of that silver was instrumental in the future economic and political expansion of North America.

1549

*Luis de Velasco is appointed viceroy of New Spain (Mexico), replacing Antonio de Mendoza who was appointed to head the viceroyalty of Peru, and enters Mexico on November 25, 1550. Among the hallmarks of his regime were the emancipation of over 150,000 Black slaves in 1551, and the inauguration of the University of Mexico, the first to function in the Americas, on June 3, 1553.

1552

*Francisco López de Gómara publishes his celebrated work, *Historia general de las Indias* (General History of the Indies).

*A professorship of cosmography and navigation is established at Seville under the control of the Casa de Contratación, which all candidates for pilotship were required to take. By order of King Philip II, all pilots and ship-masters had to keep an accurate daily record of their course, the ocean currents, the weather, as well as a detailed description of all coastlines which they had to deposit with the pilot-master in Seville. This regulation had great importance to the development of early navigational science.

1553

*Friar Alonso de Veracruz becomes the Americas' first professor of philosophy at the University of Mexico.

1554

*Francisco de Ibarra conquers Nueva Vizcaya, founding in 1563 the towns of Nombre de Dios, Guadiana and Durango, and opening many new silver mines, including San Lucas, Sombrerete, Chalcuites, San Martín, and Fresnillo. Agriculture was soon developed and the Franciscan and Jesuit missionaries began founding several missions.

1555

*Juan Gaytán discovers Hawaii. It is fair to say that this discovery remains in dispute. To the English, it was James Cook who discovered it in 1778. To the Spanish, it was Juan Gaytán in 1555 based, among other sources, on various maps of the period such as the map of the Flemish Ortelius of 1587 and the one of Mercator, where Hawaii appears under the name of "Desgraciada." In one of the maps of the 18th century (preserved at the Naval Museum in Madrid), there is a note that says that the Sandwich or Hawaii islands were discovered by Juan Gaytán in 1555 which he called "isla de Mesa." As further proof of this, in 1778 Cook himself found in Hawaii pieces of a Spanish sword and armor (today at the British Museum.) It is also believed that the islands were well-known by the crew of the galleon Manila but they kept it a secret fearing possible pirate attacks.

1556

*The Spaniards reach Virginia 30 years before Sir Walter Raleigh attempts to establish a colony there, and half a century before the visit of John Smith. By this year, Chesapeake Bay was already known by the Spaniards who named it "Bahia de Santa María," where they had sent an expedition which ultimately failed.

1559

*By order of King Philip II, Tristán de Luna y Arellano explores the eastern cost of Florida, including Tampa, then proceeds to Mobile and founds a port at Ichuse (Pensacola.) He continues inland to Manipacana (Alabama river) and sends an expedition to Coca (north of Alabama.) He also dispatches three ships to explore Santa Elena (South Carolina) but they are forced by a storm to return to Mexico.

1560

*The first Catholic church in North America is built in Saint Augustine, Florida, by Friar Francisco de Pareja.

1565

*After driving out the French from Florida, the Spanish set out to establish other missions in the Carolinas, Georgia and as far north as Virginia.

*Pedro Menéndez de Avilés founds North America's first city, "San Agustin" (Saint Augustine) in Florida and establishes various "presidios" (a garrison or military fort) throughout the peninsula.

*Fray Martín Francisco López de Mendoza consecrates the first parish in Saint Augustine.

*Andrés de Urdaneta discovers the shortest and fastest route from Asia (the Philippines and the Moluccas) to North America (Mexico), via the North Pacific following the Kuroshio current along the 42° parallel, thus becoming one of the greatest explorers of the Pacific Ocean.

*Miguel López de Legazpi founds the first permanent Spanish settlement on the Island of Cebu and begins the conquest of the Philippines. In addition, he lands on the "islas de los Barbudos" (today's Marshall Islands) and a bit later on the "islas de los Ladrones" (the Marianas) taking possession of Guam. Earlier, a captain of Legazpi, Alonso de Arellano, had discovered several islands of the Marshall and Carolinas Archipelago (Ruc, among them), and had sailed to Mindanao where he picked up a load of cinammon. In Cebu, Legazpi founds San Miguel de Cebú, the Philippines' first Spanish city. It is interesting to note that here he found a statue of the Virgin Mary, most likely the one given to the queen of the island by mariner Pigafetta of Magellan's expedition.

1566

*In this year and through 1567, Menéndez de Avilés establishes several forts in eastern Florida in San Antonio, Ays, Tocobaga (Tampa Bay), Santa Lucía and Tequesta; and in Georgia (Guale); and in South Carolina (Santa Elena). One of the men of his expedition, Captain Juan Pardo, builds a series of blockhouses inland near the slopes of Blue Mountain.

*Also in this year and through 1572, the Jesuits build ten missions at various sites ranging from Virginia (near Jamestown) to Miami (South Florida.)

1567

*Gastón de Peralta founds in Mexico the Americas' first hospital for the elderly and the mentally ill.

1568

*Alvaro de Mendaña de Neira discovers the Islands of Santa Isabel, Ramos (Malaita), Guadalcanal and San Cristóbal of the Salomón Archipelago. He continues sailing north and reaches the Marshall Islands. Twenty-six years later, in 1595, Mendaña sails again and discovers the Marquesas de Mendoza Archipelago which he names in honor of the viceroy of Peru. On September 7th he discovers Santa Cruz Islands, east of the Salomon Archipelago. Upon his death, his wife, Isabel Barreto, takes over the command of the expedition reaching Manila in 1596.

1570

*The Spanish Jesuit Segura founds a mission in Virginia.

1571

*First voyage of the "Galeón de Manila" (Galleon of Manila) between Acapulco, Mexico, and Manila in the Philippines. The other voyages lasted until 1734. On the way to Manila it brought from Mexico Spanish-made articles, such as fabrics, weapons, tools, etc., and on the way back to Mexico varied merchandise from the Orient (including China, India and Japan). Such voyages contributed greatly to the expansion and development of the California coast.

1573

*The 'New Royal Orders for New Discoveries' is issued, by which the Spanish Crown states that, "... preaching the holy gospel is the principal aim for which we order new discoveries and settlements to be made in the New World."

1575

*Franciscan missionaries arrive in Florida for the first time.
*Founding of the city of Saltillo, in today's New Mexico. This

was one the cities occupied by Zachary Taylor during the Mexican-American War. In Colonial times it was well known for its fairs, where products from Spain and the Philippines were exchanged for Mexican ones.

1578-1584

*Spain commissions a survey to be done by Spanish officials in Mexico—"Relaciones Geográficas," as part of a project to learn about its territories in the New World following the conquest of Mexico by Cortés, which included the making of local maps as well as descriptions of local resources, history, and geography. The survey made a total of sixty-nine maps and was instrumental in the future explorations of Mexico and North America.

1579

*First autopsy performed in the Americas of an Indian at the University of Mexico, to investigate the nature of an epidemic that had hit Mexico.

1580

*Saint Toribio de Mogrovejo founds the Americas' first convent for poor and abandoned women (Lima.)

1581

*Following the Royal Orders of 1573, Friar Agustín Rodríguez rediscovers the Pueblos of New Mexico and founds the San Bartolomé mission there.

*Expedition of Friars Agustín Rodríguez and Francisco Sánchez Chamuscado to New Mexico.

1582-1583

*Expeditions of Antonio de Espejo to western Arizona where he finds silver mines.

1587

*Pedro de Unamuno lands at Morro Bay on the California coast (he was one of the captains of a ship from the Philippines.)

1588

*Captain Vicente González reaches Chesapeake Bay which he calls "Bahia de Madre de Dios."

1590

*Publishing of *Historia Natural y Moral de las Indias* (Moral and Natural History of the Indies), by the Padre José de Acosta.
*Expedition of Gaspar Castaño de Sosa to New Mexico.

1592

*100 years after Columbus' discovery of America, another foreigner in the service of Spain for 40 years, Juan de Fuca (his real name as told to Micahel Lok the British Consul in Aleppo—Syria, was Apostolos Valerianos) discovers the strait bearing his name—Juan de Fuca Strait, between Vancouver Island in British Columbia and Washington State. It was named by the British captain Charles W. Barkley in 1787 in honor of its discoverer. It is interesting to note that a great many modern historical records make no mention of the fact that de Fuca, although a Greek, was in the service of Spain for over 40 years, up to the time of his discovery. For example, in *The American Peoples Encyclopedia*, the entry of de Fuca partially reads: "... It was named by Capt. Charles Barkley in 1787 in honor of a Greek sailor who was said to have sailed through the strait at an earlier date ... ." The author should have added de Fuca was under the service of Spain.

*By royal decree of this year, Friar Pedro de Gante founds in Mexico the Colegio de San Francisco, the Americas' first technical and vocational school.

1593

*King Philip II orders the conquest of Formosa (present-day Taiwan), and Antonio de Valdés founds on May 12th the port of "La Santísima Trinidad" (Holy Trinity) in Kilung or Pacan. The island was discovered by the Portuguese in 1590, who gave it its name ("Formosa" = Beautiful), then occupied by the Dutch in the south and by the Spanish in the north. The Spanish left it in 1641. The first Spanish governor of the island was Antonio Carreño who governed it until 1630.1t is worth noting that while the island was under Spain's domain, the Spanish missionaries labored long and hard to introduce Western Culture there.

*Expedition of Leiva Bonilla y Gutiérrez de Humaña to Kansas or Nebraska.

1595

*Captain Sebastián Cermeño, sailing from the Philippines, reaches Drake's Bay and renames it "San Francisco Bay."

1596

*Sebastián Vizcaíno takes possession of the California Peninsula, which he names "Nueva Andalucía." He continues his exploration through San Diego Bay, and on December 16 discovers Monterey Bay, the long-sought port by the Spanish fleet sailing to and from Philippines. Vizcaíno's voyage was instrumental in widening the knowledge of the California coast. Humboldt himself acknowledged it, and had high praise for the map drawn by the Spanish engineer Enrico Martín, detailing it. Despite the fact that Vizcaíno and his ships sailed by it several times, they inadvertently overlooked San Francisco Bay.

1598

*Juan de Oñate sets out for New Mexico taking with him a large caravan that included 130 soldiers and their families, several missionaries, 83 wagons and 7,000 head of cattle. He crosses the Río Grande through El Paso and continues inland until he reaches the Pueblo Indians. He settles in "San Juan de los Caballeros" and founds San Francisco in 1599, later re-named San Gabriel, both constituting North America's second and third European cities (the first was St. Augustine in Florida). In the same year, he sends Vicente de Zaldívar to explore the east while he explores the west, and passes through the steep Acoma, Zuñi and Mogul toward the Pacific. In the same year, Zaldívar reaches the Colorado River. In 1601, Oñate sets out again on another expedition toward the east and reaches Kansas, crossing the Canadian and Arkansas Rivers. In 1604, he leads another expedition crossing Arizona and reaching in 1605 the mouth of the Colorado. He also founds "San Juan" in northern New Mexico. The expeditions cost Oñate the equivalent of 1 million dollars. The ten missionaries that accompanied Oñate found North America's second Catholic church at "San Gabriel" (today called "Chamita"), in New Mexico.

*Gaspar Castaño de Sosa explores New Mexico, up the Pecos River and crossing the Río Grande.

1599

*Publishing of the important work *Milicia y descripción de las Indias* (Militia and Description of the Indies), by Bernardo de Vargas Machuca.

The 17th Century

Now, after discovering and exploring most of North America, Spain set out to build it and settle it, to make it part of the Western world. With regard to the term "colonize," it must be noted that the term used by the Spaniards from the very beginning was "poblar," or populate, as Spain never considered its possessions in the Americas as colonies, like all other European powers did. They also used the term "ennoblecer" (which loosely translated means "to ennoble".) The Spanish historian Salvador de Madariaga, in his book *El auge y el ocaso del imperio español en América,* explained it this way:

> The Spaniards sought to ennoble the lands they had discovered. Where today we say "to develop" or "to civilize", the Spaniards said "ennoblecer"... This is precisely what Cortés meant when he wrote to the Emperor Charles V in 1524: "In another five years [Mexico] will become the most noble and populated city in the known world." Or Don Francisco de Toledo when he also wrote to the Emperor: "... and now, after the fields have been enriched, we are able to produce it all, and men are settling down and taking root, and buildings are sprouting everywhere ennobling the cities." The task of the state and church was to propagate the faith as an indispensable means to propagate "la policía" (the police), that is to say, the civilization and culture, extending equally to Spaniards and Indians, as men different in character, tendencies, and aptitudes, but equal before the law and the cross.[127]

For the task, Spain turned to the noble and honorable missionaries, who became not only crusaders for Christ but teachers of all trades, as well as builders, cattle raisers, and farmers. The long list of apostolic missionaries included, among many others, Friar Junípero Serra (his first name was Miguel), who came to be revered not only by his own people but by the natives as well. Unwavering dedication, patience, caring, and a profound sense of purpose, were the driving forces behind this man who, almost single-handedly (with some help from his companion Father Francisco Palau), was able to found numerous missions (still standing), some of which served as the foundation of some of today's United States most important cities—San Francisco, Los Angeles, Monterey, and San Diego. In addition, he was a fundamental force in spreading the use of the Spanish language, of intermarriages between whites and Indians, and of introducing in California the first herds of cattle and superior agriculture methods.

In this regard, of calling the Spanish possessions in America "colonies," English historian Sir Arthur Helps had also this to say: "... Colonies is a convenient term to describe the Spanish American possessions, but it is hardly a correct one; they were really attached to the Crown, and regarded as the personal possession of the sovereign." And we add, just as Castile or Aragon were, in other words, former kingdoms that had become provinces dependent on the Crown.

Much is owed to this legion of missionaries and to many of the Spanish viceroys who, from Mexico, organized and sponsored many of the famous North American Spanish expeditions, especially to Viceroy Antonio de Mendoza, who was responsible for the expeditions of Francisco de Ulloa, Friar Marcos de Niza, Francisco Vázquez de Coronado, Rodríguez Cabrillo, Hernando de Alarcón, and others. Archbishop Juan de Zumárraga of Mexico also deserves a very special mention for his efforts in developing early North America.

1600

*Franciscan monks establish several missions in Hopi, Arizona.

1601-1615

*Publishing of the celebrated *Historia general de los hechos de los castellanos en las islas y tierra firme del Mar Océano* (General History of the Spaniards in the Islands and Mainland of the Ocean Sea) by Antonio de Herrera.

1605

*Luis Váez de Torres sights Australia without realizing that he had found what he was looking for. Then, together with Fernández de Quirós, they discover the "Espiritu Santo" island, which the latter thinks is Australia and so names it in honor of the "Austrias" or Hapsburgs.

*The Inca Garcilaso de la Vega publishes his famous work, *Historia de la Florida y jornada que a el la fizo el gobernador Hernando de Soto* (History of Florida and of the Expedition of Hernando de Soto.)

1606

*Luis Váez de Torres discovers the strait that bears his name (between Australia and New Guinea.) He did not realize, however, that the land to his left was Australia or "Tierra Austral" sought by so many other explorers, including Pedro Fernández de Quirós. He did find, however, "Australia del Espíritu Santo" and the magnificent city of "Nueva Jerusalén".

*North America's third Catholic church is built in Santa Fe, New Mexico.

1607

*Publishing of the ethnographical work *Origen de los indios del Nuevo Mundo* (Origin of the Indians of the New World), by Friar Gregorio García.

1609

*After the occupation of Jamestown by the British (1607), Spain is infuriated over the intrusion in its territory and sends Captain Pérez de Ecija to seize it and expel the British. However, Ecija later withdraws and sends Indian allies in his place. Spain tries again in 1611, but King Philip III finally abandons the idea, thinking that the colony would be short-lived.

1610

*Pedro de Peralta, the new governor of New Mexico (then called the Kingdom and Province of New Mexico) establishes its capital at Santa Fe.

*Gaspar Pérez de Villagrá of the Oñate expedition publishes in Spain (Alcalá) his *Historia de la Nueva México* (History of New Mexico), an epic poem in which he describes in detail that expedition. Today, it is widely one of the first works of poetry written in North America.

1611

*Sebastián Vizcaíno is first to navigate from Mexico to Japan.
*Fernando de Trejo y Sanabria founds the first school for girls in the Americas, in Cordoba, Argentina.

*Publishing of the important work *Vocabulario manual de las lenguas castellana y mexicana* (Vocabulary Handbook of the Spanish and Mexican Languages), by Pedro de Arenas.

1612

*Friar Luis de Oré founds several missions in today's Georgia which, in less than two years, increase to 20 in that region (which included Florida), and to 44 by 1633.

1615

*Publishing of the "Historia Natural de la Nueva España" (Natural History of New Spain) is published in Mexico. It is widely considered one of the first and best books on the subject.

1619

*Publishing of the important work "Gramática Chibcha" (Chibcha Grammar) by Padre Fray.

1629

*The Carmelite missionary Antonio Vázquez de Espinosa publishes his work *Compendio y descripción de las Indias Occidentales*, an exhaustive scholarly work describing all of the Americas in detail (geography, people, natural resources, economy, etc.) and, most importantly, the medicinal properties of the "quina" (Quinine) used to combat malaria, which is extracted from evergreen trees of the madder family found mainly in the Andes Mountains from Bolivia to Colombia. The part of the tree that is extracted is called "Cinchona Bark," named in honor of the countess of Chinchón (a Spaniard) who, it is believed, was cured of a fever in 1638. She was instrumental in bringing it to Spain, and from there it was exported to Java and India where it became extremely useful and popular. The book of Vázquez de Espinosa was first translated into English by Charles Upson Clark and published in Washington in 1942. He found the original manuscript at the Vatican Library.

*Antonio León Pinelo publishes in Madrid his *Epítome de la bibliotheca oriental y occidental, náutica y geográphica* (A Summary of the Western and Eastern Library, Nautical and Geographical), the first bibliography dealing with works published in the Americas.

*Friar Antonio de Arquega founds two Catholic churches in New Mexico, one in the town of "San Antonio de Senecú," and the other in the town of "Nuestra Señora del Socorro."

1632

*Pedro Portes y Casanate brings for the first time mercury or quicksilver to the Americas.

*Publishing of the famous book *Historia verdadera de la conquista de la Nueva España* (The True History of the Conquest of New Spain), by Bernal Díaz del Castillo. The book has been traditionally acclaimed as the best on the Conquest of Mexico.

*Publishing (1632-1633) of the work *Grandiosa Conversión* (Great Conversion) by Friar Esteban de Perea in Seville, dealing with the subject of conversion to Catholicism of the Zuñi and Hopi Indians.

1634

*Expedition of Alonso de Vaca to the Arkansas River.

1642

*Friar Jerónimo de Luna founds the beautiful church of Guaray, east of the Rio Grande.

1648

*Pedro Porter y Casanate explores eastern California (which he still thought was an island), and crosses it up to the Yaqui River. He returns in 1649 and explores the western region of the gulf.

1659

*Franciscan missionaries found the mission "Nuestra Señora de Guadalupe de los Mansos" in what is today Ciudad Juárez, across the river from El Paso.

1662

*Friar García de San Francisco founds a church at "El Paso del Norte," in today's border between the United States and Mexico.

1668

*The Jesuits arrive at the Ladrones Islands (so named by Ferdinand Magellan who discovered them in 1521) in the Southern Pacific (which includes Guam) and renamed them "Islas Marianas." They were sold to Germany in 1899 with the exception of Guam which had been ceded to the United States by Spain after the Spanish-American War.

1674-1675

*Franciscan friars found the missions of "San N Nicolás," "San Carlos" and "La Encarnación de la Santa Cruz" in present-day southwestern Alabama.

1680

*Payo Enríquez de Ribera, who was a viceroy of Mexico from 1673 to 1680, seeks to settle California and sends Jesuit missionaries to the region for that purpose.

*Franciscan missionaries found churches in Zia, Santa Ana, Tesuque, Pojoaque, San Juan, San Marcos, San Lázaro, San Cristóbal, Alameda, Santa Cruz and Cochtí, east of the Río Grande.

1681

*The missionary Eusebio Francisco Kino arrives in New Spain (Mexico), and is appointed royal cosmographer of an expedition to colonize Lower California. He settles at Pimería Alta (now N. Sonora and S. Arizona) dedicating his whole life, until his death in 1711, to his missionary work. From his mission of "Nuestra Señora de los Dolores" in Sonora, he made more than 50 journeys, frequently traveling alone or with Indian companions or guides. He founded over 20 missions, among them, "San Javier del Bac" (Tucson), and built many churches. He established agriculture at all of his missions and brought in cattle, sheep, and horses, and distributed seeds among the Indians. In 1701 he made two expeditions down the Colorado River, reaching the head of the Gulf and re-establishing that California was not an island. He was the first to draw a map of Pimería Alta, which remained the basis of exploration in that region until much later. By 1702 he had baptized over 100,000 Indians and wrote several books about his expeditions. Among his collaborators were the padre Juan María Salvatierra and Captain Mange.

1686

*Friar Alonso de Posada writes the best description of the land of Teguayo, as part of a special report to the Council of the Indies. Teguayo, together with Quivira, comprised parts of Utah, Oregon and California.

1690

*Alonso de León and the padre Damián Massanet found two missions in Texas on the bank of the Neches river.
*Founding of the province of Texas.

1692

*Diego de Vargas Zapata reconquers New Mexico.
*Spanish missionaries baptize over 2,000 Indian children in New Mexico.

1693

*Domingo de Terán becomes the first governor of Texas.
*Diego de Vargas Zapata sets out on his second expedition to New Mexico, taking with him a caravan of soldiers, families, 18 priests, allied Indians, cattle and carriages, foodstuffs and tools, becoming a predecessor of the American West's Wagon Trains.
*Publishing in Mexico of the Americas' first newspaper, "El Mercurio Volante."

1695

*José Sarmiento de Valladares founds Loreto Harbor or Sacramento, the future capital of California.

1697

*Beginning in this year, Friar Juan Maria de Salvatierra founds five missions in Baja California, also exploring the region in all directions.

1699

*Cotton Mather writes North America's first book written in Spanish, *La fe del cristianismo. La religión Pura en Doze Palabras Fieles, dignas de ser recibidas por Todos* (Faith of Christianity. Pure Religion in Twelve Faithful Words, Worthy to be Received by All.)

The 18th Century

Two hundred years have passed since Rodrigo de Triana sighted for the first time American land. Most nations, giving the same circumstances, would have packed their bags and left after such a long time, if not sooner. Why stay? What else could America offer that would entice people to call it home?

If it would be true that the Spaniards came and seized all of America's gold and riches, would it not be logical that they would go back to Spain, the land they held so dear, and live the rest of their lives in comfort and luxury? Today, if you emigrate to a foreign country, work hard, make and save enough money, you then move back to your native country a rich person and live happily ever after.

But not always, not in the case of the Spaniards of the 16th century. They came to America, "made it here," and stayed, and those who went back to Spain longed to return and eventually did and immediately became "Americans." They took roots, deep roots, married, had children born here, and spent the rest of their lives living out the American dream. Hernán Cortés himself went back to Spain in 1528 but returned to Mexico two years later (1530), then back to Spain again in 1540. He died in Seville in 1547 on his way back to his beloved Mexico where he wanted to spend the rest of his years. Today he is buried in Mexico, in the

Hospital de Jesús, and although his remains were hidden during the Mexican Independence, they were re-discovered in the same place in 1946.

That bonding between Spain and her American possessions became ever so stronger and deeper with the passing of time. It must be remembered that some of South America's honorable liberators, Bolívar, San Martín, and Martí spent many years in their mother country. Bolívar to pursue his studies (in Madrid, in 1802, he married a lady from this capital city, María Teresa Rodriguez del Toro. His mother, María de la Concepción was a native of Castile, and his father's ancestors were originally from Vizcaya). San Martín (son of a Spanish officer in the New World), for the same purpose (in 1784 studying at the Real Seminario de Nobles), and while in Spain he joined the army and over a period of twenty-two years took active part in many battles and wars, 31 in total. Martí (whose father was from Valencia, and whose mother, Leonor Pérez, although born in Cuba, was the daughter of Canary Island's parents) also for the same purpose, although because of his revolutionary ideas and ties with the known revolutionary Fermín Valdés, was deported to Spain. But it was here in Spain where Martí was able to nurture and foster his ideas of independence, and where he published *El presidio politico en Cuba* (Political Imprisonment in Cuba) while studying Law and Philosophy and Letters at the universities of Madrid and Zaragoza.

Thus, the Spaniards remained in America for another 300 years up to 1898. Why? What attracted them so much about America? Why hold on to something without a need or purpose? Well, perhaps there was no need, but there was indeed a purpose, which was none other than to complete the mission to which they had committed themselves after 1492. The 18th century was no different from the previous one—more discoveries and explorations, more daring incursions into the unknown, more building and establishing of institutions, and perhaps a greater desire to understand the new surroundings and the native cultures.

Regarding American history, that is to say the history of the United States, the 18th century is very significant in terms of Spain's involvement in the American Revolution, which began many years prior to 1776, and continued for many years after. It is a known fact that Spain played a key role in achieving the just cause of the American colonists, becoming one of their stronger allies, if not the strongest, a fact that only a handful of people today know and are willing to acknowledge. In the hundreds of American history textbooks we have read over the years, no mention is made of this fact, not even in passing. It took a courageous woman, American historian Buchanan Parker Thomson to bring it to light in 1976, but in spite of this, it continued to be ignored to this day.

1702

*Bernardo de Egoy explores the islands of Uluti, Palau and Sonsorol (Carolinas).

1706

*Governor Francisco Cuerzo y Valdez founds the city of Albuquerque.

*Juan de Ulibarri explores the region of the Arkansas River.

1716

*Domingo Ramón founds in Texas (near de Neches and Angelina Rivers), four missions and the presidio of Dolores.

1718

*Martín de Alarcón founds "San Antonio de Béjar" (San Antonio, Texas.)

*Juan María Rivera discovers the Rocky Mountains.

1719

*Expedition of Antonio Valverde to the prairies.

1720-1722

*The Spaniards permanently occupied Texas, mainly through the efforts of the Marquis de Aguayo, then governor of Coahuila.

*Friar Antonio Margil de Jesús founds the Mission of "San José" and "San Miguel de Aguayo" in San José Valley in Texas.

*Martin de Alarcón is appointed first governor of Texas.

*Pedro de Villazur founds a colony in the "Rio de Jesús y María" (North Platte River, in Arkansas).

1721

*The Marquis of San Miguel de Aguayo, governor of Coahuila, establishes a presidio at Los Adaes and another at Bahía, where the Fort of Saint Louis would later be built. In total, at the end of his expedition, he had founded ten missions and four forts.

*The 10-room Spanish Governor's Palace is built in San Antonio, Texas. It served as a residence and court for the Spanish governors.

1722

*Publishing of America's first newspaper, "Gaceta de México" in Mexico City, by Juan Ignacio de Castorena. Other newspapers followed: "Gaceta de Guatemala," 1729; "Gaceta de Lima," 1743; "Gaceta de La Habana," 1764; "Gaceta de Caracas", 1808.

1731

*Spanish missionaries found a colony at San Antonio called "San Fernando" (Texas), and the first mission in Arizona.

1735

*Spanish is first taught in the schools of New York City.

1746

*From this year through 1755, José de Escalón founds a total of 21 towns, 57 Franciscan missions and 30 Dominican missions. The region extended from the north of the Río Grande to the Nueces River in today's Texas.

1748

*The Jesuit Consag explores the depths of the Gulf of California and establishes a base for the explorations of the Gila and Colorado valleys. He becomes a great protector of the Indians, and plays a key role in keeping the French and English from invading Texas.

*Publishing of the important work *Relación histórica de la América meridional, hecho de orden de S.M. para medir algunos grados del meridiano terrestre y venir por ello en conocimiento de la verdadera figura y magnitud de la Tierra*, by Antonio de Ulloa, who in 1766 was appointed governor of Louisiana and who also discovered the properties of platinum in New Granada (Colombia) in 1780. His book was translated into English in 1758 under the title *A Voyage to South America*.

1749

*José de Escandón explores "Nuevo Santander" (extending to the southern-most region of today's Texas, between the Río Grande and Nueces Rivers), and founds the city of Laredo.

1751

*The viceroy of New Spain, Juan Francisco Güemes de Horcasitas orders the construction of two presidios at Altar and Tubac, in Sonora, New Mexico to contain the attacks of the Pimas Indians.

*Publishing of the first textbook for the study of Spanish in the United States in New York, *A Short Introduction to the Spanish Language*, by Garrat Noel.

1757

*Father Andrés Burriel, a Jesuit scholar, publishes in Madrid *Catálogo de California* (Catalog of California). It was immediately translated into French, English, Dutch and German and it renewed the interest in finding the elusive Northwest Passage.

1760

*By this year it is estimated that the Spanish missionaries had baptized (christianized) over 10,000 Indians in Texas and New Mexico alone.

1761

*Spain intervenes in the Seven-Year War between France and England (1756-1763), in which the latter wins and France cedes (by Treaty of Paris) Canada and Louisiana east of the Mississippi, and Spain cedes Florida. To compensate Spain for the loss, France cedes the Louisiana territory between the Mississippi and the Rocky Mountains, its last territorial domain in North America. Thus, North America, at this juncture, is separated by two territories divided by the Mississippi: Spanish to the west and English to the east, with the French totally excluded.

1762

*The Americas' first library is established in Mexico. Other libraries that followed were: Bogota, 1777; Havana, 1793; Quito, 1792.

1765

*Juan María Rivera, coming up into the San Juan Valley (Colorado), explores the Silver Mountains which he calls "La Plata."

1766

*Antonio Ulloa takes over as governor of Louisiana.

*Spanish is added for the first time to the list of courses offered at the University of Philadelphia.

*Several presidios are established from Sonora to Texas, and José de Gálvez, Minister of the Indies, establishes the "Comandancia General de las Provincias Internas" (General Command of the Internal Provinces), which included Nueva Vizcaya, Sinaloa, Coahuila, Sonora, New Mexico, California and Texas. After the Mexican independence, the province of Nueva Vizcaya was divided into the states of Chihuahua and Durango.

1767

*The Jesuits are expelled from North America and are replaced by the Franciscans.

1768-1774

*Fray Francisco Tomás Hermenegildo leads four expeditions to the Gila and Colorado rivers.

1769

*Gaspar de Portolá discovers San Francisco Bay (called by the Spaniards "Bahia de los Farallones", and later by the Franciscans "San Francisco"), and founds the cities of San Diego and Monterey. Accompanying him was the famous Franciscan friar Juan Junípero Serra who organized the first mission of California, "San Carlos Borromeo." Much is owed to the Franciscan missionaries in developing the region (planting olive trees and vineyards, building numerous churches and teaching the Indians), and very especially to Friar Serra. The region was later organized and developed by José Gálvez.

Friar Junípero Serra is one of the glories of North American history, a tireless pioneer who not only founded numerous missions in California, but in essence was its true founder along with a legion of followers, many of them Indians who revered him. He accompanied Gaspar de Portolá to Monterey in 1970 at age 36 where he founded the above-mentioned mission. After founding two more, he returns to Mexico City with Portolá to report to Viceroy Bucareli, presenting him with a "Representación" or account of his work, which sets the basis for the final organization of California. He remained in California until his death, totally committed to his evangelical pursuits, constantly traveling the region mostly by foot as president of the nine missions he had founded, including the one in San Francisco in 1776, and the one in town of San Gabriel, which later became Los Angeles. It is believed that he personally baptized 5,800 Indians. His system consisted of grouping the Indians in towns near the missions where he taught to men and women the arts of agriculture, cattle breeding, arts and crafts, among others. He and his fellow missionaries were instrumental in spreading the use of the Spanish language, of mixed marriages between Spaniards and Indians or between christianized and non-christianized Indians. Some of the missions he founded were: San Carlos Borromeo (which he later moved to Carmel by the Sea becoming his permanent headquarters), San Antonio de Padúa (1771), San Gabriel Arcángel (1771), San Luis Obispo (1772), San Juan Capistrano (1776), San Francisco de Asís (1776), Santa Clara de Asís (1777), and San Buenaventura (1782.) These missions served as the foundations of some of North America's greatest cities, including San Francisco, Monterey, and Los Angeles. His closest companion, Friar Francisco Palau, wrote his best biography, *Relación histórica de la vida y apostólicas tareas del venerable padre fray Junípero Serra*, published in Mexico in 1787, and translated into English in 1958 under the title: *Life and Apostolic Labors of the Venerable Father Junipero Serra*. As stated, North America owes much to Friar Serra and his followers, as well as to Mexico, for it was there where he arrived from Spain in 1749 and where he remained until 1758, founding the missions of Sierra Gorda at Querétaro, and gaining the knowledge and experience that would prove invaluable in the future development of California.

1770

*The city of Saint Louis (Missouri) is transferred to Spain under an earlier agreement.

1772-1775

*Domingo de Boenechea explores Tahiti which he calls "Isla de Amat" (in honor of the viceroy of Peru.)

*Also in 1772, José Celestino Mutis publishes in Madrid his famous *Flora de Bogotá*, a monumental work on the flora of New Granada, which continues to be highly praised until this day by the world's scientific community. The book was the fruit of his scientific expedition to Colombia, which cost the Spanish Government at the time 230,000 pesos. It was profusely illustrated by the best artists of the time, containing over 6,840 illustrations (engravings), of which 6,717 are preserved today at the Botanical Garden in Madrid. It is worth noting that in 1817 General Morillo had this treasure shipped to Spain, including over 6,000 plants of all kinds and other important specimens.

1773

*Felipe Tompson explores the Islands of "Pasión" (Nagaluk) and "Bajo Triste" (Oraluk) in the Carolinas.

1774

*Juan Pérez explores the coast of the Pacific Northwest where he had been sent by the Spanish viceroy to investigate Russian intrusion down the northern coast. He then makes contact with the natives of Queen Charlotte Island, sights Vancouver Island and discovers Nootka Sound, which he names harbor of "San Lorenzo." The diary of one of his companions, Juan Crespi, narrates in detail the voyage.

1775

*Bruno Hezeta discovers the mouth of the Columbia River, which he calls "Bahia de la Asunción", and Juan Francisco de la Bodega y Cuadra reaches Sitka, and also discovers Bodega Bay, near San Francisco.

*Francisco Garcés, of the expedition of Captain Juan Bautista Anza, goes up the Colorado and crosses the Mojave Desert, becoming the first European to set foot on present day Nevada; he then crosses the Sierra Nevada and reaches the central California valley; he then recrosses the Sierra Nevada until finally reaching the Moquis in northeast Arizona. His expedition diary is one of the most famous geographical documents of the North American West. In total, he had trekked almost 10,000 miles and made a great contribution to the knowledge of the North American southwest from New Mexico to California.

*Domingo de Boenechea takes possession of the island of Tahiti.

1776

*Friars Silvestre Vélez de Escalante and Francisco Anastasio Domínguez, with seven other companions, set out from "Santa Fé de Nuevo México" toward "Sierra de Plata", and followed a northeastern route cross the Rocky Mountains to an area still unknown to white men (the tributaries of the Colorado River).

Then they continue toward the "Dolores Valley" and the "Rio de San Javier" (Grand River), cross the "Rio Buenaventura" (Green River) and discover the "Lago de los Timpanogos" (Lake Utah) and the region that would later comprise the state by the same name, the Sevier River, the northern tributaries of the Colorado River, the Wasatch Mountains, and marked a southwestern route later called The Old Spanish Trail. It is worth noting that while exploring the area they wrote detailed accounts of their expeditions as well as the customs of the natives. Two rivers and various geographical sites in that region have been named in honor of these two friars by the United States government.

*Juan Bautista de Anza founds the city of San Francisco, California.

1777

*Bernardo de Gálvez, who at one time was governor of Louisiana and Florida, takes active part in the American War of Independence seizing from the British several cities and towns, such as Baton Rouge (1779), Panmure (1779), Mobile (1780), Panzacola (1781) and all of western Florida. In addition, he chased the British contraband and fostered trade between France and the United States. Galvestown, in Texas, was named in his honor. His uncle, José de Gálvez, sent Franciscan missionaries to California and promoted the settling of that region. He established the naval base of San Blas at Tepic, and founded several colonies and towns. In 1769 he sent the first expeditions of Portolá and Rivera y Moncada, who were accompanied by Friar Junípero Serra. He also established forts along the Gulf of Mexico and the California coast, and the "Comandancia General de las Provincias Internas" (General Command of the Internal Provinces), and promoted the Solano expedition. Because of the victories of Bernardo de Gálvez, British pressure subsided on George Washington, who was then able to open the supply lines not only of money but also of military goods from Spain, Mexico, and Cuba.

*The town of San José, California is founded.

*Louisiana becomes a dependency of the Audiencia de Santo Domingo and later of Cuba.

1779

*On his second expedition, Juan Francisco de la Bodega y Cuadra and Ignacio Arteaga explore northern Alaska.

*Salvador de Muro y Salazar, Marquis of Someruelos, is first to cross the Atlantic sailing on a brigantine from Spain to Cuba.

*The Spanish establish a permanent settlement at Nacogdoches, Texas.

*The Spanish expelled the British from Honduras as allies of the American Revolution.

1781

*The "El Pueblo de Nuestra Señora de Los Ángeles de Porciuncula" (Los Angeles, California) is founded, and continues to be the capital until 1846 when it is captured from Mexico by the United States.

*The Spanish forces, led by Cruzat, defeat the British at Saint Joseph, Missouri (now under Spanish domain), as part of Spain's campaign in favor of the American Revolution.

1783

*By the Treaty of Versailles, Spain recognizes United States independence and is giving back Florida. At this juncture, most of the North American territory falls under Spanish domain, including Louisiana (comprising at the time all lands west of the Mississippi) and the entire southern region from coast to coast. In other words, most of today's United States. However, Spanish domain was short-lived. As expected, a conflict soon breaks out between Spain and the United States. By the Treaty of 1795, the border between Florida and the United States was set at the 31° degrees rather than at the 32'28 as previously set. By the Treaty of San Idelfonso of 1800, Spain cedes to France Louisiana, but before taking possession of it, Napoleon sells it to the United States which officially took it over in 1803.

1784

*Benjamin Franklin is elected the first correspondent in the United States of the Spanish Royal Academy of History. Franklin studied Spanish and read it well.

1785

*The United States and Spain sign the Pinckney Treaty grating the former the first navigational rights on the lower Mississippi.

1786

*Pedro Vial begins planning the Spanish Trail linking San Agustín and San Diego.
*The mission Santa Bárbara is founded.

1787

*Publishing in Madrid of the critically important work *Diccionario geográfico de las Indias Occidentales* (Geographical Dictionary of America and the West Indies), by Antonio de Alcedo. The first English translation done by G.A. Thompson appeared in London in 1812. A magnificent work in 5 volumes, this work contains thousands of entries and articles on New York, Cuzco, Texas (or Nuevas Filipinas), Mexico, California, Oaxaca, with dozens of charts and tables. It is worth noting that this important work was published before Humboldt's encyclopedia.

1789

*Esteban José Martínez reaches Nootka and finds that the English are trying to establish a colony there; he expels them, but by the Treaty of El Escorial of 1790 Spain cedes it to England.

*The colony of New Madrid (Missouri) is founded after having been purchased from the Spanish.

*Publishing of *Historia de California* (History of California) in Italian, by the Jesuit Francisco Javier Clavijero.

1790

*Francisco Elisa explores the coasts of Alaska. In the same year, by the Treaty of El Escorial, Spain grants England the right to occupy Nootka (Alaska), which does not take effect until 1794.

*The Spaniards explore a city in Alaska which they name "Valdés" (Valdez.)

1791

*Alejandro Malaspina explores the region between Alaska and Nootka. The Malaspina Glacier in southeast Alaska is named in his honor. His expedition sights Mounts Edgecumbe, Fairweather and "San Elías", and in June of that year readies Mulgrave Harbor and explores Prince William Sound and Montague Island. A year later, in 1792, the expedition passes through New Hebrides, New Zealand and Sidney, Australia, and Mindanao. At the end of the five-year voyage, Malaspina had gathered an extraordinary amount of scientific data and measured latitudes and longitudes with precision.

1792

*Dionisio Galiano and Cayetano Valdés, sailing on the Sutil and Mexicana, explore the Straits of Juan de Fuca and Georgia, while at the same time Jacinto Caamaño re-explores the islands of "Principe de Gales," "Reina Carlota," "Revillagigedo," and

Aristizábal (western Archipelago of the Canadian coast and southern Alaska.)

1794

*Spain takes possession of Nootka Sound in Vancouver Island. It is interesting to note that Nootka Sound was named "Bodega" (for Juan Francisco de la Bodega y Quadra, one of its discoverers), and Vancouver, which ultimately was the one that prevailed. It is also worth noting that José Mariano Mozino spent time in Nootka and carried out in-depth studies of the language, religion, government and customs of the region, writing also a dictionary about the Nootka language.

1795

*By the Treaty of San Lorenzo de El Escorial (October 27th), Spain cedes to the United States a vast area in eastern Florida, from which the United States later carves out the new state of Mississippi. Also by this treaty, their respective new borders on the North American mainland are agreed upon and set.

*Fernando Quintano explores the Island of "San Bartolomé" (Taongui) in the Carolinas.

*Carlos Fernández Martinez, Marquis of Casa-Irujo, Spanish ambassador to the United States, uncovers Senator Blount's conspiracy to seize the states of Florida and Louisiana from Spain. The Marquis was married to Theresa Mac Kean, the daughter of the governor of Pennsylvania and president of the U.S. Congress.

1797

*Work begins to build the main church of San Juan Capistrano, the most magnificent example of Spanish California to date.

1798

*The United States Congress establishes the state of Mississippi out of the lands previously ceded by Spain.

*Frontiersman Daniel Boone receives a grant from the Spanish government in Louisiana consisting of 850 acres in Missouri where he settles in 1799.

*Alexander von Humboldt arrives in Spain through the Pyrenees and meets Don Mariano Luis Urquijo, minister of Charles IV, with whom he discusses his project for a scientific expedition to America. On May 7, 1799, the king grants him permission and orders all Spanish officials in the Americas to provide assistance. He sails from La Coruña on the frigate Pizarro July 5th, taking with him various scientific instruments and books. The voyage lasted five years, and his itinerary included stops at the Canary Islands, Venezuela, Cuba, New Granada, Peru, Mexico, Philadelphia, and Bordeaux where he landed in 1804. While in America he covered over 17,000 kilometers and voyaged as far as the Orinoco jungle. Riding by mule, he traveled from Cartagena de Indias to Lima, and then from Acapulco to Veracruz and to most of New Spain. In Quito he climbed the Chimborazo, the highest altitude reached by man until that time. In those five years he observed and studied all of America, took geographical and astronomical measurements, studied animals and minerals, as well as people, customs, the colonial history, economy and society, writing incessantly and recording every detail. Humboldt's work comprises an incredible 30-volume encyclopedia, which he wrote with the collaboration of his close friend A.J.A. Bonpland, and which he titled *Voyage aux regions équinoxiales du nouveau continent*, published in Paris in 1807-1827. This important scientific expedition by Humboldt was entirely sponsored and financed by Spain.

The 19th Century

The Thirteen Colonies, now free and independent, look beyond the Mississippi seeking control of the entire continent. Toward this end, they devised a daring and ingenious (and rather unpopular) political plan which quickly bore fruit. In just a few short years, the fledging nation was able to claim a vast territory extending west all the way to the Pacific Ocean and to the south to the Gulf of Mexico and the Caribbean Sea. The present-day geographical configuration of the United States was just about to take shape. The immense territory—actually two-thirds of today's United States—was no Mexico or Peru of the 16 century; in fact, by the mid-1800s, when that expansion was in full swing, most of North America had been transformed from a desolate wilderness into a fairly developed area with the seeds of Western Civilization sprouting everywhere. Texas, California, Arizona, Louisiana and others areas were well on their way to join the civilized world.

That world was created by Spain and jointly developed with Mexico, and, as stated before, had it not been because of them, that expansion would have never taken place, or would have been delayed for at least another one hundred years. After all, the American West was now in far better shape than Mexico or Peru when the Spaniards arrived in the 16 century. On the other hand, Spanish-America, mostly following the lead of its northern neighbor, seeks to also sever the umbilical cord and carve out its own destiny. First Argentina in 1810, then Paraguay in 1813, Nueva Granada in 1819, Mexico, Venezuela and Peru in 1821; one by one, in a span of just a few years, steered away from their mother country seeking to stand on their own two feet. By 1898 it was all over, prompting Segismundo Moret y Prendergast, foreign minister of Spain at the time of the Spanish-American War, to exclaim in front of the Spanish Parliament: "We come from a glorious but tired race!"

Indeed, Spain was tired, exhausted, with all of its blood drained after 300 long years in America. No other nation in modern times has been able to hold on to such an awesome task, especially when being constantly harassed by so many powerful countries, almost since the day it set foot in America. After its departure, climaxing with the Spanish-American War, it took Spain many years to realize that in life all must come to an end, including the mightiest of empires.

At the beginning of this century the Jesuit Order, founded by the Spaniard San Ignacio de Loyola in 1540, had established missions in the following present-day U.S. states: Michigan, Illinois, Indiana, Ohio, Iowa, and Missouri, and some years later in Arkansas, Louisiana, Mississippi, Pennsylvania, and others.

1800-1801

*Juan de Ibargoitia explores the islands of Palau, Unup, Puluot and others in the Carolinas.

*President Thomas Jefferson is informed of Spain's plans to cede the Louisiana territory to France, and is alarmed by the consequences as he considers France, or rather Napoleon a formidable opponent.

1802

*Juan Lafita explores the Island of "Matalotes" in the Carolinas.

1803

*After Spain cedes the Louisiana territory to France, it is then sold to the United States, which also claims that the western portion of the Florida territory, which belongs to Spain, should be included in the purchase. Thus, while the United States' representatives, Pinckey and Monroe, are negotiating the Louisiana purchase, Thomas Jefferson signs the 1804 law declaring that the western coast of Florida, between the Mississippi and Perdido Rivers, now belongs to the United States, prompting a strong protest by the Spanish ambassador, the Marquis of Casa Irujo. Taking advantage of the Spanish War of Independence, under President Madison, the United States residents of Baton Rouge declare the independence of western Florida, September 26, 1810, with the consent and support of President Madison. By a secret authorization of the U.S. Congress, Madison seizes Amelia Island on the Atlantic coast in 1811, and Mobile in 1813, both occupied by General Jackson. By the end of 1813, all of the Florida territory had been taken forcefully by the United States, though not at war with Spain. In 1818 General Jackson invades eastern Florida and occupies Panzacola, with much praise from President Monroe and Secretary of State John Quincy Adams. In 1819 the United States and Spain sign a treaty (January 22nd), by which Spain renounces any claim to Florida upon payment of 5 million dollars, which was never paid. By July 17, 1821, the Spanish domain in Florida had formally ended, and most of the Spanish residents left for Cuba.

*The book *Historia verdadera de la Conquista de la Nueva España*, (The True History of the Conquest of New Spain), by Bernal Díaz del Castillo is published in Salem, Massachusetts.

1804

*The Spanish surgeon Francisco Javier de Balmis introduces the smallpox vaccine in Texas. It had been discovered by the English Edward Jenner in 1796. In this regard, historian Robert Ryal Miller wrote:

> At the beginning of the 19th century, when the use of vaccine to immunize against smallpox was newly discovered, the Spanish government sent the Balmis expedition to the New World with medical

teams, who penetrated mountains and jungles vaccinating American Indians by the thousands.

But Balmis went a step further. In 1805 he sailed from Acapulco to Manila and from there to Macao to introduce the vaccine in China.

*Luis de Torres explores the Island of Uleai in the Carolinas.

1806

*Juan B. Monteverde explores the Island of Nuguor in the Carolinas.

1809

*Publishing of the important work *Viajes* (Travels), by the Spanish naturalist Félix de Azara. Published in French by his brother, the Spanish Ambassador to France, José Nicolás. He is also the author of several other important works relating to the flora and fauna of Latin America.

1810-1813

*The United States occupies Texas and takes it away from Spain, mainly by deception.

1813

*Father Narciso Durán, of the San José Mission in California, publishes a choir book which is soon after used by all the Catholic missions of the southwest, whose members are mostly Indians.

*Francisco de Paula Marín proposes the cultivation of the pineapple in Hawaii which, by the end of the century, becomes one of its principal industries.

1815

*"The Smith Chair" for the study of Spanish is established at Harvard University on the donation of $20,000 by Abiel Smith, who was a graduate from that university.

1819

*By the treaty of this year, Spain cedes to the United States the last territory it held in east Florida and the entire northern region comprising Oregon, Washington, and Columbia, keeping only for herself Texas, New Mexico, California, Arizona, Nevada, Utah, and Colorado. The triumph of the Mexican Revolution in 1821 included all of these territories, which were then "ceded" to the United States by the Treaty of Guadalupe Hidalgo in 1848.

1820

*Moses Austin asks permission from Spain to settle 300 North American families in Texas, and the Spanish Governor of Texas grants the charter one year later (1821.) Spain's loss of Texas had thus begun.

1821

*Mexico declares its independence from Spain.

1823

*Mexico, now independent, provides new land grants to Moses Austin's son, Stephen for further North American settlements. By 1836 the North American population in Texas had grown to thirty thousand, and by 1846 had reached a total of 142,000. The loss of Texas looms and in a few years it would become imminent. In the case of California, the governors dispensed land grants more generously than in Texas. For example, some of these lands or "ranchos" were about 11 leagues in size, or 48,000 acres, with the proviso that family members could add new holdings to the acreage. By the end of the Mexican rule in California, approximately 700 of these grants had been given away for free or for a nominal fee, mostly to foreign colonists who had become Mexican citizens only to qualify. These colonists also had to convert to Catholicism.

1825

*The Republic of Mexico (it became a republic in 1824) sends José María de Enchenadia to establish California as a territory and to set up government there.

1826

*A new development intensifies Mexico's mistrust of Stephen Austin's intentions. Benjamin Edwards takes camp at Nacogdoches, Texas and declares himself ruler of the Republic of Fredonia. Although he is quickly defeated by Austin, Mexico sees it as a step in trying to control the area.

*Spanish is for the first time offered at Yale University.

1828

*The fate of California as a Mexican territorial possession looms in the horizon. The "Californianos" or "Californios", the Mexican settlers of California, rebel against Mexican rule and seek, among other objectives, the secularization of the Spanish missions, especially the one at San Gabriel, which they achieved. However, a few more rebellions break out between 1828 and 1843 which have a debilitating effect on Mexico and pave the way for other settlers in the area, mainly North Americans.

1829

*The inevitable happens. President Jackson makes an attempt to purchase Texas from the Mexican Government and is refused. By now, the North American population in the area has grown to over 4,000, while the immigration into the area continues uninterruptedly both legally and illegally.

*While Mexico had freed its slaves in 1825, Mexican President Guerrero declares Texas excluded or exempt from slavery for motives unknown.

1830

*Mexico decides against further North American incursions in Texas and forbids any importation of black slaves into the region.

*H. W. Longfellow publishes his *Novelas Españolas* (Spanish Novels). And, in "The North American Review," appear his two essays, "Spanish Devotional and Moral Poetry" and "Spanish Language and Literature." His translation of *Coplas de Jorge Manrique*, was published in New England in a little book in 1833, in which he includes Manrique's own version as well as his own adaptation. In 1843 he also publishes *The Spanish Student*. In 1845 his magnificent anthology, *Poets and Poetry of Europe*, is published, in which he includes such Spanish literary masters as Cervantes, Lope de Vega, Calderón de la Barca, Ercilla, Garcilaso de la Vega, and others.

1831

*Manuel Victoria becomes the new Governor of California following a conflict between natives of California and the Mexican army.

1832

*The end of Texas as a Mexican territorial possession nears as Samuel Houston crosses the Red River and makes his entrance in Texas. He notifies his friend President Jackson that those who are now called "Texans" are planning to draw up their own constitution and ultimately become part of the Union.

*The Mexican Government promises Californians a voice in self-government provided it remains part of the Republic of Mexico. They agreed.

*Washington Irving publishes *The Alhambra,* in London.

1833

*"Texans" now vote to separate from Mexico at San Felipe. War between the two nations is now imminent. Stephen Austin petitions separate statehood from Mexican President Santa Ana. He is imprisoned for almost a year for so asking. His petition does not include Cohauila.

*"Texans" under the command of William B. Travis capture the Mexican fort at Anahuac, which is soon to be followed by other armed clashes. "Texans" continue to voice their discontent with Mexican rule under Santa Ana.

*Stephen Austin, after being freed from prison in Mexico, reveals his plans to go to war with Mexico as the only alternative to achieve statehood. Later at a convention, "Texans" voice their desire to separate from Mexican rule in favor of self-government and the army captures San Antonio.

1835

*Siege of The Alamo by Mexican President Santa Ana, commanding an army of 6,000 men. The defenders do not give up the fort and are all killed.

*Sam Houston becomes President of Texas and will serve his term until 1841.

*The celebrated Bostonian William H. Prescott publishes in Boston his work *Ferdinand and Isabella* (Spain's Catholic Monarchs), which was soon translated into Spanish, French, Italian, and German. With this publication, Prescott sparked wide interest about Spain and Spanish-American history in the United States.

1837

*José Joaquín Estudillo founds the city of San Leandro, located in present Alameda County near San Francisco.

1839

*France recognizes the independence of Texas, being the first European nation to do so.

1842

*United States writer Washington Irving is named Minister Plenipotenciary of the United States in Madrid. His official writings about the Spain of the time were so captivating that Secretary of State, Daniel Webster is said to have enjoyed reading them immensely. In all, he had written some 3,000 pages about Spain or one million words.

1843

*The celebrated historian William H. Prescott publishes his *History of the Conquest of Mexico*, in three volumes.

1845

*The annexation of Texas to the United States is effectuated, being the principal cause of the war between both nations. Also in this year, "Texans" approve the plan for Annexation and adopt a new state constitution. A little later, on December 29, Texas is incorporated into the Union as the twenty- eighth state.

*President Polk, who had publicly stated his desire to acquire Texas, California, and Oregon, sends John Slidell to Mexico to negotiate a settlement of hostilities and to offer the purchase of California and New Mexico, which Mexico declines to accept. However, he already had his own plans for annexing California when he names Thomas Larkin (October 17, 1845) to be a consul of the United States in Monterey. Both territories (California and

New Mexico) had been claimed by Texas. In view of the fact that Polk could not get his wish diplomatically, he decides to get it by force. Polk is known at the time he was elected (December 4, 1844) as the most expansionistic president the United States had elected up until that year. In his inaugural address he states that: "… the United States has clear and unquestionable title to Oregon and that the annexation of Texas is a matter solely to be resolved between the United States and Texas." In other words, Mexico has absolutely no say in the matter. He also reaffirms the Monroe Doctrine and enunciates his own, the "Polk Doctrine", opposing an attempt by European nations to maintain a balance of power. We must say here that the war was favored mainly by North American imperialists and by those wishing an extension of slave-holding territory. Then, when the Mexican army crosses Brownsville, Texas, President Polk calls it an invasion of United States territory and war is officially declared on May 13th, 1846. By that time California had also fell under United States rule, after Commander John B. Montgomery seizes San Francisco and Lt. James W. Revere occupies Sonoma, and later by the occupation of Santa Barbara and Los Angeles. Earlier, Commodore Thomas Catesby had seized Monterey, the capital of California. The Mexican army is confused. After all, during the armed conflict the presidency of Mexico had changed hands several times. The final campaign of the war takes place with the landing of the United States army at Veracruz under General Winfield Scott, and then on to Mexico City, where President Antonio López de Santa Ana is defeated at Cerro Gordo in 1847. Mexico, defeated and humiliated, signs the Treaty of Guadalupe-Hidalgo by which it cedes to the United States a fifth of its territory, receiving also an indemnity of $15 million. It also accepts all other United States claims over its former territory, like, for example, the addition of 1,193,061 square miles into the Treaty. During the Mexican-American War, the United States had presented a united front while Mexico had not.

Thus, the outcome of the conflict was, from the very beginning, quite clear and obvious. A very costly mistake indeed for Mexico. The North American expansion was almost complete.

*William H. Prescott publishes his other famous work, *The Conquest of Peru*.

*The Spanish friar Rosendo Salvado founds the "Nueva Nursia" mission in western Australia, to which he dedicated his entire life and made it prosper.

1848

*The noted United States Hispanist, George Ticknor, publishes his celebrated work *History of Spanish Literature*. Later he left his extensive collection of Spanish literature books (over 10,000 volumes) to the Boston Public Library, which he assisted in founding.

1853

*Franklin Pierce becomes the fourteenth President of the United States. Among his plans are the acquisition of Hawaii and Cuba as part of his "peaceful expansion." The seeds for the future Spanish-American War have thus been planted.

*The United States Ambassador to Mexico, James Gadsden is instructed to negotiate purchasing the land south of the Gila River, west to the 37th parallel boundary of California, and east to the Río Grande border of Texas. The agreement, known as the Gadsden Purchase, is finally reached on December 30th of this year, whereby Mexico cedes to the United States that territory consisting of 29,640 square miles at a purchase price of $10 million, thus completing what is now the southern borders of New Mexico and Arizona. As part of the purchase, the United States also acquires rich fields of gold and silver. There was indeed no end in pushing the United States frontier as far south and southwest as possible. The continental map of the United States, as we know it today, was indeed getting closer and closer. A final point of interest. The mines acquired by the United States in the Gadsden Purchase yield over $2 million in gold, especially the one in Gila City. And the Comstock Lode mine, located in the Washoe Mountains of Nevada, yield, in an approximate twenty-year period, the nice sum of $300 million in silver and gold.

1854

*On October 14, the United States once again makes an offer to Spain to purchase Cuba for $120 million, through the "Ostende Manifest", hinting that it would use force if necessary.

1855

*William H. Prescott publishes his *The History of Philip II*, which he did not finish. Volume I and II were published in this year; volume III in 1858. What is amazing about this famous writer and scholar is not only his total dedication to the study and writing about Spain, but even more so the fact that he lost his sight at an early age, despite which he was able to accomplish so very much. His life is truly a fascinating story.

1858

*Spanish soldiers from the Philippines joined the French in a four-year intervention in Vietnam. At the end, Spain was kicked out and the French took all the laurels. A Spanish military officer commented: "Once more we carried within ourselves the spirit of Don Quixote in this chimerical engagement in Indonesia."

1863

*The Scientific Commission of the Pacific docks in San Francisco in October 9. This was a reconnaissance scientific expedition sponsored by Spain from 1862 to 1866, one of the greatest ever undertaken. As Robert Ryal Miller said in his book,

For Science and National Glory—The Spanish Scientific Expedition to America, 1862-1866:

> Spanish monarchs sponsored scientific expeditions to the New World over a period of four centuries, but the last great reconnaissance was in the 1860s when a royal commission visited a dozen countries of Latin America. Although the naturalists crossed the Argentine Pampas, surveyed the Atacama Desert, examined Andean archeological sites, photographed people and places from Brazil to California, descended the full length of the Amazon River, and sent home crates containing 82,000 specimens of plants, animals and minerals, the story of their adventure is virtually unknown. There is no published account of it in English, French, or German, and the two printed summaries in Spanish are rare and not well known.

1872

*George Santayana, born in Madrid in 1863, immigrates to the United States and graduates from Harvard in 1876, where he teaches philosophy from 1889 until 1912. Among his most celebrated works is *The Sense of Beauty*, published in 1896. According to the *Stanford Encyclopedia of Philosophy*, "... Using contemporary classifications, Santayana is the first and foremost Hispanic-American philosopher."

1874-1890

*United States publisher and historian, Hubert Howe Bancroft publishes his prodigious work, re-issued in 1882-1890 as *The Works of Hubert Howe Bancroft*, a 39-volume encyclopedia covering the history of Central America, Mexico, and the Far West of the United States, in which he has much to tell about Spanish history in those areas. In 1905 he donated his 50,000-volume library to the University of California, containing a magnificent collection of maps, rare manuscripts, books, and narratives of early pioneers. The collection remains one of the best in the world.

1878

*William Cullen Bryant publishes his poem "Cervantes," in New York. Mr. Bryant, who was a partner and manager of the "Evening Post" for over fifty years, was a Hispanist at heart. He translated into English numerous Spanish classics, including Fray Luis de León, the novel *Jerilla*, by Carolina Coronado, which was published in "The New York Ledger," circa 1869, and others. He also authored *Toured of the Old South*, in which he deals in part with the Spanish influence in North America, and in particular with a group of some 1,000 Spaniards from the Balearic Islands who had settled in Florida in the early l 800s.

1885

*The study of Spanish is offered for the first time at the University of California.

1890

*United States Hispanist, Hubert Howe Bancroft, donates his magnificent library of Spanish History of North America to the University of California. It consisted of well over 50,000 volumes, and is widely considered among the world's best.

1895

*The United States, which for many years sought to control the Cuban economy, takes advantage of its 10-Year War with Spain and declares an embargo on Cuban sugar imports through the Dingley Tariff, thus adding to the Cuban unrest and their subordination to the Union.

1898

*USS *Maine*, a battleship built between 1888 and 1895, was sent to Havana in January 1898 to protect American interests during the long-standing revolt of the Cubans against the Spanish government. In the evening of 15 February 1898, *Maine* sank when her forward gunpowder magazines exploded, and nearly three-quarters of the battleship's crew died as a result of the explosion. When the Maine exploded, suspicion immediately fell upon the Spanish. Despite the best efforts of experts and historians in investigating this complex and technical subject, a definitive explanation for the destruction of *Maine* remains elusive. However, there is ample evidence, mostly from the United States, which determined the cause of the explosion to have been internal rather than external. At the time of the incident, T.B. Reed, president of the U.S. Congress, called for a more thorough investigation by neutral countries as he was not convinced that Spain was to blame. Then, he requested that Admiral Melville, of the Army's Corps of Engineers, render his own personal report which stated (January 29, 1902) that Spain was not at fault. His report was published by "The North American Review," in June of 1912. Prior to this year, in 1910, the U.S. Government salvaged the Maine's hull, and in July of 1911, General Bixley, head of the Army's Corps of Engineers, confirmed that the explosion had been due to an internal explosion of ammunition, and that no external explosion could have damaged the ship that way. Finally, Admiral Sigsbee, the Maine's former commander, attested to the fact that there was absolutely no proof that Spain had been in any way involved in the incident. His statement was later published in the "New York."

Clearly, the Maine incident was used as a clever pretext by the United States Government to intervene in Cuban affairs and to help throw out or diminishes Spanish control over the island in favor of its own. This was the beginning and basis of the Spanish-American War. It should have never happened. The people were against it, as well as half the world. As a result of the war, which the United States won, Spain lost her last possessions in the Americas—Cuba and Puerto Rico, and also the Philippines.

*First publishing in the United States of "Brevísima relación de la destrucción de las Indias" (Brief Description of the Destruction of the Indies) by Friar Bartlomé de las Casas. The timing could have not been better chosen, precisely at the time that the United States was at war with Spain. The Spanish Black Legend now took new life in North America.

1899

*By the Treaty of this year, Spain sells to Germany the Islands of Carolinas, Palau, and the Marianas for a total of 25 million Pesetas. They later belonged to Japan and then to the United States.

The 20th Century

In terms of U.S.-Hispanic relations, much happened in this century. For one thing, Fidel Castro came to power in Cuba and millions of Hispanic immigrants flocked to the United States in search of a new life. No one knows to this date where all of these events will lead and how they will ultimately affect future relations between the north and the south. We are restricted by time and space to elaborate further, and will let it pass until another edition of the book. We are, however, mentioning here a few interesting facts.

1904

*Hispanist Archer M. Huntington founds the Hispanic Society of America in New York City, still standing. Among its many treasures is a very rare first edition of *Don Quixote*.

1918

*Historian Roger Bigelow Merriman published his work in New York, *The Rise of the Spanish Empire in the Old World and the New*, in three volumes.

1921

*United States historian and teacher, Herbert Eugene Bolton publishes *Texas in the Middle of the Eighteenth Century*, and *The Spanish Borderlands*, followed in 1931 by *The Outpost of Empire*, the story of the founding of San Francisco, and in 1936 *Rim of Christiandom*, with the biographies of Father Eusebio Francisco Kino and Coronado. After teaching at the Universities of Stanford, Texas, and California, he became an outstanding authority on the Spanish West during the colonial era.

1949

*The Smithsonian Institution publishes for the first time *Compendio y descripción de las Islas Occidentales* (Compendium and Description of the West Indies), by Friar Antonio Vázquez de Espinosa.

APPENDIX B

MORE HISTORICAL FACTS

Contents

MORE HISTORICAL FACTS

Introduction

"If Spain had not existed 400 years ago, the United States would not exist today."
—Charles F. Lummis,
Former professor emeritus at Harvard
and among the U.S's greatest scholars

"By the time of the British landfall, the Spaniards had already etched an indelible mark on the North American landscape, and had claimed almost half of the continent for Spain. Coronado, de Soto, Ponce de León, Cabeza de Vaca, and literally hundreds more, had criss-crossed the immense uncharted territory in one of the greatest and most fascinating epics in the annals of discovery and exploration. In sharp contrast, once on North American soil, the British set up camp on the narrow strip of land along the northeastern coast and never ventured beyond its borders ...France had but managed to make a few uneventful forays in the continent, and Portugal had only settled a few spotted colonies in South America."
—Carlos B. Vega

"Spanish, bestow great attention on this and endeavor to acquire an accurate knowledge of it. Our future connection with Spain and Spanish America will render that language a valuable acquisition."
—Thomas Jefferson, 1787

"Till near the end of the eighteenth century not Boston, not New York, not Charleston, not Quebec, but Mexico City was the metropolis of the entire Western Hemisphere."
—Herbert E. Bolton

"During the fifteenth and sixteenth centuries, two nations, Spain and Portugal, pioneered the European discovery of sea routes that were the first channels of interaction between all of the world's continents, beginning the process of globalization in which we live in today."
—U.S. National Parks Service

The discovery, exploration, settlement, and development of North America, although initiated by Spain in the early 1500s, became soon after a joint enterprise of Spain and the newly discovered lands in the Caribbean first, and later of Mexico and South America. Although Spain maintained control of its America's enterprise, most of the discoveries, conquests, explorations, settlements, even conflicts and wars with rival nations, originated in the Americas, such as Cortés and the conquest of Mexico, Pizarro of Peru, Balboa and the discovery of the Pacific, and the expeditions of Ponce de León, Cabeza de Vaca, Coronado, de Soto, and Menéndez de Avilés to North America, among countless others. Thus, in this book, when we say Spain, Spanish, Spaniards, it should be understood in a wider sense as Hispanic, especially after the mid-1500s.

Yet, the contributions of all of these countries have been systematically ignored, glossed over, or repudiated by historians in the long 500 years since America was discovered. The fact is that, without all of these countries, the North America that we know today would be very different, and here is why: instead of starting in the early 16 century, U.S. history would have been set back at least 100 years, at least in the early 18 century. All of the major expeditions would have never occurred, and all of the gold and silver that poured into North America from the mines of Potosí, Zacatecas, and others, would have ended-up somewhere else.

In this appendix we are presenting historical facts that may seem at first to have been carried out solely by Spain or by Spaniards, mainly because all of the leaders that undertook them were Spaniards. However, as we have already said, with few exceptions, the events themselves were organized and launched from American soil, from many of the countries above mentioned. Even American natives contributed greatly to many of these enterprises by informing Spaniards where to go to find what they were after, as was the case with Cortés, Pizarro, Balboa, Coronado, de Soto, and others. And, of course, the natives were also the ones who mined the gold and silver. When King Charles III of Spain lent millions of pesos to the leaders of the American Revolution, all of those funds came from the mines of Ecuador, Peru, and Mexico which the natives had to work under horrible circumstances. Indeed, Spain was the conduit of all of those funds, but they did not come directly from Spain but from the Spanish possessions in America. It is something like a bank, which lends you money that belongs to the depositors. The bank is the conduit. The depositors are the originators.

In this regard, countries such as the Dominican Republic, Cuba, Puerto Rico, Guatemala, Panama, Peru, Bolivia, and Ecuador were as vital to the development of North America as Spain or any other European nation was. Again, we repeat what we have said many times before: Christopher Columbus was the man with the idea and the plan to find a shorter route to Asia (stumbling upon America without even realizing it at the beginning), but without Spain and the Catholic Monarchs, Columbus's dream would have been gone up in smoke, as it has happened to so many good ideas. Here also Columbus was the conduit, but the support and all of the resources to launch his voyage came from Spain, no one else.

The purpose of this appendix is to illuminate those coming upon its pages about the large and far-reaching contribution of Spain and Hispanics to the forging of what is today the United States. To support it, we have gathered hundreds of irrefutable historical facts dating all the way back to the beginning of the 16th century, when the North American continent was first put on the map. To think that U.S. history began in the 17th century and later expanded exclusively to the Thirteen Colonies, is a fallacy and a distortion of history that demands immediate correction. U.S. history did not begin with the founding of Jamestown, but with the landing of Juan Ponce de León in Florida in 1513, almost 100 years earlier. Nor did U.S. history originate in the northeast, but in the southwest, nor did Western Civilization found its way through the northeast, but through the southwest, through Mexico. The seeds of Western Civilization were firmly planted in North America much before the English and others ventured to cross the Atlantic following Spain's footsteps.

The appendix is divided into 14 parts or sections, each one presenting those facts to which they correspond. It has drawn all of its information from reliable, well-documented sources, many of which are quoted throughout. It is, therefore, an appendix based on facts long established by distinguished historians and scholars.

Here we are expanding on some of the topics presented earlier, including Spain's aid to the American Revolution, and to Spain's so-called "Black Legend." The reader will find some duplication of the material covered in the main section of the book, which we have provided in order to allow the appendix to be used independently, if so desired.

Part A

SPAIN OPENS AND LEADS THE WAY TO THE NEW WORLD

America was discovered in 1492. Although the discoverer, Christopher Columbus was Italian, the man with the idea and the plan, it was Spain the nation that lent the necessary support and the resources needed to carry out the mission. Without one or the other, America would have not been discovered, at least at that time.

By discovering America it is meant that the event was transcendental and had consequences, that it was recorded and made known to the world. It is possible that the Vikings may have discovered it before, but that "discovery" led to nothing and had no consequences of any kind. The landing on the moon was a world event, known to all mankind and had consequences. The Vikings came and left, and nothing happened. This cannot be called a discovery.

As soon as America was discovered, the whole world was put on high alert. All of the nations of Europe sought expansion, longing for new horizons that would take them out of poverty and of century of warfare and darkness. A new era, the Renaissance, was taking root and with it humanity looked within the individual for his own preservation, happiness, and wellbeing, rather than upwards to the heavens. What can I do to better myself, to better understand life and the world, to attain some basic goals for a brighter and safer tomorrow? Because of Spain's pioneering efforts, all of that was soon to change. What this means is that Spain led the way in more ways than one, especially by charting the Atlantic Ocean and making it navigable. Now the other European nations could follow and be able to also reach America and share in the hopes and the bonanza. With the discovery and conquest of Mexico and later of Peru, America presented itself to Europe as a land bursting with riches and opportunity. In view of this, who in their right mind would stay behind and just let one nation take it all in?

But, inasmuch as each one of them strived to follow Spain's footsteps, Spain was so far ahead of them that for 100 years they were unable to catch up with her. In fact, during the first 50 years after the discovery, Spain was all over the place, both in the Americas and around the world, as far as China and Japan. After the Philippines were discovered by Magellan (under the service of Spain) in 1521, Spain's presence was firmly established throughout Asia, especially after the successful completion of the first circumnavigation of the world by the Spaniard Sebastián Elcano in 1522, began by Magellan in 1519. In the Americas, Spain's domains extended as far south as the Strait of Magellan, and as far north as mid-North America, east to west. Any nation trying to trespass these domains had to confront a formidable and determined enemy ready to protect and defend them.

Spain charted the route from Europe to America and made it viable for other nations to follow, although reluctantly. The reason for that reluctance was that Spain had been granted the sole domain of all the lands discovered and yet to be discovered west of the Azores by the Papal Bull (Inter Cetera I, confirmed later by another bull, Eximiae Devotionis, and yet later by another, Dudum siquidem, all three in the same year) of Alexander VI in 1493 and that included all of North America according to the Line of Demarcation. Of course, the whole of Europe was infuriated, specially Portugal which had already established a foothold in Brazil, and the bull was challenged and changed repeatedly to maintain the fragile peace. Nevertheless, at the end, Spain kept all of the Americas with the exception of the Brazilian mainland. With Portugal out of the way, the other nations, namely England, France, and Holland, began their maneuvers to gain access to the new "promised land." But, despite the odds and having literally the whole western world in an unrelenting pursuit to obliterate her, Spain kept pushing and was able to carry out her mission, a mission that took four centuries to complete and her total economic devastation. In 1898, when Spain's supremacy in the New World took the last blow, she was totally drained, exhausted, almost reduced to ashes. She simply gave up and began a long and arduous road to recovery that took 100 years through the Franco regime.

Part B

THE DISCOVERY OF
NORTH AMERICA

We have already mentioned that the Vikings and others may have landed in North America prior to the actual discovery by Christopher Columbus in 1492. Most of these voyages, however, are based on hypothesis, which, to this day, have not been fully authenticated.

The first known and scantly recorded voyage to North America was that of John Cabot (an Italian) ordered by King Henry VII of England. In 1497, Cabot discovered the coast of Newfoundland and the Gulf of St. Lawrence, and a year later traveled with his son, Sebastian, from Labrador to Cape Hatteras. Regarding John Cabot's discovery of the North American mainland, here are the comments of some well-established historians. American historian Edward Gaylor Bourne wrote:

> The date of the landfall, June 24, does not appear earlier than the so-called Cabot map of 1544. It was probably derived from Sebastian Cabot. In regard to the landfall, controversy has been as busy as with the identity of the San Salvador of Columbus, but the results are not as satisfactory. The Canadian scholars Dawson and Prowse advocate respectively Cape Breton and Newfoundland. Harrisse has been insistent for Labrador, but with slight assent from those familiar with the region. In view of this uncertainty, it has been questioned whether John Cabot's report that he

found the mainland should be accepted as final. He may have been as much mistaken as was Columbus about Cuba.

And a group of American scholars commented on the same subject: "The voyages of John Cabot and his son Sebastian in 1497-1498 provided the basis for the English claim to North America, though there was nothing that could be called a British empire in the New World until the settlement of Virginia in 1607." On the other hand, the discovery of America by Christopher Columbus in the name of Spain changed the world forever. After Columbus, as historian Charles Norman asserts, "Africa was rounded, the earth circumnavigated, the world remapped." And on the same point, historian-producer Zvi Dor-Ner said:

> In the final chapter, we look at the explosion that followed in the wake of Columbus. Thirty years after the discovery of the Americas, the first ship circumnavigated the globe, an act that defined and united our planet. The ideas that emerged then changed our notions of God and religion, of science and technology, of trade and industry, and put us decisively on a path to a world whose fate-history, geography, and resources is shared for better or for worse. ... No one before Columbus had achieved anything similar to that.

Further on John Cabot, he sought the auspices of the king of Spain (and also Portugal) for his planned voyage, according to Pedro de Ayala, Spain's ambassador to the English court in a letter to the Catholic Monarchs. And we wonder what would have happened had he succeeded in this endeavor and made the trip under the banner of Spain instead of England. History always has its twists and turns which leave us dumbstruck.

In 1500, the Portuguese Gaspar Corte-Real reached Greenland and Newfoundland, returning to the latter in 1501 and then disappearing just like his brother Miguel in 1502. The area of Newfoundland was soon after visited by mariners from various countries, including the Basques, for fishing. In 1502 Europe had already a notion about the existence of Florida, as it appeared in the maps of Cantino and Caverio (1502.) Also, there may have been an anonymous voyage between 1500 and 1502, although it was soon forgotten. In 1514, King Ferdinand of Spain had arranged an expedition to Newfoundland by Sebastian Cabot (now under the service of Spain), but it never materialized due to the king's death. This takes us to 1513, when the Spaniard Juan Ponce de León landed in Florida.

Ponce de León was named governor of Puerto Rico in 1510. In 1512 he set out to find the Island of Bimini, to the north of Cuba, lured, it seems, by an Indian legend about a marvelous fountain that had magical powers to rejuvenate (known to us as the "Fountain of Youth.") On March 27, 1513 (there is some controversy about the precise month and year of the discovery) he discovered what he thought was an island, naming it *Florida* because of its fertility and also because of Easter Sunday *(Pascua Florida,* in Spanish.)

Part C

HISPANIC DISCOVERIES AND EXPLORATIONS IN NORTH AMERICA.

—The first flag to fly over what is now the United States was the Imperial flag of Spain, carried by Juan Ponce de León when he landed in Florida in 1513. Then came the French flag, the Dutch (Dutch West India Company), and later the Union Jack. The Liberty Flag may have been used in Boston to protest the Tea Act of November 23, 1 773. The Star Spangled Banner was not used until after May 1, 1795, when the states of Kentucky and Vermont became part of the Union. The first Stars and Stripes, which is also called the Betsy Ross flag, was used in 1776. Thus, the Spanish flag was used in what is now the United States 260 years before the Liberty Flag, and 282 years before the Star Spangled Banner, counting from the time of the landing of Juan Ponce de León in Florida in 1513

—Most of Spanish America, but especially Peru, Mexico, Cuba, Puerto Rico, and the Dominican Republic, were the places where most Spanish explorers honed their skills. Had this not been so, explorers such as Coronado, de Soto, Avilés, Cabeza de Vaca, and others, would have been ill- prepared to carry out their missions.

The epicenters of the Spanish empire in America shifted from the Dominican Republic, first, then Cuba and from there to Mexico. As for the Spanish explorations in the Pacific, all expeditions sailed either from Mexico or from Peru.

—Half of our present states were discovered, explored, and colonized by Spaniards in the 16th and 17th centuries. They were: Alabama, Arizona, Arkansas, California, Colorado, Florida, Georgia, Illinois, Indiana, Kansas, Kentucky, Louisiana, Mississippi, Montana, Nebraska, Nevada, New Mexico, North Carolina, Oregon, South Carolina, Tennessee, Texas, Utah, Washington, Wyoming. We should also include Hawaii and Alaska, thus making it a total of 27.

—Most of the famous voyages to America by foreign nationals in the 16th, 17th, and 18th centuries were organized and sponsored by Spain, including those of Sebastian Cabot (Italian), Ferdinand Magellan (Portuguese), Alexander von Humboldt (German), Amerigo Vespucci (Italian), and Juan de Fuca (Greek), whose real name was Apóstolos Valerianos. It is interesting to note that Magellan first named the strait he discovered (the Strait of Magellan) "de Todos los Santos" (of All the Saints). Following Magellan's discovery, two other Spaniards crossed the strait, García Jofre de Loasia and Sebastián Elcano, both in April and March of 1526. Included also, of course, must be Christopher Columbus.

—The Spanish discovered many of North America's greatest natural wonders, and gave them Spanish names, such as El cañón del Colorado (Colorado Canyon), Montañas Rocosas (Rocky Mountains), Sierra Nevada, Bahía de los Farallones (San Francisco Bay), Puerto de San Miguel (San Diego Bay), Río del Tizón (Colorado River), Bahía del Espíritu Santo (Tampa Bay), Lago de los Timpanogos (Lake Utah), and Madre de Dios del Jacán (Chesapeake Bay). To these we would have to add the many other natural wonders discovered by Hernando de Soto and his army, such as the Salina River, the Ozark Mountains (Arkansas), Lake Michigan (July 8, 1541), and, of course, the Mississippi River. From the Wabash River he went down to a town called "Quiguate" which we call today "El Dorado," in Illinois.

—The Spaniard Pedro de Coronas tried to establish a post in Chesapeake Bay.

—Francisco Vázquez de Coronado and his men discovered and explored a vast territory in the American Southwest, namely the Far West, the Praderas, the Rocky Mountains, the Colorado River, the Grand Canyon, the depth of the Gulf of California, the culture of the Pueblo Indians, the Llano Estacado, plus the states of New Mexico, Arizona, and Kansas, and trekked thousands of miles through today's Texas and Oklahoma. The narrative of his expedition, written by Pedro de Castañeda spurred further explorations of the vast area. It would take another 200 years before the Jesuit Francisco Garcas looked again in awe at the Grand Canyon. By the way, "Colorado" is the Spanish word for "coppery-red," which is precisely the color of the Canyon.

—The Santa Lucia Mountains in California were originally named "Sierras de San Martín" by Juan Rodríguez Cabrillo in honor of the day of San Martín, November 11th. And Cabrillo also discovered the Islands of the Channel of Santa Barbara in 1542.

—Álvar Núñez Cabeza de Vaca not only pioneered the exploration of the entire Southwest, but was the first to discover and write about primitive North America, and the first to sight the North American bison, which he called "vacas corcobadas," or hunchback cows. With his other three companions, Alonso del Castillo Maldonado, Andrés Dorantes, and Estebanico, an Arab from Morrocco, they trudged over 10000 miles across the North American Southwest. Cabeza de Vaca's *Naufragios* stands today as the first narrative of North America. Another companion of de Vaca, Andrés Docampo, trekked the longest distance from

Northern Kansas to the South of Mexico, which took him nine years to complete.

—The Sacramento River, California's largest (384 miles from source to sea), was discovered by the Spaniards in 1808 on the Holy Day of the Sacrament, hence its name.

—The city of Monterey in California was named for the viceroy of Mexico, Don Gaspar de Zúñiga y Acevedo, Count of Monterrey, who dispatched the Vizcaíno expedition in 1596. Incidentally, when Vizcaíno entered the Gulf of California and took possession of the peninsula, he named it "Nueva Andalucia."

—The first relatively detailed map of Florida was published by Pedro Mártir de Anglería in 1511, showing the isle of Beimeni (Bimini) to the north of Cuba. On the reverse of the map he noted "to the north of this isle wonderful countries and lands had been discovered."

—In 1556 the Spaniards reached Virginia, 30 years before Sir Walter Raleigh and half a century before the visit of John Smith. By this year, Chesapeake Bay was already known by the Spaniards who named it "Bahia de Santa María." In 1588, Captain Vicente González also reached Chesapeake Bay and re-named it "Madre de Dios del Jacán." He also discovered many rivers in that region, including the Susquehanna River, which they named "San Juan de las Rocas."

—Hernando de Soto not only discovered the Mississippi but also ten of today's states, and the writings of his explorations fueled further European expeditions resulting in the settlement of a vast territory. True, it is conceivable that someone else could have done it at a later date, but this would have set back the birth of our nation for, perhaps, as many as 100 years. But de Soto's importance to American history goes even further. On leaving Cuba, he commanded an expedition unparalleled up to that time; and, in fact, he has been rightly called the United States' first true pioneer and settler. His expedition consisted of a fleet of nine vessels, five navíos, two caravels, and two brigantines, over 620 soldiers, hundreds of settlers, including artisans and men of all trades and professions, approximately 300 horses, all kinds of domestic animals, including dogs and pigs, many priests and missionaries, hundreds of women, an extensive variety of plants and seeds, tools of all kinds, and Indian and Black slaves from Cuba. In the words of American historian Theodore Maynard: If no expedition to the New World had ever consisted of better human material, so also no expedition to the New World was ever better equipped. But de Soto did much more. Besides discovering the Mississippi and discovering or exploring ten of our states (Florida, Georgia, the Carolinas, Tennessee, Alabama, Mississippi, Arkansas, Oklahoma, Texas), he journeyed farther north crossing the Wabash River in today's El Dorado, Illinois, and reaching Lake Michigan in today's Chicago. In addition, he discovered the Ohio River at Henderson, Kentucky, and the Ozark Mountains in Arkansas, and the Missouri mountains. Thus, in reality, he discovered not ten but thirteen states, the ones already mentioned plus Illinois, Indiana, and Missouri. With regard to North American pioneers, the significance of De Soto's expedition was extraordinary. What he had really envisioned was to establish absolute Spanish domain in what he thought was an island, with the ultimate purpose of finding a shorter trade route to the Orient via the Mississippi to the Pacific Ocean (already discovered by Balboa). With this purpose in mind, he brought with him many skillful explorers, carpenters, ship builders, farmers, blacksmiths, merchants, navigators, and engineers, as well as many domestic animals and tons of supplies, such as seeds, axes, saws, and nails. With de Soto, and later with Coronado, Cabeza de Vaca, and many others, the building of present-day United States had thus begun. Although incredible to believe, de Soto and his army had trudged over 4,000 miles across North America, from Florida to Chicago and then on to Texas. The entire Mississippi basin and far, far beyond. And, believe it or not, it took over 200 years before other Europeans climbed the Appalachians or canoed down the Mississippi River.

—And talking about de Soto, he crossed the Appalachians 200 years before the famous frontiersman Daniel Boone. Also, after his death, his troops, led by Moscoso, were the first Europeans to stand on the site of present-day Louisiana.

—The Gulf of Mexico, when first discovered by the Spaniards, was called "Spanish Sea." In the map of Johann Baptist Homann (circa 1730) it is named "Sinus Mexicanus."

—The present state of Oregon was discovered by the pilot Bartolomé Ferrelo (a Portuguese in the service of Spain) in 1543. Ferrelo continued the expedition when Cabrillo died in that same year. He also discovered Cape Mendocino.

—The Pacific Ocean was discovered by Vasco Núñez de Balboa in 1513, which he named "Mar del Sur" (South Sea). It was later renamed "Pacific Ocean" ("Mare Pacificum") by Magellan in 1520. It established that such an ocean divided America from Asia.

—When it was discovered by the Spaniards, Texas was named "Nuevas Filipinas" (New Philippines) also in honor King Philip ll of Spain. And many years later, Domingo Terán de los Ríos, the first governor of Texas appointed by Bernardo de Gálvez on January 23, 1691, renamed Texas "Nuevo Reyno de la Montaña de Santander y Santillana."

—In 1519 Alonso Alvarez de Pineda discovered the northern coast of the Gulf of Mexico and the coast of Texas, while ascertaining that Florida was not an island but a peninsula. This discovery paved the way for the future exploration and settlement of North America. He was also credited with opening the sea route between Texas and Florida, and the first to come upon the mouth of the Mississippi River, which he named "Río del Espíritu Santo."

—Many of the present-day territorial possessions of the United States in the South Pacific were discovered or explored by Spain.

The Marianas Islands were discovered by Magellan (under the service of Spain) in 1521. In 1565 the Spaniard Miguel López de Legazpi took possession of the islands. The name "Marianas" was given by father Luis Diego Sanvítores in honor of Mariana de Austria, queen of Spain and wife of Philip IV. The island of Guam (in the Marianas) was also discovered by Magellan in 1521, and further, Sanvítores founded there a mission and several schools (1668). Spain ceded the island to the United States in the Treaty of Paris, 1898. And the Carolina Islands were discovered by the Spaniard Francisco Lazcano in 1686, which he named in honor of King Charles ("Carlos") II of Spain.

—The discovery and subsequent conquest of Mexico, and the discovery of the Gulf of Mexico, made possible all future discoveries and explorations of the North American mainland by the Spanish. Without these two events, the history of the United States would have been pushed back, possibly, at least 150 years.

—Mendocino Cape (northern coast of California) was named in honor of the viceroy of Mexico Antonio de Mendoza. It was discovered by Bartolomé Ferrelo, pilot of Juan Rodríguez Cabrillo, in 1542.

—Who discovered Hawaii? To the English, it was James Cook in 1778. To the Spanish, it was Juan Gaitán in 1555, based on some maps of the period, such as the maps of the Flemish Ortelius (1587), and of Mercator, where Hawaii appears under the name of "Desgraciada." As further proof of the Spanish discovery, there is a map in the Naval Museum of Madrid on which it says that the Sandwich or Hawaii Islands were discovered by Juan Gaytán in 1555, which he named "Isla de Mesa." Also, in 1778, Cook himself found in Hawaii pieces of a Spanish sword and armor preserved today at the British Museum. It is also believed that the islands were known to the crew of the Galleon of Manila who kept it a secret fearing pirate attacks.

—The very first group of Europeans from all nationalities came to America in the expedition of Ferdinand Magellan (sponsored by Spain). It included, besides Spaniards, Portuguese, Italians, Flemings, French, Greeks, Germans, Jews, and one Englishman, Master Andrew of Bristol.

—In 1564 the Legazpi expedition took possession of the Island of Guam, in the Marianas, in the name of Spain.

—In 1524, Esteban Gómez (or Gomes), a Portuguese in the service of Spain, reached New Brunswick (Canada), and continued south along the coast to Florida. On this voyage he sighted the Penobscot river, Cape Cod, the Massachusetts Bay, Narragansett Bay, and the mouths of the Connecticut, Hudson (named "San Antón"), and Delaware Rivers. It is worth noting that on the Ribero map the entire coastline, stretching from New Jersey to Rhode Island, was called "Land of Esteban Gómez." In this regard, American historian Charles Gibson noted: "On the map of Ribeiro in 1529 that part of North America, now New York and New England, is inscribed "Land of Esteban Gómez," who discovered it by his majesty command in 1525. Trees and fruits like those of Spain abound, and turbot, salmon, and pike." And another American historian, Samuel Eliot Morison, added:

> Spanish explorers had now minutely examined the coasts of North America, from Mexico to Labrador, with results of great importance for the history of geography, but of little importance to the building of their colonial empire. That they should have neglected that region where the English were to lay the foundations of a great nation and to embody on a grander scale their most valuable contribution to the political life of mankind, may seem strange, yet it was wholly natural. No empire of plantation appealed to Spain, for she had little surplus population, and too many political irons in the fire to do everything for which opportunity offered.

—In 1592, one hundred years after America was discovered, Juan de Fuca, a Greek under the service of Spain, discovered the strait bearing his name (Juan de Fuca Strait), between Vancouver Island in British Columbia and Washington state. This is further proof that Spain moved in all directions in North America, and not only in the Southwest.

—A major pioneer of North America and the future United States was Juan de Oñate, who in 1598 led an expedition to New Mexico where he founded several cities, including the United States' second city—San Francisco, later re-named San Gabriel.

—In 1601 he reached Kansas where he crossed the Canadian and Arkansas Rivers. In 1604 he crossed Arizona and a year later reached the mouth of the Colorado River. (Oñate's expedition consisted of a large caravan of people, animals, and supplies: 130 soldiers, several missionaries, 83 wagons, and 7000 heads of cattle. Altogether, it cost him today's equivalent of $1 million. One of the missionaries founded North America's second church in San Gabriel, in New Mexico, today called "Chamita." Two more churches were founded in New Mexico by Friar Antonio de Arquega in 1629—one in the town of San Antonio de Senecú, and the other in the town of Nuestra Señora del Socorro.

—Although Francis Drake stumbled upon what is believed to have been San Francisco Bay (July, 1579), which he named "Nova Albion" (New England), such event passed unnoticed until 1769 when it was actually discovered by the Spaniard Gaspar de Portolá. He re-named it "San Francisco," in honor of the Franciscan friars who accompanied him, especially Friar Junípero Serra. Portolá also founded the cities of San Diego and Monterey. As it is well-known, the Franciscan missionaries, led by father Serra, greatly developed the region planting olive trees, vineyards, and constructing numerous buildings. Today, California is one of the world's leading wine-makers thanks to the vision and efforts of Father Serra and his missionaries. The region was later organized and developed by José de Gálvez (uncle of Bernardo de Gálvez).

—The Peede River at Winyah Bay was named "Rio de San Juan Bautista" by its discoverer Francisco Gordillo (1521), of the expedition of Lucas Vázquez de Ayllón.

—The territories comprising present-day Texas, Louisiana, and Mississippi, were known to the Spaniards in the early years as "Tierra de Garay" (Land of Garay). Francisco de Garay was at the time the governor of Jamaica and had planned to establish a province or discover a strait leading to the Pacific.

—Comparable to Juan de Oñate, de Soto, and Coronado, was Sebastián Vizcaíno, a leading pioneer of California. In 1595 he took possession of California for Spain and explored San Diego Bay. A few months later (December 16), he discovered Monterey Bay, the port long-sought by the Spanish fleet sailing to and from Philippines. The California map by one of his engineers, Enrico Martín, drew much praise from Humboldt.

—The Columbia River was discovered by the Spaniard Bruno Heceta in 1775, which he named "Bahía de la Asunción."

—When discovered by Juan Ponce de León, Cape Canaveral was named "Cabo de las corrientes" because of the strong currents. Together with Cape Raso in Newfoundland, they were the earliest place names on the eastern coast of North America.

—The Sea of Cortez, discovered by Francisco de Ulloa in 1539, was first named "Mar de Cortés" by Ulloa in honor of Hernán Cortés. And the California Peninsula was discovered by Ortún Jiménez in 1533 or 1534, who had been sent in a reconnaissance expedition to the area by Cortés himself. It is curious to note that on the Ortelius map of 1584, showing the Caribbean, Florida, and California, California is still shown as an island and not as a peninsula with a northern passage.

—Los Angeles was originally named by the Spaniards: "El Río de Nuestra Señora la Reyna de Los Angeles de Porciuncula" (The River of Our Lady the Queen of the Angels of Porciuncula). That was the full, complete original name. It was given by Father Juan

Crispi of the expedition of Gaspar de Portolá in 1769. It was actually a river so named. In 1781, Governor Felipe de Neve gave that name to the town, which eventually became "Los Angeles." The name "Porciuncula" was taken from the first convent of the Franciscan Order in Asia, and it refers to the jubilee of Plenary Indulgence that is gained on August 2nd in the church of said Order. "Purciuncula" is also the birthplace in Italy of Saint Francis of Assisi.

—And what about the name "California?" Where does it come from? The Spanish writer Garci Ordóñez de Montalvo wrote in 1510 the book, *Sergas de Esplandián* (The Exploits of Esplandian) in which he describes an Amazonian Queen, "Califa," in a kingdom named "California" in her honor. That name was fresh in the memory of the Spanish explorers, such as Juan Rodríguez Cabrillo for he named it in 1542, only 32 years after the book was written.

—And talking about California, its true discoverer was the Spaniard Ortún Jiménez who first sighted it in 1533 or 1534, and which the named, thinking that it was an island, "Isla de Santa Cruz."

—Let's now see how the names of some of our western present-day states originated:

Texas: The word is Spanish but it was most likely derived from the Hasinai tribe of that region meaning "Friendship."

Colorado: From the river meaning "red or ruddy" in Spanish. So named because of the large amount of red mud and sand the river carried when swollen by downpours.

Nevada: Spanish for snowy or snow-clad.

Arizona: Most likely from the Spanish "árida zona" (arid zone), but it could also be derived from the Aztec "arizuma" meaning silver bearing.

Florida: So named by Juan Ponce de León when the region was discovered on Sunday, March 27, 1513, in honor of "Pascua

Florida," or Easter Sunday.

Montana: Spanish for mountain or mountainous country.

New Mexico: Obviously, "a new Mexico," just as Mexico was named "New Spain."

Oregon: Most likely from the Spanish "Orejones," literally meaning "men with big ears or big-eared men."

—The city of Albuquerque, New Mexico, was originally named "San Felipe de Albuquerque." In was so named in 1706 by the then Governor Francisco Curvo y Valdés in honor of the Viceroy of Mexico, Francisco Fernández de la Cueva Henríquez, Duke of Alburquerque.

—Approximately 30% of all U.S. geographical names are Spanish or were designated Spanish names when they were first discovered, and in the Southwest, that percentage may reach over 50%. Of all the states, California and Texas have the most Spanish names, and between the two, the percentage of Spanish names may exceed 80%. Even in the state of Ohio, there is a town called "El Toboso," in honor of Don Quixote's heroine, "Dulcinea del Toboso."

On this subject of U.S. Spanish names, we would like to again quote H.L.Mencken:

> According to Harold W.Bentley, no less than 2000 American cities and towns have Spanish names, and thousands more are borne by rivers, mountains, valleys and other geographical entities. He says that there are more than 400 cities and towns of Spanish name in California alone. They are numerous all over the rest of the trans-Mississippi region, and, curiously enough, are even rather common in the East. And then this most striking revelations: Many names originally Spanish have been translated, e.g., "Río de los Santos Reyes" into Kings River, and "Río de las Plumas" into Feather River, or mauled by crude attempts to turn them into something more "American, " e.g., "Elsinore "in place of "El Señor, " and "Monte Vista" in place of "Vista del Monte. " It is estimated that about a fifth of the Spanish place-names in California are the names of saints, derived from the New Testament rather than from the Old. Other

modified or shorten Spanish names in California are: "Ventura," from "San Buena Ventura," "San José," from "San José de Guadalupe," and "Santa Clara," from "Santa Clara de Asís."

—Although short-lived, North America's first colony was San Miguel de Gualdape (Virginia), founded by the Spaniard Lucas Vázquez de Ayllón in 1526. The significance of this expedition is better explained by American historian Paul E. Hoffman:

All the Spaniards must have appreciated the importance of discovering what to them was a previously unknown land north of the Bahama Islands. But none could have known that their reports about this land would plant the seeds for one of the more important, if neglected, legends connected with North American explorations. Relocated and worked upon by men's imaginations until the discovery assumed the form of a new Andalucia flowing with milk and honey, not to mention laden with pearls, gold, silver, wine, grapes, and olives, it was to spawn a legend that, together with another legend about the continent born three years later, would motivate Spaniards, French, and Englishmen to explore and attempt to colonize the coast of North America between the latitudes 32° and 39° north.

—The discovery of the Gulf of Mexico by the Spaniards was a most significant event in the future discovery of North America. On this subject, American historian Robert S. Weddle wrote:

...The vital conduit for the first real European access to the North America mainland—the Gulf of Mexico—has been grossly neglected, never having been treated as the distinct entity that it is...Following Columbus' initial discovery of the fringe islands, the Andalusian voyagers groped their way through the maze, seeking a continent. Running uphill, as it were, they found Central and South America. Not for sixteen years did the first navigator find the crucial passage into the Gulf of Mexico. Another decade passed before the discoverers realized that a second continent lay beyond the Gulf. Only then could the actual discovery of mainland North America begin. Through this `Spanish Sea'—which the Gulf remained for almost two centuries after the first European entry—the discoverers and explorers advanced onto the continent. The Gulf and its environs were the theater for the earliest and most determined efforts to conquer the natives and explore and settle the interior.

—Although Juan Rodríguez Cabrillo had named San Diego Bay "San Miguel" (1542), Sebastián Vizcaíno renamed it "San Diego" for both his flagship and for the feast of San Diego de Alcalá on November 12. Incidentally, Cabrillo, before voyaging to North America (1540), had fought with Hernán Cortés in the conquest of Mexico and with Pedro de Alvarado in the conquest of Guatemala.

—An additional note about Vizcaíno and Cabrillo. Vizcaíno chartered the coast of California with such detail and accuracy that his maps were used until about 1790 (the map was actually drawn by the engineer Enrico Martín). And the map of Cabrillo was published by Archbishop Lorenzana in 1770. Indeed, both explorers contributed immensely to the knowledge of the entire region and to its future development.

—It was Spain the nation that chartered the sea route to the South Pacific, making it viable for all the voyages and explorations that followed. In addition, it paved the way for future voyages to China and Japan and for much of the commerce that ensued to those countries, particularly from North America. The known route for return from the Philippines was to steer north to latitude 30° to find favorable winds, and then to turn south immediately upon seeing seaweeds as a sign of approaching land. Such course brought ships to the lower end of Baja California from where they would continue south to Acapulco.

—Sebastian Cabot, son of John Cabot, was in the service of Spain for thirty years and married a Spaniard, Catalina Medrano, daughter of a Mexican colonizer. While in the service of Spain, he discovered the Paraná River and the interior of Argentina and Paraguay. Another famous explorer in the service of Spain, Ferdinand Magellan, married a Spaniard, Beatriz Barbosa, daughter of his Spanish mentor Diego Barbosa.

—The Spanish viceroys in Mexico sponsored many of the famous expeditions to North America, including those of Cortés and Francisco de Ulloa to the Gulf and the California Peninsula in 1535 and 1539; Marcos de Niza to Cibola (New Mexico), 1538; Francisco Vázquez de Coronado, 1540-1542; Rodríguez Cabrillo to Upper California, 1542; and Villalobos to the Pacific in 1542. Ortún Ordóñez, of the expedition of Cortés, discovered Baja (Lower) California in 1533. The viceroy of Mexico Juan Francisco Güemes de Horcasitas, First Count of Revillagigedo, during 1746-1755, many expeditions to North America, especially those carried out by the Jesuits, including Father Consag who explored the Gulf of California as a base for the colonization of the Gila and Colorado valleys and founded two presidios at Altar and Tubac. Another of these great viceroys (1789-1794) was Juan Vicente Güemes Pacheco de Padilla, son of the former and second count of Revillagigedo, who also dispatched an expedition to California mainly to safeguard the Spanish claim in that region against the British. It is interesting to note that it was he who preserved many of Mexico's historical documents and ordered a series of excavations throughout the country, one of which discovered the famous Aztec Calendar. The Spanish Viceroy of Mexico, Martin Mayorga (1779-1783) had to deal with the increasing hostilities of England during the American Revolution. One of his first measures was to fortify Veracruz in view of an imminent attack by a British fleet sent from New York in 1778, and Colonel Rosado seized the English colony of Belice. One of New Spain's greatest viceroys and the first in the Americas was Antonio de Mendoza (appointed by Charles V in 1535). One of his greatest achievements was to contain the great epidemic that devastated Mexico in 1545 in which over 800,000 people perished. He was also an ardent protector of the Indians, established the first archbishopric of Mexico, the first "Audiencia" (court) in the province of New Galicia (1548), the first national mint (1535), and during his government the Americas' first printing shop was established. He also founded the college of Tlaltelolco for the natives (1536) and the college of San Juan de Letrán for mestizos, and in 1537 the College of Santiago which was granted a charter as a university in 1551. He also expanded cattle ranching and the cultivation of the silkworm, constructed new roads and many other public works. And under his auspices new expeditions were launched to North America, including the ones already mentioned at the beginning of this section. And the Viceroy Fernando de Alencastre Noreña y Silva (1711-1716) founded many missions in Texas and strived to found many towns there. Finally, the viceroy Luis Enríquez de Guzmán (1650-1653) encouraged the further exploration of California. All of this progress in Mexico, barely a dozen years after it had been conquered by Cortés, had a major bearing on the future development of the United States. Finally we should mention the Viceroy José Sarmiento de Valladares, Count of Moctezuma y Tula (1696-1701), who married the fourth granddaughter of the Emperor Moctezuma, Andrea Moctezuma Jofre de Loaisa. He was responsible for the expedition of Father Salvatierra to California and helped him found his mission there. Father Salvatierra also discovered Loreto Harbor. In this regard, it should be noted that the Viceroyalty of New Spain comprised all lands north of the Isthmus of Panama up to the then known and unknown confines of North America, including New Mexico, Texas and California (these last two were part of the Audiencia of New Galicia). The list of able and dedicated viceroys of Mexico is extensive from the first Viceroy Antonio de Mendoza in 1535 to the last, Juan O' Donojú, in 1821 for a total period of 286 years. Many of the viceroys were first assigned to Peru and later to Mexico, or viceversa. Thus, future exploration and expansion of North America was greatly enhanced by the establishment of the viceroyalty of New Spain (Mexico) by Charles V in 1535. In this same year, Charles V also authorized the Americas' first mint

("Casa de la Moneda") in Mexico City, from which most of the gold and silver that freely circulated in Colonial America came.

There were a total of four Spanish viceroyalties in America, comprising all known lands in the New World separated by the Isthmus of Panama:

México, established in 1535 by Charles V with its capital in Mexico City. The first viceroy was Don Antonio de Mendoza. Originally it was named "Nueva España" (New Spain).

Perú, established in 1 544, also by Charles V with its capital in Lima. The first viceroy was Don Blasco Núñez de Vela.

New Granada, in 1739 with its capital in Santa Fe de Bogotá. The first viceroy was Don Antonio de la Pedrosa.

Río de La Plata, in 1777 with its capital in Buenos Aires. The first viceroy was Don Pedro de Cevallos.

The Americas' first viceroy was Christopher Columbus so named in the Capitulations of Santa Fe, and the second his son, Diego Colón. The Americas' first woman viceroy was María de Toledo, Diego Colón's wife.

—North and South America were first named on the map of Gerard Mercator of 1538, now preserved today in the New York Public Library.

—The discoveries of Mexico and Peru were as important to Spain as they were to the rest of Europe, and very especially to the future United States and to its expansion westward and beyond the Pacific. From the ports of these two countries, numerous voyages originated to the Pacific, including the one by the "Galleon of Manila" which paved the way to all future trade routes to the Pacific and most of Asia. Its first voyage began in 1571 and continued until 1734, and it contributed greatly to the commerce between Mexico and Japan, China, and India, and to the expansion of California and the entire North American northwest.

And in 1565, the San Lucas, sailing to the north of Japan discovered the route across the Pacific from west to east.

In terms of the discovery and exploration of the Pacific, the entire 16th century belongs to Spain. Then came the others, one hundred years later—the Dutch, English, and Germans. Micronesia, Melanesia (New Guinea, Salomon, Santa Cruz, Espiritu Santo, Guadalcanal), and Polinesia (Marquesas. Tuamotu, Manihiki, Tokelau), Islas de los Barbudos (today Marshall Islands), Islas de los Ladrones (Marianas), Carolina Islands, all discovered and explorered by Spain in the 16th century. The discoverers and explorers were all Spaniards, with the exception of Alexander Malaspina, another Italian in the service of Spain. Some of them were: Alvaro de Saavedra, García Jofre de Loaísa, Juan Sebastián Elcano, Ruy López de Villalobos, Íñigo Ortiz de Retes, Juan Gaitán (discoverer of Hawaii in 1555), Bernardo de la Torre, Gaspar Rico, Pedro Sarmiento de Gamboa, Miguel López de Legazpi (founder of the city of Manila, Philippines in 1571), Andrés de Urdaneta, Alvaro de Mendaña de Neira, Juan Fernández, Luis de Torres, Sebastián Vizcaíno.

—The North Platte River, in Nebraska or Wyoming, was originally named "Río de Jesús y María" by Pedro de Villazur (1720).

—The Spaniard Luis de Torres, of the Quirós' expedition, made many discoveries in the Pacific which enabled others to delineate many of the archipelagos in a 100,000-mile area of the Pacific. Many future cartographers based their maps on such important discoveries.

—Of California's fifty-eight counties, thirty-two have Spanish names, such as: Alameda, San Benito, San Luis Obispo, El Dorado; and of the sixteen largest metropolitan areas, fourteen have Spanish names, such as: Los Angeles, San Francisco, San Diego, Sacramento, San José, Santa Ana, and also many of its bays, such as Monterrey, San Pedro, Santa Bárbara, Santa Monica. And in New Mexico, there are also many counties with Spanish names, such as Cibola County (formerly Valencia County),

Socorro County, as well as throughout most of the southwestern states.

—In Alaska, there are over one hundred major Spanish place names or toponymes, such as: Ulloa Channel, Saint Nicholas Lake, Mexico Point, Madre de Dios Island, El Capitán Peak, Cape Suspiro, Isla de la Desgraciada, Mariposa Reef, and Isla del Totí. One of them in particular caught our attention, the last one, "Isla del Totí." Is there here a direct connection with the "totí," the black bird so common in the Caribbean?

—Five Spanish explorers and missionaries trekked over 100,000 miles in North America by horse, mule, or by foot. They were: Alvar Núñez Cabeza de Vaca, Hernando de Soto, Francisco Vázquez de Coronado, Friar Junípero Serra, and Father Juan Crispi. And this they did after also trekking many more miles in South America through jungles, swamps, and mountain ranges. Here are the specific numbers for two of them: De Soto's expedition traveled 3,000 miles over a five and a half-year period; Coronado, 3,500 miles over a three- year period. And here is a sixth: In Texas, the Marqués de Aguayo, in order to hold back the British, marched over one thousand miles and then returned to the Rio Grande on foot. Five hundred horses perished in a blizzard.

—The Americas' first navy was built in Mexico City during the conquest by Cortés. In the words of American historian James Norman:

> Martín López was a sixteenth century carpenter of Spain who joined Cortés' expedition to Mexico. He longed to become an adventurous swordsman, and he did. But it was his carpentry one of the greatest factors in the defeat of the Aztecs. Centuries before the word `prefabricated' was coined, López designated a prefabricated navy. He built thirteen ships, disassembled them, and had the parts carried acroos the tortuous mountain route to the huge lake fronting the capital city of Moctezuma. Reassembled, the little navy was indispensable in the storming of Tenochtitlán.

And, in North America, the first ships were built by Hernando de Soto's army on the banks of the Mississippi River in 1542.

—And the Americas' first-built large vessel was "Jesús María de la Limpia Concepción," commonly called "La Capitana." It was built in Ecuador and launched at Puna Island in 1644. It weighted 1,150 tons with a length of 122 feet and a beam of 40 feet. It was the flagship of the Viceroralty of Peru. It was sank in 1654.

—In 1548 Juan de Tolosa discovered the silver mine of Zacatecas, in Mexico, from which much of the silver flowing into Colonial America came. Around the same time, in Nueva Vizcaya, Francisco de Ibarra opened other silver mines, namely those of San Lucas, Sombrerete, Chalcuites, San Martín, and Fresnillo. Again, the direct beneficiaries of such treasures were mainly the American colonists who used it to finance their struggle against England. About thirty-five years later (1582-1583) the expedition of Antonio de Espejo discovered several silver mines in western Arizona.

—Other significant North American explorations by Spaniards were the expeditions of Fray Agustín Rodríguez and Francisco Sánchez Chamuscado to New Mexico in 1581, Antonio de Espejo to western Arizona in 1582-1583, where he discovered a silver mine; Gaspar Castaño de Sosa (1590), Leiva Bonilla and Gutiérrez de Humaña to Kansas or Nebraska in 1593.

—Another Spaniard, Diego Gutiérrez, drew a map of the northern part of the New World in 1562 which is preserved at the British Museum. It is the largest and most greatly detailed and engraved map up to that time. The famous mapmaker Mercator based the New World part of his map of 1569 on this map.

—One of the earliest maps of the Western Hemisphere was drawn by Joan Martínez, a Spanish (or Catalan) of Messina, Sicily, in 1578. It is preserved at the British Museum in London. He also published an atlas in the same year which is likewise preserved at the British Museum.

—And talking about maps, the famous Ortelius Map was mostly based on the book *Dell'historia del la China*, authored by the Augustinian Juan González Mendoza, and published in Venice in 1586. It deals with travels to China and Japan in the early 16th century, and provided much data on those countries as well as others. This is an Italian translation of the first Spanish edition published in Rome in 1585.

—Another great pioneer of the future United States was the missionary Eusebio Francisco Kino. He founded over twenty missions, among them, San Javier del Bac, in Tucson, and several churches. Sometimes alone, and others accompanied by natives, he made more than 50 journeys inland, bringing with him cattle, sheep, and horses, and distributing thousands of seeds to the natives. In 1701, he made two expeditions down the Colorado River, reaching the head of the Gulf and re-establishing that California was not an island but a peninsula. He was first to draw a map of Primería Alta, which remained a key source of exploration in that region until many years later. By 1702, he had baptized over 100,000 natives and written several books about his expeditions.

—Another major U.S. pioneer was Diego de Vargas Zapata, who led an expedition to New Mexico in 1693, bringing with him soldiers, priests, many natives, cattle, and carriages, foodstuffs and tools, thus becoming a predecessor of the American West's Wagon Trains

—Much of the knowledge gained on the territory of the land of Teguayo, comprising parts of Utah, Oregon, and California, is owed to the description made by Friar Alonso de Posada.

—The Peninsula of California was originally given the name "Nueva Andalucía" (New Andalucia –Andalucía is a province in southern Spain—), by Sebastián Vizcaíno in 1596.

—In 1718, Juan María Rivera discovered the "Montañas Rocosas" (Rocky Mountains).

—The survival of what has been labeled the United States' first colony, Jamestown, may have depended on a twist of fate. Here is the story in brief. Spain, infuriated by the English intrusion in its territory, dispatched Captain Pérez de Ecija to seize the colony and expel the English. At the last moment, Ecija had a change of heart and sent Indian allies in his place to do the job, but they were unsuccessful. Spain tried again in 1611, but it was now King Philip III who changed his mind believing that the colony would be short-lived.

—The beautiful island of Tahiti was explored by the Spaniard Domingo de Boenechea in 1772-1775, who named it "Isla de Amat" in honor of the viceroy of Peru, Manuel de Amat y Junyent. The island was discovered by the Englishman Wallis in 1767.

—Two major discoveries by the Spaniards took place in 1775: the discovery of the mouth of the Columbia River, on the border of Oregon- Washington, by Bruno Heceta, which he named "Bahia de la Asunción," and the discovery of Bodega Bay (California), named in honor of its discoverer, Juan Francisco de Bodega y Quadra. Other major discoveries in that same year included: Francisco Garcés, of the expedition of Captain Juan Bautista Anza, explored the Colorado River and the Mojave Desert, becoming the first European to set foot on present-day Nevada. He then traversed Sierra Nevada up to the Central California Valley, and later reached the Moquis in northeastern Arizona. His expedition diary is one of the most accurate and famous geographical documents of the North American West. In total, he had trudged almost 10,000 miles and made a great contribution to the knowledge of the North American southwest from New Mexico to California. One year later (1776, the year of the U.S. Independence), Friars Silvestre Vélez de Escalante and Francisco Anastasio Domínguez led an expedition toward Sierra de Plata. Following a northeastern route, they crossed the Rocky Mountains reaching an area then unknown to white men—the tributaries of the Colorado River. They continued toward the Dolores Valley, the Río de San Javier (Grand River), crossed the Río Buenaventura (Green River), and discovered "Lago de los Timpanogos" (Lake Utah) and the present-day state by this name, the Sevier River, the northern tributaries of the Colorado, Wasatch Mountains, and marked a southwestern route later called "The Old Spanish Trail." They wrote a detailed account of the expedition, including many of the customs of the natives. Two rivers and several other geographical sites were named by the U.S. Government in honor of these two friars. Also in this year, Juan Bautista de Anza founded the great city of San Francisco, California.

—In 1863, another Spanish scientific expedition, "The Scientific Commission of the Pacific," docked in San Francisco (October 9th). This was a reconnaissance scientific expedition sponsored by Spain between 1862-1866, one of the greatest ever. As Robert Ryal Millar stated:

> Spanish monarchs sponsored scientific expeditions to the New World over a period of four centuries, but the last great reconnaissance was in the 1860s when a royal scientific commission visited a dozen countries of Lain America. Although the naturalists crossed the Argentine Pampas, surveyed the Atacama Desert, examined Andean archeological sites, photographed people and places from Brazil to California, descended the full length of the Amazon River, and sent home crates containing 82,000 specimens of plants and minerals, the story of their adventure is virtually unknown. There is no published account of it in English, French, or German, and the two printed summaries in Spanish are rare and not well-known.

Principal also among these expeditions was the one led by Alejandro Malaspina (an Italian in the service of Spain since 1776) and José Bustamante y Guerra in search of the fabled Northwest Passage (named by the Spaniards Strait of Ferrer Maldonado) in 1791, collecting hundreds of celestial observations data to determine accurate longitude, as well as botanical and zoological specimens of all sorts and including detailed artists' renditions of many of them. Among these artists was the celebrated Tomás de Suria who had studied in Mexico. In addition to these, they recorded visually the people and customs of the region which are now kept at the Naval Museum in Madrid. A map of the area was also drawn by the Spanish artist Bauzá. As it had been common practice among the Spaniards from the beginning, the officers of the expedition, on specific orders by the Spanish Crown, strived to learn the language and culture of the local aborigines, the Tlingits, whom they treated affably and with much understanding. The interpreter for the expedition was Gabriel del Castillo, from Guadalajara. The expeditioners bestowed many of the areas they had visited with Spanish names, such as "Puerto del Desengaño" (today Disenchantment Bay), Mount "Buen Tiempo" (Fairweather), "Cape Engaño" (called by Captain Cook before Edgecumbre Cape), "Isla de Santiago" (St. James Island), "Hezeta Strait" (now the Columbia River), "Point Muñoz," "Príncipe Guillermo" (Prince Williams Sound), "Cabo Chupador (Cape Suckling, these two along the Alaska coast), "Santa Cruz de Nutka", etc. En route to Prince Williams Sound, they bestowed these other names: "Islas de Magdalena" (Hinchinbrook), "Cabo Arcadio" (Cape Hinchenbrook), "Isla Triste" (Seal Rocks), "Ensenada de Castilla," "Entrada de Aragón," "Bahía de Palma," "Puerto de los Remedios," "Islas Mazarredo" (Nootka Island), "Cala de los amigos" (Friendly Cove), "Puerto de Córdoba" (Esquimalt Harbour), Canal de Nuestra Señora del Rosario (Strait of Georgia), Angostura de loa Comandantes (Arran Rapids), etc. Incidentally, Vancouver Island was originally called "Vancouver and Quadra Island," and, besides the North American Pacific Coast, Malaspina voyaged also to the remote lands of Guam, the Philippines, Macao, Australia, New Zealand and many islands in Oceania. On his voyage of five years, he had circumnavigated the world, arriving in Cádiz September 21, 1794 (he had sailed from Cádiz on July 30, 1789). Today, the glacial of Mount Saint Elías bears his name.

Following on the heels of the Malaspina expedition, was the one led by Dionisio Alcalá Galiano and Cayetano Valdés, sailing from Acapulco on the *Sutil* and *Mexicana* schooners in 1792, in a reconnaissance mission of the Juan de Fuca Strait.

Here again, in the exploration of the vast region north of California, or the Pacific Northwest, the Spanish enterprise has been minimized or undermined by the British first and later by the United States, beginning with the erasing or substitution of original Spanish place names. All told, little merit and recognition has been afforded to the Spanish exploration of the U.S. Pacific Coast, as a result of which Donald C. Cutter wrote his book: *Malaspina and Galiano: Spanish Voyages to the Northwest Coast*. In it, historian Cutter lamented that, "The Spanish heritage of the Pacific Northwest has long been overshadowed by that of the region 's more persistent colonizers, the English." And, as stated therein, "With this book, commissioned to honour the two- hundredth anniversary of the Malaspina expedition," Donald C. Cutter sets right the historical balance, telling the rich story of Spain along our shores. To Mr. Cutter, both expeditions constituted" Spain 's major contribution to eighteenth century science."

For several years, Spain and England vied for control of the North American Pacific Coast, and the time came, inevitably, in which both nations came very close to the brink of war. This is how the event unfolded: In 1789, while in China, John Meares dispatched two ships, the Argonaut and the Princess Royal to meet another ship, the Iphigenia, in Nootka Sound, which was the first to arrive. Two Spanish ships, the San Carlos and the Princesa, seized the Iphigenia and the North-west America, and later the Argonaut and the Princess Royal, on the grounds that they were intruding on Spanish territory, as Spain had claimed the entire northern coast and all adjacent seas. The Spanish commercial code forbade any foreign ships from trading in the area, considering them guilty of smuggling and even piracy. England protested and threatened Spain with war. At the end, Spain backed down and signed the Nootka Convention in 1790, whereby she returned the confiscated ships and relinquished all claims to the Northern Pacific coast. At the time Spain's monarch was Charles IV (1788-1808), a Bourbon, known for his weakness and inefficiency and for ceding Louisiana back to France and losing Menorca to the British.

It is interesting to note that Francisco Antonio Maurelle, a second pilot in the Bodega y Quadra journey to the northwest coast of North America in 1775, wrote a journal of the voyage that Spain never published fearing intrusion in her domains by the English and the Russians. However, in 1781, a Briton by the name of Daines Barrington, got hold of a copy of the manuscript and published it in a book entitled *Miscellanies*. Maurelle's journal was a significant source of information and proved invaluable for Cook's third voyage. And while on the subject of the Malaspina and Galiano and Valdés expeditions, we should also take notice that the Spaniards were the first Europeans to establish a settlement in what it is known today as the northwestern United States, at Port of Núñez Gaona. It is depicted in a detailed ink and wash drawing made by José Cardero and preserved at the Museo de América in Madrid.

—How did other Europeans get to America during the 16th and 17th centuries? They voyaged on ships built following the Spanish and Portuguese techniques unknown to them before. And they voyaged following a route delineated by Christopher Columbus: Out-ward bound via the northeast trades to the south of the Sargasso (or the mid-Atlantic), and back via the Westerlies to the north of the Sargasso.

—Sacramento is the capital of today's California. In 1695, José Sarmiento de Valladares founded Loreto Harbor or Sacramento, which later became this capital.

—A woman, Isabel de Bobadilla, wife of Hernando de Soto, was not only governor of Cuba but also a key contributor to her husband's expedition to North America. Over and over again she helped him by providing all of the supplies needed for the expedition. Another woman, María de Toledo, was not only the America's first woman governor (Santo Doming, 1515), but also served her husband (Diego Colón, son of Christopher Columbus) both as a confidant and supporter of the many expeditions he sponsored. A third woman, Isabel Barreto y Quirós, added much navigational knowledge of the South Pacific. In fact, when her famous husband (Alvaro de Mendaña) died unexpectedly, she took the reins of command and completed the voyage. She is the only woman named an Admiral of the Spanish Navy. The actions of these three women impacted greatly the future development of the U.S. Pacific Coast.

—Although a Russian mariner, Aleksei Chirikov, is credited with having sighted Alaska in 1741 (probably Prince of Wales Island), two Spaniards, Juan Francisco de la Bodega y Quadra and Ignacio Arteaga, explored most of the region in 1779. It should be mentioned that a Danish sea captain, Vitus Bearing, passed by the area in 1728 but may have missed land due to dense fog. In 1790, another Spaniard, Francisco Elija, also explored the coast of Alaska, and other Spaniards founded a city they named "Valdés" (Valdez). Also, in 1791, another Spaniard, Alejandro Malaspina, explored the region between Alaska and Nootka (the Malaspina Glacier is named in his honor.) He then sighted Mounts Edgecumbe, Fairweather, and San Elías in southeast Alaska, and in June of the same year reached Mulgrave Harbor and explored Prince Williams Sound and Montague Island. A year later, 1792, the expedition of Malaspina passed through New Hebrides, New

Zealand, Sidney (Australia), and Mindanao. At the end of a five-year voyage, he lead gathered an extraordinary amount of scientific data and measured latitudes and longitudes with precision. It should be mentioned that in 1794 Spain took possession of Nootka Sound in Vancouver Island, and José Mariano Mozino conducted there a detailed study of the language, religion, government, and customs of the region. He even wrote a dictionary of the Nootka language.

—Spain discovered the Caribbean Sea, the Gulf of Mexico, the Pacific Ocean, and charted the Atlantic route to America. Think what all four bodies of water have meant to the development of the United States, and what they mean today.

—The first European women and children arrived in North America with the expedition of Lucas Vázquez de Ayllón in 1525, and the first African-American woman, Isabella, arrived in Jamestown in 1619 on a Spanish cargo ship bound for the West Indies.

—The island of Bermuda, in the Bahamas, was discovered by Juan Bermúdez in 1522, who named it after himself. It was later changed to its present name.

—Jamaica was first named by Columbus, who discovered it on his second voyage (May 5, 1494) "Isla de Santiago" but later he changed it to "Yamaye" from which "Jamaica" is derived.

—At the time of Hernán Cortés' death (1547), North America was divided into two parts: New Hispania (Mexico) and La Florida. This according to Ptolemy "Geografía" published in 1508.

—Here is a most interesting fact although not directly related to U.S. history. The name of the continent of Australia ("Terra Australis Incognita") was taken from *"Australia* del Espíritu Santo,"* the name given by Pedro Fernández de Quirós to a large island in the "Archipiélago de Nuevas Hébridas" in honor of the "Casa de *Austria"* or House of Hapsburgs.

—A key event in the future development of North America, was the conquest, exploration, and colonization of Nueva Galicia (northern Mexico) by Nuño de Guzmán in 1530-31. It soon became the focal point of future explorations northward, especially after the establishment of a permanent government in Guadalajara and the founding of its capital, Compostela.

—Many people think that the Spanish presence in North America was mainly in the south and the Southwest. Although it may be partially true because of the proximity to Mexico and the Caribbean, the Spanish also explored and settled many areas of the Southeast. For example, as early as 1520, Francisco Gordillo and Pedro de Quejos landed near Cape Fear in North Carolina, called "Chicora" by the natives. Five years later, in 1525, Pedro de Quejos explored the eastern seaboard and reached New Jersey.

—Louisiana was indeed purchased from France in 1803, but that vast territory (double the size of the United States) had been explored and settled previously by Spain. It opened the heartland of America, the United States, to all future discoveries, explorations, and settlements.

—Without the U.S. expansion in the 19th century into territories discovered, colonized, and settled and explored by Spain, we would be seeing today a United States occupying a territory less than half of its present size, with no direct outlet to the Pacific Ocean, the Gulf of Mexico, or the Caribbean Sea.

—The town of Ponte Vedra, in Florida, was named after the city of "Pontevedra" in Galicia, Spain.

—And Bourbon Street in New Orleans was named after the Bourbon Kings of Spain.

—Explorer Amerigo Vespucci, while in Spain, married the Spaniard María Cerezo. He was also made a naturalized citizen of Spain in 1505, and from that moment forward was in the service of Spain. His nephew, Juan Vespucci, was appointed royal pilot in 1512.

—Some of our greatest present-day cities were founded by Spain, such as San Francisco and Los Angeles, as was America's first city: St. Augustine in Florida. And so were the discoveries of many of our natural wonders, including the Grand Canyon, the Mississippi River, Lake Utah, Sierra Nevada, the Rocky Mountains, Sierra Nevada, the Mojave Desert, as well as the Gulf of Mexico, the Pacific Ocean, and the Caribbean Sea. Think of today's United States without of all of these marvelous works of nature including Yosemite (California) or Yellowstone (Wyoming).

—In 1763, 13 years before the Declaration of Independence, all lands west of the Mississippi, north and south, were under Spanish domain, about two-thirds of present-day United States if Florida is included. As American historian E.G. Bourne wrote: "More than half of the present territory of the United States at one time or another has been under Spanish rule." Louisiana, back then, was not as it is today; in fact, it was called "país" (country, just as Florida was) by the Spaniards, and it comprised the territory of the present-day states of Louisiana, Arkansas, Oklahoma, Kansas, Missouri, Nebraska, Iowa, the Dakotas, Montana, and parts of Minnesota, Colorado and Wyoming. Spain held the Louisiana territory for forty-one years, from 1763 to 1803, and reached its maximum territorial domain in North America from 1783 to 1803, when it extended from Florida to California.

Part D

EARLY HISPANIC SETTLEMENTS IN NORTH AMERICA

—Of the thirteen original U.S. colonies, Spain was first in establishing settlements in:

Virginia: Jesuit missionaries from Mexico (New Spain) founded a mission at Chesapeake from 1570 to 1572. At that time, the area was considered part of northern Florida. This was almost 40 years before the settlement of the Virginia Company of London in 1607;

South Carolina: The Spanish established a colony at Santa Elena (Hilton Head) in 1566;

Georgia: The Spanish established a colony on Santa Catalina Island in 1566, and in 1573, Franciscan missionaries established a mission on Cumberland Island. This was about a century and a half before the British settlement at Fort King George (Darien) in 1721.

And what role did Spain play in the founding of some of the other present- day U.S. states? Plenty, as detail below (listed in alphabetical order):

Alabama: The first to establish a settlement was the Spaniard Tristán de Luna in 1559 at Mobile Bay, and later missions were founded by the Franciscans. France claimed it in 1699 and it remained under its control until 1763. Then England took it over until 1783 when the area became part of West Florida. On that same year, Mobile was ceded to Spain while the rest of Alabama was incorporated into Georgia. Mobile became part of the United States in 1813 following the War of 1812.

Arizona: The Franciscans founded the first missions in the northeastern area in 1629, and then the Jesuits in the southeast in 1692. These, plus other missions came to be known as Primera Alta, on the Arizona-Sonora frontier in 1701. In 1751 the Spaniards built a presidio at Tubac and later at Tucson in 1776. In 1810 Arizona became part of Mexico and in the mid- nineteenth century of the United States.

Arkansas: Although established by the French in 1686, the part known as Upper Louisiana was ceded to Spain in 1763.

California: The first settlement was the Mission of San Diego de Alcalá. Then other missions were founded as follows: Monterrey in 1770; San Gabriel in 1771; San Antonio de Padúa in 1771; San Luis Obispo in 1772; San Francisco in 1776 (the same year of the U.S. Declaration of Independence); San José in 1777; Los Angeles (town) in 1781; and Santa Bárbara in 1782. In 1822 California became part of Mexico and annexed to the United States in 1850.

Florida: The first settlement was a presidio at Saint Augustine in 1565. The Franciscan monks settled in the area in 1572. In 1763 it was ceded to England and divided into West and East Florida. In 1784 it was returned to Spain. In 1812 most of West Florida was annexed to Mississippi and Louisiana, and in 1819 the rest of the territory was ceded to the United States.

Louisiana: In 1762 France ceded to Spain the area known as Lower and Upper Louisiana, west of the Mississippi.

Minnesota: in 1762 it was ceded by France to Spain and in 1763 by Spain to England.

New Mexico: The first settlement was San Juan de los Caballeros founded in 1598. Its two major cities, Santa Fe (the capital) and Albuquerque were founded in 1610 and 1706 respectively. Then it became part of Mexico in 1821 and ceded by Mexico to the United States in 1848 by the Treaty of Guadalupe Hidalgo.

Tennessee: In 1775, the Spaniards built Fort San Juan de los Barrancos, in present-day Memphis.

Texas: In 1659 the Franciscans founded a mission near El Paso and a presidio also at El Paso in 1682. In 1690 two missions were founded: San Francisco de las Tejas and Santísimo Nombre de María, both on the Neches River. In 1700, another mission, San Juan Bautista, was founded, and in 1716 various presidios were established. The presidio of San Antonio de Béjar was established in 1718. In 1779 the cities of Nacogdoches and Laredo were founded. Texas became part of Mexico in 1822, an independent republic in 1836, and was annexed to the United States in 1845.

So now we have that, of the thirteen original colonies, Spain had the first settlement in three of them; that of the rest of those present-day states, Spain also established the first settlements in most of them, actually in nine of them; and that, of the present-day fifty states, Spain discovered or explored twenty-eight of them, or over half. This in itself speaks volumes about Spain/Hispanics contribution to the making of the whole United States. Modern historians and teachers of American History from across the nation should take good note of this indisputable fact.

In summary, Hispanics established 28 settlements extending from California to North Carolina between 1526 and 1782. Listed below are the settlements by states:

Arizona:
Tubac in 1752. Tucson in 1752.

California:
San Diego in 1769. Monterey in 1770.
San Francisco in 1776. San José in 1777.
Los Angeles in 1781. Santa Barbara in 1782. Santa Cruz (Brancifuerte) in 1787.

Florida:
Saint Augustine in 1655.
San Luis de Apalache in 1650. San Marcos de Apalache in 1660. Pensacola in 1698.

Louisiana:
Los Adaes in 1716.

New Mexico:
San Gabriel in 1599. Santa Fe in 1605.
Santa Cruz in 1695. Albuquerque in 1706. Taos (18th century).

North Carolina:
San Miguel de Gualdape in 1526.

South Carolina:
Fort San Felipe in 1566.

Texas:
Béjar (San Antonio) in 1718. La Bahía in 1749.
Laredo in 1755.
Dolores in 1755.
San Luis in 1757.
Nacogdoches in 1779.

Washington:
Núñez Gaona in 1792.

Part E

HISPANICS LAY THE FOUNDATION OF THE FUTURE UNITED STATES

—Hispanics set many firsts in North America, one hundred years before any other European nation. Here is a partial list:

Professions and trades:

Doctors, surgeons, dentists, astronomers, anthropologists, archeologists, botanists, theologians, pharmacists, veterinarians, nurses, law-makers and enforcers, teachers, lawyers, accountants, assayers, bankers, engineers, architects, musicians, artists, governors, mayors, councilmen, chemists, physicists, linguists, historians, mathematicians, writers, poets, judges, politicians, administrators, mariners, seamen, sailors, mechanics; carpenters, masons, bricklayers, locksmiths, blacksmiths, miners, lumbermen, bakers, ranchers, farmers, cowboys, cooks, seamstresses, weavers, tailors, midwives, grocers, florists. It is worth noting that the Americas' first autopsy of an Indian was performed at the University of Mexico in 1579 (to investigate the cause of an epidemic that had devastated Mexico).

—Hispanics also:

Introduced the wheel and all metals including iron, copper, tin, bronze, brass, steel; all fabrics, including wool and silk; weapons and tools; milked the first cows and goats; made the first cheeses and wines, cooked the first European meals and wore the first European clothes; introduced coffee and tobacco; fruits, such as apples, pears, oranges, peaches, grapes, sugar cane, wheat, flour, spices, and many of today's fragrant plants and flowers, such as the rose, the geranium, and the carnation; cattle, horses, pigs, bulls, and poultry, and we must not forget soap. As early as 1501, the horse, bovine cattle and fowl had been introduced in the Dominican Republic.

—On the subject of winemaking, it is an established fact that Spanish soldiers but mainly the Spanish missionaries pioneered the industry throughout the Southwest, including California, Texas, and New Mexico during the 17th and 18th centuries. This came with the founding of the missions and with the valuable winemaking techniques (such as irrigation) that the missionaries brought with them and later taught to the natives. The so-called "Mission grape," planted by the missionaries, became the basis of wine production throughout the region. Today, California produces 90% of the grape crush and 85% of all the wines produced in the United States, mainly in the Sonoma and Napa Valley regions, and the early Spanish missionaries are to be thanked for that. In Texas, the Spanish missionaries planted in the 1600s about 50% of the world's known grape species, and the same applies to New Mexico. In Texas, Father García de San Francisco y Zúñiga established a vineyard in 1650 using the black grape, where he produced the sacramental wine. Later, around 1680, the Spanish army fleeing from the Pueblo revolt in New Mexico established several missions which quickly began to produce wines. In 1830 the Islatta Winery opened in El Paso, one of the oldest wineries in North America.

—More on the subject of food. Hispanics also introduced the red beans (the "Habichuelas") to Louisiana which quickly spread throughout the region and far beyond, They were brought from the Caribbean, as well as oranges to Florida, today one of this state's most formidable industries. Red beans with rice, so typical in Spanish-America, became one of Louisiana's main staples, particularly during the forty years that it was under Spanish domain. Cooking wine, introduced by the Franciscan friars in Texas (El Paso) in the eighteenth century, is an integral part of many gastronomical dishes in that region as well as in others. Rum was brought into Florida by Juan Ponce de León and the conquistadors, as was the chickpeas and a large variety of other legumes and spices, such as peppers (especially the *Capsicums* kind), garlic, and safflower. It is interesting to note that in the northern region, the Puritans later banned the cultivation of many of these spices, including peppers, believing that they stirred up passion in their consumers. Chile peppers are widely cultivated today throughout the Southwest, especially in California, Arizona, New Mexico, and Texas. Other popular dishes introduced by the Spaniards, particularly in California, was the roast pork, as was the "arroz con pollo" (chicken with rice). The avocado, although originally of South America, was brought to the North by the Spaniards. It is said that Hernán Cortés was first to taste it and liked it, and so was George Washington when he first took a bite at it while in Barbados. Hispanics also brought it to Hawaii around 1825, and some years later a man by the name of Henry Perrine cultivated it in Miami. And they also perfected the barbecue *(Barbacoa)* by marinating the meat in sauces with hot peppers and garlic, and by substituting the crude woods with charcoal.

—Hispanics also fostered many other principal industries in America with the introduction of iron and other metallurgies, new textiles such as wool, cotton, linen, silk; glass, weaponry, gunpowder, tools of all types; the wheel, the wax candle, machines, such as lathe, pulley, the water and animal-pulled mills, the waterwheel, the sugar mill. Mexico alone, by 1540, produced over 15,000 pounds of silk, and similar industrial expansions were achieved in Peru and Ecuador with sheep wool, leather, and cotton, and also in Havana, Campeche, Guayaquil, and El Callao with shipbuilding, first in Santo Domingo and then in the rest of the Caribbean and New Spain with the production of sugar cane, plus flour, tobacco, cheese, soap, shoes, saddles, ceramics, baskets, hats, silverwork, foundry, especially of precious metals and bronze in the manufacturing of cannons, bells; minting, lumber, furniture, smithy; alcoholic beverages, fishing, dyes etc. Alexander von Humboldt estimated that in Mexico the industrial production totaled 7 to 8 million pesos, mining 25 million pesos, and agriculture 30 million pesos. All of these industries greatly benefited the future colonization of North America by Hispanics and set the economic foundation of what it was later to become the United States.

—Built the infrastructures of the first cities and towns, such as roads, bridges, ports; established the first museums, libraries, botanical gardens, zoos, forts, hospitals, shelters, community and social institutions, printing presses, schools, convents, monasteries, churches, post offices, charities, workers' unions, and stores. Regarding the roads, they were built in all directions, starting from the south toward the north, northwest, northeast, as well as west to east. It is interesting to note that in 1505 father Hernán Suárez founded the Americas' first school and Franciscan convent in the Dominican Republic which he called "San Francisco." The first cathedral was also built in the Dominican Republic in 1512, and the first high court (Audiencia) also in the Dominican Republic in 1510. The first technical and vocational school—"Colegio de San Francisco"—was founded by Friar Pedro de Gante in Mexico City in 1592. The first Catholic church in North America was built by Friar Francisco de Pareja in Saint Augustine, Florida, in 1560, and the first parish consecrated by Friar Martín Francisco López de Mendoza in 1565. It is also worth noting that in 1567 Bernardino Alvarez, a conquistador from Peru, founded in Mexico the America's first mental hospital called "Hospital y Asilo de Convalescientes de San Hipolito." He also founded many more hospitals throughout Mexico (in contrast, the first U.S. hospital was founded in Philadelphia in 1752). The Spaniards also founded North America's first hospital in Florida in 1597. In this regard, it should also be noted that at that time Spain was way ahead of Europe in caring for the mentally ill, being the first to found psychiatric hospitals in Europe. Further, none of Spain's hospitals in the Americas discriminated against social status or race, as all patients were welcomed along with the Spaniards. The first convent for the poor and abandoned women was founded by Saint Toribio de Mogrovejo in Lima in 1580. The America's first charity—San Nicolás—was established in the Dominican Republic by a pious black women of unknown name in 1501. The first workers' union in the Americas was established in Mexico City in 1546. North Americas' first forts were established by Pedro Menéndez de Avilés between 1566-1567 in today's eastern Florida (San Antonio, Ays, Tocobaga –Tampa Bay—, Santa Lucía, Tequesta), Georgia (Guale), and South Carolina (Santa Elena). They also established the first army and navy. The Americas' first library was established in Mexico City in 1762, followed by Bogotá, 1777, Quito, 1792, and Havana, 1793.

—Hispanics introduced printing in Los Angeles in 1640.

—Introduced western medical knowledge in the New World.

—Navigated the first rivers and lakes, including the mighty Mississippi, and climbed the first mountains and valleys.

—Founded the Americas' first city, Santa María de la Antigua (Isthmus of Panama) in 1510, by Alonso de Hojeda, preceded only by Hispaniola (founded on January 6, 1494), almost 100 years before Jamestown (1607).

—We would like to elaborate further on this subject of city planning and building. Hispanics built not only the first but also the best cities in America. In fact, the "... Laws of the Indies, proclaimed by Philip II in 1573, were America's First City Planning Legislation," according to historian John W. Peps. He continued:

> As the Spanish extended their settlements throughout the Caribbean Islands and to Mexico and Central and South America, and as the pace of colonization accelerated, the issuance of individual orders and directives for each expedition became inefficient and unnecessary. In 1573 Philip II proclaimed the Laws of the Indies to establish uniform standards and procedures for planning of towns and their surrounding lands as well as for all the other details of colonial settlement. While parts of these royal ordinances established new requirements and regulations, virtually of all the sections governing town planning represented a mere codification of practices that had become fairly standardized a score of years earlier. This conclusion is supported by an examination of plans of cities founded before 1573, which appear to coincide in all essential features with the prescriptions of the Laws of the Indies.
>
> Because of the relative inflexibility of Spanish colonial policy, the regulations of 1573 remained virtually unchanged throughout the entire period of Spanish rule in the Western Hemisphere. Literally hundreds of communities were planned in conformity to their specifications—a phenomenon unique in modern history. A brief review of some of the more important town planning aspects of the Laws of the Indies is essential for an understanding of the urban forms which were to be used by the Spanish settlers in the area of the United States."

And then Mr. Peps goes on to describe in detail the specifics of city planning as per the regulations prescribed in the Laws of the Indies. "These remarkable regulations," he continues, "stand out as one of the most important documents in the history of city planning."

Mr. Peps brings out an interesting point in the way Spain laid out cities as per the type of settlements: Missions to house religious orders and to work on the conversion of the Indians;

Presidios as military outposts for the protection and defense from foreign invaders; and Pueblos for normal civilian life, including trade and farming. Such planning, although clear in theory, not always worked in practice as the distinction between one and the other often disappeared. In North America, Mr. Peps cites as a perfect example of such mixture—religious, military, and civil— the town of San Antonio, Texas, as it was originally laid out: The presidio of San Antonio de Béjar, founded by Martin de Alarcón in 1718; the Mission of San Antonio de Valero (which was later to become the Alamo) and the pueblo of San Fernando founded by families brought in from the Canary Islands in 1730. As near perfect examples of cities laid out in conformity with the Laws of the Indies, Mr. Peps gives San José and Los Angeles in California, i.e. streets, plaza, and building sites: A redrawing of an early survey of Los Angeles shows the regular design of the plaza and the buildings around it in the town proper and, at a scale reduced to one-fifth that of the town, the checkerboard pattern of the farm fields beyond.

City planning and building was one of Spain's greatest contribution to the Americas, more so in the south than in the north, the reason being that city planning in North America was almost confined by necessity to the coastal areas, as it was in the case in St. Augustine where a fort was erected to guard the port from the French.

—During the Spanish colonial period (we used the term "colonial" freely as Spain never thought of their possessions in America as "colonies" but rather as "provinces"), the cities built rivaled those of Europe in every aspect, and in the case of Mexico City and especially Lima, even surpassed them. Certainly, there were no cities in the U.S. colonial period—New York, Boston, Philadelphia—that could even stand a basic comparison with any of the Spanish American cities, be them Mexico, Lima, Santo Domingo, Havana, or Guatemala. Alexander von Humboldt was filled with awe, truly mesmerized when he set eyes on Mexico City and Lima, and even the English Franciscan friar Thomas Cage, no friend of Spain at all, was struck by the beauty and majesty of Guatemala which he visited between 1625 and 1637.

—Hispanics were also the first priests, nuns, preachers and evangelists, who celebrated the first masses, organized the first church choirs, lumbered the first trees, and painted the first structures. Friar Bartolomé de las Casas celebrated America's first mass in the Americas at Ciudad de la Vega, Dominican Republic, in 1512.

—They were even the first martyrs. Friar Juan de la Cruz, who was killed by the natives at Tigüex, New Mexico, and his brother Luis de Escalona at Pecos, also in New Mexico in 1541.

—They also authored and published the first histories, geographies, and narratives of the Americas, such as *Décadas* (Decades), by Pedro Mártir de Anglería in 1516; *Summa de Geografía*, by Martín Fernández de Enciso in 1520, and *Geografía y descripción universal de las Indias* (Geographical and Universal Description of the Indies), by Juan López de Velasco in 1519.

Other pioneering publications in the 16th and 17th centuries were (partial list):

Letters of Relation to the Emperor (Charles V) by Hernán Cortés;

Historia natural de las Indias (Natural History of the Indies), by Gonzalo Fernández de Oviedo in 1535;

Vocabulario trilingüe en castellano, en latín y mexicano (Trilingual Vocabulary in Spanish, Latin, and Nahualt), and *Vocabulario y gramática del Nahualt* (Nahualt Vocabulary and Grammar), both by Friar Bernardino de Sahagún in 1535;

Historia general de las Indias (General History of the Indies), by Francisco López de Gómara in 1552;

The Narrative of the Expedition of Francisco Vázquez de Coronado, by Pedro de Castañeda,1550-1552;

Naufragios (published with the Comentarios), by ÁlvarNúñez Cabeza de .Vaca in 1555;

True Relations of the Hardships of Governor Fernando de Soto and Certain Portuguese Gentlemen During the Discovery of the Province of Florida, by the Gentleman of Elvas. The first Portuguese edition was published in 1557;

Relación de la jornada que fizo el general Sevastián Vizcayno al descumbrimiento de las Californias el eno de 1602 (Relation of the Journey of General Sebastina Vizcaino to the Discovery of the Californias in the Year 1620), by Father Antonio de la Ascensión in 1620;

Islario General (first atlas of the Americas), by Alonso de Santa Cruz in 1560;

Historia natural y moral de las Indias (Natural and Moral History of the Indies) by father José de Acosta in 1590;

Historia general de los hechos de los castellanos en las islas y tierra firme del mar Océano(General History of the Spaniards in the Islands and. Mainland of the Ocean Sea),by Antonio de Herrera in 1601-1605;

Historia de la Florida y jornada que a ella hizo el gobernador Hernando de Soto (History of Florida and of the Expedition of Hernando de Soto), by the Inca Garcilaso de la Vega in 1605;

Origen de los indios del Nuevo Mundo (Origins of the Indians of the New World), by Friar Gregorio García in 1607;

Historia de la Nueva México (History of New Mexico), by Gaspar Pérez de Villagrá (of the Oñate expedition) in 1610. The first poetical work published in North America;

Vocabulario manual de las lenguas castellana y mexicana (Vocabulary Handbook of the Spanish and Mexican Languages), by Pedro de Arenas in 1611;

Epítome de la bibliotheca oriental y occidental, náutica y geográphica (A Summary of the Eastern and Western Library,

Nautical and Geographical) by Antonio León Pinelo in 1629, the first bibliography of works published in the Americas;

Historia verdadera de la conquista de la Nueva España (The True History of the Conquest of New Spain), by Bernal Díaz del Castillo in 1632;

Historia natural de las Indias (Natural History of the Indies) by Francisco Hernández, published in Mexico in 1615. In 1570 he was appointed by Philip II Surgeon General of the Indies and the Spanish possessions in the Pacific;

Geografía y descripción de las Indias (Geography and Description of the Indies) by Juan López de Velasco;

Milicia y descripción de las Indias (Militia and Description of the Indies), by Bernardo de Vargas Machuca, published in 1599;

Origen de los indios del Nuevo Mundo (Origin of the Indians of the New World), by Fray Gregorio García, published in 1607;

Historia del Nuevo Mundo (History of the New World), by Juan Bautista Muñoz (only volume I was published in 1793);

Diccionario geográfico-histórico de las Indias Occidentales (Geographical and Historical Dictionary of the Indies), by Antonio de Alcedo y Herrera, published in 1786-89;

Compendio y descripción de las Indias Occidentales (Compendium and Description of the Indies), by Fray Antonio Vázquez de Espinosa, published by the Smithsonian Institution in 1942;

Historia de los indios de Nueva España (History of the Indians of New Spain), by Toribio de Benavente or Motolinia, published in parts in 1848 by Lord Kingsborough;

Monarquía Indiana (Indian Monarchy), by Juan de Torquemada, published in 1613;

Virtudes del indio (Virtues of the Indians), by Juan de Palafox, published circa 1650;

Historia de la conquista de México (History of the Conquest of Mexico), by Antonio de Solis, published in 1648;

Historia de la conquista de Nueva Galicia (History of the Conquest of New Galicia), by Matías de la Mota Padilla, published in the 18th century;

Historia de la Nueva México (History of New Mexico), by Gaspar de Villagrá, published in 1610.

Another critically important work was *Diccionario geográfico de las Indias Occidentales* (Geographical Dictionary of the West Indies), by Antonio de Salcedo, published in 1787. The first English translation by G.A. Thompson appeared in London in 1812. It is a magnificent 5-volume edition containing thousands of articles, e.g. New York, Cuzco, Texas, Mexico, California, Oaxaca, with dozens of charts and tables. It must be mentioned that it was published several years before Humboldt's encyclopedia.

But by far, the most important work of the time was *Arte de navegar* (Art of Navigation), by Friar Pedro de Medina, published in Valladolid in 1545, the first treatise to provide authoritative navigational information on American waters. It was intended to be an instructional manual for voyaging to the New World. In addition to charts and sailing directions, Medina made astrolabes, quadrants, compasses, fore staffs and other navigational instruments. His table of the sun's declinations was straight forward and his illustrations of how to hold instruments and apply the rules for finding latitude by celestial observations were excellent (Waters, *Art of Navigation in England*, p. 163). It is quickly translated into other European languages and used as a vital source for voyaging to the Americas. Thus, by the middle of the 16th century, the route to America had been paved for all other European nations, thanks to Spain, Father Medina, and a large contingent of Spanish explorers.

To this list, we would have to add the monumental work of Alexander von Humboldt's *Travels to the Equinoctial Regions of the New Continent Made Between 1799 and 1804*, which he wrote with his associate and companion Amado Bonpland, published in 30 volumes in 1807-27. Although Humboldt was German (born in Berlin), he was in the service of Spain during his 5-year voyage to South America, which was made possible by the intervention of Mariano Luis de Urquijo, Spain's Prime Minister.

—In 1751 the Jesuit Andrés Burriel published in Madrid, *Catálogo de California* (Catalog of California), which was immediately translated into French, English, Dutch and German, spurring new interest in finding the Northwest Passage.

—In 1590, the Spanish Jesuit José de Acosta published his *Natural and Moral History of the Indies*, in which he argued that the New World natives resembled the people of Tartary, who crossed from northeastern Asia into America, a theory that has survived through today.

—In 1699, Cotton Mather published the first book written in Spanish in North America: *La fe del cristianismo. La religión pura en doce palabras puras, dignas de ser recibidas por todos* (Pure Religion in Twelve Pure Words which Should be Well-received by All).

—The *New Testament* in Spanish was published by the American Bible Society in 1819. It was the first printing of any part of the Bible in the New World.

—Much of our present knowledge of the flora of the Americas (which includes North America), was derived from the magnificent book *Flora de Bogotá*, authored by José Celestino Mutis and published in Madrid around 1772. The work was the result of his scientific expedition to Colombia, which at the time cost the Spanish government 230,000 pesos. It was profusely illustrated by the best artists of the time, featuring over 6,840 illustrations (engravings), of which 6,717 are preserved today in Madrid's Botanical Garden. It is worth mentioning that in 1817 General Morillo had most of these plants (approximately 6,000) and specimens shipped to Spain for further study and analysis.

—Although we have not counted or included all of the published works about the discovery, conquest, exploration, and colonization of the Americas written by Hispanics, it is but certain that altogether the list must exceed at least 1,000 works between the 15th and the 18th centuries, covering all regions of the world, including North America, in all areas of human knowledge. There were books written about Mexico, Peru, Chile, Colombia, Argentina, Venezuela, Central America, the Caribbean, and Philippines. Most were published in Spain and others in Mexico and also Peru. The vast majority were translated into many European languages, but mainly English and French, and German. Many of the first editions of these extraordinary books can be found at some of the U.S. leading libraries, including the Library of Congress, Brown University, Harvard University, Yale University, the Bancroft Library at the University of California, the Rosenbauch Foundation, the Newberry, the Sutro, the University of Texas, the New York Public Library and the Hispanic Society of America. However, as outstanding as they are, none can compare with the *Archivo General de Indias* (National Archives of the Indies) in Seville, Spain, or with The Biblioteca Nacional de Madrid (the Madrid National Library) in the historical holdings of the Americas. Mexico and Peru also hold many of these historical treasures.

—In 1539 printing was introduced in Mexico by the Italian Juan Pablos (Paoli), who worked for the German printer John Cromberger in Seville, and under the auspices of Bishop Juan de Zumárraga. Although it is believed that the first book printed in Mexico was *Escala spiritual*, by Saint Juan Clímaco, published by Esteban Martín in 1535, the first known book was *Breve y más compendiosa doctrina christiana en lengua castellana y mexicana*, published by Juan Pablos in 1539, as ordered by bishop Zumárraga. The only known copy was that of M. Jiménez de la Espada in 1877, which later disappeared. Other books that followed were: *Manual de adultos* (1540), *Doctrina breve*, written by Zumárraga (1543-4). Juan Pablos died in 1560, and the Spaniard Antonio Espinosa opened the second printing shop. Engraving appeared in 1547. In Lima, printing was introduced in 1584 by the Italian Antonio Ricardo, and in Manila n 1593. In contrast, printing in the U.S. Colonies was introduced in Cambridge, Massachusetts, in 1638, over 100 years later. The first two printed books were *The Freeman Oath*, and *Almanak*,printed by Stephen Daye or Day. The Spaniards established New Orlean's first printing shop in 1769.

More on the Italian Juan Pablos and the origin of printing in Mexico. In 1490 the Catholic Kings, Ferdinand and Isabella, sought to establish printing in Seville and put it in the hands of a German and a Pole: Meynardus Ungut and Stanislaus Polunus, who, together, printed some of Spain's finest books (among them, *Processionals Dominican*, in 1494). After their death, the press passed to the hands of the Cromberger family who sent Juan Pablos to Mexico to introduce printing in the Americas. Thus, the introduction of printing in the New World is owed to its true mentors, Ferdinand and Isabella. In the sixteenth century the art of printing itself was greatly influenced by two other such events, the Reformation and the discovery of America.

Jacobo and Juan Cromberger (father and son, born in Germany) established printing in Seville in 1503, and produced some of the period's best and finest books, among them the *Cartas de Relación de Hernán Cortés* (Letter of Cortes to Charles V), and the *First Decade* of Peter Martyr's. Juan Cromberger married a Spanish woman and printed one of the first edition of *Amadís de Gaula* in 1535. Their press lasted well over fifty years and was considered one of Europe's finest.

The succession of printing in Mexico after the death of Juan Pablos in 1560, was as follows:

Antonio de Espinosa (former worker of Juan Pablos) in 1559; Pedro de Orchate, in 1563 (through the marriage to a daughter of Pablos); Antonio Ricardo of Turin (an Italian), in 1577. In 1580 Ricardo moved to Peru and established a press there by a royal letter dated at El Escorial in 1584. His first work was *Pragmática sobre los diez días del año*, in that same year, making it the first South America imprint. The total book output of both Mexico and Peru, before 1820, according to José Toribio Medina, was for Mexico 12,412 titles, and for Lima 3,948. These are known titles, of which copies have survived and have been documented. However, many, about twice that output, was lost, leaving little or no traces, Lima being the heaviest loser since most of what was printed appealed to the populace.

In Hispanic America, except for Lima, Spain introduced printing as follows:

In La Paz (by the Jesuit Order) between 1610-1612;

In Paraguay, in 1703;

In Cuba in 1707;

Another one in Oaxaca, Mexico, in 1720;

In Santa Fe de Bogotá, since 1738;

In Quito, Ecuador, in 1754;

In Cartagena, Colombia, 1759;

In Nueva Valencia (Venezuela), in 1764;

In Córdoba, Argentina, in 1766;

In Santo Domingo in 1782;

In Santiago de Cuba in 1792;

In Guayaquil, Ecuador, in 1793;

In Puerto Rico in 1808.

During the 16th century a total of 251 books were printed in Mexico, and during the Spanish colonial period, the total reached, as stated, 12,412 titles. Although no records exist to this effect, it is believed that in Colonial America (U.S.) the number of books (titles) printed may not have exceeded 500.

In California, it is known that in 1833 a printer carried a press from Mexico to Monterey, and that a year later Agustín Vicente Zamorano established a press there. Incidentally, for those who may wonder where rag paper came from, it came from China first to Spain and from there to the rest of Europe.

—Hernán Cortés introduced cattle in Mexico which was later introduced in North America, and also the cultivation of the silkworm in Mexico. In addition, he is credited with having introduced in Mexico, thus in America, the art of ship-building and mining, and the metallurgical procedures for the benefit of gold and silver, as well as the invention of the wheel applied to transportation. He should also be credited with being the precursor of Mexico's modern agrarian politics, and with implementing the democratic system of municipal government in Mexico (see the introduction by G.R. Conway to the book: *The Last Will and Testament of Hernán Cortés, Marqués del Valle*). Also, he not only conquered Mexico but also introduced sugar cane to the Americas, and its first grower. In fact, the method he devised and implemented in Cuba was so productive and successful that it has been the only one used ever since.

—Western Civilization did not enter North America via de northeast in 1607, as it is commonly believed, but one hundred years before through quite an opposite route. Originally, it went from Spain to Cuba (discovered by Columbus October 12, 1492); then to Santo Domingo (December 5, 1492); then to Puerto Rico (November 19, 1493); and finally to Mexico. The entryway through the Southeast was first and it came from Puerto Rico (Juan Ponce de León, 1513); the second also through the southeast came from Cuba (Hernando de Soto, 1539); the one through the southwest was third and came first from Cuba and then from Mexico (first in 1508 in the expedition of Vicente Yáñez Pinzón y

Diego de Solís; then Juan de Valdivia in 1512; Francisco Hernández de Córdoba, 1517; Juan de Grijalva, 1518; and finally Hernán Cortés in 1519). Pánfilo de Narváez was the first to lead and expedition from Florida to Texas, which failed. Then Álvar Núñez Cabeza de Vaca continued until he arrived in Mexico in 1536. Fray Marcos de Niza entered New Mexico in 1539 searching for Cibola, and then Francisco Vázquez de Coronado led another expedition through the southwest in 1540.

In summary, there were four main entryways to North America: two through the Southeast in 1513 and 1539, and two through the Southwest in 1539 and 1540. The English landed on the northeast coast of North America in 1607, 94 years after the Hispanics.

And with Western Civilization came Christianity, which was given a big boost in America after it had dwindled considerably during the Middle Ages. This is owed to the Spanish missionaries, primarily to the Franciscans and also to the Jesuits, whose zeal and passion spread throughout two continents in less than 100 years. One of these missionaries alone, Saint Pedro Claver, baptized over 300,000 Indians during his thirty years of service in America. And the friar Bartolomé Olmedo, thought to have baptized Doña Marina or "Malinche," and the first apostle of New Spain, baptized over 2,500 natives. In North America, it should suffice to mention that after the city of Santa Fe was founded in 1610, Spanish missionaries scattered throughout the region baptizing some 30,000 Indians in about 40 tiny churches. We cannot fail to mention also that every year Spain sent to America two-hundred missionaries at a cost to the Spanish Crown of sixty million pesos. Christians in America, both in the north and in the south, are forever indebted to these venerable monks, not only for this, but also for their enterprising spirit and the greatest of lofty deeds.

—The importance of the Spanish missions in North America (and around the globe) set the foundation, the basis, the very essence of what we proudly call today "Northamericanism." Historian Herbert

E. Bolton described it as accurate as it can possibly be. He interprets the mission as "an economic, a social, and a political as well as a religious institution—an affair of the State as well as the Church." Indeed it was, and from these missions sprouted cities, towns, industries, trades, religious, civic, and community beliefs, in short, most of our present way of life.

—In America, Spain sent six principal religious orders: the Franciscans, since 1493 in the West Indies; the Dominicans who came to America (to the Spanish Main) in 1508 as collaborators of the Franciscans; the "Mercedarios," or Order of Our Lady of Mercy, to Santo Domingo in 1514; and the Augustians in 1513; the Jesuits in 1567; the Capuchins in 1647; and the Discalced Carmelites since 1585.

We feel compelled to mention a few of these venerable monks: Saint Francis Solano, the Apostle of the America slaves.

Friar Junípero Serra, the great North American pioneer and the Apostle of California.

Eusebio Francisco Kino, the great scholar and explorer.

Father Francisco Garcés, the great founder of many missions and also a explorer.

Father Juan María Salvatierra, the founder of numerous missions and explorer of California.

Friar Bernardino de Sahagún, the great scholar of America's native languages.

Pedro de Gante, a relative of the Emperor Charles V and builder of over one hundred churches and hospitals in Mexico.

Father Alonso Barzana, who was fluent in eleven Indian languages and wrote copiously about them.

Father José de Anchieta, who spent a lifetime evangelizing the Indians, especially the children, in Brazil where he built many churches and schools in the impenetrable jungles of the Amazon basin.

Father Florián Baucke, the great teacher of music to the Indians and organizer of the America's first native orchestra in Paraguay.

St. Toribio de Mogrovejo, the great explorer who all by himself trudged over 3000 kilometers through Peru, where he founded America's first seminary and convent for poor maidens.

Father Bartolomé Olmedo, considered the Apostle of Mexico. Friar Antonio Margil who founded many missions in Texas.

The Americas' Twelve Apostles who, from 1524 to 1531 baptized over one million natives in Mexico. Their names were: Martín de Valencia, Francisco de Soto, Martín de Jesús, Juan Juárez, Antonio de Ciudad Rodrigo, Toribio de Benavente (Motolinia), García de Cisneros, Juan de Ribas, Francisco Jiménez, Luis de Fuensalida, and the laymen Juan de Palos and Andrés de Córdoba. They arrived in Mexico on May 13, 1524 and welcomed with great honors by Hernán Cortés who, in their presence, kneeled in reverence to the amazement of the natives. They could not believe that the great conqueror would prostrate himself in front of humble men, dressed in in simple garb, skinny, and barefooted.

And we should also include another great missionary, the Augustian San Juan de Rivera who, in his long thirty years of mission work in Japan and China, built numerous churches and convents.

And also the Dominican friar Vicente Valverde, great benefactor of the Indians in Peru. He was the one who approached the Emperor Atahualpa at Cajamarca with a bible and crucifix.

On this subject, we would like to bring these words by historian John Gilmary Shea:

> A few years since the labors of the Catholic missionaries were ignored or vilified: now, owing to the works of Bancroft, Sparks, O'Callaghan, Kip, and others, they occupied their merital place in our country's history...One remarkable fact will, at all events, appears in the course of this work, that the tribes evangelized by the Spanish and the French subsist to this day, except where brought in contact with the

colonists of England and their allies or descendants; while it is notorious that the tribes in the territory colonized by England have in many cases entirely disappeared and perished without even having had the gospel preached to them. The Abnaki, Caughnawagas, Kaskakis, Miamis, Ottawas, Chippeways, Arkansas, and the New Mexican tribes remain and number faithful Christians, but where are the Pequods, Narragansetts, the Mohegans, the Mattowas, the Lenape, the Powhatans? They live only in name in the rivers and mountains of our land.

And then these other eloquent and poetic words about Fray Junípero Serra from historian Francis Bret Harte:

> He approaches us laboriously across the southern plain. He is old and thin, too thin, friendless, alone. He has left his tired muleteers a league behind, and has walked on ahead without a knapsack or wallet, carrying no more than a bell and a crucifix. The plain is typical of the region, one of those the tourists do not like. At once, sun-scorched and glacial, windswept, seared to its very core, cracked and open crevices. As the cruel sun sets the old man falters, bends forward and falls to the ground in exhaustion. There he lies all night long. The following morning, some Indians find him there; they belong to a weak and simple race, and with clumsy friendliness they offered him food and drink. But, before accepting these, the old man kneels, matins and baptises them into the Catholic faith... This was Fray Junípero Serra, and the sun rose this morning over Christian California ... There is no more heroic figure than that of this Franciscan monk, thin, consumed by his journeying, independent, and self-denying.

Father Serra was a tireless traveler while in California, where he traveled by foot more than 5,500 miles from mission to mission. And he did so half crippled after being bitten by a mosquito in his leg while walking from Veracruz to Mexico City. The after-effects of his leg lingered for the rest of his life making walking very painful. Despite the excruciating pain, he still managed to walk once again from San Diego to San Francisco (a total of 600 miles) to visit the nine missions he had founded. This he did during the last three years of his life, or in his late 60s (he died in 1784). On this trek he also suffered from pains in his chest but refused medical treatment or medications.

Father Junípero Serra not only founded 21 missions in California (San Carlos Borromeo was the first one), but worked the land and taught the natives to cultivate it. In addition, he brought in hundreds of plants that were later planted through most of the west of North America. Most of our agricultural methods of today were first implemented by this saintly friar.

The Spanish missionaries founded almost as many missions along the U.S. southeastern coast as others did in the west. Many of those western missions later flourished and became some of North America's greatest cities, such as Los Angeles and San Francisco. By 1617, in New Mexico alone, the missionaries had founded twenty-five missions, eleven churches, and the first school for the teaching of reading and writing to the natives. Regarding the missions founded in the southeast, the Jesuits alone founded ten in an area extending from South Florida to Virginia (near Jamestown). Contrasting the labor of the French and Spanish Jesuits, it must be noted that in colonial times there were in Mexico alone many more Jesuits as in New France. One of these Jesuits was father Segura, who founded a mission in Virginia in 1570. And, in 1612, Friar Luis de Oré, of the Oñate expedition, founded several missions in Georgia, increasing to 20 in two years and to 44 by 1633. Also, in 1674-1675, Franciscan friars founded three missions in present-day Alabama— San Nicolás, San Carlos, and La Encarnación de la Santa Cruz. But the Spanish missionaries did not stop in the Americas. Their missionary work extended to vast and distant regions such as China, Japan, Cochin China, Tonkin (now North Vietnam), and Formosa (Taiwan). Regarding Vietnam, it is interesting to note that the Spanish and the French jointly occupied it and that, had it not been for the bravery of the Spanish army, it would have been lost to the local rulers. However, in a surprise and covert move at the end of the conflict, the French managed to dispose of the Spanish army and established absolute control in 1863. This is how Vietnam became a French colony. Finally, these words by historian Trevor Davies are worth quoting:

> Spanish missionaries, like St. Francis Xavier and Cosmo de Torres, were to be found in almost every heathen land from Morocco to Japan. It was they who first made known to Europe the most inaccessible parts of Asia and Africa as well as the American continents. At the same time, Spain was the land towards which every Roman Catholic in the world looked for support in time of persecution.

The first to document the natives' own account of life in Mexico before and after the conquest was the Friar Bernardino de Sahagún. Through his work, *Historia de las cosas de la Nueva España* (History of the Things of New Spain), we were able to learn about many aspects of life in the Americas, such as food, rituals, medicines, relationships, crafts, and an extensive variety of animal and plant life. The natives themselves drew many of these images, which Sahagún included in his famous work. They are known today as the *Códice Matritense*, which is preserved in the Royal Palace of Madrid, and *Códice Florentino*, preserved in the National Library of Florence. A partial translation of the Códices was published by Pedro Robredo in Mexico in 1938 in five volumes. In addition to these, Friar Sahagún wrote copiously about the life and customs of the natives as well as many catechisms in Spanish and Nahualt. Friar Sahagún is considered today the Father of Modern Ethnology.

Had it not been for the Spanish missionaries and their labor of love working the fields and teaching the natives how to cultivate the land, many of our present-day agriculture (the best in the world) and industries would have never evolved, or would have been delayed indefinitely, such as wine-making, the citrus industry, and many others. In terms of the cattle industry (also the best in the world), author Bruce M. Schackelford stated:

Christopher Columbus brought spotted Castilian range cattle that became the basis of future herds in the Americas. By the 1520s over 8,000 cattle were herded on the island of Hispaniola. Nearly every expedition to the northern frontier of Mexico, now Texas, brought cattle as part of the expedition...In the mid-1500s, ranching exploded on the northern frontier of Mexico in the area called Nueva Vizcaya. Cattle were brought from Spain, the Canary Islands, and the islands of the Caribbean to populate the huge ranches called estancias. A traveler in Northern Mexico reported in 1579 that some ranches had as many as 150,000 cows and that 20,000 cattle were considered a small herd. In 1586, two of the estancias branded a total of 75,000 calves...By 1685, Spanish livestock operations had been established in the areas of present-day East Texas, Arizona, California, and New Mexico... The Franciscan missionaries that founded the missions of San Antonio continued to bring cattle to Texas with breeding annually greatly increasing the number of cattle. Each mission operated a ranch manned by Indian converts to Catholicism under the supervision of the Franciscan friars. By the 1760s, the ranches contained large cattle herds. An inventory of livestock made in 1762 lists almost 5,500 cattle running on the mission ranches. By 1860, Texas alone had more than three and a half million head of cattle.

—The Castillo de San Marcos, built by Spain in St. Augustine, Florida, is the oldest permanent seacoast fortification in the United States. It was begun in 1672 and became part of the United States when Spain ceded Eastern Florida in 1812. Although it was renamed Fort Marion (in honor of Francis Marion in the American Revolution) in 1942, Congress declared it a national monument and changed its name back to what it was originally. Other early U.S. forts were: Fort Whetstone, Baltimore, 1776; Fort Mifflin, Philadelphia, 1798-1803; and Fort McHenry (perhaps the best known), Baltimore, 1800, among others.

—The first currency of the Americas was the Spanish *4 maravedís,* minted in the Dominican Republic in 1504. In Columbus' time, a *maravedí* was worth about two-thirds of a penny (as of the early 20 century). And in South America, the first minted coin was the *Rincón 1 Real,* minted in Lima in 1568 and 1570 under Philip II, by assayer Alonso de Rincón, the best at the time. The obverse depicts de Pillars of Hercules, and the reverse, the shield of Spain with lions and castles.

—After they first settled in Mexico in 1572, and within a period of 100 years, the Jesuits founded a total of thirty colleges from Guatemala to California.

—Florida and Mexico, but mainly Mexico, were the entryways through which all of the livestock, fruits and plants unknown in the New World came to North America, including the horse, cow, pig, and the now famous Texas longhorns, plus wheat, flour, sugar, cinnamon, peaches, grapes, and oranges, among hundreds more, all of which were brought in from Spain. And from Spanish America, came imports of cocoa, bananas, tomatoes, potatoes, and innumerable other products.

—Many U.S. statutory and common laws, although perhaps somewhat modified, can be attributed directly to the long-standing "regulamientos" of Spain, such as mining and property.

—Among the first cities founded in America were: Santo Domingo or Isabella, in 1496, by Christopher Columbus' brother, Bartholomew; Baracoa, in Cuba, 1512 (which became the capital), by Diego Velázquez; and San Juan, Puerto Rico, in1521, by Juan Ponce de León. La Habana (then called "San Cristóbal de la Habana," and before "Fernandina," in honor of King Ferdinand), was founded in 1514, along with Santiago de Cuba. The island of Puerto Rico was first named "San Juan Bautista" by Columbus (in honor of Spain's Catholic Monarchs' great devotion for that saint). The city of San Juan was first named "Caparra," but later changed to "Puerto Rico" as per the king's wishes. Later the country became Puerto Rico and the city San Juan. The original indigenous name of Puerto Rico was Borinquen.

Other cities founded by the Spaniards during the early years were, in Cuba: Bayamo in 1513, Sancti Spíritus and Trinidad, San Juan de los Remedios, and principally Santiago de Cuba in 1514-

1515. They were all founded by Governor Diego Velázquez de Cuéllar, who also sponsored the first expeditions to Culúa (México), including the one by Hernández de Córdoba in 1517, the one by Juan de Grijalva in 1518, and the famous one by Hernán Cortés on November 18, 1518.

—Most of today's pharmaceutical knowledge was derived from an incredible amount of medicinal plants regularly used by the natives in South America to cure a variety of illnesses, including the common cold, headaches, cataracts, and others. How did that knowledge get to us? For that we have to thank many of the Spanish missionaries who wrote extensively about such plants and their healing properties, especially father José de Acosta and his laudable book: *Historia natural y moral de las Indias* (Moral and Natural History of the Indies), published in Seville in 1590, and soon translated into different languages. Alexander von Humboldt praised his work and considered him the Founder of the Earth's Physics. It is also interesting to note that in 1571, a Spanish doctor named Nicolás Monardes published another book about the history of medicinal plants of the Americas, in which he wrote that tobacco could cure over 36 illnesses.

—North America's first church was build in Saint Augustine, Florida, by Friar Francisco de Pareja in 1560, and the first parish consecrated in that same city by Friar Martín Francisco López de Mendoza in 1565.

—In 1578-1584 Spain ordered its officials in Mexico to undertake a survey to learn about its territories in the New World. It was called "Relaciones geográficas," and it included the making of local maps as well as detailed descriptions of local resources, history, and geography. The survey produced a total of sixty-nine maps which were rendered most valuable in the future exploration and expansion of Mexico as well as North America.

—Spain founded the Americas' first university, the University of San Marcos in Lima in 1551, eighty-five years before Harvard in Cambridge, Massachusetts, one hundred and ninety-five years before the Presbyterian College of New Jersey, later renamed Princeton, eighty-three years before the Jesuit College of Quebec (founded 1635), which later became Laval University, and two-hundred and twenty years before Yale (founded in 1771). It must be noted, however, that the very first university was Santo Tomás de Aquino, founded by the Spaniards in Santo Domingo in 1538; however, it did not open officially until many years later. And not only the first university, but also the first library, founded in Mexico City in 1762. The second university was the University of Mexico, inaugurated by the Viceroy Luis de Velasco. By the end of the colonial period, Spain had founded in the Americas a total of twenty-five universities, and the first in Philippines, the University of Manila, in 1648. In contrast, in North America, the first public library was established by Benjamin Franklin in Philadelphia in 1731. And the first public school was the Boston Latin School, founded in Boston in 1635.

Incidentally, the universities of San Marcos in Lima and in Mexico were founded by the royal orders of Charles V of May 12th 1551 and September 12th of the same year respectively. The University of Mexico opened January 25, 1553, and the University of Lima May 12 of the same year. However, the universities required the approval of the Pope, thus the University of Lima was granted the Pontifical title in 1571 and the University of Mexico in 1595, making San Marcos the oldest. Between the 16th and 17th centuries, 28,000 students graduated from the University of Mexico, and during the colonial period a total of 1400 students received doctoral degrees. All universities founded by Spain in America were organized on the basis of the University of Salamanca, thus enjoying full autonomy and certain basic privileges. For example, the viceroy had no authority to appoint the faculty.

Both universites had five basic schools or colleges which were established in 1624: Theology, Law, Medicine, Indian Languages, Canons, and universities, as in the Philippines and Chile, also offered courses in Grammar, Art, and Latin Studies. Friar Alonso de la Veracruz was the Americas' first philosophy professor in 1553.

Other universities founded by Spain in the Americas were:

Mexico, besides the University of Mexico, the universities of Mérida and Yucatán, between 1622 and 1625, and the University of Guadalajara, founded by the Jesuits in 1791.

Havana, in 1721.

Guatemala, in 1625, which later became the University of San Carlos (1676).

New Granada, the University of Santo Tomás in 1624 or 1639.

Venezuela, the University of Caracas in 1721.

Quito, the University of San Gregorio Magno (Jesuit) in 1620 and the University of San *Fernando (Dominican)* also in 1620, and the Real Univesidad de Santo Tomás in 1786.

Lima, besides San Marcos, the University of Cuzco in 1682, the University of Huamanga in 1677, the University of Chuquisaca of Saint Francis Xavier in 1623.

Argentina, the University of Córdoba in 1622.

Chile, the University of San Felipe in 1738.

The Philippines, the University of Santo Tomás de Manila in 1645.

In total, seven universities were founded in Spanish America before Harvard University.

The first school was founded in the Franciscan Convent of Santo Domingo in 1505, by Friar Hernán Suárez, and the second Santiago de Gorjón y de la Paz in 1558, with monies provided by the rich merchant Hernando de Gorjón; it was elevated to a university by the Jesuits in 1748.

—In 1632, Pedro Porter y Casanete introduced mercury or quick silver in the Americas.

—A Spaniard, José de Escandón, founded in Texas between 1746 and 1755, 21 towns, 57 Franciscan missions and 30 Dominican missions.

—In 1770, the city of Saint Louis, Missouri, was transferred to Spain, thus becoming part of its many territorial holdings in North America.

—In 1735, Spanish is taught for the first time in New York City schools. And in 1751, Garrat Noel published the first textbook for the study of Spanish titled, *A Short Introduction to the Spanish Language*. Some years later (1766), the study of Spanish is added to the courses offered by the University of Philadelphia. And, in 1815, Harvard University established the "Smith Chair" for the study of Spanish with a grant by Abiel Smith, a former graduate of this university. At Yale University, Spanish is first taught in 1826. At the University of California, which opened in 1869, Spanish was first taught in 1885.

—In 1693, the Americas' first newspaper, "El Mercurio Volante" is published in Mexico City. The first United States' newspaper, the "Boston News-Letter," was published in 1704.

—In 1761, Spain intervened in the Seven-Year War (1756-1763) between France and England, in which the latter won. By the Treaty of Paris, France ceded Canada and Louisiana East of the Mississippi, while Spain ceded Florida to the United States. To compensate Spain for the loss, France ceded the Louisiana territory between the Mississippi and the Rocky Mountains, its last territorial domain in North America. Thus, at this juncture, North America is divided into two territories marked by the Mississippi: Spanish to the west and English to the east, with the total exclusion of the French.

And talking about Louisiana, New Orleans greatest benefactor and real estate tycoon was the Spaniard Andrés Almonester y

Roxas, an Andalusian who arrived in Louisiana in 1769. After the two fires that devastated New Orleans in 1788 and 1794, this man of extraordinary piety built at his own cost the magnificent Saint Luis Cathedral, costing 100,000 pesos, and the New Charity Hospital of Saint Charles (named in honor of the king of Spain), also costing 100,000 pesos. He also contributed most of the funds to the construction of a leper hospital on Metairi Ridge in 1785. Leprosy had become almost epidemic in the 1780s and had almost vanished by the end of the Spanish dominion thanks to this hospital. Other great Spanish governors of Louisiana were Francisco Luis Héctor, called the "City Builder," for his many civic improvements, such as a lighting system and by spawning New Orleans' new industry, syrup made from the sugar cane that had been introduced by the Jesuits in 1751; Marqués de Casa Calvo, who served from 1799 to 1801, and Juan Manuel de Salcedo, who served from 1801 to 1803. In total, Louisiana was under Spanish domain for a period of forty years, from the Treaty of Paris in 1763 to 1803 when it was formally transferred to France and later sold to the United States. It should be noted that the Jesuits established two universities in Louisiana: Loyola University in 1911 and Xavier University in 1925.

How can those forty years of Spanish control be categorized? Historians Joan B. Garvey and Mary Lou Widmer put it this way:

> By the end of the Spanish period, Louisiana was more self-sufficient in foodstuffs. Natives had also been encouraged to cultivate indigo, tobacco, flax, hemp and cotton, as commercial crops ... The population had increased sixfold in Louisiana during the Spanish period. Settlers trickled down from the North until the end of the American Revolution, after which the trickle became a torrent... Many people came from West Florida... The Acadians began coming in the 1750s and continued to come throughout the Spanish period

Our Spanish ancestors are to be thanked for three decades of stable government, for the city's first fire and police protection, for the Old Basin Canal, and for the first attempts made at establishing public schools in 1771. They are to be thanked for a reconstructed Vieux Carre, with its Hispano- American architecture, which is a monument to the period of Spanish domination. Credit goes to them for roofing the Indian Market on the riverfront. The market has always been a vital place of business and continues to be today.

Further on Louisiana, during the term of Governor Alejandro O' Reilly (an Irish national in the service of Spain) in the mid 1700s, the use of the Spanish language was declared mandatory and many Spanish institutions were established. And, when Louisiana became Spanish, it was a dependency of Santo Domingo and later of the "Audiencia de Puerto Príncipe" in Cuba. And the Marqués de Someruelos, who presided the ceding of Louisiana in 1803, provided shelter in Cuba for the French Army (led by Leclerc) and more than 30,000 French refugees who were fleeing from the Black Terror in Haiti (by the Peace of Ryswick in 1697 Spain had ceded the western part of Hispaniola, or today's Haiti, to France.)

—In 1885, a group of U.S.'s leading architects voted Trinity Episcopal Church in Boston the best building the United States. It is a massive Gothic Revival structure located on that city's famous Copley Square. Their criteria were based on its splendid adaptation of Spanish ecclesiastical architecture. The architect was Henry Hobson Richardson, one of the most prestigious architects of that era.

Here are some most interesting facts about the Sephardic Jews who emigrated to the United States during the early years, especially those who settled in New York. To their much honor and glory, it has been established that many Sephardic Jews were among the immigrants who arrived aboard the Mayflower.

—New York City is the banking and financial capital of the world, which New Yorkers, all Americans, and the world owe to the Spanish Sephardic Jews who pioneered both industries in the 18th century.

The Sephardic Jews, that unique breed of enterprising and visionary people, whose ancestry dates back to Medieval Spain, pioneered countless industries and businesses, and either founded or contributed to founding, many charitable and community-based institutions ever since they arrived in 1654. Among the many prominent Sephardic families were the Nathans, the Seixases, the Hendricks, and the Cardozos. Here are but a few of their achievements:

A relative of Emily Da Silva Nathan, Emma Lazarus, was the author of that historic poem now inscribed at the base of the Statue of Liberty in New York Harbor: "Give me your tired, your poor/Your huddled masses."

Another Nathan, Annie Nathan Meyer, was the founder of New York's prestigious Barnard College, part of Columbia University.

The father of Mr. Piza Mendes helped found New York's Montifiore Hospital.

Mosey Levy was among the seven Sephardic Jews who in 1711 contributed financially to build the steeple of New York's Trinity Church;

Mendes Seixas Nathan was one of the drafters of the constitution of the New York Stock Exchange.

The Hendricks (an Anglicized/Germanized version of the Spanish surname "Henríquez") became the U.S. premier merchants in copper processing, which was mined in the vicinity of Newark, New Jersey;

One of the members of this family, the Hendricks, donated an impressive private collection of rare books and manuscripts to the New York Historical Society. It contained, among other treasures, 17,000 manuscripts dating back to 1758.

The Seixas family immigrated to Germany after the Jews were expelled from Spain in the 15th century. Their name was Germanized to Sachs or Saks, founders of New York's premier department store;

New York City's first synagogue was built by the Sephardic merchant Louis Gomez (he later changed his name to "Lewis') on Mill Street, and was also among the men who contributed to build the steeple of New York's Trinity Church. One of his sons, Daniel, became a tycoon in colonial times dealing in wheat and numerous other commodities.

Little introduction is needed for Mr. Benjamin Nathan Cardozo, who served on the New York Court of Appeals and later as an Associate Justice of the United States Supreme Court. Cardozo is remembered for his significant influence on the development of American common law in the 20th century, and his vivid prose style.

We would like to add, as an interesting fact that between 170,000 to 400,000 Jews emigrated from Spain in the 15th and 16th centuries, and that Spain was not the only country that expelled them. In fact, they were also expelled from England much earlier, in 1290, for trying to convert Christians to Judaism. Big, irreparable loss for both countries. The term Sephardic, in Spanish "Sefardita," derives from the Hebrew "Safarad" which appears in the Bible, and which means, in all likelihood, a native from the Iberian Peninsula. It is worth noting that many Sephardic Jews became excellent printers, a tradition that continues into today. They wrote and printed many books in Spanish, or Castilian, and adapted many of the metric innovations of classic Spanish writers, such as Boscán and Garcilaso de la Vega. One of the leading Sephardic literary figures was León Hebreo, author of *Dialogs of Love*. Other modern notables were Benjamin Disraeli, count of Beaconsfield, a well-known figure in England's politics, and the Schombery, who excelled in medicine in England. In today's

Israel, there are approximately one million Sephardic Jews, of whom some 275,000 still speak Spanish, and worldwide the total is estimated to be over two million, of whom about 900,000 still speak "ladino" (the mixed dialect of Hebrew and Spanish). In the United States, mainly in New York, it is estimated that there are as many as 40,000 Sephardic Jews, and in South America it may totaled up to 120,000.

As the Arabs, the Jews were also very intimately related to Spain's history, especially during the Middle Ages. In fact, many of Spain's literary luminaries were of Jewish ancestry, namely Saint Teresa of Avila, Fray Luis de León, Mateo Alemán, Luis Vélez de Guevara, Luis de Santángel, Baltasar Gracián, and even perhaps the famous Inquisitor Torquemada. It is also contended that Miguel de Cervantes, the author of *Don Quixote*, may have been wholly or partially Jewish. And many Spanish kings, such as Alphonse X of Castile, James I, James II and Peter IV, maintained very close ties with Jewish financers. Also, it must be remembered that the Jew Abraham Señor, a banker, provided considerable assistance to Spain's Catholic Kings during the first arduous years of their reign. And the figure of Juan Hispalense, another Jew, truly shines in the famous Translators' School of Toledo.

—Spain sponsored many of the famous scientific expeditions to the New World, among the most important being the expedition of Martín Sessé and José Mariano to Mexico, Central America, and California in 1791, and 1795-1803. Also of monumental importance is the1893 expedition of Francisco Javier Balm is, in which he introduced the vaccine against smallpox in Latin America, the United States, and Asia. Some of the other famous expeditions sponsored by Spain and carried out by foreign nations under its service, were: the one by the Elhuyar brothers to Mexico and New Granada in 1793; the one by Nordenflycht to Mexico in 1788; the one by Peter Loeffling to Guayana in 1755-1756; and of course the one by Humboldt to Latin America in 1799-1804. In this regard, Harvard historian Robert S. Chamberlain noted: "A vast body of historical writing, much of it of high quality, was produced during the Spanish colonial period, and important anthropological and linguistic studies were made."

Balmis was a Spanish surgeon who first introduced the vaccine for smallpox in Texas, which had been discovered by Edward Jenner in 1796. In this regard, historian Robert Ryal Miller had this to say:

> At the turn of the nineteenth century, when the use of vaccine to immunize against smallpox was newly discovered, the Spanish government sent the Balmis expedition to the New World with medical teams, who penetrated mountains and jungles vaccinating American Indians by the thousands.

But Balmis went further. In 1805 he sailed from Acapulco to Manila and from there to Macao to introduce the vaccine in China. Not surprisingly, the English took the credit for his good work.

—For over three centuries Texas was under Spanish domain. In 1720-1722 it was permanently occupied mainly through the efforts of the Marquis de Aguayo, then governor of Coahuila. The first official governor was Martin de Alarcón, appointed in 1720. He also founded the city of San Antonio (San Antonio de Béjar) in 1718.

—The first trader in British America may have been a Hispanic by the name of Rodríguez, who started trading pots and pans right after the purchase of Manhattan Island from the Dutch.

—The United States is a capitalist nation as are most of the nations of Western Europe. How did capitalism originate?

Modern capitalism originated from the wealth mined in Peru, Bolivia, and Mexico, brought to Europe via Spain. It must be said, however, that only a fraction of that wealth reached Spain, with its bulk ending up in the other European nations, mainly England and Holland. It must also be said that about half of that wealth never left America as it was used for exchange, seized by pirates, or lost at sea. Finally, it must also be said that American wealth made some of the nations of Europe very rich while it totally bankrupted Spain. Spanish historian Pedro Aguado Bleye said in this respect: "Neither the monopoly nor the part of the precious metals (especially silver) which corresponded to the royal treasury benefited Castile, but, rather, the industrialists and businessmen who advanced to the kings large sums of money at high interest rates, which were paid largely with the remittances coming from America." As Spain was unable to produce the goods that were needed in the Western Hemisphere, it turned to the other European nations for manufacturing and exports. In economic terms, they gained, while Spain lost.

American historian Mendel Peterson had this to say on the same topic:

> Increasing production of gold and silver was the most important cause of the price revolution of the 16th and 17th centuries. As by far the greater part of this metallic wealth came from America, the function of Spain in the movement was a significant one. She became the distributor of the precious metals to the rest of Europe. It should be noted that the Potosi mines alone yielded in 1602 over 42,000 pounds of silver which, at today's prices, would have amounted to approximately $48 millions, an astonishing sum at the time.

On the same topic, a group of Harvard University historians wrote:

> Massive imports of silver from the mines of Mexico, Bolivia, and Peru, produced such a depreciation in the value of silver that quantities of gold had to be hoarded for the critical transactions. Hence, for about 80 years, the European economy ran on silver. The result was a tremendous inflation. Prices and wages rose to fantastic heights in what could be considered an artificial prosperity. ... For a brief period, Spain shares this preeminence, but it was ill-fated to continue it. Spanish industrial development was too feeble to supply the demand for manufactured

products from the European settlers in the Western Hemisphere. Accordingly, they turned to the north of Europe for the textiles, cutlery, and similar products they urgently needed. By the 16th century, the Spanish economy, which had first seemed to be prospering greatly from the discoveries, lay almost completely in ruins. Also, that accumulation of wealth, which as stated revitalized the economies of such countries as England, France, and the Lower Countries, popularized the system of investments through stocks, this according to economist Max Weber.

It is indeed ironic that the mammoth efforts of Spain and the enormous wealth of Spanish America had mainly served to enrich and advance the economies of Western Europe, not of Spain's or any of the Spanish American countries. In this regard, Spanish historian Emilio Fernández Fuster said (translated by the author):

> The most notable economic centers of the time— England, France, and the Lower Countries—were the definite receivers of the treasure conquered by Spain in the Americas. Of that extraordinary accumulation of benefits, evolved the idea and almost the necessity to invest in order to gain larger yields. The big companies of America (English and Dutch) obtained extraordinary benefits and, as mentioned by Mr. Weber, developed and made popular the stock capital system which then extended to all of the other European nations. The importance of this fact is undeniable. During the 17th century, the capitalists who increased enormously the wealth of their countries were British and French, not Spanish.

And English economist Lord Maynard Keynes also said in this regard:

> The period of maximum English prosperity began really upon the return of Drake's first important voyage in 1573, and was reaffirmed with the immense riches he brought in after his second of 1580 and without disregarding the third of 1586. The value of gold and silver of this combined treasure has been estimated at between 300,000 and 1,500,000 sterling pounds, although professor W.R. Scott thinks that it was much larger. The effect of these great sums of money had to be a predominant factor in England's eleven years of prosperity from 1575 to 1587. Francis

Drake seized and plundered Spanish ships and ports repeatedly and took all those riches to England and shared them with his many investors, among whom was Queen Elizabeth herself. And so did the pirates Hawkins, Morgan, Cavendish, and the Dutch and French corsairs.

—An estimated 2,800 Spanish galleons, laden with gold, silver and other treasures, sunk off the Florida cost in the 16th, 17th and 18th centuries. One of them, the Atocha, was salvaged by an American adventurer in the 1980s, yielding almost a billion dollars in revenues, and this is only thought to be less than 10% of the total cargo. Although the rights to such discoveries are now in dispute between the United States and Spain, it is conceivable that in the years ahead many more ships will be found, making many of our citizens multi-millionaires, and adding more tax revenues to the U.S. treasury. Incidentally, the Atocha, or rather, "Nuestra Señora de Atocha" sank off the coast of Havana in 1621 and was the flagship of the Spanish fleet of the Spanish Main. The famous Spanish mariner Bartolomé Nodal perished in that shipwreck.

—North America's first native student of Spanish was Francisco de Chicora (Christian name after he was baptized) of the expedition of Lucas Vázquez de Ayllón. He learned Spanish well and accompanied Ayllón to Spain in 1523, where he related in very good Spanish his fantastic tales of the land of Chicora.

—The United States's first Spanish-language book was written by the preacher Cotton Mather and published in 1699. Its title was *La religion pura en doce palabras fieles, dignas de ser recibidas de todos.*

—In 1748 Jacob Rodríguez Rivera introduced the sperm oil industry to the colonies while residing in Newport, Rhode Island. He is also credited with introducing the manufacture of spermaceti candles.

—Spanish was the first European language spoken in North America- 100 years before English.

—When the United States expanded westward in the 19th century, it did not enter barren territory, but lands that had already been explored, settled, and colonized, first by Spain and later by Mexico. Think of what would have happened to American history if the American pioneers had to do what it took Spain and Mexico 300 long years to accomplish.

—Spain's presence in North America outlasted both England's and France's. In total, it lasted over three centuries, from the time of the arrival of Ponce de León in 1513 to the ceding of Florida by Spain in 1819. It outlasted England by sixty-seven years, 1607 to 1846, when England ceded the Oregon territory, and France by seventy-seven years, from the time of the arrival of Jacques Cartier (Newfoundland) in 1534 to its cession of Canada and lands east of the Mississippi to England, and its holding west of the Mississippi to Spain in 1763 by the Treaty of Paris. On this subject, American historian Philip Ainsworth Means said: "... of the nearly 450 years that Europeans have known about America, 325 were years during which Spain was the dominant power in the most enviable parts of the Western Hemisphere."

—At one time, parts of Mexico, Lower and Upper California, Texas, and New Mexico belonged to the "Provincias Internas" (Internal Provinces), established by José de Gálvez.

—In 1795, Carlos Fernández Martinez, Marquis of Casa-Irujo, is appointed Spanish ambassador to the United States. He then married Teresa Mac Kean, daughter of the governor of Pennsylvania and President of the U.S. Congress. The Marquis held his post for twelve years, and was the one who discovered Senator's Blount's conspiracy to seize the states of Florida and Louisiana from Spain.

—In 1781, the "Pueblo de Nuestra Señora de Los Angeles de Porciuncula" is founded. That was the original name given by the Spaniards to today's Los Angeles, California, which was the capital of the state until 1846 when it was occupied by the United States.

—In 1798, the Spanish governor of Louisiana granted American Daniel Boone 850 acres of land in Missouri, where he settled in 1799.

—By the beginning of the 19th century, the Jesuit Order, founded by the Spaniard Saint Ignatius of Loyola in 1540, had established missions in Michigan, Illinois, Indiana, Ohio, Iowa, and Missouri, and a few years later in Arkansas, Louisiana, Mississippi, and Pennsylvania, among other states. One of these colleges was Saint Charles College in Grand Coteau, Louisiana, founded in 1837, and in 1847 they had founded another one, in New Orleans, the College of the Immaculate Conception.

—By the Treaty of San Lorenzo del Escorial (1795) Spain ceded to the United States all of eastern Florida, from which the United States later carved out the new state of Mississippi.

—In addition to the Spaniards, many other Hispanics labored hard in developing the future United States, particularly Mexicans from the 18th to the 19th centuries in the vast area of the North American Southwest, many of whom served as governors and key government officials of some of the incipient states. For example, the Cuban-born Joseph Marion Hernández was the first Hispanic to serve in the U.S. Congress from 1822 to 1823. Another, the Spaniard Miguel Antonio Otero, served also as a delegate of the Territory of New Mexico from 1856 to 1861. And yet another, José Manuel Gallegos, served also as a New Mexico delegate to the U.S. Congress from 1853 to 1853, and later again from 1871 to 1873. In truth, it must be remembered that, after two hundred years in America, the Spaniard of the early years had been transformed into a "Criollo," or Creole, or better said in today's terms, into a Hispanic, a new generation born out of the three predominant races: Spanish, Indian, and Black. In actuality, they should be referred to as "Spaniards" up until the end of the 17th century and Hispanics after that. In other words, the contribution to the United States was Spanish at the beginning but Hispanics later. And even in this case it was never totally Spanish, as we have already demonstrated. Yes, the people were Spaniards at the beginning, but the credit must be equally shared between them, the indigenous Americans and America itself.

—In 1802, Col. David Humphreys brought for the first time one hundred merino sheep from Spain, where he was the U.S. Minister.

—By the Treaty of 1899, Spain sold to Germany the islands of the Carolinas, Palau, and the Marianas for a total of 25 million pesetas. They were later acquired by Japan and ultimately by the United States.

Part F

HISPANICS AND THE AMERICAN REVOLUTION

During the American (U.S.) Revolution Spain was the United States' biggest and most-trusted ally. Its aid continued through the battle of Yorktown, which was won partially through the help coming, not from Spain, but from Havana, Cuba. In desperate needs for funds, the colonists, under the command of George Washington, turned to France for help but it was denied. At that critical moment, the Spaniards in Cuba volunteered to launch a massive national appeal for funds and collected 1.5 million livres tournoises which were sent to Washington immediately.

In a letter dated in Virginia December 19, 1785, addressed to the Count of Floridablanca, George Washington begins with these words: "My homage is due to his Catholic Majesty (King Charles III) for the honor of his present (a loan)." And in another letter, dated at Mount Vernon January 20th , 1786, addressed to Diego de Gardoqui, Spain's Representative to the American Congress, George Washington wrote: "To meet the approval (of a loan) of such gentleman, whose good wishes were eagerly engaged in the American cause, and who has attended to its progress through the various stages of the Revolution."

More about the Spanish aid to the American Revolution.

Spain provided large sums of money, made available through a secret third party, and payable in livres tournoises and reales de vellón: one million livres tournoises in June, 1776 (just one month before the Declaration of Independence), and four million reales de vellón on August 5th, 1776, plus letters of credit and war supplies, including weapons, such as brass cannons, bayonets, gun carriages, mortars, ammunition, shells, bullets, power, plus clothing, blankets, threads, buttons, needles, uniforms, shoes, tents, and countless other supplies. By orders of the king, carried out through his representatives Aranda and Gardoqui, cities and towns across Spain feverishly pulled together to manufacture the goods needed by the American colonists. In this regard, American author Ms. Parker Thomson wrote:

> Gardoqui gave the order for the weaving, collection and baling of the blankets and other woolen articles to the weaving centers of the province of Palencia of which Vitoria is the capital. Palencia was at this time the center of the finest of the wool-weaving industries in the country. Gardoqui's orders threw this peaceful province into a fever of activity; in every pueblo, men, women, and children worked furiously in order to complete the work. The plazas in the small towns were piled high with the product of their hands while being bailed for shipment to the city of Palencia. Excitement spread throughout the province when it became known that the blankets were destined for the army of Washington in America.

Those loans and supplies were never re-paid, nor did Spain expect it. In one of his many letters to Arthur Lee, the Count of Floridablanca (Charles III's Prime Minister) stated: "That these things the King did and would do out of his generosity, without stipulating any recompense." Altogether, all of the various loans and supplies amounted to 7,944,906 reales, which at the rate of 20 reales to one hard peso, it would have totaled 52,966 hard pesos. At the time of the loans, the peso was worth 40 continental dollars;

thus, in today's dollars, they would have amounted to $2,118,640, an astronomical sum of money at that time. And Benjamin Franklin, while Minister to France, strongly disagreed with giving up the Mississippi River as a way of repaying Spain for all those loans. Not that we criticize Mr. Franklin for refusing to give up such treasure as the Mississippi River, but Spain should have been paid somehow (with the accrued interest) and shown more respect and goodwill.

Bernardo de Gálvez, governor at the time of Louisiana, for a period of three years (1779-1881) led five successful campaigns against the English in Western Florida, thereby reclaiming all of the Louisiana territory that England had obtained by the Treaty of Paris and limiting their power and threat within that area. A beautiful statue in his honor was erected in the nation's capital. But governor Gálvez went far beyond that. In June of 1778, he gave to Oliver Pollock, commissioner of the Colonial Congress, 24,023 pesos; in October of the same year, an additional 15,948 pesos to refurbish the frigate Rebecca; in July of 1779, another 22,640 pesos for the same frigate; and in 1781, another 5,000 pesos. This money was in addition to the official loans made by Spain to the colonists. José de Gálvez, uncle of Bernardo de Gálvez, was instrumental in getting the funds intended for the American Revolution. A statue of Bernando de Gálvez stands today at the Spanish Plaza in New Orleans, a gift from Spain in 1977.

More on Governor Gálvez's campaign against the British. In September of 1779 he took Baton Rouge and forced the British to forfeit Natchez. He then launched an offensive toward the British stronghold of Mobile, assembling a small armada with a force of 1,200 men, and sailed from New Orleans in 1780. Hurricane winds almost destroyed it before they landed on Mobile Bay. At this moment, and unexpectedly, four ships arrived from Havana as reinforcements and Gálvez marched on to Fort Conde (called Fort Charlotte by the British who, under the command of Elias

Dumford, surrended on March 14, 1780). Gálvez then captured Pensacola, Florida, on May 9, 1781, an action that prevented the British from gaining a foothold in the lower Mississippi Valley and forcing them to abandon West Florida.

But before Governor Gálvez was his immediate predecessor, Louisiana's second Spanish governor Luis de Unzaga y Amezaga. In fact, the American Revolution began during his administration, and he was also instrumental in helping the American patriots by purchasing arms and ammunition and by beefing up the Spanish forces in the event of a British attack. It is interesting to note that these two Spanish governors married Creole women from Louisiana. Gálvez's wife's name was Felicie de St. Maxent d'Estrehan. And Gálvez's successor, Esteban Rodríguez Miró, also married a native Creole, Marie Celeste Elenore de McCarty.

On the war front, in 1781, the Spanish forces, led by Cruzat, defeated the English at Saint Joseph, Missouri, which at the time was under Spanish domain. But there is more Spanish aid to the American Revolution. Beginning in 1777, one year after the U.S. Declaration of Independence, Bernardo de Gálvez (who was then governor of Louisiana and Florida) seized from the English several cities and towns, such as Baton Rouge (1779), Mobile (1780), Pensacola (1781) and all of western Florida. Because of his victories, the British pressure was lessend on George Washington, thus opening the supply lines not only of funds but of military goods from Spain, Mexico, and Cuba. And the Spaniard Gabino Gaínza was very successful in helping seize Panzacola from the British in 1780.

We could fill pages and pages with detailed information about Spain's aid to the American Revolution, most of which would greatly surprise a vast number of readers. In all fairness, and adhering to the hard historical facts, France's aid to the American cause was mostly through diplomacy while Spain's aid was entirely through actions, money, and supplies. Both of them were important, but Spain's was decisive, firm, sincere, and long-lasting. Yet, most of the credit has been afforded to France and little or none to Spain.

We have said it many times before and say it again, so we never forget. Hispanic gold and silver built Colonial America. No one knows what would have happened without it. This is all irrefutable historical fact, documented by the brightest minds of our own scholars and historians. Huge amounts of the precious metals made everything possible and helped build the economy of the incipient republic. Let's look at some of the facts:

Galvestown, in Texas, was named in honor of Bernardo de Gálvez, governor of Louisiana (and later of Cuba and also viceroy of New Spain) and a key ally of the American Revolution. The name should have preserved the original Spanish spelling— "Galveztown," with a / z /.

Spain provided the coinage system that would prove invaluable during colonial America, and that would form the basis of today's U.S. currency. In fact, during Alexander Hamilton's era, all foreign coins in circulation could be accepted as legal tender for a period of three years. After that, only Spanish silver could be legal tender, a standard that was in effect from 1792 to 1834, and a single Spanish gold standard thereafter until 1857. The "piece of eight," as it was called, had a value of 8 reales. Merchants would break the coin into eight pieces or bits. English-speaking colonists were the first to refer to it as the dollar, and throughout most of the 18th century, it was the standard monetary unit for settling all debts and contracts. In 1793, the United States government passed a law making the 8 reales silver dollar part of the nation's monetary system. On February 17, 1776, the Continental Congress issued a note of 2/3 dollar to help finance the war. It totaled $4 million payable in Spanish Milled Dollars or the equivalent in Spanish gold or silver. For over 100 years, all of those gold and silver coins were minted in Spanish America, in the same countries where the mines were located: Peru, Bolivia, and Mexico. It is interesting to note that the College of William and Mary, in Williamsburg, Virginia, was built from the ground up, during the governorship of Thomas Jefferson, with Spanish silver.

Our current dollar sign ($) is also derived from the Spanish Milled or Pillar Dollar (the pillar and scroll on the coin's obverse), which was used by a government clerk as early as 1788 and came into general use shortly thereafter. So critically important was Spanish money at the time, that England's George II counter-stamped many thousands of Britain's Half Guineas with the gold seized by Admiral Anson off the coast of Philippines, and put his own image on it. As an aside, the counter-stamping was of very poor quality, mainly because of poor taste and because it was done hastily to help finance the war.

In 1788, Spain minted a $1 coin for use in the American colonies. It is considered to be the United States' first One Dollar coin.

Part G

THE SPANISH ROYAL ANCESTRY OF GEORGE WASHINGTON AND THOMAS JEFFERSON

George Washington.

To the surprise and amazement of many, George Washington, the hero of the American Revolution and the first president of the United States, was a direct descendant of Spanish royalty and of one of Spain's greatest military heroes going all the way back to the Middle Ages. John Inclán, a well-established genealogist, wrote an article for the Website Genealogy.com entitled "The Spanish Ancestry of George Washington," dated August 29, 2010, in which he documents President Washington's pedigree, stating: "Our First President carried undisputable Hispanic DNA." <http://genforum.genealogy.com/washington/messages/1681.html>:

> George Washington's ancestors, Princess Joan, was the daughter of Saint Fernando III King of Castile and León and Jeanne Dammartin, Countess of Ponthieu (daughter of Simon II, Count of Dammartin, Aumale and Ponthieu, and Marie (Jeanne), Countess of Ponthieu. King Fernando was the son of Queen of Castile Berengaria and Alfonso IX, King of Leon

(son of Fernando II, King of León and his Queen Urraca of Portugal.) Elvira, A.K.A. Cristina, was the daughter of Don Rodrigo Díaz de Vivar, known as El Cid and Jimena de Gormaz (daughter of Diego Rodríguez de Oviedo and Cristina Fernández.)

Thomas Jefferson.

Thomas Jefferson, the third president of the United States, was a descendant of a Spanish king of the Middle Ages, which came through his mother's lineage. The king was Ferdinand III, called "the Saint," who reigned in Castile and León in the 13th century between 1230 and 1252. He was born circa 1201 and died in Seville in 1252. He married Joanne De Dammartin, born in France circa 1216 and died also in France in 1279. Gregory Schaaf, author of, *On Religion and the State: Franklin, Jefferson, and Madison*, published by CIAC Press, Santa Fe, NM, 2004, page 97, states:

> Thomas Jefferson's mother, Jane Randolph (1720-1776), was born in London, the daughter of a prominent family resettled in Virginia as part of the landed gentry. Her aristocratic family tree originated in Old England and Scotland ranging as far back as Charlemagne (742-814), Emperor of the Holy Roman Empire. One genealogist documented her as a direct descendent of both King Henry III Plantagenet (1207-1272) of England and King Ferdinand III de Castile (1201-1252) of Spain.

Here we can see that Jefferson's direct Spanish royal ancestry came through his mother, the aristocrat of the family.

Another source, which confirms President Jefferson's ancestry, is the book, *Americans of Royal Descent*, compiled, edited and copyrighted by Charles H. Browning, Philadelphia, Porter and Coates, 1883, page 9. Mr. Browning summarizes President Jefferson's family lineage as follows:

> Edward I, King of England, m. in 1254 Lady Eleanor, only **child of Ferdinand III, King of Castile and Leon,** and had:
> Princess Joan D'Arce. D. in 1307, who married 1st Gilbert de Clare,

ninth Earl of Clare, seventh Earl of Hertford and third Earl of Gloucester, d. in 1295, and had:

Lady Eleanor de Clare, who m. Hugh Le Despencer, beheaded in 1326, and had:

Edward Le Despencer, Baron Despencer, who m. Lady Elizabeth, daughter of Bartholomew, Baron Burgghersh, and had:

Thomas Le Despencer, Earl of Gloucester, who m. Lady Constance Plantagenet, daughter of Edmund, Duke of York (by his wife Princess Isabel, **daughter of Peter, King of Castile and Leon**), son of Edward III, King of England.

Thus, George Washington and Thomas Jefferson, the third president of the United States and author of the "Declaration of Independence," were blood related through King Ferdinand III, called "the Saint," and Washington to El Cid, Spain's greatest hero of the Reconquest.

Thomas Jefferson was well-versed in the Spanish language, literature, and history. In fact, he boasted of having improved his Spanish by reading *Don Quixote* in nineteen days, even though when told, John Quincy Adams noted the remark in his diary saying that "Mr. Jefferson tells large stories." He was an avid reader of *Don Quixote* and mentioned him several times in his writings, even referring to Don Quixote's horse "Rocinante." As Fawn M. Brodie said in her book, *Thomas Jefferson: An Intimate History*, W.W. Norton & Company, New York, 1974, p.283: "And in an importantly revealing metaphor he likened his whole earlier career to that of Don Quixote: "I have laid up my Rosinante in his stall, before his unfitness for the road shall expose him faltering to the world."

He was also a great admirer of Hernán Cortés, the Spanish conqueror of Mexico. In his magnificent library he had fine editions of these four famous books <http://www.monticello.org>:

-Francisco Javier Clavijero: *Storia del Messico dell' Abate Clavigero.*

-Hernando Cortez: *Historia de la Nueva España*, 1770.

-Francisco López de Gómara: *Historia de México con el descubrimiento de la Nueva España*, 1554.

-Antonio de Solís: *Historia de la conquista de México*, 1783-1784.

-Juan de Mariana: *Historia de España*.

Also in his library, Parlor, upper tier, he had magnificent portraits of Fernando Cortez (Hernán Cortés) and Christopher Columbus.<http://www.monticello.org/site/research-and-collections/catalogue-paintings>

Benjamin Franklin's interest in the Spanish language.

Benjamin Franklin spoke good Spanish and urged his compatriots to learn it as one of the world's most important languages. He made it part of the curriculum of the Philadelphia Academy in 1733. Also, in 1784, he was named a correspondent of the Spanish Royal Academy of History.

And so impressed was Benjamin Franklin with the ideas and writings of the Spanish economist Pedro Rodríguez, Count of Campomanes, that he invited him, based solely on what had been written about him in the newspapers, to join the prestigious American Philosophical Society. Count Campomanes was a minister of Charles III who became famous in fostering Spain's economy, especially the textile industry and banking.

And talking about Benjamin Franklin, the Franciscan Antonio José Ruiz de Padrón, shipwrecked off the coast of North America in 1784, was his close friend and so was he of George Washington. For a while he preached in Philadelphia against the Inquisition.

Part H

THE U.S. HISPANIC "FOUNDING FATHERS"

We said before that Hispanics founded the country—or at least most of it—and that the Anglo-Saxons founded the republic, which is a historical fact hard to contradict although admittedly hard to accept like so many of the other facts contained in this book.

But much before there were founding fathers of the United States, there was a founding mother of America—Queen Isabella of Spain, the one who initiated it all and whose many virtues as a mother, wife, homemaker, statesman, and warrior, will continue to be an inspiration to men and women throughout the ages. As we celebrate Columbus Day, we should also celebrate the memory of this outstanding statesman, or stateswoman, rightly called by many throughout the Hispanic world, the "Mother of America."

The United States had many founding fathers: Washington, Jefferson, Adams, Madison, Franklin, all great and honorable patriots who helped forged this great republic. But before them, there were others who deserved to be included in this prestigious group.

From a list of many Hispanic U.S. founding fathers, we are including only the following nine:

Juan Ponce de León First European to land in what is today the United States (1513) and the discoverer of Florida.

Hernando de Soto Discovered the Mississippi (1541) and many of our present-day states.

Francisco Vázquez de Coronado Discovered and explored most of North America's Southwest.

Álvar Núñez Cabeza de Vaca Trekked North America from Florida to Texas and wrote the first account ("Naufragios") of the region and culture of the natives.

Pedro Menéndez de Avilés Founded North America's first city, St. Augustine, Florida (1565) and fostered further explorations along the Florida, North Carolina, and Virginia coast.

Friar Junípero Serra Founded innumerable missions in California and fostered agriculture throughout the region. Founder of the city of San Francisco.

Antonio de Mendoza As viceroy of Mexico was instrumental in launching many of the North American famous expeditions.

Juan de Oñate Founded North America's second city, San Francisco de los Caballeros, in New Mexico (1599), and explored much of New Mexico and Arizona. Brought with him a large contingent of settlers and their families (some 400 people in total), and over 7,000 heads of cattle, thus setting the basis for one of the U.S. greatest future industries.

Bernardo de Gálvez One of the greatest allies of the American Revolution.

The United States is well aware of the contributions of all of these pioneers, and has paid homage in numerous ways to them. In the nation's capital, for example, there are statues of father Serra at the Capitol and of Gálvez in one of the city's main streets. Also, at the Capitol, there is a large painting depicting de Soto's discovery of the Mississippi. Roads, bridges, national parks, monuments, coins, stamps, and many other sites and objects have been designated to honor these great men. Also, of Queen Isabella, there is a beautiful statue outside the Pan American Union, in Washington, and other sites throughout the country have been named in her honor. In California, the memory of Father Serra has been enshrined everywhere, and so have many of the Spanish explorers, including Cabrillo and Vizcaíno. What the United States has not done is to recognize them among the founders of the nation as a whole, and not only of a particular area or region. Perhaps the time has come to do so, to set aside a national holiday in their honor, and, above all, to include them in all school curriculums and in every textbook of American history. This we should and must do.

Part I

HISPANICS AND THE
UNITED STATES CIVIL WAR

And what about Spain's aid during the U.S. Civil War?

On June 12, 1864, Queen Isabella II of Spain dispatched two armies to help the Confederacy defeat the Union. Soon after, an army of 25,000 troops arrived in Norfolk, Virginia, and another in Savannah, Georgia. These reinforcements lent great support to General Robert E. Lee against the Army of Tennessee. Obviously Spain was on the wrong side of the war as eventually General Lee surrendered to General Ulysses Grant in 1865.

One of the heroes of the famous Battle of Gettysburg, General Daniel Edgar Sickles, was Minister to Spain in 1869-1874. He received the coveted Medal of Honor in 1897. And General George Gordon Meade, Commander of the Union Army of the Potomac at the Battle of Gettysburg (July 1-3, 1863), who was born in Spain to American parents, returned to the United States at the age of two, and was raised in Philadelphia.

And another of the great heroes of the U.S. Civil War was David Farragut whose father, Jorge Farragut, was a Spaniard born in the Island of Minorca, Balearic Islands. Jorge Farragut immigrated to the United States in 1776 and was also a hero in his own right in the Revolutionary War and the War of 1812 against the British. He married Elizabeth Shine Farragut, from North Carolina. David Farragut was born near Knoxville, Tennessee on July 6, 1801, and became the First Admiral of the U.S. Navy. His great success at New Orleans and Mobile Bay made him one of the most honorable figures in American History. Today, the gravesite and monument of Admiral Farragut is in the Woodland Cemetery, Bronx, New York, a National Historic Landmark. The mayor of New York City asked the navy to return Farragut's remains to the northern city that embraced the Virginia officer just nine years earlier. On October 1, soldiers, sailors, and politicians--including President Ulysses Grant--formed a funeral procession two miles long to escort the admiral's coffin to his final resting place at the Woodland Cemetery. (source: National Parks Service).

And about 10,000 Hispanic Americans, mostly from Mexico, fought gallantly to preserve the Union during the Civil War. And a woman native of Cuba, Loretta Janet Velásquez, joined the Confederate forces in 1860 disguised as a man, and distinguished herself as a gallant soldier at the Battles of Bull Run, Fort Donelson, and Shiloh. She was finally discovered in New Orleans and discharged.

Part J

SOME CLOSING COMMENTS: ABOUT SPAIN'S BLACK LEGEND

The infamous "Black Legend," which has tarnished Spain's image for five hundred long years, must be once and for all forgotten, as we have done with the black legends of other nations. We must collectively come to the realization of the peaks and valleys of the human race, of all of its inherent flaws as well as its goodness. In this regard, American historian Theodore Maynard, in his book, *De Soto and the Conquistadors*, had this to say:

> It is true—especially as applying to the one hundred glorious years then begun, during which occurred that explosion of Spanish energy which is perhaps the most brilliant chapter in history. While that energy exploded around the globe, the rest of Europe watched the succession of astonishing events in discovery and exploration with awe, perplexity, and increasing envy. ... The dominant position of Spain and Portugal in America at the end of the sixteenth century was truly remarkable. No other European power had established a single permanent settlement. Portugal monopolized the Brazilian seaboard. Spain had colonies all the way from Buenos Aires to the Rio Grande. Two-thirds of the Western Hemisphere was Hispanic, and so it has remained to this day. Spain's exalted position in the New World at the time is illustrated by the enemies who then rose up against her.

The North European countries and France founded no permanent American colonies in the sixteenth century. But all were interested in expanding in similar ways. All took to the sea. All desired a share in the trade of America and the Far East. All tried to break down the monopoly of Spain and Portugal. All made intrusions into the Caribbean and the South American mainland. Britons braved winds and ice floes in an effort to find a Northwest Passage. French sea dogs, Dutch sea dogs, and English sea dogs alike plundered vessels and sacked town all around the Hispanic American periphery. In defence [sic] Spain adopted a commercial fleet system, formed a West Indies armada, and walled her towns on the Caribbean coasts. ... The French intruded into Brazil, Carolina, and Florida, but were effectively expelled from all three. Raleigh attempted to found colonies in Carolina; his Orinoco project sent him to the block. Drake became a millionaire by plundering Spaniards, was crowned Great Hioh by the Indians near San Francisco Bay, and talked on a New Albion in California, long before there was a New England on the Atlantic Coast.

And on the subject of Spain's "Black Legend" it was, as we have stated before, nothing more than a scheme concocted by protestant Europe to undermine Catholic Spain, and fueled all over the world by William of Orange, staunch enemy of Philip II and writers such as Robertson's *History of America* (London, 1777) and Raynal's *Histoire philosophique et politique*, (Amsterdam, 1770), and during the governance of Oliver Cromwell in the mid-seventeeth century, especially by exploiting Bartolomé de Las Casas, *A Short Story of the Destruction of the Indies*, and using it as propaganda. The Black Legend has thrived to this day.

During their years of glory, the Spanish kings were goaded by the insidious jealousy and envy of their European counterparts: First, King Francis I of France with Charles I of Spain, and later Elizabeth I of England with King Philip of Spain. The French King sent out Jacques Cartier to counterbalance Spain's accomplishments in the New World and elsewhere, and Queen Elizabeth, unable to compete openly and squarely with Spain, sent out a band of adventurers, called by many "sea dogs," to plunder what had been gained with much effort by the nation of the two Spanish kings.

An influential Englishman, key in awakening England's interest in America, was the geographer Richard Hakluyt, a clergyman of the Angelical Church. In his 1584 *A Discourse on Western Planting*, he argued that:

> If you touch him in the Indies [King Philip II], you touch the apple of his eye; for take away his treasure, which is "nervus belli ", and which he hath almost out of his West Indies, his olde bandes of soldiers will soon be dissolved, his purposes defeated, his power and strength diminished, his pride abated, and his tyranny suppressed.

In analyzing and understanding Europe's eagerness to seek gold (not only Spain but all the other nations as well), it must be brought to bear that the general economic theory of the time measured the wealth of a nation by the possession of precious metals. This explains, and perhaps even justifies, at least to a large measure, the conduct of those nations in securing the Americas' treasures, a theory, which, to us, does not much differ from the one prevailing in our own time.

But that was 500 years past. There is no logical reason for anyone in the United States today to leave as a blank page the first two hundred years of his own history—1513 to the middle of the 18th century—negating or ignoring such a glorious beginnings while embracing the belated contribution of others. Indeed, many great nations contributed to the making of today's United States, for which they should be very proud. After all, they helped forged a nation that, in just two hundred plus years, escalated the highest peak which has so profoundly dignified humanity. One of those nations, and the first, was the nation of Spain, even at a time when its energy had been drained as a consequence of its own pursuit for unity, sovereignty, and internal tranquility. At the time of the discovery of America, Spain was a nation impoverished and barely of eight million people, treasuring many dreams but lacking the vital resources to attain them. A land of "Don Quixotes," searching for an impossible quest in a world of darkness. The fact that it succeeded is truly remarkable. The spirit of the old "Man of La Mancha" lived on for almost half a millennium.

U.S. history books, but especially those used in schools, should be thoroughly revised to reflect the historical truth with regards to Spain in America. The distinguished American historian Charles F. Lummis said it best one hundred years ago:

> When the reader finds out that the best English textbook does not even mention the name of the first mariner who circumnavigated the globe (a Spaniard), nor the explorer who discovered Brazil (another Spaniard), nor of the discoverer of California (also a Spaniard), nor of the Spaniards who discovered and settled colonies in what is today the United States, and that said book contains such blatant omissions and a hundred historical accounts that are as false as the omissions are inexcusable, he will then understand that the time has come for us to do more justice to a subject that should be of the utmost interest to all true Americans.

For five hundred years, historians have been mystified about Spain's ability to achieve so much in America in so short a time. In barely fifty years, a continent and a half had become an integral part of Western Civilization. How was this done? The only reasonable explanation is this: 800 hundred years of a mammoth crusade to rid the homeland of the Moors, fitted the Spaniards to undertake the awesome task laying across the Atlantic. Indeed, they had harnessed the spirit of the *Reconquista* in its purest form. The gallant warrior of the Middle Ages had found in America a new frontier in which to give wings to his dreams of fame and glory. The legends of "El Dorado," the "Fountain of Youth," and the "Seven Cities of Cibola," gave new impetus to his hope and determination to succeed. Once on American soil, the men of chivalry had been transformed into Conquistadors, a new breed of warriors "forged in America." Their character was best described by Bernal Díaz del Castillo, one of the conquerors of Mexico and author of the famous chronicle of the conquest: "We came to serve God and our king, and also to seek fame and fortune, as all men do."

It is often said that Spain came to America for the sole purpose of seizing all of its riches and wealth, the only nation in Europe so driven from the outset. Was she really? Such assertion must be challenged and there is no better place for us than here and now. Supposing that it was true, that Spain's only aim in crossing the ocean was to seize those riches, she was by no means the only one. In fact, there were many others, including England. We shall explain.

In 1576, Queen Elizabeth I of England sent Martin Frobisher on an expedition to the northeast coast of North America searching for gold. He returned with a load he claimed was a gold ore, and the Queen immediately rewarded him with a second voyage, although this time she, personally, demanded to be an investor. Indeed she invested one thousand pounds of her own coffers. He returned with a similar load and was sent out again but this time returned empty-handed. The Queen was disillusioned and gave up her dreams of wealth and glory for her country and for herself.

Here we shall let historian T.H. Watkins continue:

Elizabeth died in 1603, but the dreams [of finding gold] survived her. The vision of New England as a country rich in all that had fed the coffers of Spain was irresistible, as suggested by John Marston's contemporary play, "Eastward Ho!" in which one of the characters extols the mineral virtues of the country: "I tell thee, gold is more plentiful there than copper is with us; and for as much red copper as I can bring, I'll have thrice the weight in gold. Why, man, all their dripping pans and their chamber pots are pure gold; and all the chains with which they chain up their streets are massy gold." ... The canny James I, Elizabeth's successor and never one to discount possibilities, specified in the royal charters he granted to various American colonization companies that one-fifth of all the gold and silver discovered by them in America would accrue to the crown.

The settlers of Jamestown in 1607 had hardly landed before they were around and about, digging after gold. One member of the colony complained in 1608 that there was "… no talk, no hope, no work but to dig gold, wash gold, refine gold, load gold." That same year, Captain John Smith discovered what he thought was rich ore during an expedition up the Chickahominy River. He sent a load back to London, but his ore, like that of Frobisher, was worthless. The Jamestown colonists went on to the more immediate problem of surviving in the American wilderness, a task that left little time for chasing after someone else 's hopes.

Those who followed them had no better luck, and gradually the dream of gold faded from the New England consciousness, until by the time of the American Revolution it was considered an incontestable fact of life that there were no precious metals on the American continent, as Benjamin Franklin testified in 1790: "Gold and silver are not the produce of North America, which has no mines.

And it is a known fact that the western nations of Europe, namely England, Holland, and France, sought to seize Spain's newly discovered America's riches on land and sea. The raids of the English despoilers Francis Drake, John Hopkins, Thomas Cavendish, Henry Morgan; of the French corsairs, Jacques de Sorie and Gramont; of the Dutch sea-rovers, Piet Heyn, Cornelius Holz; and even of the Chinese with Limahon, are legendary, and once again serve as ample proof of man's insatiable thirst for gold. As late as 1718, the Gentlemen Adventurers' Association of London contracted George Shelvocke to lead a privateer on behalf of England to raid the Spanish fleet along the Pacific Coast of the Americas. Regarding the legend of "El Dorado," not only were the Spaniards the ones who gave it wings, but Sir Walter Raleigh contributed much in this regard with his book *The Discovery of the Large, Rich and Beautiful Empire of Guiana*, published in 1596. By the way, Sir Walter Raleigh was the brother of Sir Humphrey Gilbert who, in 1578, was given a charter by the English Crown to colonize North America and to implement a piracy plan to plunder the Spanish possessions in America, and in which Raleigh took active part. One of his cousins was Richard Greenville who in 1585 attempted to establish a colony at Roanoke, Virginia, but failed. Raleigh also took active part in the battle of the Invincible Armada.

According to historians Michael Coe, Dean Snow and Elizabeth Benson:

> Many explorers, particularly those that penetrated the interior, hoped to duplicate the profitable conquests of Cortés and Pizarro. Initial coastal settlements by the English and French during this century (16 century) were established in large part to provide bases from which to raid Spanish treasure ships, and Spanish coastal settlements were established mainly to protect them.

And it is also an established fact that most of the riches of America never reached Spain, and that those which did quickly ended up in the coffers of other European nations. Spain was a conduit of the gold and silver and never the ultimate beneficiary. And it is also an established fact that much of those treasures remained in America as confirmed by many historians, including J.H. Parry: "Much of the silver which came from the mines [of South America] was sent to Spain; but much also remained in the Indies and was coined and spent there."

And on this very same subject, Zvi Dor-Ner had this to say:

> In the end, .Spain 's dreams of following the routes of its silver trade to a permanent place among the wealthy nations of the world proved evanescent. In 1600, Seville had been the richest city in Europe, but as the seventeenth century wore on, even the vast resources of Spain 's colonies were rapped. Spain became a mere conduit, through which her colonial wealth flowed to the northern European countries that supplied her with credit for her adventures and goods that silver could buy but not replace. Spain, in a blunt analogy of the day, was said to be like a mouth that receives the food, chews it, and passes it on to the other organs,

returning no more than a fleeting taste of the particles that happen to stick on its teeth. The real nourishment was directed to the Protestant countries of northern Europe, where the old Italian inventions of investment banking and venture capitalism ere being refined into the instruments of modern economic interdependence.

Historian J.H. Elliott agrees: "... much of the Spanish king's share of the New World's silver was consigned to their foreign bankers for debt service immediately upon reaching Seville."

This is a subject requiring the time and space we lack. However, so much has been written on this topic and Spain's vindication that we urge the reader to pursue it further knowing that in the end reason will prevail.

We close the subject with these words from historian Evarts Boutell Greene:

> Much has been said about the Spaniard's greed for gold and his cruelty to the Indians; but in the former respect, Frenchmen and Englishmen, though less successful in their search, were not far behind the Spaniard. In their treatment of the Indians, the Spanish conquerors, from Columbus down, were often cruel and treacherous; but in their efforts to give the natives some kind of Christian civilization, they were more persistent and successful than the French or the English. Unlike the English colonists, before whom the Indians gradually disappeared, the Spaniards established communities in which Europeans and Indians have for three and a half centuries been able to live in tolerable relations.

And with these other words from the "Catholic Encyclopedia":

> While lamenting the disappearance of the Indians of the Antilles, writers of the Columbian period have, for controversial effect, exaggerated the numbers of these people; hence the number of victims charged to Spanish rule. It is not possible that Indians constantly warring with each other, and warred upon by an outside enemy like the Caribs, not given to agriculture except in as far as women worked the crops, without domestic animals, in an enervating climate, would have been nearly as numerous as, for instance, Las Casas asserts. The extermination

of the Antilles Arawaks under Spanish rule has not yet been impartially written. It is no worse a page in history than many filled with English atrocities, or those which tell how the North American aborigines have been disposed of in order to make room for the white man. The Spanish did not, and could not, yet know of the nature and the possibilities of the Indian. They could not understand that a race physically well-endowed, but the men of which had no conception of work, could not be suddenly changed into hardy tillers of the soil and miners. And yet the Indian had to be made to labor, as the white population was entirely too small for developing the resources of the new-found lands. The European attributed the ineptitude of the Indian for physical labor to obstinacy, and only too often vented his impatience in acts of cruelty. The Crown made the utmost efforts to mitigate and to protect the aborigine, but once the period of experiments was over, the latter had almost vanished.

Regarding the United States, and not in the 16th century, but in the 19th, we all remember the words of U.S. General Philip Sheridan when he said: *The only good Indians I ever saw were dead.* Harsh and horrific words pronounced just one-hundred and fifty years ago. And the Indians or native Americans were in no way kind to their foe. In fact, as it is well-known, Sitting Bull leading the Sioux and Cheyenne at the Battle of Little Bighorn (Custer's last stand) June, 15, 1876, took no prisoners, meaning that he obliterated the enemy leaving no survivors.

And in a brief reference to Black slavery, this established historical fact would prompt many of our readers to deep meditation: By the dawn of the U.S. Civil War, the Black slaves held in the southern states totaled almost half of all the slaves brought to the New World (not by Spain but by England and Holland) between 1521 and 1870, or four and a half million. The slave trade was first in the hands of the Portuguese (and before them the Arabs) and later of the British and the Dutch who perfected it.

Again, cruelty toward one's own kindred has always cast a shadow over man's universal existence and no nation, race or culture ever can claim exception. But as we have said repeatedly, Spain strived consistently to prevent and eradicate chattel property and the serf-like existence of the Indian. On Columbus's second voyage, Queen Isabella and King Ferdinand made abundantly clear to him on May 29:

> Their highness charge and direct the said admiral, viceroy and governor, to strive by all means to win over the inhabitants of said island and main lands to our Holy Catholic Faith. ... to treat the said Indians very well and lovingly, and abstain from doing them any injury, arrange that both people have much conversation and intimacy, each serving the others to the best of their ability.

And when Columbus envisioned and put into effect the marketability of the Indian, i.e. selling him as a commodity, Queen Isabella blurted out: "What right does my Admiral have to give my vassals to anyone!"

We would rather refrain at this juncture to further discuss and bring to light the cruelty and atrocities perpetrated by other nations, namely England and Holland, for example, in South Africa and in many of their other far-flung colonies. To do it, would truly serve no good purpose other than instill-will and draw further apart the already fragile and volatile relations between races and cultures. We are in no way interested in this day and age to place such a wedge of discord and resentment by emulating those who persisted in creating and espousing a venomous Black Legend of Spain. One Black Legend is enough.

Obviously, no one can deny that the acquisition of fortune has consistently been the quintessential pursuit of man throughout the ages.

In the United States, that thirst of gold also struck, perhaps even to a larger degree, with the California Gold Rush of the mid-1800s, three hundred years after Cortés set foot on Mexico and Pizarro in Peru. The entire country, from all four corners, followed that quest with frenzy, unparalleled in U.S. history. It is not an exaggeration to assert that the entire country simply appeared insane, each man dreaming of finding, finally, "El Dorado," which so eluded Coronado and other Spaniards. So much was the greed and paranoia that it prompted many newspapers in 1849 to headline: "No coming of the Messiah, or the dawn of the millennium would have excited anything like the interest [for gold]." In total, that California Gold Rush yielded, in only 50 years, $1,500,000,000, in contrast to Spain's total yield, in 325 years in the Americas (from 1495 to 1820), of $10,438,000,000. The major difference was that the California gold stayed in the United States and eventually ended up in the U.S. Treasury, while most of Spain's riches ended up in the coffers of other nations, including the United States. But the gold of California was not the United States' only rush. There were others, many others, although not as generous. These few come to mind: The discovery of gold in New South Wales in Australia; in the Frasier River in British Columbia in 1858; in the Colorado Rockies in 1858 and 1859, which yielded $25,000,000 in just ten years; and the discovery of the Gold Canyon silver mine in Nevada in 1850, along the Carson River. The American West was conquered by men seeking for gold, among other motives, just as in Mexico and Peru. That frantic quest took gold-seekers all across the southwest as well as the northwest—Washington, Idaho, Oregon, Montana, Alaska, and beyond. Adventurers, prospectors, investors, went around and about searching for the mighty metals, taking with them whole families and abandoning their towns and homes. By the way, it should be mentioned that Mexicans taught the California gold-seekers how to pan for gold and use mercury to separate silver from ores.

On this subject we could write volumes on how all of Western Europe vied with Spain for the same purpose of finding the precious metals at all cost. However, the above will suffice to refute as absurd such claim that Spain was the only one. But let's add a few last words on this subject. According to historian Terence Wise author of *The Conquistadores*: "At the end of the 15th century, Europe's entire store of gold did not exceed 88 tons: cast in a single ingot it would have formed a cube only six feet in each dimension." This was all the gold Europe had in its reserves, which amounted to nothing. After the discovery by Columbus, Mexico yielded an estimated $6,300,000 in gold, and Peru 1,326,000 gold pesos, or $6,169,000, and 52,000 silver marks, or $681,240. This is what Cortés took from Moctezuma and Pizarro from Atahualpa, respectively. Add to these the silver discovered in the Potosi mines in 1545, and those of Zacatecas in 1547, which resulted in an estimated 6,765 tons of silver which were shipped to Spain in the short period of forty years. It is an established fact that of all of that immense wealth, only a small fraction reached Spain with all the rest going straight to the coffers of all of Europe, mainly of England, Holland, and France. These countries, plus many others, would have remained in economic obscurity had it not been for the "generosity" of Spain, Peru, Bolivia, and Mexico.

And we wonder, could we draw a parallel between that gold rush of California in the mid-1800s and today's rush of Mexicans and others to cross the Rio Grande in search of another "El Dorado"—the prosperity, opportunity, and promise that this country offers to the immigrant? Many gold-seekers ventured to California during the Gold Rush, from Mexico, Panama, South America, not to mention China, and the same could be happening today. To them, it seems, "El Dorado" is the United States, and no matter what it is done to discourage the wave of these immigrants, and knowing human nature, as we all do, it will not likely succeed. Dreams never die, never, and the United States was, is, and will continue to be, a dream for all of mankind. It is a price we have to pay for our own successes, just as other nations paid it in the past, Rome during her glorious years and Spain in the Middle Ages.

Something else we must know. Not only were the European nations after Spain's riches but also after its navigational knowledge which they badly needed to catch up with Spain. Such was the case of an English subject named Bartholomew Sharp who, in 1680, seized from a Spanish vessel a collection of charts and sailing data ("derrotero") for the Pacific coast. They were later copied by the buccaneer William Hack of Wapping, published by him under the title "Wagoner of the South Sea", and presented to England's Charles II who honored him with a captain's post in the navy.

The first emancipation of Indians in North America took place as early as 1543, when the Spaniard Luis de Moscoso, of the expedition of Hernando de Soto, freed some five hundred slaves (men and women) on his return to Mexico City. And the first emancipation of Black slaves in the Americas was ordered by Viceroy Luis de Velasco in Mexico in 1549, freeing over 150,000 slaves. And, regarding the emancipation of the Black slaves in America, it was Spain that was the first nation to do so, nine years before the British, 37 years before President Abraham Lincoln's Proclamation, and 40 years before the 13th Amendment to the United States Constitution. Spain abolished it in Mexico in 1825, England in 1834, President Lincoln in 1862, and the 13t[h] Amendment in 1865. It must be noted, however, that by the treaty of September 23, 1817, the Spanish King Fernando VII convinced England to agree to abolish the trade, which it did not do until 1834. The treaty was signed on behalf of Spain by García de León Pizarro and by Henry Wellesley for George III. In other words, Spain had sought the emancipation as early as 1817. And much earlier than that, in 1753, the Spanish King Charles III abolished the Black Trade in the Spanish possessions and set them free in 1789. Also, circa 1770, the new Spanish governor of Louisiana,

Alejandro O'Reilly, an Irishman in the service of Spain, abolished Indian slavery in that territory. It is interesting to note that by 1725 the black slave population in the U.S. colonies had reached 75,000, and that five years earlier, in 1720, the population of the colonies had reached 475,000. Thus, at that time, the black slaves represented approximately a fifth of the total population.

But Spain's deep commitment to protect the Americas' natives from bondage goes back to the beginning of the 16th century during the reign of Queen Isabella who, on June 20, 1500, declared that the "Indians were free vassals of the Crown of Castile and, therefore, could not be enslaved." And, on embarking from Spain in 1501, Nicolás de Ovando, newly appointed governor of the Indies by King Ferdinand, was specifically instructed to look after the Indians "as free vassals" of the Crown and that they should be *paid a salary for their work.* It must be noted here that in 1515 the Crown issued a royal order authorizing Spaniards to marry the Indians, and in 1513 issued another royal order making it mandatory to instruct the children of the Indian chiefs of Hispaniola in the Latin grammar. In summary, the Spanish Crown always stood firm and never wavered in pressing forward the rights and well-being of the America's native and in mitigating their suffering, notwithstanding occasional actions of their local commanders and overseers. The Emperor Charles V himself suspended in 1550 all future conquests in America pending the recommendation of theologians and court advisers as to the best and most humane way to carry them out. Also, in 1531, Bishop Juan de Zumáraga was granted a royal order forbidding Indian slavery in Mexico.

Regarding the Spanish Inquisition, so vilified over the centuries, it was not the nation of Spain which initiated it but Pope Gregory IX in 1233 against the heretical sect of the Albigenses and then introduced in Spain (in Aragón) two years later. In Castile, King Alphonse X refused to allow it, and it was not until the 15th century that it was permitted. But in this regard, English historian (professor at Oxford) Trevor Davies wrote:

> Popular tradition dies so hard that it is still necessary to point out that the Spanish Inquisition, judged by the standards of the time, was neither cruel nor unjust in its procedure and its penalties. In many ways it was more just and humane than almost any other tribunal in Europe. ... [It] should be remembered also that the Inquisition did much to save suspects from the violence of fanatical mobs and much to combat ignorant superstitions, and so—to give one example—saved Spain from those hideous witch-hunts that were a common feature of life in Northern Europe as late as the eighteenth century.

In any event, it is important to point out that the Indians in the New World were never subjected to the Inquisition as dictated by the Spanish Crown but placed under the jurisdiction of each individual bishop in all matters pertaining to the faith. And further on the comment by historian Davies, the Spanish Inquisition, with all of its flaws, paled in comparison with the witch-hunting practices of most of the countries of Europe at the time in which thousands were burned to death.

The first person to protect and defend the native population of the Americas was Queen Isabella of Spain which she did in many different ways. First by the royal decree of 1503, which stated all Indian slaves be set free and be paid wages for their work. Excluded from work were women, children, the sick, and the elderly. When departing for the New World, Nicolás de Ovando was given these specific orders from Spain's Catholic Monarchs:

> That all the Indians in Hispaniola should be free from servitude and be unmolested by anyone, and that they should live as free vassals, governed and protected by justice, as were the vassals of Castile. ... The Indians should be treated with much love and kindness, so that no wrongs done to them should hinder their reception of our Holy Faith by creating an abhorrence of the Christians ... That he should take care that natives and Spaniards live in peace, administering justice with an equal

hand, since this will be the best way to ensure that no violence is done to the Indians.

And in her testament, she begged and encouraged her husband King Ferdinand:

> Wherefore I very affectionately supplicate my lord the King, and charge and command my said daughter (Juana) that they act accordingly, and that this (the conversion of the Indians) should be their principal end, and that in it they should have much diligence, and that they should not consent or give occasion that the Indians who dwell in those islands, or on the Tierra Firme, gained, or to be gained, should receive any injury in their persons or goods, but should command that they be well and justly treated. And that if the Indians had received any injury, they should remedy it and look that they do not infringe in any respect that which is enjoined and commanded of the said concession.

The second person was the Emperor Charles V who, in his royal decree of 1520, declared the unconditional freedom of all Indian slaves.

And regarding the treatment of married women, a 1515 royal decree declared that they should be subject to a very special care, and not being allowed to work while pregnant, to breast-feed a white woman's child while breast-feeding her own, and by being exempt from paying taxes. All of the aforesaid points to the fact that from early on Spain resisted and condemned the idea of any discrimination against native Americans and Blacks and that, if there was any, it was mostly based on religion and not on race or ethnicity, nor on culture, background, social status of general beliefs. In this regard, Spain was quite unique when compared with others, and even though those laws were at times ignored or abused, it was never intended to be so. Laws are passed to be enforced; sometimes they do and others they do not. That is the way it was, and that is the way it is in our present era.

Part K

OTHER RELATED HISTORICAL FACTS OF INTEREST

—En route to the New World in 1492, Martín Alonso Pinzón convinced Columbus to steer south instead of continuing west after passing the Azores (October 7). Had Columbus continued west as he had planned, the Spanish would have landed somewhere in the eastern coast of North America, possibly between Virginia and Florida, changing U.S. history forever, and probably turning today's United States into one or more Hispanic countries. What evolved in the South may have evolved in the North.

In our estimation, this is an extremely important event. In fact, it is so important that we would like to expand on it. For that we are turning to the magnificent work on the Columbus Diary of historian Edward Gaylord Bourne:

Saturday, 6th of October.

The Admiral continued his west course, and during day and night they made good 40 leagues, 33 being counted. This night, Martin Alonso [Pinzón] said that it would be well to steer south rather than continuing west, and it appeared to the Admiral that Martín Alonso did not say this with respect to the island of Cipango.* He saw that if an error was made the land would not be reached so quickly, and that consequently it would be better to go at once to the continent and afterwards to the islands ... For this reason he [Columbus] resolved to give up the west course, and to shape a course WS. W. for the two following days. He began the new course one hour before sunset. And then this footnote: Las Casas [Father Bartolomé de las Casas] remarks 1.285. If he had kept up the direct westerly course and the impatience of the Castilians had not hindered him, there is no doubt that he would have struck the main land of Florida and from there to New Spain...

*Cipango: Name given to Japan by Marco Polo.

And since we are talking about Friar Bartolomé de Las Casas, it is of great interest to note that the Columbus's log, which he kept in minute detail the record of the voyage, disappeared and no one to this day has been able to locate it. A copy was made which was also lost. So how do we know the contents of the log or "Diario"? For this we have to thank Friar de Las Casas who transcribed verbatim its most important parts in his *History of the Indies*. This is the only source which has served as the basis of all modern knowledge about the voyage.

—The only interpreter in Columbus's first voyage was Luis de Torres, a converted Jew who knew Hebrew and Arabic, both of the principal languages of the time. It should also be noted that one of the principal financiers of Columbus' first voyage was another converted Jew, Luis de Santangel, born in Valencia. He met Columbus in Córdoba in 1486 and contributed some 140,000 maravedís to the voyage. He later became one of Columbus's best and most trusted friends.

—The Spanish pilot Vicente Yáñez Pinzón, who accompanied Christopher Columbus on his first voyage, discovered later, on January 20 or 26, 1500, the world's largest (widest) river, the Amazon, which he named "Santa María de la Mar Dulce" (Saint Mary of the Sweet Sea). At the same time he discovered Brazil, traveling in total all incredible 3600 kilometers and also confirming the existence of a the new continent of South America.

—What language did Christopher Columbus speak? He did not speak formal Italian but Genovese dialect of his native Genoa, which was mainly spoken rather than written. The language he spoke and wrote and in which he became literate was Castilian, or Spanish. He also spoke broken Portuguese.

—The Spaniard Pedro Alonso Niño de Moguer was the pilot of the "Niña" on Columbus' first voyage, a ship owned by his family, and the "Pinta" was owned by Cristóbal Quintero, a Spaniard and also a native of Palos.

—How much did Columbus's first voyage cost? According to John Boyd Thacher, approximately 1,167,542 maravedís or $151,780 in 1991 U.S. dollars. In modern times, the maravedí would have a gold-standard value of 13 cents.

—Mount Vernon is today a national shrine in the United States, home of George Washington and his family. Where does the name "Mount Vernon" come from? It was given by George Washington's half brother, Lawrence Washington, in honor of his commander in the British Navy during the War of Jenkin's Ear, Admiral Edward Vernon ("Old Grog"). While in England, Lawrence Washington was named a captain to fight in the Jenkin's Ear War and was present in the siege of Cartagena. This war, The Jenkin's Ear War, was fought against the Spanish for the control of the Caribbean and the Spanish Main following England's declaration of war on October 19, 1739. It was called "War of Jenkin's Ear" because Admiral Vernon had claimed that the Spaniards had cut off his ear, an incident that irritated England and gave her an excuse to launch a major offensive against Spanish possession in Panama and Cartagena. If Lawrence Washington had led, not accompanied, Admiral Vernon to Cartagena, it is probable that his estate in Virginia may have been given a different name.

—Here are some interesting facts about Mexico's "transfer" of half of its territory to the United States.

By the Treaty of Guadalupe-Hidalgo, after the Mexican-American War of 1848, Mexico ceded to the United States five states comprising as much land as its entire Northeast. The five states were: California, Nevada, Utah, Arizona, and New Mexico, a "gift" long to be treasured by the United States and long to be regretted by the Mexican Republic. Spain also has its regrets, for it ceded after the Spanish American War of 1898 such prized possessions as Cuba, Puerto Rico, the Philippines, and Guam. But perhaps the biggest regret for Spain was the sale of Louisiana to the United States in 1803 for a mere $15 million, an immense territory she had held previously. And what about the big state of Texas? It was annexed in 1845, thanks to Sam Houston who was able to carve out his own independent republic of Texas. The Mexican-American War, over a period of two years, cost the United States one hundred million dollars and eleven thousand U.S. lives. It was indeed a shameful war, meant only to render Mexico powerless and incapable of holding on to its vast southwestern lands. We would like to echo these words from an American president: "I do not think there was ever a more wicked war than that waged by the United States on Mexico." The president was Ulysses S. Grant, a veteran of that war.

More on the benefits derived by the United States on this "transfer" of Mexican lands. The Treaty of Guadalupe-Hidalgo partially states:

New Mexico and Upper California have been ceded by Mexico to the United States, and now constitute a part of our country. Embracing nearly ten degrees of latitude, lying adjacent to the Oregon territory, and extending from the Pacific Ocean to the Rio Grande, a mean distance of nearly a thousand miles, it would be difficult to estimate the value of these possessions to the United States. They constitute by themselves a country large enough for a great empire, and their acquisition is second only in importance to that of Louisiana in 1803. Rich in minerals and agricultural resources, with a climate of great salubrity, they embrace the most important ports on the whole Pacific coast of the continent of North America. The possession of the ports of San Diego and Monterey and the bay of San Francisco, will enable the United States to command the already valuable and rapidly increasing commerce of the Pacific. The number of our whale ships alone now employed in that sea exceeds seven hundred, requiring more than twenty-thousand seamen to navigate them, while the capital invested in this particular branch of commerce is estimated at not less than forty million dollars. The excellent harbor of Upper California will, under our flag, afford security and repose to our commercial marine, and American mechanics will soon furnish ready means of ship-building and repair, which are now so much wanted in that distant sea. By the acquisition of these possessions, we are now brought into immediate proximity with the west coast of America, from Cape Horn to the Russian possession North of Oregon, with the islands of the Pacific Ocean, and by a direct voyage in steamers we will be in less than thirty days of Canton and other ports of China. In this vast region, whose rich resources are soon to be developed by American energy and enterprise, great must be the augmentation of our commerce, and with it new and profitable demands for mechanic labor in all its branches, and new and valuable markets for our manufacturers and agricultural products.

If he had only known? On April 4, 1837, Mexican President Corro decreed a bond issue to repay his country's foreign debt, especially a loan from England. As security or collateral he put up 100,000,000 (that's one hundred million) acres of land of Mexican territory. That "territory" comprised lands in the Californias, Texas, New Mexico, Chihuahua, and Sonora. After the Mexican-American War, when those lands became U.S. property, the bondholders received only $2,500,000 of the U.S. payment to Mexico. With such ineptitude and short-sightedness on the part of that supposedly public servant, Mexico continued to risk losing half of its land holdings, which it eventually did. President Corro should have implemented a more sensible and austere plan of fiscal discipline to repay that debt, rather than gamble with such invaluable possessions.

—In 1820, three hundred American families settled in Texas marking the beginning of the end of the Spanish rule. How did it happen? Moses Austin requested permission from Spain to settle in Texas, which was granted by the 1821 charter, and the Americans moved in. Then in 1823, Mexico, now independent from Spain (1821), provided new land grants to Moses Austin's son, Stephen to settle in the area. In 1832, Samuel Houston crossed the Red River and entered Texas. He then notified his friend President Jackson that *those who now called themselves Texans,* were planning to draw up their own constitution and ultimately become part of the Union. In 1833, "Texans" voted to separate from Mexico at San Felipe, and Stephen Austin petitioned separate statehood from Mexican President, the venal Santa Ana, and was imprisoned for so asking. In this same year, "Texans," under the command of William B. Travis, captured the Mexican fort in Anahuac, which was soon to be followed by other armed conflicts. Stephen Austin, after being freed from prison, revealed his plans to go to war with Mexico as the only alternative to achieve statehood. Later, at a convention, "Texans" voiced their desire to separate from Mexican rule in favor of self-government and captured San Antonio. Then came the siege of the Alamo by Santa Ana in 1835. The "Texans" did not surrender and they were all killed. Later in that same year, Sam Houston became President of Texas serving his term until 1841. In 1845, Texas is annexed to the United States and on December 29th is incorporated as the twenty-eighth state. The rest is history. By 1836 the American population in Texas had grown to thirty thousand, and ten years later (1846) reached 142,000. In 1839, France is the first European nation to recognize Texas' independence.

—And what happened in California? In the case of California, its governors dispensed land grants even more generously than in Texas. Some of these lands or "ranchos" were about 11 square leagues, or 48,000 acres. By the end of the Mexican rule, approximately seven hundred of these grants had been dispensed for free or at a nominal fee. Most of the settlers were foreign colonists who had only become Mexican citizens in order to qualify. The only pre-requisite for the settlers to receive a land grant was to convert to Catholicism. In 1828, the "Californianos" or "Californios," Mexican settlers, rebelled against Mexican rule and sought, among other measures, the secularization of the Spanish missions, especially the mission of San Gabriel. A few more uprisings broke out between 1828 and 1843, having a debilitating effect on the Mexican government and paving the way for new settlers, mainly Americans.

More historical facts about California and Texas.

In 1845, President Polk, who had publicly stated his desire to acquire Texas, California, and Oregon, dispatched John Slidell to Mexico to negotiate a settlement of hostilities, and to offer the purchase of California and New Mexico, which Mexico refused. However, he had already developed his own plans for annexing California when, on October 17th, he named Thomas Larkin to be consul of the United States in Monterey. Both territories, California and New Mexico, had been claimed by Texas (Polk was known to be at the time he was elected in1844, the U.S.'s most expansionist president). In his inaugural address, he stated that he regarded the question of annexation "belonging exclusively to the United States and Texas, and that our title to Oregon is "clear and unquestionable." At this time, President Polk reaffirmed the Monroe Doctrine and enunciated his own doctrine, "The Polk Doctrine," opposing any attempts by European nations to maintain a balance of power. Then, when the Mexican army crossed Brownsville, Texas, President Polk called it an invasion of U.S. territory and war was officially declared on May 13, 1846. By that time, California had also fallen under U.S. rule, after Commander John. B. Montgomery seized San Francisco and Lt. James W.

Revere occupied Sonoma, and later by the occupations of Santa Barbara and Los Angeles (earlier, Commodore Thomas Catesby had seized Monterey, the capital of California). The Mexican army grew confused, especially for the numerous times its government had changed hands during the period. The final campaign of the conflict took place with the landing of the U.S. army in Veracruz under General Winfield Scott, which later proceeded to Mexico City, where President Antonio López de Santa Ana was defeated at Cerro Gordo in 1847. Mexico, crushed and humiliated, signed the Treaty of Guadalupe-Hidalgo (1848), whereby Mexico ceded to the United States a large portion of its territory for which it received and indemnity of $15 million. As part of the Treaty, Mexico also accepted all other U.S. claims over its former territory, such as the inclusion of an additional 1,193,061 square miles.

—Also, it is a known fact that U.S. General James Wilkinson attempted with Aaron Burr to conquer Mexico in 1806, but later changed his mind and notified Thomas Jefferson of his covert plan. He was named governor of Louisiana (the first after the acquisition by the United States) in 1805. He died in Mexico in 1825 where he had gone to claim some lands.

—In 1853, the United States Ambassador to Mexico, James Gadsden, is instructed to negotiate the purchase of land south of the Gila River, West to the 37 parallel boundary of California, and east to the Rio Grande border of Texas. The agreement is finally signed on December 30th of that year, whereby Mexico ceded to the United States this territory comprising 29,640 square miles, for which it was paid $10 million, thus completing what is today the southern borders of New Mexico and Arizona. Also as part of the purchase, the United States acquired rich fields of gold and silver. This is known as the "Gadsden Purchase." As a point of interest, these mines yielded an enormous amount of revenues for the U.S. Treasury, especially the one located in Gila City. And, in a short thirty years, the Comstock Lode Mine in the Washoe Mountains in Nevada had yielded over $300 million in revenues. This alone covered the $10 million paid to Mexico for the land, plus a profit of $290 million. In California, by 1938, the cumulative of the gold found in mines totaled $2 billion, and of the gas and oil found in that same year amounted to $5 billion.

—Here is an interesting fact of particular interest to the Irish in New York City and elsewhere. The Irish are indeed closely related to Spain's history, especially from the 16th century on. Many of them immigrated to Spain in the late 1500s and King Philip II strived to aid and protect them against the persecutions of Protestant England; in fact, he sent an armada to Ireland in 1596 under the command of Martín de Padilla, and King Philip III also sent various expeditions with the same purpose in 1601. The new Irish immigrants flourished in Spain and were educated in Spanish universities, particularly at the University of Salamanca where Philip II established a school for Irish noblemen in 1592. Other schools were established in Santiago de Compostela in 1605, in Seville in 1612, and in Madrid in 1621.

—The *turkey* Spanish connection. Is it true? What is true is that the turkey has been indigenous to the Americas for the past 10 million years. And what is also true is that both Christopher Columbus and Hernán Cortés had a taste for it and took it to Spain where it became very popular and then throughout Europe, especially in England and France. What follows may or may not be true but it nonetheless makes for entertaining reading. It seems that Columbus, believing that he had reached Asia, called the turkey "tuka," which means peacock in the Tamil language of India. In Spain it was later called "tukki," which is a Hebrew word and from which the English "turkey" derived.

Thus, when the Pilgrims came to North America they were already familiar with the turkey which the Spaniards had brought into Europe and the rest is history. That may be the Spanish connection with the U.S. traditional feast of "Thanksgiving." The first Thanksgiving Proclamation was enacted June 20, 1676.

—The very first Italian opera played in New York was "The Barber of Seville," introduced in 1825, with the famous Spanish tenor Manuel García.

—More on the U.S. acquisition of Florida and other territories. How much is Florida worth? The United States paid $15 million for Louisiana, $7 million for Alaska, and even paid Denmark for the purchase of the Virgin Islands (formerly the Danish West Indies), but nothing to Spain for Florida, which it simply ceded to the United States. Here is the story: In 1803, after Spain ceded Louisiana to France, it was then sold secretly by this country to the United States for the above-stipulated amount. At this juncture, the United States approached the Spanish government claiming that the western region of Florida should be included in the purchase, and without waiting for a reply, two U.S. representatives, Pinckey and Monroe, traveled to France to clinch the deal. In 1804, Thomas Jefferson signed a law declaring that the western coast of Florida, between the Mississippi and the Perdido River, was now under U.S. domain, prompting a strong protest from the Spanish Ambassador, the Marquis of Casa-Irujo. Later, on September 26, 1810, under President Madison, and taking advantages of the Spanish War of Independence, the residents of Baton Rouge declared the independence of western Florida. By a covert authorization of the U.S. Congress, President Madison seized Amelia Island on the Atlantic Coast in 1811 and Mobila in 1813, both occupied by General Jackson. In 1818, Jackson invaded eastern Florida and occupied Penzacola with much praise from President Monroe and Secretary of State John Quincy Adams. On January 22, 1819, the United States and Spain signed a treaty, whereby Spain would give up Florida upon receiving $5 million, which was never paid. By July 17, 1821, the Spanish domain in Florida had officially ended with most of the Spanish residents leaving for Cuba. This territory ceded by Spain included today's Oregon, Washington, and Columbia, keeping only Texas, New Mexico, California, Arizona, Nevada, Utah, and Colorado, which in 1821 were taken over by Mexico after the Mexican Revolution. However, by the Treaty of Guadalupe- Hidalgo, this vast territory was ceded by Mexico to the United States.

—In 1521, sailing on the Victoria, the Spaniard Juan Sebastián Elcano is first to complete the first circumnavigation of the world, began by Magellan in 1519. After traversing the Indian Ocean and passing the Cape of Good Hope, he finally reaches Seville in 1522. During the voyage, Elcano measured the circumference of the world, thus proving that it was indeed round, and established that the other side of the world is habitable, a most remarkable discovery for future explorations. The second circumnavigation of the world was also completed by a Spaniard, Andrés de Urdaneta in 1536. The voyage took him eleven years to complete. Further, the Spaniards found a new sea route from Mexico to Philippines, made the first map of the world (Juan de la Cosa, 1500), and the first historical atlas (1560), and were also the first to observe the currents of the Gulf of Mexico.

—To the amazement of many, there are more than 320 places in Australia bearing Spanish names.

—The Spanish Jesuit St. Francis Xavier (1506-1552), co-founder of the Society of Jesus, is the patron saint of all of Oceania, which includes Australia.

—The Spanish dollar was an international currency for most of the 16th and 17th centuries.

—For 25 years (1803 to 1828) the Spanish dollar became the legal currency of Australia but with a hole in the center. It had been brought there by the British in 1792.

—Do you like pineapples? If you do, you have to thank the Spaniard Francisco de Paula Marín who, in 1813, proposed its growing in Hawaii. By the turn of the century, it became one of its leading industries.

—And those with a taste for sugar, it was Christopher Columbus who brought sugar cane to the Americas (Hispaniola) on his second voyage from the Canary Islands. It is believed that sugar cane originated in Polynesia (Guinea) and brought to Spain by the Moors after they had cultivated it in North Africa.

—And corn, "maíz" in Spanish, "maize" in English, the staple of both Americas, most likely evolved in what is today Mexico and Central America where it was developed by the Aztecs and Mayas.

—And the potato, or "papa," was first harvested in Peru and Bolivia, high above the Andes. The Spaniards, who were the first Europeans to eat it, brought it to Europe where it became the main staple that it is today.

—The great American poet H.W. Longfellow did much to foster Spanish language and literature in the United States. In 1830 he published his *Novelas españolas* (Spanish Novels), and in "The North American Review" appeared his two essays "Spanish Devotional and Moral Poetry," and "Spanish Language and Literature." His translation of *Coplas de Jorge Manrique* was published in New England in 1833, and in 1843 published *The Spanish Student*. Two years later, in 1845, he also published *Poets and Poetry of Europe*, in which he included such Spanish literary masters as Cervantes, Lope de Vega, Calderón de la Barca, Ercilla, Garcilaso de la Vega, and others. In all, he had written about 3000 pages on Spain or some 1 million words. In 1842 he was named Minister Plenipotentiary of the United States in Madrid.

—In 1832, another prominent American Hispanist, Washington Irving, published *The Alhambra* in London.

—In 1835, the celebrated American historian William H. Prescott published in Boston *Ferdinand and Isabella*, which was soon after translated into Spanish and other languages. With this publication (plus many others that followed, *Conquest of Mexico*,

1843, *Conquest of Peru*, 1845, *History of Philip II*, 1855-1858) Prescott sparked wide interest about Spain and Spanish America. It should be noted that in his writings he depended greatly on his close Spanish collaborator, Pascual de Gayangos.

—Much is owed to the distinguished American Hispanist George Ticknor for the knowledge of Spanish literature. In 1848, he published his classic work *History of Spanish Literature*, and also donated his extensive private collection of Spanish language, literature, and history (over 10000 volumes) to the Boston Public Library, which he himself helped found. The great American philosopher George Santayana was born in Madrid (1863). He immigrated to the United States in 1872 and graduated from Harvard in 1876, where he taught philosophy from 1889 until 1912. Among his most celebrated works is *The Sense of Beauty*, published in 1896. He is widely considered one of the United States' pre-eminent philosophers.

—One of the United States' greatest Hispanists, Hubert Howe Bancroft, published in 1882-1890 (re-issued), *The Works of Hubert Howe Bancroft*, a 39-volume encyclopedia covering the history of Central America, Mexico, and the Far West of the United States. In 1805 he donated his 60,000-volume personal library to the University of California (1890), which contains a magnificent collection of rare maps, manuscripts, books, and narratives of early Spanish explorers. The collection remains one of the best in the world.

—Another Hispanist at heart was Cullen Bryant, a partner and manager in the "Evening Post" for thirty years. In 1878 he published in New York his poem "Cervantes." In addition, he translated many of the Spanish classics, including Fray Luis de León's novel *Jerilla*, by Carolina Coronado, which was published in "The New York Ledger" circa 1869. He also authored *Toured of the Old South*, in which he deals in part with the Spanish influence in North America, and in particular with a group of some 1,000

Spaniards from the Balearic Islands who settled in Florida in the early 1800s.

—The acquisition of Cuba, as a state or commonwealth, had long been sought by the United States. Such was the plan of President Franklin Pierce (thirteenth U.S. president) who had envisioned the acquisition of Hawaii and Cuba as part of his "peaceful expansion." In 1859, Florida's Senator Stephen R. Mallory, addressing the U.S. Senate, dreamed of an American slave empire in the Caribbean, arguing that the acquisition of Cuba had been a bipartisan cornerstone of American Foreign Policy, and adding:

> ...its purchase (Cuba) is the necessary consequence of the purchase of Louisiana ... and unless Cuba is acquired, the United States will sit by helplessly while the island is Africanized' by sentimental and misguided emancipation policies of Spain and England. (Baltimore, John Murphy, 1859.)

Also, in 1859, the U.S. Senate proposed Bill S.497, "making appropriations to effect the acquisition of the island of Cuba by negotiation" (U.S. Congress, Senate Committee on Foreign Relations, 1859). In this regard, American historian James W. Cortada said:

> During the 1820s evidence of American interest in Cuba was consistently there. John Quincy Adams, for example, envisioned Cuba being drawn into the sphere of North American influence in years to come through the dint of geographic proximity and intimate trade relations.

The plan or plans for the acquisition of Cuba became inoperative only because of the U.S. Civil War. An earlier attempt to purchase the island was made in 1854, when the United States offered to purchase it from Spain for $120 million (Ostende Manifest).

—Three hundred years before the California Gold Rush, the discovery of the gold and silver mines in 1543 and 1544 in the province of New Galicia, Mexico, and of more significance of silver ore in Zacatecas in 1546, should count as North America's first "rush." Just a few years later, over thirty companies were operating in the area under fierce competition. So was the abundance of silver, that from 1550 to 1820, one year before Mexico declared its independence from Spain, Mexico, or New Spain back then, coined over two billion dollars and about the same amount was exported worldwide, or two-thirds of the world supply. As stated earlier, much of this silver ended up in the United States before, during, and after the colonial period. Undoubtedly, such wealth, when first found in the middle of the sixteenth century, both in Mexico, Peru, and elsewhere in South America, ushered Europe's "rush" to the New World, with Queen Elizabeth I of England leading the way. As South America was under Spanish domain, England and the others—France, Holland—directed their attention to the northern lands. Said differently, they sought to do in the north what Spain had achieved in the south with one major difference: their motives. In the case of Spain there were many while in the case of the others there was only one: the sheer acquisition of wealth for self-preservation and power. Not that such in any way diminishes their many accomplishments in settling and colonizing North America, but that came later and not at the beginning, when they were only driven by the glimmering metals, just as all humans are since time immemorial.

—The Santa Fe Trail was crucial to the expansion of the United States into the Southwest after Mexico's Independence in 1821. It extended from western Missouri through Kansas and Colorado to Santa Fe in New Mexico. It was pioneered by William Becknell in 1821 and it remained an important commercial route for over 50 years until the Santa Fe Railways were built.

—The first Catholic bishop of the Americas was the Franciscan Juan de Quevedo at the Santa María de la Antigua in the Darien in 1513. He came to the New World on the expedition of Pedrarias Dávila.

—1898. Explosion of the Maine in Havana Harbor. Who was at fault? One thing is certain: Spain had absolutely nothing to do with it. Let's look at the historical facts: At the time of the incident, T.B. Reed, President of the U.S. Congress, called for a more thorough investigation by neutral countries, as he was not convinced that Spain was to blame. He asked Admiral Melville of the Army's Corps of Engineers to render his own personal report, which stated (January 29, 1902) that Spain was not at fault. His report was published in the "North America Review" in June of 1912. Prior to this year, in 1910, the U.S. government salvaged the Main's hull, and in July of 1911 General Bixley, head of the Army's Corps of Engineers, confirmed that the explosion had been due to an internal explosion of ammunition, and that no external explosion could have damaged the ship that way. Finally, Admiral Sigsbee, the Maine's former commander, attested to the fact that there was absolutely no proof that Spain had in any way been involved in the incident. His statement was later published in the "New York." However, the theory still persist that William Randolph Hearst was the "inventor" of the Spanish- American War for his own personal gain, a theory that has not yet been substantiated.

—The first to circumnavigate the earth was the Spaniard Juan Sebastián Elcano in 1522, and the second another Spaniard, Andrés de Urdaneta, in 1536 after voyaging for a total of eleven years. It is but most disheartening that such a major accomplishment, the first circumnavigation of the globe, has been credited only to the great navigator Ferdinand of Magellan with little or no mention of Elcano who, in addition to being the first, proved also the sphericity of the earth in doubt at the time. Because of his great feat, Charles V honored him with a crest bearing the inscription "Primus circumdedisti me."

—The Americas' first native to learn Spanish was an Arawak Indian who Columbus brought to Spain where he was baptized Diego Colón (name of Columbus' son and heir). He served Columbus as an interpreter and accompanied him on his second voyage. He is to be considered the Americas' first interpreter/translator of a European and indigenous languages.

—Although the reader may not realize it or perhaps not recognize some of them, thousands of words of common English usage are of Spanish origin.

Besides the obvious ones—taco, enchilada, sombrero, siesta, rodeo, fiesta—, there are many more that have been assimilated into English. They have come to us from three main sources: via the Southwest from Mexico, the Caribbean, mostly through commerce, and from foods with no direct English equivalents. Other Spanish words have come to us through other languages, such as French and even Arabic. Of these, most English words beginning with "al" are of Arabic origin, like "alfalfa", from the Arabic "Alfasfasah." Other words are of South American origin, coming to us from some of the indigenous languages such as Quechua or Guaraní. In some of the words the spelling may vary somewhat and so may the pronunciation, although, remarkably, in most cases they preserve their original Spanish pronunciation, such as "Embargo," "Margarita," "Conquistador" (without pronouncing the "u" in "qui," as to sound /kee /), "Piñata" (pronouncing the "ñ" as in /onion/), "Garbanzo." Most of these words came into American usage before the Civil War.

First, we will give a sampling of words assimilated into English from the three sources mentioned above, and then list about 50 common or not so common words with a Spanish origin. The words are listed randomly rather than in alphabetical order.

Via de southwest from Mexico: Chocolate (from the Nahualt "xocolati".) From the Caribbean (Haiti): Barbecue (from "Barbacoa").

Listing of words:

Conquistador
Banana
Sombrero
Tobacco (Caribbean, from *"tabaco "*)
Guerrilla
Tornado (from *"Tornada"*)
Hurricane (from *"Huracán "*)
Margarita ("daisy" in Spanish)
Armada (from the Spanish Armada)
Mosquito
Desperado
El Niño (relating to the weather, and to the child, "Niño" (Jesus Christ), appearing during Christmas)
Garbanzo
Cafeteria (most likely from Cuban-Spanish, originating in Chicago in around 1918)
Tomato (from the Spanish *"tomate "*)
Pimento (from the Spanish *"pimiento"*)
Oregano
Plaza
Ranch (from the Spanish *"rancho "*)
Cigar, cigarette (from the Spanish *"cigarro "*)
Comrade (from the Spanish *"camarada"*)
Siesta
Stampede (from the Spanish *"estampida"*)

Embargo
Vanilla (from the Spanish *"vainilla "*)
Jaguar (from the Guarani, *"Yaguar"* via the Spanish)
Barracuda
Vigilante
Incomunicado
Adobe Alligator
Aficionado
Avocado (from the Nahualt *"ahuacatl "*)
Bonanza
Bronco ("wild" in Spanish)
Burro
Chaps (from the Mexican *"chaparreras "*)
Puma (from Quechua)
Condor (from Quechua)
Cocaine (from Quechua)
Canoe (Caribbean)
Lasso (from *"lazo "*)
Papaya (from *Arawak)*
Esparto (meaning long and wiry grass)
Creole (from *"criollo, "* a native of the land)
Cannibal ("caníbal " in Spanish, from the Caribbean)
Hammock ("hamaca" in Spanish, from the Caribbean)
Coyote (possibly from the language of the Chinook, or perhaps
from the French *"Cailloux, "* meaning "pebbles")
Canyon ("cañón," in Spanish)
Cinch ("cincho," in Spanish)
Corral Bronco Poncho
Peon (peón)
Tornado
Presidio
Buckaroo (from *"vaquero "*)
Calaboose (from "calabozo ")

These last ten were adopted after the Mississippi was crossed, and especially following the Mexican-American War.

Three words stand out as most curious: "spaniel," derived from "Hispania" which is the name given to Spain by the Romans); "hoosegow (judged)," from "juzgado," past participle of the verb "juzgar," "to judge"; and "yanki," ("Yankee") which is not Spanish, and not even applied to the English originally but to the Dutch. It was a common nickname applied as early as 1683 among the Buccaneers who ravaged the Spanish Main. The name is derived from "Janke", a diminutive of the Dutch given name "Jan."

For those interested in the semantics of Spanish-derived English terms, they will be well-served by consulting these four capital books: *A Dictionary of Spanish Words in English*, by Harold W. Bentley, *Geographical Terms in the Far West*, by Edward E. Hale, *Geographical Terms from the Spanish*, by Mary Austin, American Speech, October 1933, and *The English Language in the Southwest*, by T.M. Pearce, New Mexico Historical Review, July 1932.

We are not including in the above listing many more thousands of Spanish toponyms (names of places) as originally given by the early Spanish discoverers and explorers, especially in the south and southwest of the country. In fact, according to H.L. Mencken, The Spanish contributions to the American vocabulary are far more numerous than those of any other continental language, and that includes German, Dutch, French, and Italian. Mr. Mencken maintains that most of them were adopted after the Louisiana Purchase, and also declares that by 1806 Spanish was already considered the second language of the United States.

—Prior to 1492, North America was linguistically linked by a common language: "Utoaztec," among which were the Aztec group in the central region and the Nahualt to the south.

—Had Spain. not intervened and held them back in Alaska in the late 1800s, it is quite probable that the Russians would have gained full domain of the United States' entire Northwest.

—The Americas' first postal system was established by Emperor Charles V in 1525, and the America's first Postmaster was Lorenzo Galíndez de Carvajal.

—Mexico was originally named "Nueva España" (New Spain), a name proposed by Hernán Cortés to the Emperor Charles V. And it was Cortés who, in 1522, after the conquest of Mexico, proposed to Charles V to name himself Emperor of the Indies.

—North America's first Annual Fair was the Taos Fair, established by Spanish officials in 1723 in New Mexico. It functioned uninterruptedly for almost a century and was an important source of contact for the trading and commerce with the Plains Indians and French fur trappers

—"Sangre de Cristo Mountains" is the name given by the Spaniards to Blood of Christ Mountains, part of the Rocky Mountains, extending from south-central Colorado into north-central New Mexico.

—When the British landed in North America in 1607, they set foot on lands that had been claimed by Spain 100 years before. And they were claimed by Spain based on the Line of Demarcation, a north-south line drawn by Pope Alexander VI in 1493, thus settling the dispute between Spain and Portugal by common consent in the Treaty of Tordesillas in 1494. Such line ran about 45 degrees west, with Spain keeping all lands to the west and Portugal to the east. At the time, all the nations of western and central Europe were loyal to the Pope and thus, although perhaps reluctantly, accepted his decision. It could then be argued that they were trespassing on private domain, making all of their settlements and future actions both illegitimate and illegal. In other words, they could have been branded as our very first "illegal aliens."

—Spanish missionaries were often accompanied by Mexican Indians or charges, and many of them suffered miserable deaths at the hands of North American tribes, such as the Comanches. In 1758, many Trascalan Indians were massacred together with Spanish missionaries soon after they had founded the San Sabá Mission in central Texas. These Trascalans were of the same tribe that so befriended Hernán Cortés on his overland march to Mexico City. After they were reconstructed, the walls of the mission stand today as a memorial of the bloody encounter.

—According to historian W.H. Hutchinson, the Spanish tripod of civilization in North America were Missions, Presidios, and Pueblos, with which we must fully agree. This helps understand Spain's motives in coming to the New World: Faith, Conquest, and Settlement or Colonization, in that order.

—Further on the Line of Demarcation, and as we have already said, all Europeans nations agreed with the Pope's decision. In the case of England, however, it did so deceptively. In fact, while apparently agreeing with the decision, the king of England was already planning to dispatch John Cabot on his voyage knowing that he would infringe on Spain's domains. According to Cabot:

> The King of England has often spoken to me on this subject. He hoped to derive great advantage from it. I think it is not farther that four hundred leagues [about 1200 miles]. I told him that in my opinion, the land was already in the possession of your Majesties [Ferdinand and Isabella]; but, though I gave him my reasons, he did not like it.

Cabot received his patent in February, 1498.

—Much credit should also be given to the North American natives for their contribution to the building of the nation, for many of them took active part in such important areas as construction, agriculture, the manual arts, and others. In this regard, the Spaniards welcomed and appreciated their eagerness to learn and work in sharp contrast to other later Europeans who pushed them away. On this subject, American historian David J. Weber wrote:

> In contrast to the Anglo-American frontier in North America, which largely excluded natives, Spain sought to include natives within its new world societies, Thus, Spanish missionaries labored to win the hearts and minds of Indians in what might be defined as a spiritual o cultural frontier...

—Sailing on a caravel or a galleon from Spain to America was in itself a major and dangerous undertaking, but more so on a brigantine. In 1779, Salvador de Muro y Salazar dared to cross the Atlantic from Spain to Cuba precisely on such a small vessel, and he made it safely.

—The whole world, including the United States, has profited enormously from the vast Amazon rainforest, the earth's largest. Francisco de Orellana discovered the Amazon River and traversed it east to west. Such a rich and vast territory added much to the future progress and development of all of South and North America. His odyssey through the jungles and swamps of the uncharted region remains one of the most fabulous accomplishments in the annals of discovery and exploration. In just 18 months, he traveled, starting from Quito (Ecuador), over 400 miles by land and an astonishing 4,000 miles by sea and river. And Diego de Ordás traveled the full length of the Orinoco River and explored what is today the French, British or Dutch Guiana in 1531.

Part L

SPANISH/HISPANIC GREAT HISTORICAL FIGURES. THE EARLY GRANDEES OF THE UNITED STATES: DISCOVERERS, EXPLORERS, PIONEERS, NATION BUILDERS.

The following list is intended to include mainly individuals in the area of discovery and exploration. Therefore, it does not purposely include many other prominent figures in areas such as politics, the arts, literature, science, etc., particularly of the Modern or Contemporary Ages. Although most of them are Spanish, it must be remembered that all of their famous deeds originated from what was then the Indies, or Hispanic America, which is to say that the America to the south was the fertile land and the inspiration that greatly contributed to the creation of the America to the north. Indeed, the future Spanish North American explorers honed their skills in South America, and it was from the main Spanish outposts of Havana and Mexico City that most of these great explorations originated. In this regard, it could also be said that the Spain that was before the discovery was transformed into a new Spain, or rather, into a new world known today as "Hispanism." In essence, Spain was reborn in America. Hernán Cortés was Spanish, yes, but, after he set foot in the Dominican Republic in 1501, then in Cuba in 1511, and in Mexico in 1519, he had become unmistakably a Hispanic. So much so, that while in Spain on his last trip he longed to return to his "Beloved Mexico," and on his way back he died. And so it is with every honorable immigrant coming to these shores, then, and now. In colloquial Spanish it is called "aplatanarse," something like "becoming Americanized."

The list is by no means exhaustive or even complete, but only partial. It is logical to assume that in three hundred plus years of constant discoveries, explorations, and nation-building, Spain and Hispanics, or rather, the Hispanic World, would have engendered thousands of other similarly great historical figures, which in fact it did. The ones appearing below shall speak for the rest.

Queen Isabella
Mother of America, as she is called throughout the Hispanic world ("Madre de América.)

King Ferdinand
After Queen Isabella's death, he managed all of the America's affairs during the early years.

Emperor Charles V of Spain
Father of all America. Established the viceroyalties of Mexico and Peru, and ordered the foundings of the Americas ' first universities: The University of San Marcos in Lima, and the University of Mexico.

King Philip II of Spain

Central figure in the history of the Americas.

King Charles III of Spain

Great ally and supporter of the American Revolution.

Martín Alonso Pinzón

Christopher Columbus ' pilot.

Vicente Yáñez Pinzón

Christopher Columbus pilot.

Alonso de Hojeda

Early discoverer and explorer of America.

Juan de la Cosa

Drew first map of the world.

Nicolás de Ovando

First European to bring to America a large group of whole families totaling over 2500 people, between men, women, and children.

Diego Colón

Son of Cristopher Columbus and first viceroy of America. Sponsored th conquests of Cuba by Diego Velázquez, of Puerto Rico by Ponce de León, and of Jamaica by Juan de Esquivel.

María de Toledo

First woman governor of the Americas and key supporter of her husband's (Diego Colón) undertakings in the Caribbean.

Francisco Hernández de Córdoba
Discovered de Yucatan Peninsula and the Mayas.

Juan de Grijalva
Discovered the island of Cozumel, the Mexican coastline, and established first European contact with the Aztecs.

Sebastián Elcano
Completed the first circumnavigation of the world.

Hernando de Soto
Discovered/explored the U.S. Southeast.

Francisco Vázquez de Coronado
Discovered/explored South-Western United States.

Álvar Núñez Cabeza de Vaca
Discovered/explored region between Florida and Texas.

Hernán Cortés
Conquered Mexico and discovered/explored Baja California.

Friar Junípero Serra
Founded 21 Spanish missions in California.

Juan Ponce de León
Discovered/explored Florida.

Vasco Núñez de Balboa
Discovered the Pacific Ocean.

Juan de Fuca

Discovered the strait bearing his name.

Esteban Gómez

Discovered and explored an extensive area in north-eastern North America.

Juan Pardo

Led an expedition from Santa Elena to North Carolina and explored the Tennessee Valley.

Pedro Menéndez Márquez

(Nephew of Pedro Menéndez de Avilés). Explored the Chesapeake Bay area.

Juan de Ulibarri

Explored the area of the Upper Arkansas River.

Pedro de Quejos

Explored the eastern seaboard of the United States, including New Jersey.

Francisco Gordillo

Explored the region near Cape Fear (North Carolina).

Lucas Vázquez de Ayllón

Founded North America's first colony and explored the southern east coast of the United States.

Pánfilo de Narváez

Governor of an extensive area from Tamaulipas Mexico to Florida, and led an expedition to present-day Tallahassee.

Alonso Álvarez de Pineda
Discovered the northern coast of the Gulf of Mexico and the coast of Texas.

Diego Hurtado de Mendoza
Explored the region around the Gulf of California.

Gaspar Castaño
Explored New Mexico.

Ortún Ordóñez
With Cortés, discovered/explored Baja California.

Viceroy Antonio de Mendoza
Fostered many of the North American expeditions.

Friar Juan de Zumárraga
First Bishop of Mexico and patron of the arts.

Nuño de Guzmán
Fostered many expeditions to North America after conquering Nueva Galicia (northern Mexico).

Francisco de Ulloa
Explored the Gulf of Mexico.

Friar Marcos de Niza
Explored an extensive region in Arizona.

Juan de Tolosa
Discovered the Zacatecas silver mine in Mexico.

Friar Agustín Rodríguez
Re-discovered the Pueblos in New Mexico and founded there the San Bartolomé mission.

Juan Rodríguez Cabrillo
Discovered Upper California and Sierra Nevada.

Juan Gaytán
Is credited with discovering Hawaii.

Tristán de Luna y Arellano
Explored the eastern coast of Florida.

Pedro Menéndez de Avilés
Founded the U.S. 's first city, St. Augustine.

Andrés de Urdaneta
Discovered the shortest route between Asia and North America.

Friar Pedro de Gante
Founded in Mexico City the America's first technical and vocational college.

Juan Bautista de Anza
Explored a vast area from Sonora, Mexico, to San Diego and Monterey. Together with other colonists, founded the mission and presidio of San Francisco, which later became the great city in California.

Leiva Bonilla
With Gutiérrez de Humaña led an expedition to Kansas.

Pedro Cebrián y Agustín
Led an expedition to Florida which included many colonists from Mexico.

Lope Díaz de Armendariz
Fostered many expeditions to California.

Álvaro de Mendaña y Neira
Explored the South Pacific.

Isabel Barreto y Quirós
Explorer of the South Pacific.

Payo Enríquez de Ribera
As viceroy of Mexico, sent a large group of Jesuits to settle California.

Friar Alonso de Posada
Published a detailed account of the land of Teguayo, comprising parts of Utah, Oregon, and California.

Francisco Cuerzo
Founded the city of Albuquerque, New Mexico.

Antonio Valverde
Explored the American prairies.

Antonio de Espejo
Explored western Arizona.

Vicente González

Explored the region around Chesapeake Bay.

Sebastián Vizcaíno

Explored California and discovered Monterey Bay.

Juan de Oñate

Explored a large area in the U.S. Southwest.

Pedro de Peralta

Explored New Mexico and founded the city of Santa Fe.

Friar Luis de Oré

Founded several missions in today's Georgia.

Alonso de Vaca

Explored the area around the Arkansas River.

Pedro Porter y Casanete

Explored eastern California.

Friar Juan Lairos

Founded several missions in Texas.

Eusebio Francisco Kino

Founded many missions in Arizona.

Friar Damián Massanet

With Alonso de León founded several missions in Texas.

Diego de Vargas Zapata

Explored New Mexico.

José Sarmiento de Valladares
Founded the city of Sacramento, California.

Friar Juan María de Salvatierra
Founded five missions in Baja California.

Domingo Ramón
Founded five missions and the Presidio of Dolores in Texas.

Martín de Alarcón
Founded San Antonio, Texas.

Juan María Rivera
Discovered the Rocky Mountains.

Friar Antonio Margil
Founded several missions in Texas.

Pedro de Villazur
Founded a colony near the North Platte River.

Marquis de San Miguel de Aguayo
Founded ten missions and five forts in Texas.

Father Consag (Jesuit)
Explored the depths of the Gulf of California and the Gila and Colorado valleys.

José de Escandón
Explored a large area in Texas and founded the city of Laredo.

Friar Francisco Tomás Hermenegildo
Led four expeditions to the Gila and Colorado Rivers.

Gaspar de Portolá

Discovered San Francisco Bay and founded the cities of San Diego and Monterey.

Juan Pérez

Explored the Pacific Northwest and discovered Nootka Sound.

Bruno Heceta

Discovered the mouth of the Columbia River.

Miguel López de Legazpi

One of the great explorers of the South Pacific. Founded in the Philippines the first Spanish city which he named San Miguel de Cebú. One of his pilots discovered the sea route between the Philippines and Mexico. Legazpi also founded the city of Manila in 1571. By establishing a base in Philippines, he opened the sea trade between Manila and China and Japan.

Francisco Garcés

Explored the Mojave Dessert and is first European to explore Nevada.

Friar Silvestre de Escalante

With friar Francisco Anastasio Domínguez explored a vast area around the Rocky Mountains and discovered Lake Utah and other natural wonders.

Juan Bautista de Anza

Founded the city of San Francisco, California.

Bernardo de Gálvez

Key ally and supporter in the American Revolution.

José de Gálvez

Uncle of Bernardo de Gálvez. Fostered the founding of many missions in California and was a key figure in organizing Mexico and California.

Pedro Pablo Abarca de Bolea

Instrumental figure in Spain 's aid to the American Revolution. Was Charles III' Spanish Ambassador to France.

Gerónimo Grimaldi

Instrumental figure in Spain's aid to the American Revolution. Was Spanish Prime Minister during reign of Charles III.

José Moñino y Redondo, Count of Floridablanca

Instrumental figure in Spain 's aid to the American Revolution. Was Spanish Ambassador to the Vatican.

Diego María de Gardoqui

Instrumental figure in Spain's aid to the American Revolution. Was Spanish Ambassador to the U.S.

Juan Francisco de Bodega y Quadra

With Ignacio Arteaga explored northern Alaska. He had also discovered Bodega Bay (Nootka Sound) near San Francisco and reached Sitka.

Esteban José Martínez

Explored Nootka Sound.

Francisco Elisa

Explored the coasts of Alaska.

Alejandro Malaspina

Explored a vast region in Alaska.

Dionisio Galiano

With Cayetano Valdés explored the Straits of Juan de Fuca and Georgia.

Francisco Javier de Balmis

Introduced the smallpox vaccine in Texas. To this list we should have added all the leading discoverers/explorers of foreign nationality who were under the service of Spain, and that also includes Christopher Columbus. We did not do so because they have already been mentioned in the previous pages.

Here also belong other prominent figures, such as Doña Marina ("Malinche"), and Doña Luisa Xiconténcalt, both native Americans, who should be considered mothers ofthe Hispanic race as known today; Francisco Pizarro, for the knowledge gained by Western Civilization in the discovery and exploration of the entire South Pacific following the conquest of Peru; Estebanico, an Arab from Morocco of the expedition of Coronado who served as interpreter to friar Marcos Niza and who, in fact, was first to come upon the "Pueblo Indians" and to hear about the "Seven Cities of Cibola"; the Fidalgo de Elvas, for his narrative of de Soto's expedition which spawn many future explorations to North America; and Juan Ortiz (of the Narváez expedition) who was de Soto's interpreter. Also included on the list should be Cabeza de Vaca's companions: Alonso de Castillo Maldonado and Andrés Dorantes.

Part M

OTHER FAMOUS HISPANIC EXPLORERS OF NORTH AMERICA

As we have been saying, the list is long and will get even longer as scholars and historians dig deep into North America's history for the first three hundred years. We are including below more Spanish explorers who distinguished themselves in charting the vast continent lands. Their names should also be etched in our memories for having contributed in so many ways to what this nation is today. To the names we have added a brief description of their most relevant deeds. This is only a partial list.

Francisco Sánchez

In 1581-82 crossed the Rio Grande and traveled through the Jumani Indians.

Juan de Salas

In 1629-1632 led various missionaries to western Texas.

Diego Dionisio de Peñalosa

In 1662 commanded an expedition to the northeast looking for Quivira, and between 1661-64 was governor of New Mexico.

Juan Josef Pérez Hernández

In 1769 lead a group of colonists to the Alta California region and in 1774 explored the Northwest Coast.

Diego Ramón

In 1707 explored a vast region north of the Rio Grande.

Martín de Rivas

In 1686-1688 traveled along the coast of the Gulf of Mexico.

Agustín Rodríguez

In 1581-2 led an expedition to New Mexico.

Domingo Ramón

In 1716-9 led an expedition to reconquer Eastern Texas.

Juan María de Rivera

In 1761 traveled into today's Colorado and crossed the San Juan Mountains into present-day Durango, and in 1765 explored a vast area near the Gunnison River in Colorado.

Esteban José Martínez

In 1774 accompanied Pérez Hernández to Alaska and also in 1788 where he met a Russian settlement on the Aleutian Island.

Antonio de San Buenaventura y Olivares

In 1770 founded the San Francisco Solano Mission in Texas, and in 1718 the Mission of San Antonio de Valero in Texas.

Juan Domínguez de Mendoza

In 1683-4 founded a mission among the Jumano Indians in Texas.

Diego Pérez de Luxán

In 1582-3 wrote an account of the voyage of Antonio de Espejo.

Andrés de Pez y Malzáragga

In 1687-89 navigated for the first time the Rio Grande.

José de Azlor y Virto de Vera, Marqués de San Miguel de Aguayo

In 1721-22 took Texas back from the French and also founded several missions.

Alonso de León

In 1686 commanded an expedition to the Rio Grande and in 1690 founded a mission in Texas.

Marcos Farfán de los Godos

In 1598-99 founded several mines in New Mexico.

Isidro Pérez de Espinosa

In 1709 founded a mission in San Antonio, Texas.

Pedro de Aguirre

In 1708 traveled through Texas along the Colorado River.

Juan Enríquez Barroto

In 1686 was first to circumnavigate the Gulf of Mexico. Also explored the region in Pensacola Bay, Mobile Bay, and the Mississippi.

Hernando del Bosque

In 1674 commanded an expedition to Texas.

Hernando de Alvarado

In 1540 Coronado dispatched him to explore the northeast.

Dionisio Alcalá Galiano

In 1792 explored the Strait of Juan de Fuca and traveled around Vancouver Island

Francisco Tomás Hermenegildo Garcés

In 1771 crossed the California and Yuma desserts, and in 1776 voyaged up the Colorado River and crossed the Mojave desert.

Pedro de Iriarte

In 1686-87 explored the coasts of the Gulf of Mexico.

José Mares

In 1787 opened a trail from Santa Fe to San Antonio.

Alonso de Vaca

Led an expedition up the Arkansas River in 1634.

Part N

HISPANIC HERITAGE IN THE U.S. NATIONAL PARKS

In recognition of its great Hispanic Heritage, the United States named/ designated many of its national parks after a selected group of Spanish discoverers and explorers. Included below are some of the best-known.

Castillo de San Marcos National Monument
Oldest masonry construction in the United States, started in 1672 to protect the city of Saint Augustine from English and pirate attacks.

Coronado National Park
Commemorates the exploration of the Southwest by Francisco Vázquez de Coronado.

De Soto National Memorial
Commemorates Hernando de Soto's landing in Florida in 1513.

Fountain of Youth. A National Archaeological Park
Commemorates Juan Ponce de León 's discovery of Florida.

Cabrillo National Monument

Memorializes Juan Rodríuez Cabrillo's discovery of San Diego Bay.

Dry Tortugas National Park

The cluster of islands discovered by Juan Ponce de León in 1513.

El Morro National Monument

Features the "Inscription Rock" with many carved inscriptions by the Spanish explorers.

Salinas Pueblo Missions National Monument

Preservation of three Pueblo Indian villages and six mission churches founded in the 17 century.

Pecos National Historic Park

Preservation of the pueblo of Pecos, two Spanish missions, and the Santa Fe Trail sites.

San Antonio Missions National Historic Park

Memorializes four Spanish missions.

San Juan National Historic Site

It includes three Spanish fortresses and historic city walls.

The Presidio

Commemorates the military post established by the Spaniards in 1776.

Salt River Bay National Historical Park and Ecological Preserve

Area of North America believed to have been visited by members of Christopher Columbus 'voyage.

Fort Matanzas

Built to protect Saint Augustine from foreign attacks.

Juan Bautista de Anza National Historic Trail

Vast area traveled by Juan Bautista de Anza stretching from Sonora, Mexico, to San Francisco, California.

ENDNOTES

1.   Charles F. Lummis, *Los exploradores españoles del siglo XVI*, Ediciones Araluce, Barcelona, 1959, p.2

2.   Charles Gibson, *Spain in America*, Harper & Roe Publishers, New York, 1966, p.2

3.   Samuel Eliot Morison, *The Oxford History of the American People*, Oxford University Press, New York, 1965, p.38

4.   Bern Keating, *Famous American Explorers*, Rand McNally, Chicago, 1972, p.177

5.   Charles F. Lummis, op.cit., pp. 20-21

6.   Charles F. Lummis, op.cit., p.23

7.   Buchanan Parker Thompson, *Spain, Forgotten Ally of the American Revolution*, The Christopher Publishing House, North Quincy, MA 1976, p.44

8.   Lorenzo G. LaFarelle, *Bernardo de Gálvez—Hero of the American Revolution*, Eakin Press, Austin, Texas, 1992. p.68

9.   Buchanan Parker Thomson, op.cit., p.5

10.   Buchanan Parker Thomson, op.cit., p.135

11.   Buchanan Parker Thomson, op.cit., p.25

12.   Buchanan Parker Thomson, op.cit., pp. 248-249

13.   Buchanan Parker Thomson, op.cit., p.56

14.   Theodore Maynard, *De Soto and the Conquistadors*, Longmans, Greene & Co., London-New York, 1930, p.1

15.   Philip Ainsworth Means, *The Spanish Main: Focus of Envy, 1492-1700*, Charles Scribner's Sons, New York, 1935, pp. 22-23

16.   Philip Ainsworth Means, op.cit., pp. 47-48

17.   Robert Sténuit, *Treasures of the Armada*, E.P. Dutton & Co., Inc., New York, 1973, p.18

18.   Edward Gaylord Bourne, *Spain in America, 1450-1580*, Barnes & Noble, New York, 1962, p. xvii

19.   John Keats, *Eminent Domain: The Louisiana Purchase and the Making of America*, Charterhouse, New York, 1973, p.4

20.   James Cortada, *Spain and the American Civil War: Relations at Mid-Century, 1855-1868*, The American Philosophical Society, Philadelphia, 1980, p.7

21.   James Cortada, op.cit., pp.9-10

22. Joseph Burkholder Smith, *James Madison's Phony War—The Plot to Steal Florida*, Arbor House, New York, 1983, p.15
23. Joseph Burkholder Smith, op.cit., p.13
24. Milton Meltzer, *The Hispanic Americans*, Harper Collins, New York, 1982, p.75
25. Richard B. Morris, *Encyclopedia of American History*, Harper & Row Publishers, New York, 1953, p.257
26. Bruce Catton and William B. Catton, *The Bold and the Magnificent: America's Founding Years, 1492-1815*, Doubleday and Company, Garden City, N.Y., p.69
27. James Schouler, *The World's Events by Great Historians*, P.F. Collier & Son, New York, 1915, pp. 2027-2028
28. Salvador de Madariaga, *El auge y el ocaso del imperio español en América*, Editorial Sudamericana, Buenos Aires, 1959, p.299
29. Salvador de Madariaga, op.cit., p.300
30. Salvador de Madariaga, op.cit., p. 301
31. Salvador de Madariaga, op.cit., p.302
32. Edward Baylor Bourne, op.cit., p.174
33. Robert S. Weddle, *Spanish Sea: The Gulf of Mexico in North American Discovery*, Texas A & M University Press, College Station, 1985, p.xiii
34. Edward Gaylor Bourne, op.cit., p.59
35. Edward McNall Burns et al, *Western Civilization: Their History and Their Culture*, W.W. Norton & Co., New York, 1980, p.589
36. Philip Ainsworth Means, op.cit., pp.53-54
37. Charles F. Lummis, op.cit., p.20
38. Charles F. Lummis, op.cit., p.22
39. Richard B. Morris, op.cit., p.221
40. Barbara and Rudy Marinacci, *California's Spanish-Place Names*, Presidio Press, San Rafael, California, 1980, pp.13-14
41. Bruce M. Schackelford, <http://www.texancultures.utsa.edu/hiddenhistory/Pages1/shackelford.htm>
42. Agnes Repplier, *Junípero Serra—Pioneer Colonist of California*, Doubleday and Company, Garden City, N.Y., 1952, pp. 298-299
43. Agnes Repplier, op.cit., pp. v, vi
44. Richard K. Morris, *Concise Dictionary of American History*, Charles Scribner's Sons, New York, 1962, p.202
45. Paul E. Hoffman, *A New Andalucia and the Way to the Orient*, Louisiana State University Press, Baton Rouge, 1990, p.4
46. Edward Gaylord Bourne, op.cit., p.42
47. Herbert E. Bolton, *Coronado, Knight of Pueblos and Plains*, University of New Mexico Press, Albuquerque, 1949, p.2
48. Trevor Davies, *The Golden Century of Spain*, Greenwood Press, Westport, Connecticut, 1984, p.22
49. Archibald Wilberforce, *Spain and her Colonies*, Peter Fenelon Collier, New York, 1898, pp. 158-159

50. Trevor Davies, op.cit., pp.24-25
51. Trevor Davies, op.cit., pp.25-26
52. Trevor Davies, op.cit., pp.26-27
53. Edward Gaylor Bourne, op.cit., p.242
54. Eleanor D. Delaney et al, *Spanish Gold*, the Macmillan Company, New York, pp. v-vi
55. Robert S. Chamberlain, *An Encyclopedia of World History*, Houghton Mifflin Company, Boston, 1960, p.500
56. Trevor Davies, op.cit., p.212
57. Salvador de Madariaga, op.cit., p.180
58. Charles Norman, Discoverers of America, Thomas Y. Crowwll Company, New Yor, 1968, p.143
59. Mendel Peterson, The Funnel of Gold, Little, Brown & Company, Boston (n.d.), p.349
60. Philip Ainsworth Means, op.cit., pp. 209-210
61. Salvador de Madariaga, op.cit., p.174
62. Salvador de Madariaga, op.cit., p.179
63. Salvador de Madariaga, op.cit, p.180
64. José Vasconcelos, Breve Historia de México, Edición Contemporánea, Fernández Editores, S.A., México, 1967, I, pp.73-74
65. Bruce Catton and William B. Catton, op.cit., p.69
66. Sir Arthur Helps, *The Spanish Conquest of America*, John Lane, London-New York, 1900, I, p. xiv
67. Salvador de Madariaga, op.cit., pp. 39-40
68. Ramón Trías Fragas, *Diccionario de Historia de España*, Revista de Occidente, Madrid, 1968, I, p.798
69. Philip Ainsworth Means, op.cit., pp. 202-203
70. Robert S. Chamberlain, op.cit., p.89
71. Américo Castro, *Los españoles: cómo llegaron a serio*, Taurus, Madrid, 1965, p.17
72. Emilio Fernández Fuster, *Diccionario de Historia de España*, op.cit., Ill, p.131
73. A.L. Rowse, *The England of Elizabeth*, the MacMillan Company, New York, 1951, p.108
74. Richard B. Morris, op.cit., p.255
75. Mendel Peterson, op.cit., p.31
76. Mendel Peterson, op.cit., pp.46-47
77. Mendel Peterson, op.cit., p.51
78. Salvador de Madariaga, op.cit., p.479
79. Dave Horner, *The Treasure Galleons*, Dodd, Mead & Company, New York, 1971, p.217
80. Pedro Aguado Bleye, *Diccionario de Historia de España*, op.cit., II, p.450
81. Salvador de Madariaga, op.cit., pp. 190-191
82. Robert S. Chamberlain, op.cit., p.347

83. Philip Ainsworth Means, op.cit., p.18
84. Daniel P. Mannix and Malcom Cowley, *Black Cargoes: A History of the Atlantic Slave Trade, 1523-1863*, The Viking Press, New York, 1962, p.59
85. Trevor Davies, op.cit., p.1 18
86. Charles F. Lummis, op.cit., pp.249-250
87. Salvador de Madariaga, op.cit., p.54
88. Sir Arthur Helps, op.cit., p.127
89. Sir Arthur Helps, op.cit., pp.151-152
90. Charles F. Lummis, op.cit., p.49
91. Charles F. Lummis, op.cit., p.63
92. Robert S. Weddle, op.cit., p.6
93. Robert S. Weddle, op.cit., p.7
94. Robert S. Chamberlain, op.cit., p.486
95. Sir Arthur Helps, op.cit., p.49
96. John McManners, Editor, *The Oxford Illustrated History of Christianity*, Oxford University Press, New York, 1990, p.304
97. Edward Gaylord Bourne, op.cit., pp. 200-201
98. Edward Gaylord Bourne, op.cit., p.209
99. Salvador de Madariaga, op.cit., pp.346-347
100. Charles F. Lummis, op.cit., p.56
101. Salvador de Madariaga, op.cit., p.459
102. Edward Gaylord Bourne, op.cit., pp. 154-155
103. John Fiske, *The Discovery of America*, Houghton Mifflin and Company, Boston, 1892, II, pp.291-292
104. Philip Ainsworth Means, op.cit., pp.242-243
105. David J. Weber, *The Spanish Frontier in North America*, Yale University Press, New Haven and London, 1992, p.12
106. Salvador de Madariaga, op.cit., pp.322-323
107. Salvador de Madariaga, op.cit., p.279
108. Salvador de Madariaga, op.cit., p.476
109. Salvador de Madariaga, op.cit., pp.476-477
110. Salvador de Madariaga, op.cit., p.47
111. Salvador de Madariaga, op.cit., p.168
112. Salvador de Madariaga, op.cit., p. 473
113. Salvador de Madariaga, op.cit., p.148
114. Salvador de Madariaga, op.cit., p.342
115. Salvador de Madariaga, op.cit., p.242
116. Philip Ainsworth Means, op.cit., p.242
117. Salvador de Madariaga, op.cit., p.487
118. Trevor Davies, op.cit, pp.13-14
119. Salvador de Madariaga, op.cit., p.64
120. John McManners, op.cit., p.318
121. Charles F. Lummis, op.cit., p.149
122. Trevor Davies, op.cit., pp.288-29

123. Francis Bret Harte, *Tales of the Argonauts*, James Osgood & Co., Boston, 1875, p.49

124. John Gilmary Shea, *History of the Catholic Missions among the Indians Tribes of the United States, 1529-1854*, Excelsior Publishing House, 1854, Preface.

125. Washington Irving, *The Life and Voyages of Christopher Columbus*, Hurst and Company, Publishers, New York (n.d.), pp.15-16

126. Edward Gaylord Bourne, op.cit., pp.141-142

127. Salvador de Madariaga, op.cit., p.111

SELECTED BIBLIOGRAPHY

Acosta, José de. Obras *(Historia natural y moral de las indias, etc.* Biblioteca deAutores Españoles, Madrid, (1591), 1954.

Aguado Bleye, Pedro, and Alcázar Molina, Cayetano. *Manual de Historia de España.* 10a. edición, Espasa Calpe, S.A., Madrid: 1974, 3 vols.

Ainsworth, Ed. *Enchanted Pueblo: Story of the Rise of the Modern Metropolis Around the Plaza de Los Angeles.* Bank of America, 1959.

Alcázar Molina, Cayetano. *Conquistadores y virreyes españoles en América.* Madrid, CIAP, 1950.

Altamira y Crevea, Rafael. *La huella de España en América.* Editorial Reus, Madrid, 1924.

Anderson, L.G. Charles. *Life and Letter of Vasco Núñez de Balboa.* New York, Fleming H. Revell Company, 1941.

Andrews, E. Benjamin. *History of the United States.* New York: Charles Scribner's Sons, 1928, 6 vols.

Arranz, Luis. *Don Diego Colón.* Consejo Superior de Investigaciones Científicas. "Instituto Gonzalo Fernández de Oviedo", Madrid: 1982, 2 vols.

Arranz Marquez, Luis. *Don Diego Colón, Almirante, Virrey y Gobernador de las Indias.* tomo 1. Madrid: Consejo Superior de Investigaciones Científicas-Instituto Gonzalo Fernández de Oviedo, 1982.

Ateneo de Madrid. *España en California y el noreste de América. Conferencia de D. Rafael Torres Campos leída el día 17 de mayo de 1892.* Madrid: EstablecimientoTipográfico, 1892.

Ballesteros, Manuel, and Alborg, Juan Luis. *Historia Universal.* Editorial Gredos, S.A., Madrid, 1967, 2 vols.

Bancroft, George. *History of the United States of America from the Discovery to the Continent.* New York, Appleton & co., 1885, 6 vols.

Bancroft, Hubert Howe. *History of Mexico.* San Francisco, A.L. Bancroft & Co., 1883.

—*Works of Hubert Howe Bancroft,* San Francisco, Bancroft & Co., 1883, 5 vols.

Bannon, John Francis. *The Spanish Borderlands Frontier, 1513-1821*. Holt, Rinehart &Winston, New York, 1970.

Bayle, Constantino. *España en Indias. Nuevos ataques y nuevas defensas*. Biblioteca Hispana Missionum, vol. viii, Vitoria, Editorial Illuminare, 1934.

Beauchesne Thornton, Francis. *Catholic Shrines in the United States and Canada*. New York, Wilfred Funk, Inc., 1954.

Bemis, Samuel Flagg. *The Diplomacy of the American Revolution*. Bloomington, Indiana University Press, 1967.

Bernhard, Brendan. *Pizarro, Orellana, and the Exploration of the Amazon*. Chelsea House Publishers, New York, 1991.

Blackmar, Frank W. *Spanish Institutions of the Southwest*. Baltimore, the John Hopkins Press, 1891.

Bolton, Eugene Herbert, Editor. *Spanish Exploration in the Southwest*. New York, Barnes & Noble, Inc., 1952.

Brinckerhoff, Sidney, and Pierce Chamberlain. *Spanish Military Weapons in Colonial America. 1700-1821*, Stackpole, 1972.

Brodie, Fawn M. *Thomas Jefferson-An Intimate History*. New York, W.W. Norton and Company, Inc., 1974.

Brownrigg, Edwin B. *Colonial Latin American Manuscripts & Transcripts in the Obadiah Rich Collection: An Inventory & Index*. New York, New York Public Library, 1978.

Bruno de Hezeta. *For Honor and Country: The Diary of Bruno de Hezeta*. translated and introduced by Herbert K. Beals, Oregon Historical Society, 1985.

Buehr, Walter. *The Spanish Conquistadors in North America*. New York, G.P. Punam's Sons, 1962.

Cameron, Ian. *Explorers and Explorations*. Magna Books, New York, 1991.

Cameron, Roderick. *Viceroyalties of the West—The Spanish Empire in Latin America*. Little, Brown and Company, Boston, 1968.

Carderera y Solano, Valentín. *Iconografía española. Colección de retratos, estatuas, mausoleos y demás monumentos inéditos de reyes, reinas, grandes capitanes, escritores, etc., desde el siglo XI hasta el XVII, con texto biográfico y descriptivo*. Madrid, Ramón Campuzano, 1855-1864, 2 vols.

Castellanos, Juan de. *Elegías de varones ilustres de Indias*. Biblioteca de Autores Españoles, Atlas, Madrid, 1944.

Castro, Américo. *La realidad histórica de España*. Biblioteca Porrúa, México, 1975.

—*Los españoles, cómo llegaron a serlo*. Taurus, Madrid, 1965.

Castro Seoane, José O. de M. *Aviamiento y catálogo de las misiones que en el siglo XVI pasaron de España a América*. Ediciones Jura, Madrid, 1957.

Catálogo de la colección de manuscritos relativos a la historia de América, formado por Joaquín García Icazbalceta, anotado y adicionado por Federico Gómez de Orozco. Monografías Bibliográficas Mexicanas, 9, México, Secretaría de Relaciones Exteriores, 1927.

Catálogo de la sección colonial del Archivo Histórico. 1944, Lima, Perú, Ministerio de Hacienda y Comercio, Imprenta Torres Aguirre.

Catton, Bruce and William B. Catton. *The Bold and Magnificent Dream- America's Founding Years, 1492-1815.* New York, Doubleday & Co., 1978.

Caughey, John Walton. *Bernardo de Gálvez in Louisiana 1776-1783.* Gretna, Pelican Publishing Company, 1991.

Cervantes de Salazar, Francisco. *Crónica de la Nueva España.* edición de M. Magallón; estudio preliminar e índices por A. Millares Carlo, Biblioteca de Autores Españoles, Atlas, Madrid, 1954.

Chadwick, French Ensor. *The Relations of the United States and Spain. The Spanish-American War.* New York, Charles Scribner's Sons, 1911.

Chapman, Charles E. *Catalogue of Materials in the Archivo General de Indias (Seville) for the History of the Pacific Coast and the American Southwest.* University of California Press, Berkeley, 1919.

Clissold, Stephen. *The Saints of South America.* London, Charles Knight, 1972.

Collingridge de Tourcey, George. *First Discovery of Australia and New Guinea: Being the Narrative of Portuguese and Spanish Discoveries in the Australasian Regions between 1492-1616, with Descriptions of the Old Charts.* Sidney, William Brooks & Co., 1906.

Columbus, Diego. *The First Extant Letter from America of Diego Columbus.* London, Maggs Bros., 1929.

Cook, Warren L. *Flood Tide of Empire: Spain and the Pacific Northwest, 1543-1819.* New Haven, Yale University Press, 1973.

Conde de la Viñaza. *Bibliografía española de lenguas indígenas de América.* Madrid, Tipografía Sucesores de Rivadeneyra, 1892.

Cortés, Hernán. *Cartas de relación de la Conquista de México.* Espasa Calpe, S.A., Madrid, 1945.

Cummins, Light Townsend. *Spanish Observers and the American Revolution, 1775-1783.* Baton Rouge, Louisiana University Press, 1991.

Cumming, W.P., Skelton, R.A., Quinn, D.B. *The Discovery of North America.* American Heritage Press, New York, 1971.

Davies, R. Trevor. *Spain in Decline, 1621-1700.* London, MacMillan, 1957.

de Gómara, Francisco López. *Cortés-The Life of the Conqueror by his Secretary.* translated and edited by Lesley Byrd Simpson, Berkeley, University of California Press, 1964.

415

Delaney, Eleanor C. *Spanish Gold.* MacMillan, New York, 1946.

de León, Cieza. *La crónica del Perú.* Espasa Calpe, S.A., Madrid, 1962.

de Ovidio y Baños, José. *Historia de la conquista y población de la provincia de Venezuela, ilustrada con notas y documentos por el capitán de navío Cesáreo Fernández Duro.* Madrid, 1885, several vols.

de Sahagún, Fray Bernardino. *Historia general de las cosas de la Nueva España.* edición, anotaciones y apéndices de Ángel María Garibay, Editorial Porrúa, México, 1979.

—*History of Ancient Mexico.* Fisk University Press, 1932.

de Salcedo, Colonel Don Antonio. *The Geographical and Historical Dictionary of the Americas and the West.* by G.A. Thompson, Lenox Hill Pub., and Dist. Co., New York, 1970, 6 vols.

deValle-Arizpe, Antonio. *Virreyes y virreinas de la Nueva España: Tradiciones, leyendas y sucedidos del México Virreinal.* México, Editorial Jus, 1947. 2 vols.

de Zárate, Agustín. *The Discovery and Conquest of Perú.* translated by J.M. Cohen, the Folio Society, London 1968.

Díaz del Castillo, Bernal. *The Discovery and Conquest of Mexico.* translated by A.P. Maudslay, Farrar, Straus and Cudahy, New York, 1956.

—*Verdadera historia de la conquista de la Nueva España.* Fernández Editores, S.A., México, 1905.

Documentos relativos a la independencia de Norteamérica existentes en archivos españoles, Ministerio de Asuntos Exteriores, Dirección General de Relaciones Culturales, Vol. 1 Archivo General de Indias, Sección de Gobierno (Años 1752-1822), por Purificación Medina Encina bajo la dirección de Rosario Parra Cala, Vol.2. Archivo General de Simancas, Secretaría de Estado: Inglaterra (Años 1750-1820) por María Francesca Represa Fernández, Carlos Álvarez García y Miguel Represa Fernández, bajo la dirección de Amando Represa Rodríguez. Madrid, 1976.

Drinker Bowen, Catherine. *John Adams and the American Revolution.* Little Brown and Company, Boston, 1950.

Instituto nacional de antropología e historia (Mexique). *El otro yo del rey: Virreyes de la Nueva España, 1535-1821.* México, Museo Nacional de Historia, Miguel Ángel Porrúa, 1996.

Elliot, J.H. *Imperial Spain 1469-1716.* Mentor Books, 1966.

Englebert, Omer. *The Last of the Conquistadors: Junípero Serra 1713-1784.* New York, Harcourt Brace and Company, 1956.

Exquemelin, A.O. *The Buccaneers of America.* translated by Alexis Brown, London, The Folio Society, 1972.

Feldman, Lawrence. *Anglo-Americans in Spanish Archives.* Genealogical Publishing Co., Inc., Baltimore, 1991.

Fernández de Oviedo, Gonzalo. *Sumario de la natural y general historia de las Indias.* Espasa Calpe, S.A., Madrid, 1978.

Ferris, Robert G. *Explorers and Settlers-Historic Places Commemorating the Early Explorations and Settlement of the United States.* United States Department of the Interior, National Park Service, Washington, D.C. 1968.

Fieldhouse, D.K. *The Colonial Empires.* London, Weidenfeld & Nicolson, 1971.

Fifer, Valerie J. *United States Perception of Latin America, 1850-1930, A New West South of Capricorn?* New York: Manchester University Press, 1991.

Floridablanca. *Obras originales del conde de Floridablanca.* Biblioteca de Autores Españoles, Madrid, 1952.

Foss, Michael. *Undreamed Shores: England's Wasted Empire in America.* Harrop, London, 1974.

García Mercadal, José. *Lo que España llevó a América.* Taurus, Madrid, 1959.

García Villada, Zacarías. *El destino de España en la Historia Universal.* Cultura Española, Madrid, 1936.

Garcilaso de la Vega. *Obras completas del Inca Garcilaso de la Vega.* Carmelo Saínz de Santa María, Biblioteca de Autores Españoles, Madrid, 1965, 4 vols.

Gibbon, Edward. *The Decline and Fall of the Roman Empire.* London, Folio Society, 1983-1990. 8 vols.

Gibson, Count D. *Sea Islands of Georgia.* University of Georgia Press, Athens, 1948.

Graham, Gerald S. *Empire of the North Atlantic.* University of Toronto Press, Toronto, 1958.

Granados y Gálvez, José Joaquín. *Tardes americanas, gobierno gentil y católico: Breve y particular noticia de toda la historia indiana.* México, Centro de Estudios de Historia de México, 1984.

Greene, Evarts Boutell. *The Foundations of American Nationality.* American Book Company, New York, 1922.

Hallenbeck, Cleve. *Cabeza de Vaca: The Journey and Route of the First European to Cross the Continent of North America.* Glendale, CA, Arthur H. Clark Company, 1940.

Hamilton, Earl J. *American Treasure and the Price Revolution in Spain, 1501-1650.* New York, Octagon Press, 1970.

Hampden, John, Editor. *Francis Drake: Privateer: Contemporary Narratives and Documents.* University of Alabama Press, 1972.

Hanke, Lewis. *The Spanish Struggle for Justice in the Conquest of America.* University of Pennsylvania Press, Philadelphia, 1959.

Haring, C.H. *The Spanish Empire in America.* Harcourt Brace & World, New York, 1963.

Henige, David P. *Colonial Governors from the Fifteenth Century to the Present.* Madison, University of Wisconsin Press, 1970.

Herring, Hubert. *A History of Latin America.* New York, Alfred A. Knopf, 1961.

Herrera Tordesil las, Antonio de. *Historia de los hechos de los castellanos en las islas y tierra firme del mar Océano.* prólogo de J. Natalicio González, Asunción, Editorial Guaraní, 1944, 11 vols.

Herrmann, Paul. *La aventura de los primeros descubrimientos-De la prehistoria al final de la Edad Media.* translated by Francisco Payarols, Editorial Labor, S.A., Barcelona, n.d.

Cortés, Hernán. *Historia de la Nueva España, escrita por el esclarecido conquistador Hernán Cortés, aumentada con otros documentos y notas por Francisco Antonio Lorenzana, Arzobispo de México.* Secretaría de Hacienda y Crédito Público, México, 1981. Facsimile edition published in 4 vols.

Hodge, Frederick W., and Lewis, H. Theodore, editors. *Spanish Explorers in the Southeastern United States, 1528-1543.* Texas State Historical Association, 1984.

Horgan, Paul. *Conquistadors in North American History.* Farrar Straus Giroux, New York, 1963.

Horner, Dave. *The Treasure Galleons: Clues to Millions in Sunken Gold and Silver.* New York, Dodd Mead & Co., 1971.

Hume, David. *History of England.* B.D. Packard, Albany, New York, 1816, 4 vols.

Jameson, Franklin J. *Dictionary of United States History.* Puritan, Boston, 1894.

—*The History of Historical Writing in America.* Antiquarian Press, New York, 1961.

Beals, Herbert K. *Juan Pérez on the Northwest Coast: Six Documents of his Expedition in 1774.* translation and annotation by Herbert K. Beals, Oregon Historical Society Press, 1989.

Lane, Kris E. *Pillaging the Empire: Piracy in the Americas 1500-1750.* M.E. Sharpe Armonk, London, 1998.

Leonard, Irving A. *Romances of Chivalry in the Spanish Indies. With some registros of Book Shipments to the Spanish Colonies.* Berkeley, University of California Press, 1933.

Lewis, B.B. Wyndham. *Emperor of the West: A Study of the Emperor Charles The Fifth.* Eyre and Spottiswoode, London, 1932.

Lewis, James A., and Still, William N., Jr. *The Final Campaign of the American Revolution: Rise and Fall of the Spanish Bahamas (Studies in Maritime History)*. Columbia, University of South Carolina Press, 1991.

Lohmann Villena, Guillermo. *El conde de Lemus, virrey del Perú*. Consejo Superior de Investigaciones Científicas, Madrid, 1946.

Lorenzo Hervás y Panduro. *Catálogo de las lenguas*. Madrid, 1805, 6 vols.

MacIntyre, Donald. *The Privateers*. London, Paul Elek, 1975.

Madariaga, Salvador de. *El auge y el ocaso del imperio español en América*. Editorial Sudamericana, Buenos Aires, 1959.

Majó Framis, R. *Vidas de los navegantes y conquistadores españoles del siglo XVI*. Aguilar S.A. de Ediciones, Madrid, 1950, 2 vols.

Malthy, Williams S. *Black Legend in England: The Development of Anti-Spanish Sentiment, 1558-1660*. Durham, Duke University Press, 1971.

Mannix, Danniel P., and Cowley, Malcolm. *Black Cargoes: A History of the Atlantic Slave Trade-1523-1863*. New York. The Viking Press. 1962.

Mariana. Padre. *Historia general de España*. Gaspar y Roig, Madrid, 1849, 5 vols.

Martin, Gilbert. *Atlas de la historia judía*. Lasser Press Mexicana, S.A., Mexico, 1979.

Martínez, José Luis. *Pasajeros de Indias. Viajes Transatlánticos en el siglo XVI*. Alianza Editorial, Madrid, 1983.

Mártir de Anglería, Pedro. *Décadas del Nuevo Mundo: vertidas del latín a la lengua castellana*. Buenos Aires, Editorial Bajel, 1944.

Marx, Jenifer. *Pirates and Privateers of the Caribbean*. Malabar, Florida, Krieger Publishing Company, 1992.

Mathes, Michael. *Vizcaíno and the Spanish Expansion in the Pacific Ocean 1580-1630*. San Francisco, California Historical Society, 1968.

McDermott, John Francis. *The Spanish in the Mississippi Valley, 1762-1804*. University of Illinois Press, 1974.

Means, Philip Answorth. *The Spanish Main: Focus of Envy, 1492-1700*. Charles Scribner's Sons, New York, 1935, pp.22-23.

Medina, José Toribio. *Cartas de Pedro de Valdivia que tratan del descubrimiento y conquista, edición facsimilar dispuesta y anotada por Sevilla*. Tipografía de M. Carmona, 1929

Medina, Pedro de. *A Navigator's Universe: The Cosmographia of 1538*. translated by Ursula Lamb, Chicago University Press, 1972.

Menéndez y Pelayo, Don Marcelino. *Historia de los heterodoxos españoles*. Librería General de Victoriano Suárez, Madrid, 1911-1917.

—*Historia de España*. Cultura Española, Madrid, 1938.

Menéndez Pidal, Ramón. *El padre Las Casas-su doble personalidad.* Espasa Calpe, S.A., Madrid, 1963.

—*España y su historia,* Ediciones Minotauro, Madrid, 1957, 3 vols.

Ministerio de Trabajo y Previsión. *Aportación de los colonizadores españoles a la prosperidad de América.* Imprenta Artística Sáez Hnos., Madrid, 1929.

Morales Padrón, Francisco. *Manual de Historia Universal-Vols.* VI & VII, *Historia de América,* Espasa Calpe, S.A., Madrid, 1975.

Morison, Samuel Eliot. *Christopher Columbus: The Voyage of Discovery, 1492.* London, Bison, 1992.

Morgan, Wayne H. *America's Road to Empire: The War with Spain and Overseas Expansion.* New York, Alfred Knopf, 1965.

Motolinia, Benavente O, Toribio. *Historia de los indios de la Nueva España.* Herederos de Juan Gill Editores, Barcelona, 1914.

Munilla, Octavio Gil. *Spain 's Share in the History of the United States of America.* Publicaciones Españolas, Madrid, 1963.

Natella, Arthur A., Jr. *Spanish in America, 1513-1974 A Chronology & Fact Book.* Oceana Publications, Dobbs Ferry, New York, 1975.

Newman, John J., and Schmalbach, John M. *United States History.* Amsco School Publications, Inc., New York, 1998.

Noguez, Xavier. *Bibliografia sobre historia de América. Obras existentes en la Biblioteca Nacional.* UNAM, Instituto de Investigaciones Científicas, México, 1974.

Norman, James. *The Navy that Crossed Mountains.* G.P. Putnam's Sons, New York, 1963.

Núñez, Cabeza de Vaca, Alvar. *Naufragios y comentarios.* edición y presentación de Dionisio Ridruejo, Taurus, Madrid, 1969.

Obras de D. Martín Fernández de Navarrete. edición y estudio preliminar de D. Carlos Seco Serrano, Biblioteca de Autores Españoles, Ediciones Atlas, Madrid, 1954, 3 vols.

Ortega, E.H. *Manual de historia general del Perú.* Historia Revisionista Los Andes, Lima, 1974.

Palma, Ricardo. *Tradiciones peruanas.* Madrid, Aguilar, 1957.

Parry, John Horace. *The Spanish Seaborne Empire.* Alfred Knopf, New York, 1966.

Parry, J.H. *The Spanish Theory of Empire in the Sixteenth Century.* reprint of Cambridge edition (1940), Folcroft Library Editions, 1973.

Parry, J.H. *Trade and Dominion: The European Overseas Empire in the Eighteenth Century.* Praeger History of Civilization, Prager Publishers, New York, Washington, 1971.

Pereyra, Carlos. *La conquista de las rutas oceánicas.* Madrid, Imprenta de Juan Pueyo, 1923.

—*Historia de la América Española.* Editorial Saturnino Calleja, Madrid, 1920.

—*Las huellas de los conquistadores.* Publicaciones del Consejo de la Hispanidad, Madrid, 1943.

Peterson, Merrill D. *Thomas Jefferson & The New Nation-A Bibiography.* New York, Oxford University Press, 1970.

Petrie, Sir Charles. *Philip II.* Editora Nacional, Madrid, 1964.

Picatoste y Rodríguez, Felipe. *Apuntes para una biblioteca científica española del siglo XVI.* Madrid, Ollero y Ramos Editores, 1999.

Pizarro, Pedro. *Relation of the Discovery and Conquest of the Kingdoms of Perú.* New York, Cortés Society, 1921, 2 vols.

Pope, John A., Jr., ed. *America's Historic Places-An Illustrated Guide to our Country's Past.* New York: The Reader's Digest Association, 1968.

Prescott, William H. *History of the Reign of Ferdinand and Isabella The Catholic.* Philadelphia, J.B. Lippincott & Co., 1882, 3 vols.

—*History of the Reign of Philip the II, King of Spain.* Philadelphia, J.B. Lippincott & Co.,1867, 3 vols.

—*History of the Conquest of Mexico.* Philadelphia, J.B. Lippincott & Company, 1843.

—*History of the Conquest of Peru with a Preliminary View of the Civilization of the Incas.* London, Swan Sonnenschein, 1890.

Pulgar, Hernando del. *Claros Varones de España.* Salvat, Madrid, 1971.

Real Academia de la Historia, Catálogo de la colección de don Juan Bautista Muñoz. Madrid, Editorial Maestre, 1954-1956, 3 vols.

Rey Pastor, Julio. *La ciencia y la técnica en el descubrimiento de América.* Espasa-Calpe, S.A., Colección Austral, Madrid, 1970.

Richardson, Rupert N., and Carl Coke Rister. *The Greater Southwest: The Economic, Social and Cultural Development of Kansas, Oklahoma, Texas, Utah, Colorado, Nevada, New Mexico, Arizona, and California from the Spanish Conquest to the Twentieth Century.* Glendale, Calif., Arthur H. Clark Co., 1934.

Richman, Irving Berdine. *The Spanish Conquerors -A Chronicle of the Dawn of Empire Overseas.* New Haven, Yale University Press, 1921.

Robertson, James Alexander. *List of Documents in the Spanish Archives Relating to the History of the United States.* Carnegie Institution, 1910.

Robertson, William. *The History of the Reign of the Emperor Charles The Fifth-With an Account of the Emperor's Life After his Abdication.* Philadelphia, J.B. Lippincott & Co., 1878, 3 vols.

—*The History of America*. Philadelphia, Johnson & Warner, 1812, 2 vols.

Rodríguez Casado, Vicente. *Primeros años de dominicaión española en Luisiana.* Consejo Superior de Investigaciones Científicas, Atlas, Madrid, 1942.

Rosenblat, Ángel. *La población indígena de América.* Buenos Aires, 1954.

Ruiz, F. González. *De la Florida a San Francisco-Los exploradores españoles en los Estados Unidos.* Buenos Aires, Ibero-Americana, 1949.

Sánchez Albornoz, Claudio. *Lecturas históricas españolas.* Taurus, Madrid, 1960.

Sánchez Albornoz, Nicolás, and Romero, José Luis. *La población en América Latina. Desde los tiempos precolombianos hasta el año 2000.* Madrid, 1973.

Sánchez, Alonso B. *Fuentes de la historia española e hispanoamericana.* Consejo Superior de Investigaciones Científicas, Atlas, Madrid, 1952, 3 vols.

Sauer, Carl Ortwin. *The Early Spanish Main.* Berkeley, University of California Press, 1966.

Selley, T. *England in the Eighteenth Century.* A & C Black, London, 1945.

Serra, Junípero. *Writings of Junípero Serra.* Edited by Antonine Tibesar, Washington, D.C., Academy of Franciscan History, 1955-1966, 4 vols.

Shafer, Robert Jones. *The Economic Societies in the Spanish World.* Syracuse University Press, 1958.

Sherry, Frank. *Raiders and Rebels: The Golden Age of Piracy.* Hearst Marine Books, New York, 1986.

Siles, Gustavo. *Incas, virreyes y presidentes del Perú. Sus biografias y retratos.* Lima, Ediciones Peisa, 1969.

Smith, Lloyd Edwin. *New International Atlas of the World.* The Geographical Publishing Company, Chicago, 1939.

Solorzano y Pereyra, Juan de. *Política Indiana.* Edición de Francisco Ramiro de Valenzuela, Madrid, Ibero-Americana de Publicaciones, 1930, 5 vols.

Sombart, Werner. *Socialism and the Social Movement.* J.M. Dent & Co., London, 1909.

—*Lujo y capitalismo.* Revista de Occidente, Madrid, 1928.

Stewart, George R. *Names of the Land -A Historic Account of Place- Naming in the United States.* Random House, New York, 1945.

Suárez, Jorge A. *Lenguas indígenas de Mesoamérica.* México, Instituto National Indiginista, 1995.

Syers, William Edward. *Texas: The Beginning 1519-1834.* Texian Press, Waco, 1978.

Tarrago, Rafael E. *Early U.S. Hispanic Relations, 1776-1860 An Annotated Bibliography.* Lanham, MD, Scarecrow Press, Inc., 1994.

Tenenbaum, Barbara A., and Dorn, Georgette M. *Encyclopedia of Latin America, History and Culture.* New York, Charles Scribner's Sons, 1995.

The American Heritage Book of Great Historic Places. by the editors of American Heritage, The Magazine of History, American Heritage Publishing Co., Inc., New York, 1957.

The Bicentennial Almanac. Edited by Calvin D. Linton, Thomas Nelson In., Publishers, New York, 1975.

The New Columbia Encyclopedia. Edited by William H. Harris and Judith S. Levey, Columbus University Press, New York, 1975.

The Oxford Illustrated History of Christianity. Edited by John McManners, Oxford University Press, New York, 1990.

The Readers Companion to American History. Edited by Eric Foner & John A. Garraty, Houghton Mifflin Company, Boston, 1991.

The Travels of Marco Polo, The Venetian. translated and edited by William Marsden, Doubleday and Company, Inc., New York, 1948.

The World Almanac of the American West. John S. Bowman, General Editor, Pharos Books, New York, 1986.

Thonhoff, Robert H. *The Texas Connection with the American Revolution.* Burnet, Texas, Eakin Press, 1981.

Torquemada, Juan de. *Monarquía Indiana.* Editorial Porrúa, México, 1986, 3 vols.

Tovar, Antonio. *Lo medieval en la conquista y otros ensayos.* Seminario y Ediciones, Madrid, 1970.

Turner, Ralph. *Las grandes culturas de la humanidad.* traducción de Francisco A. Delpiane y Ramón Iglesia, Fondo de Cultura Económica, México, 1948.

Unwin, Rayner. *The Defeat of John Hawkins: A Biography of his Third Slaving Voyage.* London, Allen & Unwin, 1960.

Vanegas, Miguel. *Juan María de Salvatierra of the Company of Jesus, Missionary of the Province of New Spain and Apostolic Conqueror of the Californias.* Cleveland, Arthur H. Clark Company, 1929.

Vargas Ugarte, Rubén. *Historia del Perú.* Barcelona, Relación Logo Press, 1966, 10 vols.

Vázquez de Espinosa, Antonio. *Compendio y descripción de las Indias Occidentales.* Smithsonian Institution, Washington, 1948.

Vedia, Enrique de. *Historiadores primitivos de Indias.* Biblioteca de Autores Españoles, Madrid, 1877, 2 vols.

Vega, Carlos B. *Conquistadoras: Mujeres heroicas de la conquista de América,* Janaway Publishing, Inc., Santa Maria, CA., 2012.

Vicens Vives, J. *Historia de España y América.* Editorial Vicens-Vives, Barcelona, 1961, several vols.

Vossler, Carlos. *España y Europa.* Ed. Instituto de Estudios Políticos, Madrid, 1951.

Walker, Geoffrey J. *Spanish Politics and Imperial Trade, 1700-1789.* Bloomington, Indiana, University Press, 1979.

Weber, David J. *The Spanish Frontier in North America.* New Haven, Yale University Press, 1992.

Weber, Max. *General Economic History.* Greenberg Publishing, New York, 1927.

—*The Protestant Ethic and the Spirit of Capitalism.* Charles Scribner's Sons, New York, 1958.

Webster, Hutton, and Wolf John B. *History of Civilization.* D.C. Heath and Company, Boston, 1947.

Wilcox, Desmond. *Ten Who Dared.* Little, Brown and Company, Boston, 1977.

Williams, Glyndwr. *The Expansion of Europe in the Eighteenth Century: Overseas Rivalry, Discovery, and Exploitation.* New York, Walker and Company, 1966.

Williams, Neville. *The Sea Dogs. Privateers, plunder and piracy in the Elizabethan Age.* Weindenfeld, London, 1975.

Winterich, John T. *Early American Books and Printing.* Dover Publications, Inc., New York, 1981.

Woodbury, Lowery. *Descriptive List of Maps of the Spanish Possessions Within the Present Limits of the United States-1502-1820.* The Lowery Collection, edited with notes by Philip Lee Phillips, Washington, Government Printing Office, 1912.

Woodroffe, Thomas. *The Enterprise of England.. An Account of her Emergence as an Oceanic Power.* London, Farber & Farber, 1958.

Zurita, Alonso de. *Life and Labor in Ancient Mexico-The Brief and Summary Relation of Lords of New Spain.* Rutgers University Press, 1963.

INDEX

A

Abarca de Bolea, Pedro, Count of
    Aranda, 16, 18, 20, 22, 330, 396
Acosta, Padre José de, 195, 297, 300,
    313
Adams, John Quincy, 38, 40, 224,
    337, 339, 370
Aguado Bleye, Pedro, 114, 323
Aguayo, Marquis de San Miguel,
    209, 271, 322, 394
Aguirre, Pedro de, 401
Ainsworth Means, Philip, 29, 30, 61,
    93, 108, 116, 130, 137, 142, 326
Alamo, The, 229, 366
Alarcón, Hernando de, 183, 187, 199
Alarcón, Martín de, 208, 209, 394,
Alarcón, Martín de, 295, 322
Alarcón, Ruiz de, 79
Alba, Bartolomé de, 80
Albigenses, 139, 358
Albo, Francisco, 176
Alcedo, Antonio de, 218, 298
Alemán, Mateo, 321
Alencastre Norena y Silva, Fernando,
    102, 268
Almagro, Diego de, the Young, 154
Almonester y Roxas, Andrés, 316
Alvarado, Hernando de, 184, 187,
    402
Alvarado, Pedro de, 78, 124, 155, 189
Alvares Cabral, Pedro, 168
Álvarez de Pineda, Alonso, 62, 176,
    185, 258, 390

Álvarez, Bernardino, 293
Alzor y Virto de Vera, José, Marqués,
    de San Miguel y Aguayo, 401
Amat y Junyent, Manuel de, 274
America's Expansionist Movement,
    32
American Bible Society, 300
American Empire, 36
American Revolution, 25, 45, 181,
    208, 217, 243, 244, 267, 329, 330,
    332, 350
Anacaona, 154, 156
Anchieta, José de, 150, 306
Andrade, Antonio de, 145, 153
Anson, Admiral John, 333
Anza, Juan Bautista de, 66, 216, 274,
    391, 395
Apartheid, 100
Apostle of California, 148
Aquino, Santo Tomás de, 314
Arawaks, 353
Arellano, Alonso de, 192
Arenas, Pedro de, 201, 297
Arqueaga, Friar Antonio de, 144,
    202, 261
Arteaga, Ignacio, 217, 279
Ascensión, Father Antonio de la, 297
Assisi, Saint Francis of, 263
Atahualpa, 27, 54, 117, 119, 120,
    154, 180, 307, 356
Augustus, Emperor, 36
Austin, Moses, 226, 366
Austin, Stephen, 226, 229, 336
Austria, Mariana de, 259
Ávila, Alonso, 118

Cabrillo, Juan Rodríguez, 54, 183, 188, 199, 255, 258, 259, 263, 266, 341, 391
Cage, Thomas, 79, 99, 111
Cajamarca, 48
Calderón de la Barca, 372
California Gold Rush, 354, 355, 356, 375
Californianos, Californios, 227, 367
Calleja del Rey, Félix María, 155
Canning-Polignac Memorandum, 103
Cantino, Alberto, 251
Caonabo, 156
Capitana, La, 272
Cardero, José, 278
Cardozo, Benjamin Nathan, 320
Caron de Beaumarchais, 15
Carreño, Antonio, 196
Carte-Real, Miguel, 250
Cartier, Jacques, 75, 326, 346
Casa de Austria, 280
Casa de Contratación, 173, 189
Casa de la Moneda, 183, 269
Casas, Friar Bartolomé de las, 116, 121, 123, 174, 237, 296, 352, 362
Castañeda, Pedro de, 255, 296
Castaño de Sosa, Gaspar, 195, 197, 272, 390
Castillo de San Marcos National Park, 403
Castillo Maldonado, Alonso del, 179, 397
Castillo, Gabriel del, 276
Castro, Américo, 108, 142
Castro, Fidel, 237
Catesby, Commodore Thomas, 231, 373
Catton, Bruce/William B., 44, 97
Cavelier, René Robert, 34
Cavendish, Thomas, 89, 92, 350
Cazador, El, 53
Cebrián y Agustín, 392
Cerezo, María, 173, 281
Cermeño, Sebastián, 196,

Cervantes, Miguel de, 65, 228, 234, 321, 372, 373
Cevallo's Expedition, 25
Cevallos, Pedro, de, 269
Chamberlain, Robert S, , 85, 124, 322
Charlemagne, 336
Charles V, Emperor, 40, 54, 78, 86, 112, 118, 123, 129, 132, 150, 167, 170, 175, 177, 178, 182, 189, 267, 268, 269, 296, 302, 314, 346, 358, 360, 376, 381, 382, 386
Chicora, Francisco de, 325
Chirikov, Aleksei, 279
Cíbola, Siete Ciudades de, 187
Cid, El, 337
Cisneros, García de, 307
Ciudad Rodrigo, Antonio de, 307
Civil War, U.S., 33, 39, 343, 353, 374
Clare, Eleanor de, 337
Clare, Gilbert de, Ninth Earl of Clare, Seventh Earl of Hartford and Third Earl of Gloucester, 337
Claver, Saint Pedro, 147, 305
Clavijero, Francisco Javier, 219, 337
Clímaco, San Juan, 181
Códice Florentino, 310
Códice Matritense, 310
Coe, Michael, 351
Coinage Act, 73
Colón, Diego, 155, 269, 377, 387
Columbus, Batholomew, 165, 313
Columbus, Christopher/Colón, Cristóbal/Colombo, Christoforo, 59, 61, 66, 78, 86, 155, 162, 163, 164, 165, 166, 169, 170, 173, 195, 243, 245, 249, 250, 254, 269, 278, 280, 304, 311, 312, 338, 354, 356, 361, 362, 363, 369, 372, 377
Comandancia General de las Provincias Internas, 216
Comisión Científica del Pacífico, 85
Concepción, María de la, 207
Consag, Ferdinand, 210, 267, 394
Contreras, Juan, 8, 156
Cook, James, 190, 259

G

Gaceta de Caracas, 209
Gaceta de Guatemala, 209
Gaceta de La Habana, 209
Gaceta de Lima, 209
Gaceta de Madrid, 26
Gaceta de México, 209
Gadsden Purchase, 34, 232, 233, 368
Gadsden, James, 232, 368
Gaínza, Gabino, 332
Galeón de Manila, 193, 259, 269
Galiano, Dionisio, 219, 277, 278, 397, 402
Galíndez de Carvajal, Lorenzo, 178
Galíndez de Carvajal, Lorenzo, 381
Gallegos, José Manuel, 327
Galveston/Galvezton, 333
Gálvez, Bernardo de, 16, 17, 2, 22, 23, 56, 69, 216, 258, 261, 331, 332, 333, 340, 395
Gálvez, José de, 16, 212, 213, 216, 261, 326, 396
Gama, Vasco de, 125
Gante, Pedro de, 150, 195, 306, 391
Garay, Francisco, 262
Garcas, Francisco, 255
Garcés, Francisco, 149, 215, 306, 395
Garcés, Francisco, 274
García de León y Pizarro, 121
García de San Francisco Zúñiga Father, 290
García de San Francisco, Friar, 203
García López de Cárdenas, 187
García, Friar Gregorio, 297, 298
Garcilaso de la Vega, El Inca, 79, 200, 297
Garcilaso de la Vega, Sebastián, 154
Gardoqui, Diego de, 16, 18, 20, 21, 22, 25, 329, 330
Garvey, John B., 317
Gaula, Amadís de, 77, 172, 186, 302
Gayangos, Pascual de, 372
Gaylor Bourne, Edward, 56, 61

Gaytán/Gaitán, Juan, 190, 270, 391
Gentleman of Elvas, 297
Gettysburg, Battle of, 343
Gibson, Charles, 142, 260
Gilbert, Sir Humphrey, 350
Godin, Louis, 84
Golden Hind, 90
Gómez de Espinosa, Gonzalo, 176, 177
Gómez Reynel, Pedro, 132
Gómez, Esteban, 104, 176, 178, 260
Góngora, Luis de, 79
González Mendoza, Juan, 273
González, Vicente, 195, 393
González, Vicente, 256
Gordillo, Francisco, 176, 262, 280, 389
Gorjón, Hernando, 315
Gormaz, Jimena de, 335
Gracián, Baltasar, 321
Gravier, Charles, 15
Green, Evarts Boutell, 352
Greenville, Richard, 59, 351
Grijalva, Hernando de, 184
Grijalva, Juan de, 175, 181, 305, 313, 388
Grimaldi, Gerónimo, 16, 18, 396
Grimaldi, Nicolás, 107
Gualdape, San Miguel de, 73, 179, 265
Güemes de Horcasitas, Juan Francisco, 210, 267
Güemes Pacheco de Padilla, Juan Vicente, 267
Guerrero, President Vicente, 228
Guevara, Hernando de, 154
Gutiérrez de Humaña, 192, 272
Gutiérrez, Diego, 272
Guzmán, Nuño de, 180, 281, 390

H

Haenke, Née y Tadeo, 84
Hakluyt, Richard, 347

K

Keating, Bern, 12
Keats, John, 36
King Alfonso IX of León, 335
King Alphonse X the Wise, 139, 321, 358
King Charles II, 92, 357
King Charles III, 16, 50, 53, 135, 243, 329, 330, 338, 357, 387
King Charles IV, 221, 259, 278
King Edward I of England, 336
King Edward III of England, 337
King Ferdinand, 86, 119, 122, 165, 251, 302, 354, 358, 360, 386
King Fernando II of León, 335
King Fernando VII, 121, 357
King Francis I, 112, 346
King George III, 27, 72, 121, 333, 357
King Henry III Platagenet, 336
King Henry III, 89
King Henry VII, 249
King Jacob I, 91
King James I, 321
King James II, 321
King Peter IV, 321
King Peter of Castile and León, 337
King Philip II, 31, 40, 54, 55, 78, 102, 107, 116, 117, 147, 190, 191, 196, 258, 298, 346, 347, 369, 387
King Philip III, 200
King Philip IV, 107, 259
King Prester John, 125
Kino, Eusebio Francisco, 149, 204, 238, 273, 306, 393

L

La Condamine, Charles Marie de, 84
La Salle, 56
Lady Eleanor, 336
Lady Managers of the Columbus Expedition, 69
Lafarelle, Lorenzo, 17
Lafita, Juan, 223
Lago de los Timpanogos, 64, 216, 254, 275
Lairos, Friar Juan, 393
Lambert, Paul F., 47
Land of Esteban Gómez, 178
Larkin, Thomas, 230, 367
Lasuén, Friar Fermín Francisco de, 149
Lazarus, Emma, 319
Lazcano, Francisco, 259
Lebrija, Antonio de, 81
Lee, Arthur, 17, 18, 19, 21, 26, 330
Lemaire, Jacob, 104
León, Alonso de, 205, 401
León, Fray Luis de, 321
Leonard, Dr. Irving, 77
Lepanto, Battle of, 55
Lepe, Diego de, 169, 171
Levy, Mosey, 319
Lewis and Clark, 35, 56
Lincoln, President Abraham, 121, 136, 148, 357
Little Big Horn, Battle of, 353,
Livingston, Robert, 36
Llano Estancado, 64, 188, 255
Loasía, García Jofre de, 180, 254, 270
Loeffling, Peter, 321
Longfellow, H.W., 228, 372
López de Gómara, Francisco, 189, 296, 338
López de Legazpi, Miguel, 192, 259, 260, 395
López de Mendoza, Fray Martín Francisco, 191, 293
López de Velasco, Juan, 176, 296, 298
López de Villalobos, Ruy, 183, 267, 270
López, Martín, 78, 271
Lorenzana, Archbishop Francisco Antonio, 266

Louisiana Purchase, 33, 35, 39, 185, 380
Loyola, Ignatius of, 153, 223, 327
Lummis Charles F., 5, 6, 12, 13, 62, 119, 123, 128, 172, 146, 164, 241, 348
Luna y Arellano, Tristán, 391
Luna, Friar Jerónimo de, 203
Lunarejo, 79

M

MacKean, Theresa, 220, 326
Madariaga, Salvador de, 49, 50, 51, 93, 100, 112, 114, 121, 127, 129, 133, 137, 141, 142, 159, 198
Madison, President James, 39, 40, 224, 339, 370
Madre de Diós del Jaén, 64, 254, 256
Mafra, Ginés de, 176
Magellan, Ferdinand, 53, 86, 104, 175, 176, 177, 186, 192, 203, 246, 254, 258, 259, 260
Maine, US, 235, 236, 376
Malaspina Glacier, 219
Malaspina, Alejandro, 84, 85, 219, 270, 275, 276, 277, 278, 279, 397
Mallory, Stephen R., 37, 374
Manchack, Fort, 23
Manhattan Island, 55
Manifest Destiny, 32, 36
Mannix, Daniel P., 117
Manrique, Jorge, 228
Mar de Cortés, 262
Mar del Sur, 258
Marcos de Niza, Friar, 54, 180, 183, 187, 199, 390, 397
Mares, José, 402
Margil de Jesús, Friar Antonio, 209, 307, 394
Mariame Indians, 131
Mariano, José, 84, 321
Mariano, Juan, 338
Marinacci, Barbara and Rudy, 64

Marion, Francis, 311
Marqués de Casa Calvo, 317
Marquis of Almodóvar, 21
Martí, José, 207
Martín de Porras, Saint, 155
Martín, Enrico, 196, 266
Martín, Esteban José, 219, 396, 400
Martínez, Ana, 154
Martínez, Joan, 272
Mártir de Anglería, Pedro, 175, 256, 296
Massanet, Padre Damián, 205, 393
Mather, Cotton, 206, 300, 325
Mather, Rev. Richard, 182
Maurelle, Francisco Antonio, 278
Mayflower, 59, 60, 143, 318
Maynard Keynes, Lord John, 91, 94, 324
Maynard, Theodore, 29, 257, 345
Mayorga, Martín, 267
McCarthy, Marie Celeste Elenore, 332
McManners, John, 125, 145
Meade, George Gordon, 343
Medici, Catherine de, 117
Medina, Friar Pedro de, 167, 299
Medina, José Toribio, 181
Medina-Sidonia, Duke of, 167
Medrano, Catalina, 86, 266
Medrano, Lucía de, 81
Meltzer, Milton, 40
Melville, Admiral George W., 376
Mencken, H.L., 264, 380
Mendaña de Neira, Álvaro de, 156, 193, 270, 279, 392
Mendes, Piza, 319
Mendoza, Antonio de, 54, 183, 187, 188, 189, 199, 259, 267, 268, 269, 340, 390
Menéndez de Avilés, Pedro, 54, 62, 191, 192, 242, 253, 293, 340, 391
Menéndez Márquez, Pedro, 389
Menéndez y Pelayo, Marcelino, 82
Mercator Map, 272
Mercator, Garardeus, 259, 269

S

Saavedra Cerón, Álvaro de, 180
Saavedra, Álvaro de, 270
Sager, Henry, 35
Sahagún, Friar Bernardino de, 149, 182, 296, 306, 310
Saint Fernando III, King of Castile and León, 335, 336, 337
Saint Maxent d'Estrehan, Felicie de, 331
Salas, Juan de, 399
Salcedo, Antonio de, 299
Salcedo, Juan Manuel de, 317
Salinas Pueblo Missions National Monument, 404
Salt River Bay National Historical Park and Ecological Preserve, 405
Salvado, Friar Rosendo, 232
Salvatierra, Friar Juan María de, 149, 204, 205, 268, 306, 394
San Antonio de Padúa Mission, 213
San Antonio Mission National Historic Park, 404
San Buenaventura Mission, 213
San Carlos Borromeo Mission, 212, 213
San Francisco de Asís Mission, 213
San Francisco Mission, 66
San Gabriel Arcángel Mission, 213, 227
San Juan Capistrano Mission, 213, 220
San Juan National Historic Site, 404
San Luis Obispo Mission, 213
San Martín José Francisco, 207
San Vítores, Luis Diego, 259
Sanbuenaventura y Olivares, Antonio de, 400
Sánchez Chamuscado, Francisco, 194, 272
Sánchez, Francisco, 399
Santa Ana, President Antonio López de, 229, 231, 366, 368

Santa Bárbara Mission, 218
Santa Clara de Asís Mission, 213
Santa Cruz, Alonso de, 297
Santa María de la Antigua, 174
Santa María de la Mar Dulce, 362
Santángel, Luis de, 321, 362
Santayana, George, 234, 373
Santo Tomás de Aquino, Universidad de, 184
Sarmiento de Valladares, José, 154, 205, 268, 394
Schiller, von Friedrich, 116
Schouler, James, 47
Schouten, Willem, 104
Scientific Commission of the Pacific, 233, 275
Scots Magazine, 37
Scott Aiton, Arthur, 54
Scott, General Winfield, 231, 368
Scott, W.R., 94
Sedgwick, Robert, 93
Sefarad, 320
Sefardita, 320
Seixas Nathan, Mendes, 319, 320
Señor, Abraham, 321
Sephardic Jews, 318, 319, 321
Sergas de Esplandián, Las, 186, 263
Serra Monument, 198
Serra, Friar Junípero, 45, 54, 56, 66, 68, 69, 147, 148, 149, 156, 198, 213, 214, 261, 270, 306, 308, 309, 340, 388
Sessé, Martín, 84, 321
Seven Cities of Cibola, 143, 397
Seven Years War, 16, 211, 316
Shackelford, Bruce M, 66, 310
Sharp, Batholomew, 357
Shea, John Gilmart, 152, 307
Shelvocke, George, 350
Sheridan, General Philip, 353
Sickles, Daniel Edgard, 343
Sigsbee, Admiral, 376
Sigüenza y Góngora, Carlos de, 79
Silent, William The, 117

U

U.S. National Parks Service, 242
Ulibarri, Juan de, 208, 389
Ulloa, Antonio de, 84, 210, 212
Ulloa, Francisco, 183, 184, 186, 199, 262, 267, 390
Ulysses Grant, President, 344
Unamuno, Pedro de, 195
Ungut, Meynardus, 302
United States Constitution, 136
University of Manila, 79
University of San Marcos, 79, 184, 314
Unzaga y Amezaga, Luis de, 332
Urdaneta, Andrés de, 184, 192, 270, 371, 376, 391
Urquijo, Mariano Luis, 221, 300
Utoaztec, 380

V

Vaca, Alonso de, 203, 393, 402
Váez de Torres, Luis, 199, 200
Valdés, Antonio de, 196
Valdés, Cayetano, 219, 277, 278
Valdivia, Juan de, 305
Valega, José M., 51
Valencia, Friar Martín de, 143, 307
Valverde, Antonio, 392
Valverde, Vicente, 307
Vargas Machuca, Bernardo de, 197, 298
Vargas Zapata, Diego de, 205, 273, 393
Vasconcelos, José, 94, 142
Vázquez de Ayllón, Lucas, 73, 74, 179, 262, 265, 280, 325, 389
Vázquez de Espinosa, Friar Antonio, 202, 238, 298
Vega, Garcilaso de la, 320, 372
Vega, Lope de, 80, 372
Velasco, Luis de, 189, 314

Velázquez de Cuéllar, Diego, 120, 174, 313
Velázquez, Loretta Janet, 344
Vélez de Escalante, Friar Silvestre, 215, 274
Vélez de Guevara, Luis, 321
Veracruz, Friar Alonso de, 190
Vergennes, 19
Vernor, Admiral Edward, 363
Verrazano, Giovanni da, 74, 178
Vespucci, Amerigo, 86, 112, 170, 173, 254, 281
Vespucci, Juan, 281
Vial, Pedro, 218
Victoria, Manuel, 228
Vikings, 71, 167, 245, 249
Villagrá, Gaspar de, 299
Villalobos, Gregorio, 66
Villazur, Pedro de, 66, 209, 270, 394
Virgin Mary, 111, 118, 192
Virginia Company of London, 283
Virginia Company, 177
Vitoria, Francisco de, 116
Vizcaíno, Sebastián, 54, 196, 201, 256, 262, 266, 270, 273, 341, 393

W

Walckenaer, Baron, 172
Wallis, Samuel, 274
Waltzemüller, Martin, 162
War of Jenkin's Ear, 363
War of the Roses, 44
Washington, George, 22, 24, 148, 216, 291, 329, 335, 338, 339, 363
Washington, Lawrence, 363
Watkins, T.H., 349
Weber, David J., 131, 383
Weber, Max, 109
Weddle, Robert S., 59, 65, 123, 265
Welde, Thomas, 182
Wellesley, Henry, 121, 357
Wesley, Charles, 135
Widmer, Mary Lou, 317

CPSIA information can be obtained
at www.ICGtesting.com
Printed in the USA
BVHW082341130820
586229BV00001B/12

9 781596 412842